Praise for

DYNASTIC, BOMBASTIC, FANTASTIC

"*Dynastic, Bombastic, Fantastic* masterfully recounts a thrilling period in Oakland A's history. Jason's storytelling vividly captures the cast of characters that made up the Athletics of the '70s, starting with their ringleader, Charlie Finley. The stories of those memorable teams come to life in the pages of this fascinating book."

— **Billy Beane, executive vice president of baseball operations, Oakland A's**

"Not to be believed, and yet 100 percent true — this is Jason Turbow's colorful, hilarious, and impossible-to-put-down account of the Swingin' A's, from their tyrannical, unhinged, and wildly innovative owner to the brawling players whose locker-room dysfunction fueled one of baseball's greatest dynasties."

— **Steve Fainaru, author of *League of Denial*; Pulitzer Prize winner for international reporting, 2008**

"Full of great characters, from Finley to Reggie to Catfish, this rollicking look at some of the most entertaining teams in baseball history is a must-read for any fan of the sport. Jason Turbow's passion and love for the game comes through."

— **Chris Ballard, *Sports Illustrated* senior writer and author of *One Shot at Forever***

"Carefully researched and often hilarious . . . *Dynastic, Bombastic, Fantastic* has plenty to offer fans both serious and casual . . . Turbow has unearthed new perspectives on brief but important chapters in team history." — ***San Francisco Chronicle***

"A must-read for A's fans." — ***San Jose Mercury News***

Dynastic, Bombastic, Fantastic

Dynastic, Bombastic, Fantastic

REGGIE, ROLLIE, CATFISH, AND CHARLIE FINLEY'S SWINGIN' A'S

JASON TURBOW

MARINER BOOKS HOUGHTON MIFFLIN HARCOURT BOSTON NEW YORK

First Mariner Books edition 2018
Copyright © 2017 by Jason Turbow

For information about permission to reproduce selections from this book,
write to trade.permissions@hmhco.com or to Permissions, Houghton Mifflin Harcourt
Publishing Company, 3 Park Avenue, 19th Floor, New York, New York 10016.

hmhco.com

Library of Congress Cataloging-in-Publication Data
Names: Turbow, Jason, author.
Title: Dynastic, bombastic, fantastic : Reggie, Rollie, Catfish, and Charlie
Finley's swingin' A's / Jason Turbow.
Description: Boston : Houghton Mifflin Harcourt, 2017.
Identifiers: LCCN 2016043921 | ISBN 9780544303171 (hardback)
ISBN 9781328570079 (paperback)
Subjects: LCSH: Oakland Athletics (Baseball team)—History. | Finley, Charles
Oscar, 1918– | BISAC: SPORTS & RECREATION / Baseball / History. |
BIOGRAPHY & AUTOBIOGRAPHY / Sports.
Classification: LCC GV875.O24 T67 2017 | DDC 796.357/640979466—dc23
LC record available at https://lccn.loc.gov/2016043921

Book design by Brian Moore

Printed in the United States of America
DOC 10 9 8 7 6 5 4 3 2 1

Endpapers: © Ron Riesterer

Insert: *p. 1 top left* © Ron Riesterer, *top right* © Doug McWilliams, *bottom* © Ron Riesterer; *p. 2 top* © Ron Riesterer, *center* Russ Reed, untitled (Vida Blue looking through mail). Gelatin silver, 8 x 10 in. The Oakland Tribune Collection, the Oakland Museum of California, gift of ANG Newspapers, *bottom* Associated Press Photo; *p. 3 top* Associated Press Photo, *center* Associated Press Photo/Sal Veder, *bottom* © Ron Riesterer; *p. 4 all photos* © Ron Riesterer; *p. 5 all photos* © Ron Riesterer; *p. 6 top left* © Ron Riesterer, *top right* Howard Erker, untitled (Oakland A's baseball game), 1975. Gelatin silver, 10 x 8 in. The Oakland Tribune Collection, the Oakland Museum of California, gift of ANG Newspapers, *bottom* © Doug McWilliams; *p. 7 top and center* © Jonathan Perry/Longhair Photography, *bottom* © Ron Riesterer; *p. 8 top and center* © Jonathan Perry/Longhair Photography, *bottom* National Baseball Hall of Fame Library, Cooperstown, NY.

Cast of Characters: *Sal Bando, Vida Blue, Campy Campaneris, Rollie Fingers, Ray Fosse, Dick Green, Ken Holtzman, Catfish Hunter, Reggie Jackson, Billy North, John "Blue Moon" Odom, Joe Rudi, Gene Tenace, Herb Washington,* and *Alvin Dark* © Doug McWilliams-National Baseball Hall of Fame. *Dave Duncan, Mike Epstein* © Ron Riesterer (background photos); National Baseball Hall of Fame Library, Cooperstown, NY (insets). *Dick Williams* © Jerry Cooke, Sports Illustrated/Getty Images (background photo); National Baseball Hall of Fame Library, Cooperstown, NY (inset).

For L, M & R

In an incidental development to threats of revenge, litigation, franchise moving and clubhouse brawls, preparations continued for the World Series game planned for 5:30 P.M. at the Coliseum. For those who can't recall, the World Series is a best-of-seven event that serves as an annual backdrop to what the A's do off the field prior to blaming the press for blowing everything out of proportion.

—*Oakland Tribune,* October 15, 1974

Contents

Introduction

Despite his bravado over recent months, Reggie Jackson couldn't help wondering what the hell he'd just gotten himself into. It was June 1976, and only months earlier A's owner Charlie Finley — the only boss Reggie had ever known — ended nine seasons of protracted acrimony between the two by shipping him to the Baltimore Orioles, COD. For 15 imperious years Finley owned the A's, and never once had he made a move that so closely resembled submission. With Catfish Hunter already gone to the Yankees, Oakland's three-time championship team was now without its best pitcher *and* its best hitter, and Finley was casting about wildly for something that resembled a solution. It was the dawn of the free agency era, and the unremitting autocrat was struggling to adapt. Reggie had been making too much noise about wanting a big-money contract, so Reggie had to go.

Since then, things hadn't exactly been smooth for either of them. Jackson claimed to be shocked by the deal and decided that if the game was going to play Reggie, Reggie would play the game right back. Free agency awaited at season's end, but he wanted to get paid *now*. He demanded multiple years at premium prices before he'd so much as consider reporting to the Orioles. *Reggie, we need you,* pleaded general manager Hank Peters. *We traded for you because we think we can win the World Series with you. Come play baseball and we will work out the money.* But by then Reggie was on a beach in Hawaii, and Baltimore was hosting the Red Sox in the season opener.

The slugger eventually settled for $200,000 to play out the year. He reported a month late, missed his new team's first 16 games, then batted .208 over the next 34. That was where things stood when the Orioles arrived in Chicago for a late-spring series, their preseason championship aspirations having given way to the second-worst record in the American

League. Jackson, frustrated and confused, was getting booed by his own team's fans.

When the Orioles pulled into Comiskey Park, he was further confused by the message that showed up in the visitors' clubhouse. It was from Finley. *Finley.* The guy who didn't so much as offer a token note of thanks after trading Reggie away. No *Sad to see you go.* No nothing. They hadn't spoken since. Reggie was indignant, but his ex-boss beckoned, so Reggie went.

Finley was based in Chicago — the vast remove from Oakland was one reason for his impotence when it came to building hometown support for the A's — and Jackson met him in Grant Park, across the street from the South Michigan Avenue insurance headquarters of Charles O. Finley & Company. They found a bench among the office workers enjoying bagged lunches in the springtime sun. Finley placed his Kelly green, double-breasted sports coat — the one he wore so prominently during the A's championship runs — across his lap. His tie was undone and his sleeves rolled up on a warm and windy day. When Finley crossed his legs, Jackson spotted a familiar hole in the sole of his upraised shoe.

The owner of the A's got right to the point.

"I still owe you $45,000 on your original contract," he said, "and I want you to know that I haven't forgotten it. I've talked to your people, and some of the papers have gotten lost, but I'll make good on the money because I owe it to you."

Jackson didn't even remember the money. For years Finley went out of his way to make investments on behalf of his favorite players, a kindness that, in the days before player agents and financial advisers, was an incredible boon. His standard offer was an unbeatable money-back guarantee: he'd return it all, even if the investments tanked. More frequently, of course, players would as much as double their outlay. But that seemed like eons ago, long before Finley eliminated such benefits as his relationship with players grew increasingly antagonistic.

The man Jackson found himself sitting next to was not the same one who so exactingly governed throughout his time in Oakland. Gone were the bluster and the grandiosity, the untarnished conviction that everything in the world would be better if only Finley himself was in charge. There they were, the young star and the old man, reminiscing on a park bench about times past, as if their heyday together had occurred in a different era instead of only eight months earlier. In Jackson, Finley saw a manifestation of the times — somebody who had outgrown Oakland just as the very structure of baseball had outgrown Oakland's owner. He had summoned Jackson under the pretext of money — did they even have a personal relationship anymore? — but he wanted to see his former player for reasons unrelated to finances. Jackson thanked him for his fiscal integrity. They paused.

"You doing all right in Baltimore?" Finley finally asked. "You comfortable?" The irony was impossible to miss. What Finley really wanted to hear was how much better things had been with the A's. You know, in the good old days.

Jackson responded in the affirmative, said that playing for Earl Weaver was a terrific experience. That was all it took. Finley began to lament. He lamented that payrolls were growing too rich for his bankbook to sustain. He lamented that baseball's new salary structure was taking his own players — the guys he signed and groomed and carefully tended — from him. They were playing out their contracts, almost to a man, and before long he'd have nobody left. Finley had put his own personal motto — *Sweat plus sacrifice equals success* — to the test and with it built one of the best teams the sport had ever known. And now he could do little more than watch as it unraveled, strand by agonizing strand. Charlie Finley had been a lonely man for many years, but perhaps was realizing it only now.

After a time the two fell silent, watching the sun filter through the elm trees all around them, listening to the breeze whistle by. After all those years, all those championships, all those words, maybe there were no words left. What, really, did they have to say? Finally, Finley tried.

"We had some time, didn't we, Reggie?"

"We had all of that," Jackson replied.

"You're all going to do all right," the older man said wistfully. Whether he was talking to Jackson or to himself was not entirely clear. What was unmistakable was that even though he was invoking the future, his mind was squarely in the past. "Every time you hit another home run, or Sal, or Joe, or Cat wins another game," he continued, "it's going to be a feather in my cap."

That was it then. Finley still owned the A's, still purported them to be of championship caliber, still employed many of the people who had been instrumental to their success — Sal Bando, Joe Rudi, Gene Tenace, Vida Blue — but something had changed. The man who couldn't sit still even as his team was winning titles, who always needed to be moving toward *next* and *bigger,* who was the closest personification of Don Quixote his generation of baseball ownership had known, seemed to be giving up and calling it a career. He continued to insist that he'd never sell the A's, but what he'd do with them — what he *could* do with them — had become an elusive question. Finley was an iconoclast among baseball owners, the most prominent and successful member of an exclusive club that couldn't stand him, and now that club was marginalizing him right out of the sport.

"You should be proud of yourself, Reggie," he said in the go-on-with-out-me tone of a dying movie hero. "You're going to make a lot of money, and you can bet that you haven't played in your last Series." Jackson could offer only a contemplative grin. Hell, Reggie himself didn't know where he'd be playing the next season.

When they sat for what seemed to both of them like long enough, the men parted ways. After his season with Baltimore, Jackson would sign a multimillion-dollar deal with the New York Yankees, hit three home runs in three swings in the deciding Game 6 of the World Series against the Los Angeles Dodgers, sweep MVP honors, then hit .391 in the following season's Series as the Yankees won him his fifth title in seven years.

Finley, meanwhile, trundled off into obscurity. Without Reggie, Oakland finished in second place in 1976 — the first time in six years they landed anyplace but first — and then, after Finley's prediction of mass player exodus was realized, nosedived into a three-year run of baseball obsolescence, finishing an average of nearly 32 games off the pace. In 1980, unable to reconcile the finances of his divorce, Finley finally stopped fighting and sold the team.

This was a young man's game, and Charlie Finley hadn't been a young man even in his youth. His meeting with Jackson represented the mortal sigh of a dying franchise, offering only the barest hints of the awful spectacle and downright brilliance of the 15 years that preceded it. A whisper into the wind off Lake Michigan is a hell of a way to go out, but for this team it was somehow fitting. The A's players were themselves about to be scattered into the breeze, to places like Anaheim and San Diego and Arlington and Milwaukee. Why not let the idea of those dominant seasons flutter off in much the same way?

Which is exactly what Charlie Finley did.

Part 1

ASCENDANCE

1961–1971

Welcome to Oakland

If the Athletics do not win the pennant in 1969, they certainly
will win more than their share of championships in the '70s.

— *Sports Illustrated*, April 14, 1969

Bob Kennedy was feeling good. The 1968 season, the A's first in Oakland and his first as their manager, had wrapped only minutes earlier. Despite a loss to the Twins, the A's final record was 82-80, 20 victories better than the previous year and their first winning mark since 1949. It was by any reasonable measure a fantastic success. Kennedy spoke easily with reporters in the postgame clubhouse about his hopes for '69. With a roster laden with up-and-comers like Reggie Jackson, Catfish Hunter, and Campy Campaneris, the manager couldn't hide his excitement about achievements yet to come.

Unlike previous lost campaigns, in which Charlie Finley's ax swung inexorably toward the managerial chopping block as early as June, the room was upbeat after the season finale. Kennedy offered warm goodbyes to his players, wished them productive winters, and urged them to keep in shape. Then he made a quick round of the gathered media. "Thank you for everything this summer," he said, shaking each reporter's hand. "I'll be seeing you next year. But right now I have to go up to see the big man." With that, he hopped the elevator to the third-floor executive suite, where he and Finley had a full agenda of off-season prep work to discuss. When the elevator returned, a contingent of newsmen followed.

They arrived to find Kennedy in the hallway, struggling with the locked glass door to the owner's office. "Where's Finley?" one of them asked. "We want to talk to him."

"I can't even get in," replied the bewildered manager.

His confusion didn't last long; a moment later the lock rattled open, the door swung ajar, and Kennedy slipped inside. When reporters attempted to follow, however, an assistant cut them off. They might have grown suspicious if given some time, but within a minute Kennedy stormed out, unexpectedly jobless. The team's PR man, Val Binns, emerged and read a handwritten statement: "Bob Kennedy has been relieved of his duties as manager and has been replaced by Hank Bauer."

Welcome to Charlie Finley's Oakland A's. The man's perpetual need for shifting sands was ever in play, with managers, with players, with cities themselves. Kennedy had succeeded, but not enough for Finley's tastes, and so the churn endured — another odd decision in an ownership résumé packed full of them.

At least the man was decisive. Hell, it's what landed the A's in Oakland in the first place. So determined was Finley to move his team from Kansas City to Northern California in 1967 that no measure of contrary advice could sway him. It might have been the cutting-edge allure of the brand-new, 50,000-seat Oakland Coliseum, but just as likely it was the chance to buck every owner who insisted that the Bay Area was a one-team market. Finley hired a firm to research the pros and cons of the East Bay, and then ordered it to "tell me to move to Oakland."

So firm were his convictions that he signed a 20-year lease agreement and at the team's welcoming luncheon said that the A's would forever have OAKLAND printed across their jerseys as a symbol of civic pride. "I bought the team in Kansas City," he proclaimed. "I have brought it to Oakland. There is a difference. I took the only team I could get. I had no choice over where it was. Bringing it to Oakland was my choice. Once I make a decision, I stand by it, I give my word of that. I will move to Oakland. I will move my family to Oakland. I will keep my team in Oakland. And the A's will succeed here."

Finley did not move to Oakland, nor did his family. He showed up a few times each season to watch the A's, and caught them when they visited Chicago. After a year he removed the city's name from the jerseys and replaced it with the letter "A," a precursor, perhaps, to perpetual rumors that the team was preparing to move someplace else.

The Coliseum's debut — opening night, April 17, 1968 — was as grand an affair as Finley could have hoped. The stadium of his dreams was packed to overflowing. The team's mascot, a mule named Charlie O, rolled in with a police escort. Baseball commissioner William Eckert and American League president Joe Cronin were in attendance, as was California governor Ronald Reagan, who threw out the ceremonial first pitch. The arena went dark prior to the National Anthem, a lone spotlight homing in on the American flag. Fans, fully invested in the experience, spontaneously fished matches from pockets and turned the ballpark into something between a candlelight vigil and a Lynyrd Skynyrd concert. Finley's last-place Athletics were in Oakland now, and things were about to change.

The very next night they did. It took only one game for all semblance of new-team sheen to dissipate, as only 5,304 fans found their way to the ballpark. "Oh my God," gasped traveling secretary Tom Corwin, eyeing the nearly empty grandstand. "What have we gotten ourselves into?" The following day, the first Friday night contest in Oakland's big league history drew 6,251.

Just like that, a decades-long conversation of *Why?* began. Why did people stay away in such terrific numbers? Why wasn't an exciting new team enough of an attraction? Why couldn't people recognize the gift they'd been given? The answers were myriad. The A's were a second-division club, and had been for more than three decades. It was too cold. It was difficult to get to the stadium. It was the Giants siphoning fans across the bay, not to mention University of California sports right there in Berkeley, plus a panoply of local entertainment options, plus working-class Oakland residents with a shortage of disposable income, plus . . . plus . . . plus . . .

Finley's hard-edged attitude did not help. When he refused to give in to the local musicians' union — which wanted him to match the Giants' use of a live band on weekends — he was forced to use recordings of the National Anthem, unable to find so much as an organist willing to work for him. The shortcomings of the Coliseum itself also became quickly apparent. The A's shared the field with the turf-shredding Raiders of the National Football League. The infield dirt was too soft for solid footing. Finley's lauded "million-dollar scoreboard," an awesome display of ballpark messaging, was inoperable, and would stay that way, he was told, until June.

Within his first month on the job A's farm director Art Parrack, theorizing that any more time spent working for Finley would be too much, resigned. Soon Finley would fire or have quit on him the vice president Bill Cutler (a protracted legal battle over back salary followed), director of scouting Ray Swallow, traveling secretary John Fitzpatrick, sales manager Bob Freitas, and 11 scouts, bringing the number of front-office personnel to leave his employ since he bought the club in 1961 to 130. The only one to stick around from the beginning was his cousin, Carl Finley.

On the field, however, the A's grew ever more stable, following that 82-win season with 88 victories in 1969, then 89 a year later. In the process Finley did his best to transform the Kansas City Athletics into his Oakland A's, adding an apostrophe-*s* to the "*A*" on the cap and shucking away almost everybody who'd made the trek from Missouri and was older than 25. In a coup, he convinced local resident Joe DiMaggio to come aboard as an executive vice president, then overlooked assigning him a desk or much work, all but ensuring that the Hall of Famer would end up as the team's de facto hitting coach and part-time spokesman. (Reported *Sports Illustrated*: "Of all the possible answers to the question, 'Where have you gone, Joe DiMaggio?' one of the least heartening is, 'To the Oakland dugout, wearing gold pants and white shoes.'") Finley realized that Midwestern promotional holdovers like Farmer's Day, featuring hog-calling and cow-milking contests, did not play in the Bay Area, so he swapped them out for events like Hot Pants Day. He hired a couple of leggy coeds from nearby Bishop O'Dowd High School to wear short-shorts and tight tops and scoop up foul balls during games.* Despite his efforts, fans continued to stay away in droves.

Since Finley was doing most of the work anyway, he also dispensed with the idea of having a general manager on the payroll. The man didn't know much about player evaluation, but he was smart enough to secure ideas from those who did. His innate salesmanship could charm even the wariest target, and his peculiar ability to spend hours on the telephone each day allowed him to incessantly mine intel from the opposition. Finley would initiate trade calls, bringing up the names of other teams' players as points of comparison, and meticulously collect ensuing assessments, free of charge. When he heard a detail repeated often enough, he knew he was on to something. Scouts and lower-level person-

---

* Finley dressed the teenagers, Debbie Sivyer (the younger sister of Mary Brubaker, a front-office secretary) and Mary Barry, in outfits that exposed their legs and accentuated their figures. The girls lent undeniable sex appeal to the games, but that wasn't all. Sivyer augmented the between-innings beverages she ferried to umpires with homemade chocolate chip cookies, baked from a recipe that she would use some years later — after marrying a businessman named Randall Fields — to found the business for which she eventually became known: Mrs. Fields Cookies.

nel from other organizations, viewing such conversations as de facto job interviews, freely offered up inside information.

The strategy fit nicely with Finley's increasing reliance on nobody but himself. Before long, the entire A's operation would be run by fewer than seven people. Reported *Sports Illustrated*:

> Finley's one-man band mocks the conventional baseball organization, with its board chairmen, executive vice-presidents, financial analysts, media liaison officers and the other impedimenta of big business. It both galls and astonishes orthodox baseball men that Finley, wearing so many hats, can accomplish so much. It is not false pride speaking, nor is it, heaven forbid, bragging when Finley refers to the team as "my A's." They are, indisputably, his.

• • •

As the teenage son of a lifelong baseball man, Rick Williams was raised around the game. His father, Richard Hirschfeld Williams — known to all as Dick — spent the summer of 1970 as third-base coach for the Montreal Expos. The two of them, father and son, would drive together to Jarry Park Stadium, where the boy would go off to work as a clubbie while his old man tended to baseball matters. It was a familiar pattern that allowed them to connect multiple times during the course of pregame activities. One day in August, however, things took a strange turn for Rick when, after they arrived at the ballpark, his father all but disappeared.

It wasn't until Dick finally emerged for batting practice that Rick had any idea where he was, but before they could connect the coach ambled over to the grandstand and began talking to an older man in the box seats wearing a conspicuously wrinkled suit.

The teenager didn't learn more until the drive home. "Dad," he finally asked as his father fiddled with the radio dial to find a ball game on an AM station out of Chicago or St. Louis, "who was that disheveled old man you were talking to?"

Dick Williams laughed out loud. "That," he said, "was Charlie Finley."

The younger Williams knew who Finley was, and took a moment to absorb the implications. "Does that mean you're going to Oakland?" he asked. Dick Williams shrugged. "It's a possibility," he said. "Don't say anything to anybody."

Rick barely had time to think about the prospect, let alone tell anybody. Within two months his dad was managing the A's.

Dick Williams was a tough son of a bitch, on that everybody agreed. He had once been an outstanding prospect in the Brooklyn Dodgers chain, where he thrived under general manager Branch Rickey's focus on fundamentals. *Hit the cutoff man. Know when to take the extra base. Bunt the ball properly and good things will happen.* He cracked the starting lineup as a 23-year-old in 1952 but only three days later separated his shoulder while diving for a ball, ruining his throwing arm and relegating himself to a career on the bench. That was where Williams learned two enduring lessons. One was from Dodgers manager and master needler Charlie Dressen, who taught him how to verbally ride the opposition to the point of distraction. The other was the realization that since he could no longer out-athlete other players, he now had to outsmart them. Strategic thinking became an integral part of his game.

Williams's playing career ended in 1964, at age 35, and his managerial career started the very next season, with Boston's Triple-A affiliate in Toronto. Within two years he was helming the Red Sox, who were coming off of eight straight losing seasons and three in a row with at least 90 defeats. Popular theory attributed the failure to a lack of toughness. This, Williams had in spades.*

He stripped Carl Yastrzemski of his captaincy, claiming, "I'm the only chief around here," and proceeded to drill the Red Sox like they'd never been drilled. Yaz responded with the finest season of his Hall of Fame career, winning his only MVP Award. The Red Sox, all but ignored in the preseason, marched to the World Series, taking the Cardinals to seven games. Williams, the newfound Sawx whisperer, became the toast of Boston.

It didn't last. The manager's steely authority quickly began to grate on his players, who seemed to miss the old relaxed atmosphere more than they appreciated the hungry new one. In 1969, with nine games remaining in the season and his team in third place, Williams was fired.

That was how he landed in Montreal, coaching for Gene Mauch. When Finley hired him in 1971, Williams knew what he was getting into. Oakland's owner had been cycling through managers like tissues from a box

---

* As a minor league manager, Williams got into such an intense fistfight with one of his own players that he ended up soiling himself. Rather than reacting with embarrassment, the manager called a team meeting, held his pants aloft, and told his players, "If this is what it takes to win, everybody in this room will be wearing diapers."

for the better part of a decade, proclaiming a desire to surround himself with "the best baseball brains available" but unable to resist telling them how to do their jobs. He insisted that his first manager in Kansas City, Joe Gordon — winner of five World Series during 11 years as a Hall of Fame second baseman — conduct his business from the press box, for better proximity to Finley's instruction. Gordon responded with a public conversation about the difficulty of managing a baseball team that's actually being managed by somebody else, and went so far as to submit a lineup card with the notation "Approved by COF." Fifty-nine games into his tenure, he was fired.

Finley proclaimed that a new era was upon the club and announced — as would soon become rote — that his new manager was the finest he had ever known. Over the coming decade he would repeat the process ten times, a rate of once each season. Now he had Dick Williams.

The manager's first step in Oakland was to implement the concrete expectation that the A's would perform to their ability *all of the time,* and he made spring training of 1971 entirely unlike anything the players had yet experienced. "Dick came in knowing we lacked one major ingredient: fundamental execution," reflected catcher Gene Tenace. "We would give games away because we made mistakes, and that's where Dick honed in. He took all the bats away. He said, 'You ain't hitting until you get these stinking rundowns right, until you can hit the cutoff man, until we can run bunt plays and we ain't beating ourselves in the late innings.'" If a team gave away only three outs a game, the manager theorized, the opposition got ten innings' worth of at-bats while the A's got only nine. What kind of odds were those?

"He made us all managers on the field," said catcher Dave Duncan. "Suddenly, we saw how things really worked in baseball. It wasn't just hitting, running and throwing the ball. It was thinking ahead, analyzing the play, anticipating the moves of the other team. He made every player think he was a leader of his own position. He made the players more intense and proud of their performance. He gave us bigger egos. He told us how good we could be."

How Williams told them was not always the nicest. After Rollie Fingers failed to back up third base one day, the manager met him on the dugout's top step at inning's end. "Where were you supposed to be?" he shouted into the pitcher's face. Chastened, Fingers muttered, "Behind third." "You bet your ass!" barked Williams. For Fingers, the confusing part was that third baseman Sal Bando had caught the throw. Fingers should have been positioned behind him as insurance, but there was no actual need for backup. "When Dick jumped into my shit about *that,* I toed the straight line," he said later.

"Dick had this emotional distaste for losing," said Duncan. "We'd lose a game, and he would go over certain fundamental things we did wrong. If we lost two in a row, you would think we had lost 20 in a row. He would actually get ill, he hated losing so much."

The manager utilized the bench-jockey skills he picked up as a player in Brooklyn, peppering the team with verbal jabs. Should somebody make an error on the field — particularly a mental error — the volume rose quickly, with Williams frequently closing himself in the dugout bathroom to bellow unfettered to the heavens. Those witnessing it with horror from the bench took it as further motivation. Still, they came to learn that Williams was fair, and that he'd unfailingly take their side if they did what was asked of them.

Then Oakland went out and lost its first game of the season, 1971's Presidential Opener in Washington, D.C., and returned home to be swept in an opening day doubleheader. By the time the A's set out on their first extended road trip they were 2-4 and their manager was downright surly.

At their first stop, Milwaukee, the team plane set down beneath stormy skies at Billy Mitchell Field. Players decamped for a bus downtown, but before they departed, a flight attendant approached traveling secretary Tom Corwin on the tarmac and whispered something into his ear. Corwin relayed the message to Williams.

It seemed that a battery-powered bullhorn, viewed by the flight crew as an essential piece of safety equipment, had been stolen. The manager immediately strode to the head of the bus aisle, eyes flashing fire, and shoved his fists deep into raincoat pockets.

"Gentlemen," he began. The word got their attention. "Some of you think you can be pricks. I've got news for you. I can be the biggest prick of all."

Williams, six games into his tenure, stared down his players. "The plane can't leave without the megaphone," he announced, "and we're not going to leave until the plane can, if we have to sit here all night."

With that, something clattered onto the pavement outside. Heads craned to see the bullhorn on the tarmac, beneath a row of open bus windows. It was slightly dented but unequivocally accounted for. Williams took note of the development and continued. "Gentlemen," he said. There was that word again. "I have no small fines. I would suggest to you that you all stay in your rooms this entire road trip.""*

The manager could not have scripted a better incident with which to tee up a display of authority. This was about more than policing juvenile behavior. In Boston, Williams had been undermined by players going over his head to complain directly to the owner, and he knew all about Finley's reputation for learning everything that happened in the Oakland clubhouse. Such was Finley's reach that back in Kansas City players took to holding clandestine meetings in a little-used storage room deep inside Municipal Stadium, and *still* he learned the details. Finley had his favorites among the players — shortstop Bert Campaneris and pitcher John "Blue Moon" Odom, primarily — but their teammates had no idea which of them was the snitch, if either, or if it was somebody else altogether, or what to do about it even if they found out. The reality was that most of the players were culpable in some capacity for information leaks — as were executives, broadcasters, and team attendants. Finley talked to them all, casually picking up details with which to direct ensuing conversations. "You could be talking to Mr. Finley about one thing," said traveling secretary Jim Bank, "and by the end of the conversation he's going to talk to you about ten other things and get information about all ten."

It was with that in mind that Williams concluded his address. "If you've got a fucking problem . . . just call Charlie," he said. "I have about five or six phone numbers where you can reach him. From what I understand about the lot of you gutless wonders, you've got those fucking numbers already. Well, go ahead, call him. But he ain't here now — I am — and you'd better learn to live with it." The message was clear: Williams was in charge, and he viewed horseplay as a privilege, not a right. This was not the way a losing team acted.

The next day Rollie Fingers shut out the Brewers on four hits. The day after that Vida Blue threw a two-hitter. Oakland won 12 of its next 13, and

---

* It was common knowledge among the players that Catfish Hunter had absconded with the bullhorn, but nobody knew whether Williams also knew. He did, but said nothing, opting instead to let the situation play itself out. The manager let on later in the season when, apropos of nothing, he asked Hunter, "Hey, you reckon that megaphone would have worked good on your dogs?" Hunter could only grin. "I'd have loved to find out," he replied.

that was essentially that; six days after the dressing-down the A's grabbed first place and never let it go.

The team's success was noteworthy, but the real story of 1971 was Vida Blue. Six feet tall and 190 well-packed pounds, the left-hander threw devastatingly hard and with disarming ease. His windup featured a uniquely high leg kick that brought his right knee almost to his chin, and a delivery in which he reached so far back with the baseball that his knuckles nearly scraped the dirt. He'd made his debut as a 20-year-old call-up the previous September, and pitched a one-hitter against Kansas City in his second-ever big league start. Blue couldn't throw anything but fastballs, but that was enough — the ones that didn't drop like bowling balls exploded so ferociously upon reaching the plate that hitters swore they saw them rise. Two starts after baffling the Royals he no-hit the Twins. "We never even saw the ball," marveled Minnesota's Harmon Killebrew afterward, "but we sure heard it good."

Blue's marvelous September earned him the nod to pitch the Presidential Opener in 1971, but the magic didn't last. The young lefty surrendered four runs in one and two-thirds innings, and Oakland lost, 8–0. Things, however, would quickly improve.

In Blue's second start of the season he set a franchise record with 13 strikeouts over six shutout innings of a rain-shortened game. His third start was the two-hitter over Milwaukee. His fourth start was an 11-strikeout victory over the White Sox. Vida, who had spent his winter working on a curveball, was somehow even better than he'd been the previous September. Following his disastrous opening assignment the lefty won 10 straight, compiling a 1.03 ERA while spinning nine complete games in 12 starts.

"There are some guys you go hitless against and it doesn't bother you," noted Baltimore outfielder Paul Blair. "What you tell yourself is, *Well, I got a piece of him,* or *At least I fouled one off.* But this guy makes you go 0-for-4 and you feel humiliated. He doesn't give you a single thing. He strips you naked right there in public. Trying to hit that thing he throws is like trying to hit dead weight."

By early May the country was paying attention. *Sports Illustrated* compared Vida to Sandy Koufax. ("That's funny," responded Blue, "I don't look Jewish.") Soon he would grace the covers of *Time* and *Newsweek,* publications that didn't ordinarily cover sports, and hold down guest spots on NBC's *Today Show* and *The Dick Cavett Show*. Talk began in earnest about his chances of winning 30.

On May 28, more than 35,000 people crammed into Fenway Park (capacity: less than 34,000; average: 16,000) to watch Vida pitch. On June 1, he attracted more than 30,000 to Yankee Stadium for a game that would have otherwise drawn about 12,000, and the A's suffered through a pre-game clubhouse so crowded with media that Dick Williams called a team meeting just to clear the room. Back home 47 percent of all Bay Area TVs tuned in as Blue won his 12th, another complete game. By that point Finley was seeing dollar signs in everything his young star touched. Vida, scheduled to pitch only once during an eight-day homestand, was given Catfish Hunter's slot on June 17, which served the dual purpose of providing Blue with an extra home date and knocking him from his previously scheduled spot ten days hence, which corresponded with Bat Day at the Coliseum. "We didn't want him to pitch on a promotion day," Williams explained. "He's enough of a promotion himself."

Vida's sheer exuberance could not be suppressed. During games in which he didn't pitch he sat in the dugout and listened to Williams rant about on-field mistakes, then would approach the skipper, a smile on his face, to say things like, "I'm going to tell Greenie [second baseman Dick Green] what you all said about him. I'm going to tell him as soon as he gets off the field." Reggie Jackson called the pitcher a "dugout instigator, like the rest of us, but always in an innocent way." Vida wore a Joe Namath–model New York Jets jersey while tossing footballs with clubhouse kids before games, then proceeded to run them ragged. "George, you my man, get me a soda pop," he'd call out. "Steve, how 'bout wringing out my shirt here? Chuck, get me a dry sweatshirt." Chuck, of course, also went by Mr. Dobson and was at the time of the request the starting pitcher for that night's game. The left-hander politely declined. "Oh," said Vida. "I knew I'd go too far."

Blue lived within Oakland city limits, in the recently constructed Acorn Projects. He and outfielder Tommy Davis shared a three-bedroom apartment on a corner lot, and Blue took to playing street ball with the kids who continuously knocked on his door. It was an exacting model of city living, a long way from the farm community of Mansfield, Louisiana, where he grew up.

Vida Rochelle Blue Jr. was born in his family's eight-room house at the end of an unpaved road. His father, Vida Rochelle Meshach Abednego

Blue, pulled in $75 per week from his job in an iron foundry, which he supplemented with gardening work in the evenings.

Mansfield was like much of the segregated South: Vida lived in a black neighborhood, went to a black school, De Soto High, and played on black youth baseball teams. He was every bit the prep phenom he ultimately became in the major leagues, losing only two games in three seasons. As a senior quarterback, he threw 35 touchdown passes in 14 games to go with 3,400 passing yards and 1,600 rushing yards, and was courted for the gridiron by Notre Dame and Purdue. "This young fellow is going to be the first big-name black quarterback," enthused University of Houston coach Bill Yeoman after Blue opted to join his Cougars. "He's going to be the best left-handed passer since Frankie Albert."

During Blue's senior year, however, his father's health failed. Vida Sr.'s heart bothered him. His lungs grew inflamed. He saw doctors, was operated on, couldn't work. Too suddenly, at age 40, he passed away. The family barely had time to grieve; Vida's mother, Sallie Blue, found herself responsible for six children, as well as her mother and grandmother. She picked up a cleaning job at a local factory while also logging shifts in the school cafeteria. Her son also changed his plans, jettisoning college in favor of something more immediately lucrative — Finley's $25,000 signing bonus and a $500 per-month minor league salary (plus another $8,000 for college in case things didn't work out). "There are times when I can shut my eyes and see myself standing behind an offensive line, calling signals for the Baltimore Colts," Vida said in the middle of his hot streak, "but that isn't how life worked out for me."

Despite Blue's burgeoning all-world status, Finley wanted more. "Baseball is a business and we have to sell it," he explained to the left-hander. "People buy colorful personalities. A colorful nickname will help you. An unusual name will help you even more. Why don't you change your middle name to True? We'll call you True Blue. We'll tell our broadcasters to call you True Blue. We'll even put 'True' on the back of your uniform. How's that?"

"That," according to the pitcher, was nothing short of an insult. "Vida was my father's name," he reasoned. "Vida means 'life' in Spanish. I enjoy being Vida Blue. Now that my father is dead, I honor him every time the name Vida Blue appears in a headline. Why would I want to be called 'True Blue'? If Mr. Finley thinks that's such a great name, why doesn't he call himself 'True O. Finley'?"

The more Vida thought about it the more racial overtones he saw in the request and the angrier he grew. "It sounded suspiciously as if old massa was finding a pet name for a favored field hand," reported the *New York Times Magazine*, never mind that Finley had already foisted a nickname on a white pitcher, Catfish Hunter, or that the phrase "true blue" implied the noble trait of loyalty. When Finley offered Blue $2,000 to acquiesce, it only made things seamier. "You want me to disrespect my deceased father — are you out of your fucking mind?" he said, looking back. "I wasn't going to change my name for any price."

Thus was Vida incredulous when, warming up in the outfield before a game in the middle of the 1971 season, he saw the scoreboard flash an announcement for an upcoming contest featuring as Oakland's starting pitcher somebody named True Blue. Despite Vida's objections, Finley had also ordered the team's broadcasters to use the name on the radio. When players began picking it up in the clubhouse, Blue could take no more. He asked sportswriters and broadcasters to kindly knock it off. He told the team's publicity director, Michael Haggerty, to keep the scoreboard and press releases free from the moniker. He offered a touch of finality by having his first name sewn onto the back of his jersey instead of his last.*

Finley was hardly cowed. He continued to capitalize by staging Vida Blue Day on June 27 (mandating another rotation shuffle at Hunter's expense to prevent Vida from pitching on his namesake day, thus banking on Vida's name two games in a row), for which he flew in Sallie Blue, as well as Vida's four sisters and brother, from Louisiana. On the field before the game Vida was presented with a baby blue Cadillac El Dorado with a license plate reading V-BLUE. (It cost $10,000, Finley told anybody who would listen.) Shortly thereafter, Blue informed Finley that his rookie-scale salary made fuel unaffordable, so his boss gave him a gas-company credit card. A week later Vida was back, saying that he couldn't be seen driving such a fine automobile in the clothes of a minor leaguer and requesting $500 to revamp his wardrobe. Finley gave him $1,000. Vida ended up filling other people's tanks with company credit, and before long

---

* The True Blue talk subsided until August, when Finley brought his number-one draft pick, a pitcher named Bill Daniels, to meet the club and informed the media through a press release of his nickname: "Sugar Bear." Finley insisted that the pitcher was so dubbed prior to signing, a story about which Vida was so skeptical that he refused to pose for a photo with the 17-year-old unless the photographer promised not to use the nickname in the caption.

jettisoned the car altogether, sending it home to Mansfield for his mother to drive while he tooled around Oakland in the car he wanted all along, a green and gold Pontiac Grand Prix, on loan from a local dealership.

By the middle of July 1971, Blue's 17-3 record and majors-leading totals in wins, shutouts, strikeouts, and ERA earned him the starting nod in the All-Star Game. Every one of his victories had been a complete game. Even his no-decisions were spectacular: on July 9, Blue struck out 17 Angels over 11 shutout innings, but the A's didn't win until the 20th. Said Jackson, "You can even get the Babe out of his grave and he'd look at Vida and say, 'The man's too much.'"

Blue's 18th win was a one-hit shutout of the Tigers in his first start after the All-Star break. It was also his 18th complete game of the season, and the innings were taking a toll. The lefty exceeded his career-high of 171⅔ innings by the second week of July, and two weeks later he passed 200. In Blue's first attempt at his 20th victory, on July 30, he gave up four earned runs in six innings — only the third time all season he'd allowed that many — and lost. "I've never been more tired," he complained afterward.

The pitcher, at first delighted by the accolades, grew overwhelmed by them. His attention was drawn taut by the national media, then segmented to slake the public's thirst, one feature story at a time. "I wake up and then I'm at the ballpark," Blue said, head spinning. "I'm pitching. Then it's all over. I'm back in the dressing room and writers are all around me. Then I'm on an airplane. I'm in a hotel. I'm at the ballpark. Now I'm back in Oakland. Now Mr. Finley is giving me a car, and my mother and my brother and my sisters are there. Now lights are flashing. Now I'm pitching again." No one ever said being a phenom was easy.

Blue's roommate, Tommy Davis, took to screening calls for him at home. Vida signed so many autographs that he began using his right hand in order to save his left one for pitching. Over the course of the summer he went from "I want to sign 'em all . . ." to "You got to sign, you just got to . . ." to "You don't got to sign. You don't got to do nothing but die." Still, he signed. By August, Vida was lamenting that "I sometimes feel like I'm going to crack up mentally."

The interview Blue gave to reporters following his 20th victory, on August 7, was so dour as to be described as "hostile" by one reporter. Somebody asked whether the win would help Vida remove the monkey from his back, and the pitcher gripped his head. "There was no monkey on my back," he yelped. "There just was the pressure, that pressure." Somebody brought up the specter of 30 wins, and Vida snapped. "There you go again," he yelled, slapping a table. "There's that damn pressure."

Vida won his 22nd with 10 starts left in the season, and though he'd have to succeed at an absurd pace to reach 30, people still held out hope. By the end, however, he was just a gassed pitcher trying to get by. Blue was blasted out of starts earlier than ever and won only twice more, ultimately finishing second to Detroit's Mickey Lolich in victories.

Still, the kid had been spectacular. Vida's final line: 39 starts, 24-8 record, 1.82 ERA, 24 complete games, eight shutouts, 301 strikeouts, and 88 walks in 312 innings pitched. It nearly obscured the brilliance of his teammate, Catfish Hunter, who, despite being consistently shuffled to accommodate Vida's draw, went 21-11 with a 2.96 ERA and 16 complete games of his own. Oakland won 101 games — 51 on the road, an American League record — and ran away with the AL West, finishing 16 games ahead of the second-place Royals. Seven A's reached double-digit homers, including Reggie Jackson's 32 (second in the league) and Sal Bando's 24.

The only guy who seemed displeased with everything was Charlie Finley. The A's became the first American League team to draw one million fans on the road (owing largely to Vida), but they didn't come close to turning the trick at home, even with the extra Coliseum starts granted Blue. (Fifteen teams topped a million customers, with the Dodgers and Mets drawing more than two million each.) When it became clear that attendance in Oakland would touch only about 900,000, Finley abruptly canceled Fan Appreciation Day and barred his players from participating in a 1,000-seat civic luncheon scheduled in their honor. The newly alienated fan base responded by buying a total of 2,660 tickets for the team's final two games of the season. With the A's Dixieland band (Finley had finally come to terms with the union) playing to some 49,000 empty seats, it barely seemed to matter that they were going to the playoffs. The atmosphere was more New Orleans funeral than Major League Baseball.

The A's showdown with the Baltimore Orioles in a best-of-five playoff was the team's first postseason appearance since 1931. They never stood a chance. The veteran Orioles — featuring superstars Frank Robinson and Brooks Robinson and a quartet of 20-game winners led by Jim Palmer — took advantage of the first two games at home, pouncing all over a fatigued Blue in a 5–3 victory in Game 1, then smacked around Hunter,

5–1, in Game 2. Oakland's primary weakness was a lack of starting pitching, a deficiency exacerbated by lefty Chuck Dobson's elbow issues and Blue Moon Odom ending the year in a self-described state of "complete fatigue." That left 34-year-old journeyman Diego Segui as Williams's best option when the series shifted to Oakland for Game 3.

The 17,000 empty seats at the Coliseum belied the game's importance, but Finley, granted a spotlight, took advantage. He dragged his mule onto the field before the game and arranged for reliever Mudcat Grant to sing the National Anthem. Then they started playing baseball and everything went to hell, Reggie Jackson's solo homer serving as Oakland's lone highlight in a season-ending 5–2 loss.

As A's players trudged toward the showers after the final out, Jackson sprawled stock-still across the dugout steps, face down in the crook of his arm. The Orioles briefly celebrated, then decamped for their clubhouse. Still Jackson lay. For nearly a half-hour while the stands emptied he remained facedown and frozen, processing what had just happened. Finally he unfolded himself and, eyes red, stumbled up the clubhouse steps. "We didn't blow this thing," he said afterward. "They just took it away from us."

The A's were good, but their youth had been exposed. It felt like an inevitable learning process, which for its pain in the present would be all the more powerful in the future. "Now we understood," said Sal Bando, looking back. "We understood that every pitch was an important pitch, that every play was an important play, that every at-bat was an important at-bat in the playoffs. And we took that with us."

Finley was proud enough to give each player five mementos of the season: a tie tack, a tie clasp, a cigarette lighter, cuff links, and a charm, all in gold. Every one of them was engraved with the phrase A's 1971 WORLD SERIES, a reminder of what, with a break here or there, could have been.

2

The Owner

[Charlie Finley] has made himself a thorough student of player talent. He calls all the shots and he's become a damn good manager. . . . That's right, I said manager.

— A's general manager Frank Lane, 1961

Charles Oscar Finley was a child of the South, born in 1918 on George Washington's birthday, February 22, and raised in the Birmingham suburb of Ensley, Alabama. His father, Oscar Finley, was a steelworker. His grandfather, Randolph Finley, from Londonderry, Ireland, was a steelworker. Finley's own future seemed similarly settled, right up until the lad's overachievement gene kicked in. Stories abound of young Charlie's endeavors at rising above — of buying reject eggs at a steep discount from a local farmer and reselling them at a profit across town, of mowing enough lawns to merit subcontractors, then fielding his first employees at age 12.*

The Finleys moved to Gary, Indiana, after Oscar lost his job at the mill when Charlie was 15. In one swoop the lad became a Midwesterner and, with his new home only 30 miles south of Comiskey Park, an avid White Sox fan.

Upon finishing high school in 1936, young Charlie followed his father into the local mills. Starting at 47½ cents an hour, he stayed on the job for five years, improving his lot all the while. He apprenticed as a machinist. He enrolled in engineering courses at Gary Junior College and the Indiana University extension. He studied in the mornings,

---

* The boy was a born salesman, with only one consistent distraction: baseball. In 1931, at age 13, he secured a job as batboy for the Birmingham Barons, where he worked for 50 cents a day and all the discarded equipment he could carry for use in his own sandlot games.

took classes by day, worked the night shift, and rarely slept. Ambition burned hot. During World War II he worked at an ordnance plant in Kingsbury, Indiana, pulling ten-hour shifts seven days a week, and was soon promoted to superintendent, with 5,000 employees under his watch.

Somehow he also managed to establish a side business selling life insurance. Finley's personal motto, *Sweat plus sacrifice equals success* — shortened over the years to $S + S = S$ — was in full effect. As usual, he was a step ahead of the game. When his job at the ordnance plant disappeared at war's end, he transitioned into insurance full-time and was soon breaking Travelers Insurance Company records for units sold.

Then, in December 1946, he got sick. It was pneumonic tuberculosis, a disease once known as galloping consumption, which offered neither treatment nor cure. Finley was trundled off to the Parramore Sanatorium, a two-story, red-brick hospital in Crown Point, Indiana. He was 28 years old, and as he sweated away half his body weight — dropping from more than 200 pounds to 96 — his chances for survival were pegged at 50 percent. He could barely sit up in bed.

Finley spent 27 months at Parramore, and his slow recovery let him see just how poorly he had planned. The guy who prided himself on his ability to sell insurance to others had somehow failed to secure a policy of his own, forcing his wife of six years, the former Miss Shirley McCartney, to move herself and their two young children in with his parents. Her husband was left to consider the repercussions of a highly valued family member being put out of commission for an extended period. Surrounded by medical professionals, Finley got to thinking about them too — how the devastation that could come to a salesman like Finley when he was sidelined must be compounded for higher earners like doctors. Individual disability policies were expensive and largely seen by the medical community as an unnecessary luxury. But what if Finley could devise a system that would cover doctors en masse with preferred rates? Group insurance policies were hardly a novelty in 1948, but nothing existed to cover entire associations of highly paid physicians.

Finley left Parramore in March 1948 ready to enact his idea. Operating with scale allowed him to offer significantly more coverage for only slightly more money than existing policies. The plans were administered via the Provident Life and Accident Insurance Company by the newly formed Charles O. Finley & Company.

Finley opened an office on the tenth floor of the Gary National Bank building and quickly outgrew the space. Money was good. He moved to a bigger office, and in 1951 enlisted the American College of Surgeons, his first national plan. Money was great. By the early 1950s, Finley was based in Chicago, where he drew the American Medical Association into his fold, along with any number of state- and county-level outfits. He became an avid follower of Wall Street, cannily picking stocks that made him even richer. He bought a 20-room house in Gary and a sprawling, 1,280-acre farm in nearby La Porte, where he would one day bus his players an hour in the wrong direction for forced cookouts while they traveled from Chicago to Milwaukee for games.

Finley was successful, but he lacked one thing he'd always wanted: a baseball team. In 1954, some two years after he struck it rich in insurance, the Philadelphia Athletics provided him with his first shot at ownership. The team had drifted from relevance at the end of Connie Mack's 50-year run, finishing in the American League's second division 16 out of the previous 17 seasons, in last place more often than not, and bottoming out in the year they went up for sale with an unsustainable season attendance of 304,666. Finley swooped in with a $3 million bid, but found his offer matched by a fellow Chicagoan named Arnold Johnson. In the story Finley liked to tell, he showed up ten minutes early to his final meeting with A's ownership in hopes of securing a deal before Johnson arrived . . . only Johnson had appeared an hour early, locking his bid down before Finley even entered the building. Sweat plus sacrifice equals success, and in that instance Johnson sweated and sacrificed just a little bit more than Finley. Lesson learned.

The reality, of course, was that Johnson simply had more contacts than Finley and knew how to play the game in ways that were foreign to the freshly minted millionaire. Johnson was already a baseball insider, having purchased Yankee Stadium from Yankees owners Del Webb and Dan Topping (his partners in a successful vending machine business called Automatic Canteen Company) a year earlier. Leasing it back allowed the team's owners to avoid real estate capital gains and gave them a good deal of additional leverage. They coerced Johnson into simultaneously purchasing Blues Stadium, the Kansas City home of the Yankees' Triple-A affiliate. This left Johnson ripe for a local offer: Kansas City politicians agreed to purchase the stadium outright from him if he bought the A's and moved them there. With strong-arming from the Yankees, baseball's owners approved Johnson's bid and permitted the move a season later. Finley never had a chance.

So he searched elsewhere. He fell short in bidding for the Tigers in 1956, and the White Sox two years later. When the American League awarded an expansion franchise to Los Angeles in 1958, Finley made frequent trips to California and waved around a $5 million offer sheet. This time he was aced out not by a baseball insider but by a California insider, former singing cowboy Gene Autry. (Upon hearing the news that Autry had thrown his Stetson into the ring, legend has it that Finley made an unexpected stop in Arizona to woo Roy Rogers into joining his ownership collective in an effort to match his opponent, cowboy for cowboy. Rogers declined.)

Then it happened. On March 10, 1960, Arnold Johnson, only 54 years old, died of a cerebral hemorrhage while driving home from a spring training game in Florida. His widow, forced to sell the Athletics to cover taxes and accumulated debts, proclaimed a preference for buyers from Kansas City. With attendance that barely reached 750,000, however, the team was hardly a hot commodity, and the leading local syndicate could wrangle only about 75 percent of its $3.5 million offer. So when Finley, all of 42 years old, proposed purchasing a 52 percent stake for about $2 million (plus an agreement to take on 30,000 overvalued shares of Automatic Canteen), the group had little choice. Civic leaders were uneasy with an outsider possessing the bulk of the stock, but Finley was nothing if not a salesman. "I'm not in this for a fast buck or any capital gains," he cooed, "but to build a ballclub that Kansas City fans can be proud of."

Finley's new partners recognized the gravity of the situation the moment he walked through the door and began running things as a sole proprietor, his majority share obviating his need to conjure consensus about anything. Under the pretense of tax benefits, he offered another $1.9 million for the outstanding shares, a proposal that his partners accepted once he agreed to strike a provision from the ballpark lease allowing him to move the club elsewhere if attendance fell below 850,000. To satisfy his promise, Finley staged an elaborate press conference in which he theatrically burned the lease on the steps of City Hall.*

With that, Finley was in charge alone. He was also in the unique posi-

---

* It presaged future public displays of arson, including one in which Finley burned a bus, pointed east toward New York, to represent an end to the practice of shipping Kansas City's best players to the Yankees for little return.

tion of seeing his brand-new last-place team actually fall in the standings, owing to the addition of two new clubs to the American League. There was nowhere to go but up, and while it would take Finley some time to get there, getting there was what he did best. How he did it would come to define the man, sometimes in not such flattering ways, but that didn't matter. Charlie Finley was heretofore the Owner, and the Owner was going to win, or die trying.

Finley repainted the field boxes at Kansas City's Municipal Stadium citrus yellow and the bleachers desert turquoise. He made the dugouts lower and longer, and installed better interior lighting, saying, "I like to see what's going on in the dugout — the strategy being planned and so on — so I figure everybody would like to see, too." He painted the outside of the stadium yellow and orange and improved walkway lighting, all at his own half-million-dollar expense. Alongside the center-field scoreboard Finley installed a programmable message board to convey snippets of text he called Fan-A-Grams. Beyond the right-field wall he deposited a flock of sheep to munch the slopeside grass, tended by a biblically dressed shepherd who rang a bell after home runs. He installed a picnic area and a petting zoo featuring six German checker rabbits, six China golden pheasants, six capuchin monkeys named after his father and uncles, two peafowl, and a German shorthaired pointer.

For the convenience of customers in the lower boxes, who had been forced to climb to the top of the grandstand before descending to their seats, Finley dug a tunnel. Radio broadcasts of the games were piped into the restrooms so that fans would not miss a pitch. He lit fireworks to punctuate big moments. (After neighborhood residents complained about the noise, the Fan-A-Gram flashed: "Thirty thousand dollars' worth of fireworks for sale cheap.") He implemented promotions that befit the surrounding farm community, like greased-pig-grabbing contests and discount days for local farmers. Finley was all about the fans.

It was just the beginning. The Owner tipped the foul poles with pink neon. He devised a metal rabbit with blinking lights for eyes and named it Harvey (after the rabbit-themed Jimmy Stewart movie from 1950). The thing stood on its hind legs and held between its ears a cage full of baseballs. Now, instead of summoning a ball boy, an umpire had only to depress a button and Harvey would rise from the ground near the plate to present his cornucopia of horsehide. Instead of bending over to whisk off the plate, the ump could press another button to summon a vent that sprayed compressed air, scattering dirt in all directions. Finley called it "Little Blowhard."

In 1965 the Owner replaced the team's staid elephant mascot with a Missouri mule — a nod to the local contribution to World War I. The mule was selected, he said, following "the greatest mule search in history." He named it Charlie O and kept it in an air-conditioned trailer on the street outside the ballpark. If Finley ever considered that such a mascot, named after himself no less, would inevitably lead to jokes about the jackass of the A's . . . and his mule . . . he never let on. He certainly didn't care.

The rest of the Owner's interactions with the people of Kansas City — not to mention with the A's themselves — were not so smooth. Upon taking over the team, Finley promised to move his family from La Porte as soon as his son, Charlie Jr., graduated from high school, the better to embrace the local populace and be embraced in return. He went on the radio and said, "Brother, I mean to tell you, I'm here to stay." He never left Indiana.

Finley's board of directors proved meaningless — the corporation to which he named them was completely fabricated. Even Finley's public display of arson, burning the stadium lease on the steps of city hall, was a sham. The thing on fire was a blank piece of paper, while the actual lease to Municipal Stadium sat safely in the Owner's office. Within months he would send out feelers to cities across the country for potential new locations for his ballclub. In the end Finley got his way. In those days, it seemed, he always got his way.

Those A's were terrible, but from their morass future championships were forged. Even as the team struggled, farm director Hank Peters was developing one of the sport's strongest scouting staffs, and Finley proved expert at signing players as they were presented — a wispy Cuban catcher named Bert Campaneris, who had just escaped Fidel Castro's ascent to power; three Californians, Joe Rudi, Rollie Fingers, and Dave Duncan; and two Southern high school pitchers, Blue Moon Odom and Catfish Hunter. It was a fortuitous time — Charles O. Finley & Company was so flush with cash that signing-bonus expenditures provided the dual benefit of improving the Owner's baseball interests while offsetting his insurance company's taxes. In 1964 the A's signed 80 players for about $650,000 — the most ever spent by one team on amateur talent in a single year.

The implementation of the amateur player draft in 1965 hardly slowed the influx. With the top overall pick, Finley selected Rick Monday, the defending NCAA Player of the Year out of Arizona State — a strapping blond with power, speed, and grace, a face-of-the-franchise type who looked good on the cover of a media guide. Within two years the A's added Sal Bando, Gene Tenace, Reggie Jackson, and Vida Blue.

With that, phase one of Finley's master plan was essentially complete. Over a five-year span the Owner spent about $1.7 million on approximately 250 signing bonuses. When his insurance profits began to dip, he shifted the bulk of his budget into player development. The A's had their ingredients. Now the stew needed time to cook.

Part 2

PINNACLE

1972–1974

3

Vida's Blues

> Vida Blue is beautiful. He is what baseball needs. I am going
> to promote him and he is going to get publicity and he is
> going to be great for the entire game. Don't you worry about
> him making money. He is going to make money. He is going
> to get more than money. He is going to get great things from
> this game. I'm going to see that he gets great things. I am
> going to protect him.
>
> —Charles O. Finley, 1971

This being America, where acclaim is a fast track to fortune, the fact that Vida Blue made only $14,500 in 1971 — barely above baseball's minimum, despite being the sport's biggest drawing card — was an undeniable subplot of his amazing season. When he won the American League's Cy Young and MVP awards, becoming at age 22 the youngest player to win either — let alone both at the same time — his bargaining power rose considerably.

The finances were impossible to ignore. Vida drew crowds of 30,000 for games that would have otherwise attracted one-sixth that amount. Oakland averaged 23,000 fans, home and road, when Blue pitched and 10,000 when he didn't. Even more stark: one out of every 12 American League tickets sold in 1971 was for a game the left-hander started. Even Richard Nixon weighed in when the A's visited the White House in August, intoning that Blue was "the most underpaid player in baseball."

It wasn't like Vida was hurting for cash. During the off-season he earned $10,000 for endorsing the California Milk Advisory Council and another $25,000 for an aftershave commercial. He took meetings for a sequel to the movie *Shaft*. He did a USO tour in Vietnam with

Bob Hope.* So inundated was the pitcher with endorsement offers, in fact, that roommate Tommy Davis introduced him to Los Angeles–based attorney Bob Gerst, a former standout third baseman at the University of Southern California. The idea was to help Vida maximize his promotional opportunities, but when Blue and Gerst started to examine what a fair-value contract with Finley might look like, they agreed that there was work to be done there as well.

Finley never expected somebody like Gerst to be introduced to contract negotiations. Player representation was the norm in other sports (11 players on the NHL team that Finley had recently purchased used agents),† but it was virtually unheard of in baseball. The Owner was able to out-bargain high-powered insurance executives, so what chance did ballplayers fresh from high school stand? Gerst, however, was different. He was 36, energetic, and as dogged as Finley when it came to getting what he wanted. They were instantly incompatible.

Before long *The Sporting News* was speculating that the pitcher would ask for $85,000 and settle for $50,000 — a 350 percent raise that would represent the highest salary ever for a second-year player. When Gerst requested a meeting, however, Finley insisted that his business was with Vida, only reluctantly allowing the pitcher to bring his lawyer if he wished.

The three men met in Chicago on January 8. Gerst had done the math. The A's drew 150,000 more fans in 1971 than the season before, earning Finley an additional $800,000. Some of that was attributable to the playoff run, but Blue's part in the process could not be denied. Hell, Vida outdrew three American League teams by himself. Finley opened the talks at $45,000. Gerst countered with the average salary paid to baseball's top ten pitchers, which he figured to be $115,000. Finley stared across his desk in disbelief. "Do you know what floor we're on?" he sputtered. "We're on the twenty-seventh floor of this building.

---

* Some of the lines from Vida's participation in Hope's USO stage routines:
  HOPE: How come you didn't get more money from Mr. Finley, the owner?
  BLUE: Well, Mr. Finley claimed I was only using one arm.
  HOPE: Would you pitch for the same money?
  BLUE: Sure. Right-handed.

† The Oakland Seals — renamed the California Golden Seals by the Owner — were awful every year of Finley's tenure as a sustained flurry of bad trades and front-office controversy held in check any improvement. As in baseball, Finley grated on his fellow NHL owners, to the degree that the NHL eventually bought the team back from him without having a replacement owner in place.

You have as much chance of getting $115,000 from me as I do of jumping out of my office window."

Finley raised his offer to $50,000. "I know you pitched 300 innings," he told Blue, staring directly into the pitcher's eyes to drive home the point. "I know you had 24 complete games and eight shutouts. I know you led the league in ERA. I know you won the Cy Young and MVP. I don't have to pay you." It was as simple as that. *I don't have to pay you.* If Vida was to pitch in 1972, it would be on Finley's terms. *You need me more than I need you.* "He said it with a smirk," recalled Blue, "and, man, it made me want to slide under the table." This was not the type of negotiation the pitcher had anticipated.

They spent five hours going back and forth, but never got any closer. Gerst had intended $115,000 as a jumping-off point and was ready to accept $93,000 immediately. Vida himself was hoping merely for $75,000. Finley, however, didn't negotiate terms, he dictated them. The meeting broke with no resolution in sight.

Things remained that way through the opening of spring training. As the rest of the team unpacked their bags in Mesa, Arizona, Vida was back home in Mansfield, with Gerst demanding that the Owner pay the pitcher or trade him. Finley responded by taking the fight public.

Until that point, Gerst had protected details of the negotiations from the press, but suddenly every figure found its way into print, provided by Finley himself. The Owner talked about his eminently fair offer and Gerst's ridiculous counter. He pointed out that while raises were unrestricted by the collective bargaining agreement, cuts maxed out at 20 percent for one year, and 30 percent over two. "This creates an inequity," Finley explained. "If a player does better than expected, he merits an increase, but if he does worse than expected, he deserves a decrease — and the increase must be kept in line with the permissible decrease." He mentioned that Vida had confided a willingness to sign for $85,000, even while begging him not to tell Gerst about it. "I will not pay you one penny more than $50,000," Finley grandly recalled himself saying.

The Owner took to bashing Gerst wherever possible, contemptuously referring to him as the pitcher's "notary." "It doesn't help [Blue] one cent," he said. "It's going to cost him money. He's going to wind up paying something to him, ten or fifteen percent. Vida's squandering his money." Gerst clarified that he was working for a flat fee and would be paid the same regardless of Vida's contract. He pointed out that even as Finley decried the presence of a lawyer on Blue's behalf, the Owner kept his own attorney on retainer. Finley suggested that if sharply escalating salaries ever forced him to raise ticket prices, he'd get out of baseball altogether. Gerst said that might not be such a bad idea. Finley had finally found somebody as stubborn as himself. Actually, between Blue and Gerst, he'd found two.

"There were a lot of things he said that weren't true, and I responded to them," said Gerst, looking back. "I didn't let them pass. I couldn't let them pass. . . . Finley was a super salesman. Do super salesmen believe in what they say, or are they just trying to use psychological pressure, create a certain impression, a feeling? Who knows?"

As spring training ticked away, Gerst, recognizing that reason would get him nowhere, sought alternative paths. He explored the idea that Blue signed his A's contract as a minor, making it invalid. He tried to show that Finley failed to pay $2,500 of Vida's incentive bonus after the pitcher spent 90 days on the major league roster. He got in touch with former Supreme Court justice Arthur Goldberg, who was handling Curt Flood's lawsuit challenging Major League Baseball's reserve clause, to discuss whether to insert Vida's case into the fray. He talked about Vida playing in Japan. He even considered becoming a trailblazer in the arena of crowdfunding, openly wondering about setting Vida up as an employee of a nonprofit corporation, his salary paid by donations from the general public, which would free him to jump to any team since he'd effectively be volunteering his services. None of it played out.

The chatter was insufficient to force Finley closer to accepting Blue's terms, but it did improbably manage to sway public opinion away from the pitcher and toward the Owner. The fans wanted only to see Vida play baseball. This was not that. Spring training was in full swing, and the team's brightest star was nowhere to be found. Someone had to shoulder the blame.

In the offices of Charles O. Finley & Company, that person was Tommy Davis, the guy who introduced Gerst to Blue in the first place. Davis was a valuable bench player for the A's in 1971, batting .324, including a .464 mark as a pinch hitter. The following March he was even better, batting .563 in Cactus League action while Vida held out in Mansfield. Finley, however, wanted to make a statement and needed a fall guy. Prior to an exhibition game against the Padres in Yuma, three hours by bus from the A's base in Mesa, Finley gave Dick Williams specific instructions: wait until the team arrives at the ballpark, then inform Davis of his release. The Owner left it up to the stunned outfielder to find his own way home.*

About a month after Blue was supposed to have reported, Gerst pulled his boldest maneuver to date, claiming that if Finley didn't set forth agreeable terms by March 16, Vida would not pitch for the A's, no matter what kind of money was offered. On that date the agent called a press conference in Oakland to announce that Blue had taken a job outside of baseball. He would theretofore be a vice president of public relations for the Dura Steel Products Company, one of whose principals was a client of Gerst's law firm, at a salary of $55,000 per year. Blue's new employer manufactured bathroom fixtures, one of which, a cabinet called the "Over-John," designed for installation above a commode, led to the lasting impression that Vida had gone to work for a toilet company. The idea was to show that Blue did not need Finley more than Finley needed Blue, and that the pitcher was able to land a high-paying job without the Owner's blessing. Instead, it illustrated what a joke the entire affair had become. Even Vida's teammates, while publicly proclaiming hope that he come away with as much money as possible, privately grumbled that for what Finley was offering, the pitcher should be among their ranks.

The Dura Steel press conference was a disaster. A statement was prepared for Vida in which he claimed he had retired from baseball—a notion that held no credibility with Vida himself, let alone anybody else. The newly minted executive, wearing neither coat nor tie, giggled his way through his recitation. "This is a wonderful opportunity for me and one that I feel I should take," he said without conviction. "It is with deep regret and sadness I announce my leaving baseball." Newsmen had many questions, but Blue's handlers did not allow time for answers. Finley, however, was all too happy to comment, wishing Vida success at his new steel industry job while pointing out that he himself had spent five years working for US Steel—adding with a wink that he began as a machine shop apprentice, not a vice president.

When Vida showed up at Dura Steel's Southern California offices to

---

* After a reluctant Williams did as instructed, Davis wandered around the ballpark, dismayed. Eventually, traveling secretary Tom Corwin took pity on him and loaned him his car. "A club doesn't release a .324 hitter even if he's been put in jail for life over the winter," Davis said. "You get him out of the penitentiary." Davis was irate but powerless, forced to "just fade away, the way [Finley] would like me to fade away."

make phone calls on behalf of his new employer, it was obviously not where he wanted to be. Against his agent's express wishes, he contacted Finley directly. A face-to-face meeting, sans Gerst, was arranged in Phoenix, but brought them no closer. Rather than counter the pitcher's demands, Finley began staging press conferences to decry the situation. In one (originally scheduled to announce what the Owner was sure would be a signing), he recalled Vida telling him, "I'm a mixed-up kid." In another, called for 11:00 P.M. in the coffee shop of the team's spring training headquarters at the Sands Motel (attended by pitcher Chuck Dobson, among others, for the simple reason that he had come down to pick up an ice cream soda), the Owner publicly revoked some of the concessions he had already offered, primarily a stipend for up to $5,000 in legal fees.*

Finley meant it when he said he was willing to let Vida sit out the season. With that possibility appearing more likely by the day, he swung a deal with Texas for right-hander Denny McLain, a guy who until very recently had been nearly as unhittable as Blue. McLain went 55-15 for the Tigers over the 1968 and 1969 seasons, picking up two Cy Youngs and an MVP along the way. The two years since, however, told another tale. In February 1970, *Sports Illustrated* ran a feature alleging McLain's partnership in an illegal bookmaking operation that included members of the Syrian mafia, a relationship that ended when a mobster named Tony Giacalone stomped on the pitcher's foot and dislocated some toes. McLain was suspended for the first three months of the 1970 season, then returned to make 14 mediocre starts before he was suspended again for carrying a gun and pouring water over two reporters. The Tigers traded him to Washington, where he led the league with 22 losses. Still, he was only 28 and, owing primarily to his $75,000 salary, could be had for a song. Finley acquired him for two marginal prospects, hopes high that he could perform capably in Blue's stead. Even with Texas kicking in some cash to even things out, Finley proved that he would rather pay a premium to substandard strangers than budge from his stance to appease his star.

As opening day approached, Gerst peppered the Owner with offers. He suggested using an outside arbitrator. He requested a multiyear con-

---

* Finley even began a recruitment campaign, sending catcher Gene Tenace to woo Blue. Tenace had known Vida since the pitcher was a 17-year-old in the Arizona Instructional League. They were so close that Blue babysat Tenace's kids. It didn't matter. When Tenace came up empty, Finley turned to utility man Curt Blefary, who also failed to convince the pitcher to return.

tract, or a bonus based on attendance from the previous season, or a bonus based on attendance for the upcoming season. He proposed being paid $42,500 by ARCO for Vida to appear in a gas-station commercial with Finley. No, said the Owner. No, no, no.

Blue's teammates began to respond to the situation with increasing candor. Reggie Jackson, who had staged his own holdout two seasons earlier, tried to counsel the pitcher but got nowhere. Pitcher Chuck Dobson said, "I'd like to see Vida take the $50,000 Finley offered him and go out and have another great year. If Vida puts together two spectacular seasons back to back, he'll eventually get the kind of money he wants."

"I'm for a guy getting all he can," added Sal Bando, "but Charlie has offered Vida a fair contract."

One more factor was yet at play. Also holding out was Catfish Hunter, largely to see how much Blue would get. Unlike Vida, however, Catfish wanted to be in camp. He made it clear to Finley that as a seven-year veteran coming off his own 20-win season, he would not be satisfied earning less than his young teammate. Finley assured him that Blue's demands would not be met, then offered Hunter the same $50,000 he offered to Vida. This represented a $15,000 raise. Catfish accepted immediately.

In the short term, Vida's holdout was overshadowed by the first full-scale strike in baseball history. The players wanted a 17 percent increase in their pension plan to keep up with inflation, which union boss Marvin Miller claimed would not cost "a damn cent" more if the owners funded it with an existing surplus rather than placing the money in reserve, as they'd been doing. In response, management branded the players as greedy and entitled.

Over this relative pittance, the final days of spring training were obliterated, then the opening of the regular season. As cries for settlement grew louder, baseball's ownership became more entrenched. Ironically, the owners' greatest source of expertise was the guy they least wanted to lean upon.

Finley had been tormenting his baseball peers from the moment he first bullied his way into their ranks. The Owner was a man of change — it was a quality upon which he built his entire business career — and of little patience. Much of baseball's old guard viewed anachronism as a virtue, and did not sit easily with Finley's refusal to jump through their hoops, let alone the furious pace at which he built hoops of his own. Finley was tone-deaf to the fact that as the low-man newbie on baseball's ownership totem, his best chance to have his ideas considered was to manage them upward, gently massaging conversations with his colleagues right up to the point that nobody was certain where they came from in the first place.

For a man like the Owner, of course, that simply wasn't possible. The bluster that played in his insurance office stood out like a green-and-gold jersey amid a sea of gray when it came to baseball. The man was a force of nature, Hurricane Charlie bearing down on the very beachfront where his colleagues had their heads buried in the sand. By 1971 he had been barking so loudly, for so long, and in the altogether wrong pitch, that baseball's ownership circle had taken to tuning him out as a matter of reflex.

This time, however, was different. Insurance was Charlie Finley's business, and the terms in question were part of his regular lexicon. After negotiations faltered through what should have been the opening days of the regular season, Finley convinced the owners to gather in New York in conjunction with a players' union meeting across town. "A strike never has been settled without a compromise," he told his colleagues. "It can't be a one-way street. Baseball must not suffer any longer and must not be made to suffer again. A fair offer must be made and then accepted." The stance did little to endear him to ownership's hard-liners, but Finley had few friends there anyway.

At the Owner's urging, a settlement was reached. The players agreed to a bit more than half of what they wanted (instead of a 17 percent increase, to $960,000, they accepted $500,000), and games got under way 11 days after the season was supposed to start. Instead of a 162-game schedule, the A's now had 154 games to play. Finley's unflinching rationality was instrumental in solving the dispute, but it didn't reach as far as Oakland. When the season finally began, the A's were eager to take the field. All of them, anyway, but Vida Blue.

The A's may have opened their season late, but at least they looked good. Finley introduced new uniforms during the off-season, doing away with vests and buttons and even the greens and yellows that caused such a stir when he introduced them in 1963. Somehow the new outfits were even gaudier, unlike anything baseball had seen. The Owner had been obsessed with a green-and-yellow palette ever since Shirley Finley dressed their infant daughters in those colors decades earlier, and he implemented it everywhere, from the NHL team he purchased in 1970 to the blazers he wore as a matter of sartorial exclamation.

The A's new look offered a bold stance. Polyester pullover tops in gold or green, both colors more vibrant than their predecessors', tucked into white, beltless pants with striped elastic waistbands. Monochrome options, pants and jerseys both, of yellow, green, and white, never mind the white cleats that by then were de rigueur in Oakland. (Finley insisted that the shoes were made from the hides of albino kangaroos.) The secret to the all-yellow combination, joked Bando, was that opponents "don't think we're ballplayers, they think we're bananas."

The brilliance of the uniforms could not obscure the fact that Blue was nowhere to be found. "I guess I'm a lousy businessman," said Finley, reinforcing his hard-line stance. "Here we are talking about $20,000 when there is the possibility of Vida Blue sitting out the entire season. I stand to lose $500,000 at the gate, but I'll lose that before I go any further." Actually, Blue had been responsible for three times that amount in 1971 — $1.5 million in gate receipts — and a single crowd of 30,000 would more than recoup his salary demands. New to Finley's discourse was that Vida would be docked for every day he missed, and the Owner's $50,000 offer would be prorated to whenever the pitcher returned.

Replacing Blue with Denny McLain was a long shot, but Finley didn't stop there. In November he traded golden-boy center fielder Rick Monday — who by season's end in 1971 was being platooned with rookie Angel Mangual — to the Cubs for 26-year-old left-handed pitcher Ken Holtzman. In so doing, the Owner acquired a two-time 17-game winner with stuff electric enough to pitch two no-hitters over six seasons with Chicago.*

Holtzman went 4-1 over his first five decisions with the A's in 1972, with a 2.30 ERA and four complete games — a huge factor in Oakland win-

---

* When Holtzman received his first contract from Finley, he stared in disbelief at the 10 percent cut by the Owner from his $56,500 salary. The pitcher didn't yet recognize this as a rite of passage. Each December many of Holtzman's new teammates went through a similar ritual: receive an envelope from Charles O. Finley & Company, shout some profanities upon opening it, and return the contract unsigned, sometimes in pieces. The Owner met such responses with angry bluster, which was enough to get some players to fold. Those who didn't had a chance at a small raise. Occasionally, one of them would take things a step further, like Vida did, and hold out.

ning 12 of its first 16. McLain, however, with nothing left on his fastball, was not working out. The problem was that with Odom still working his way back from arm surgery in 1971, Dobson out with elbow trouble, and Diego Segui having fallen out of favor, McLain was Dick Williams's best option. It didn't end well. The right-hander struck out eight men in three weeks, and with his ERA sitting at 6.04 on May 12, was optioned all the way down to Double-A Birmingham.*

The A's already knew it, but it became clearer every day: they needed Vida.

They weren't alone. Major League Baseball's key drawing card of 1971 was out of commission, with his employer showing no urgency to rectify the situation. Enter Commissioner Bowie Kuhn. It wasn't that Finley's $50,000 offer was outrageous, the Commissioner said, but that "Finley had a way of making it seem so." On April 27, Kuhn called the parties together in his suite at the Drake Hotel in Chicago, where he, Finley, Gerst, Blue, and MLB attorney Sandy Hadden spent 22 straight hours going back, forth, and back again on contract minutiae. "Finley loathed everybody," recalled Kuhn. "Sadly, Blue seemed as ill-tempered as Finley." Kuhn's only motive was to get Vida's name on a contract, but the Owner was adamant in his refusal to compromise. Blue drifted in and out, growing upset whenever Kuhn seemed to side with Finley, and at about 6:00 A.M. he finally left to get some sleep in his own room.

In Blue's absence, the group spent three hours hammering out details. Eventually Gerst came up with some wording that allowed Finley to stick to his $50,000 figure (which, prorated to April 27, came to $41,667), but which kicked in a $5,000 bonus for Blue's 1971 performance and reanimated the long-since-expired $8,000 set aside in Blue's first contract to cover college tuition. Kuhn was delighted. Gerst was happy. Finley remained sour, yet still went to fetch doughnuts for the group. ("You know where he went, don't you?" Hadden asked Gerst when they had a moment alone. The agent figured that it had something to do with doughnuts. "He went to talk to the press," Hadden informed him. Finley paid close atten-

---

* The demotion wasn't aimed at helping McLain improve. The Owner wanted the pitcher to see it for the insult it was and refuse the assignment, thus taking Finley off the hook for the remainder of his exorbitant salary. When McLain refused to play along, Finley offered to buy him out for $25,000. McLain declined and kept cashing his major league paychecks in Birmingham.

tion to print deadlines and wanted to make sure that his version of events was the one to make the afternoon papers.)

When Gerst presented the package to Blue, however, the pitcher recoiled. Not about the money — that, he was willing to accept — but about Finley's insistence on announcing it as a $50,000 deal while stripping the bonuses from the narrative. To publicly accept the amount that the Owner had offered all along was to admit defeat. If Vida was to earn $63,000 in 1972, that was what he wanted on the record. Shocking everybody in the room, Gerst returned with the news: the deal was off.

Each party stormed off to his respective corner of the country — Blue to Oakland, Gerst to Los Angeles, Kuhn to New York, and Finley up South Michigan Avenue, back to his office. Before long the news of what was supposed to have been a secret meeting circulated among the press — the result of the Owner's doughnut run — and soon included details of the rejected offer. "Had Mr. Finley been willing to continue to work in confidence," said a discouraged Gerst, "we would have been able to work it out."

It was too much for the Commissioner to stomach. Shortly after returning to New York, Kuhn ordered Finley to keep the offer open for three days, "in the best interests of baseball" — a phrase he would use repeatedly over the coming years to justify his actions against Finley. The Owner, who had already considered such an idea and was not altogether opposed to it, raged at the audacity of what he felt was an overreach. "I will obey his order to keep the offer open only if he orders the player to accept it," he blustered at reporters. Finley need not have worried — Blue was equally sick of the process and instructed Gerst to consent.[*]

Kuhn called a May 2 meeting at the Boston office of American League president Joe Cronin, where both sides would sign the contract in conjunction with an A's trip to Fenway Park. When Finley told him to go to hell, Kuhn calmly replied, "Charlie, either you show in Boston and sign a contract with Blue, or I will make him a free agent." Such a situation was virtually unheard of, but Finley already had some experience with the process. In August 1967, the Owner rashly cut the A's leading hitter, Ken

---

[*] Gerst made an extra $10,000 for his client by selling the rights to break the news on Howard Cosell's ABC TV show *Monday Night Sports,* which meant that everybody had to sit on the deal for an extra day, until the program aired.

Harrelson, after he reportedly called Finley a "menace to baseball," then watched in horror as the first baseman signed a $150,000 contract with Boston — an enormous increase over the $12,000 the Owner had been paying him. Finley did not want to revisit similar circumstances.

At the appointed time, the Owner strode through the door, suitably dour. He, Kuhn, Cronin, and a room full of reporters prepared for the season's biggest event, and for Blue's arrival. Thirty minutes turned into an hour. Officials began to draft contingency plans as newsmen composed *What do we do now?* stories in their heads. Finally, an hour and 40 minutes after everybody got settled, Vida strolled in. If Finley's habit of making private negotiations public was simply a factor of working with him, Blue's inability to get places on time was equally inevitable. The principals grabbed pens and signed the contract, then all four of them — Finley, Kuhn, Cronin, and Blue — faced the press. Blue, the man of the hour, answered questions with something approaching misery. "I signed it and I'm happy," said the stone-faced pitcher. *Then why do you not look happy?* "I said I'm happy." Finley spat out a "no comment" when asked how he felt about Kuhn's handling of the situation, and seemed shocked when Blue informed the room that he'd need up to a month to get ready to pitch. "I'll be lucky if I win ten," Vida said. Little did anybody know how optimistic that prediction would be.

Vida joined the A's that night at Logan Airport for their charter flight to Oakland, so traumatized that he came close to leaving baseball for good. In a daze, the pitcher mindlessly followed his teammates to the boarding ramp, but as he reached the plane did a sudden about-face and hightailed it back to the terminal. "I just kept thinking, *I lost forty grand,*" said Blue. "I was so angry." The pitcher had been governed by his emotions about the contract for so many months that when rejoining the team *felt* wrong, he figured it had to *be* wrong. He ended up walking circles in a corner of the airport, head aswirl, before belatedly racing back to the aircraft. He barely made it, the last passenger aboard, but said later that "if the plane would have left me, that's all right." Once they were airborne, Blue twice tried to approach Finley and unburden himself, but failed to create the necessary space. The frustrated pitcher finally summoned *Oakland Tribune* reporter Ron Bergman and Jim Street of the *San Jose Mercury News* to his seat. "He treated me like a damn colored boy," Vida told them amid an avalanche of commentary. "Charlie Finley has soured my stomach for baseball." Blue also said that the holdout was less about money than pride, and that if he ever gave anything but full effort on a ball field he'd quit on the spot.

"Tonight isn't tell it like it is," he said, elucidating a notion that would become increasingly prominent in his interactions with team and media alike over the coming years. "Tonight is tell it like I feel."

4

Sweet Smell of Success

We finally built those big names that other teams recognized. "Who the heck is a doggone Catfish Hunter and Vida
Blue? Or Blue Moon Odom? Who are these guys? Who is
Oakland, period? They're not even on the map." Until you
play us, and then we put the fear in you.

—Blue Moon Odom

It was late May when the A's reached Arlington Stadium, the new home of
the Texas Rangers, freshly relocated from Washington, D.C., and things
were terrific. With Vida recently back, Oakland was 23-11, two games up
in the American League West. It was the start of a 14-game road trip, and
as players filtered into the clubhouse they began to settle into their travel
routines. The team's pass lists sat atop a picnic table at the far side of the
room: a blue sheet for players to leave tickets for family members (the
better seats), and a white sheet for friends. Reggie Jackson hovered above
them, eyes squinting in scrutiny, until one name in particular caught
his eye. "Berman?" he asked, perusing the blue list. "Who put down for
these?" Per Rangers policy, players were allowed four seats from the blue
list and only two from the white, so first baseman Mike Epstein had used
his family passes for friends of his father — the delightfully named Sher-
man Berman and family — to ensure that they sat together. This was not
unusual practice.

"I did," said the slugger, "and it's none of your business."

"I'm appointing it my business," replied Jackson.

Epstein had arrived in the middle of the 1971 season, along with reliever Darold Knowles, via a trade with Washington. The six-foot-three,

230-pounder had hit 30 home runs for the Senators in 1969, but soon thereafter fell into platoon use, during which time he was increasingly described as temperamental. ("Moodiness," Epstein rationalized in response, "is an outgrowth of pride in a person.") Still, he was just what the A's needed, slugging 18 home runs in 104 games after coming over, and becoming a staple in the heart of their order. Now he was in a staredown with the team's biggest star. "Don't buy more than you can handle," Epstein warned.

Years' worth of proximity enabled the players who came up with Jackson — Duncan, Rudi, Bando — to differentiate his confrontational, bark-not-bite nature from something actually nefarious. For guys like Epstein who were new to the team, however, such distinctions were not always so easy.

Most of the players had only just arrived at the ballpark and were still dressing when the exchange took place. Watching the brewing confrontation warily, Joe Rudi was the first to pipe up. "Back off," he sternly warned Reggie. "Don't mess with him."

Reggie did not back off. "Those are family tickets, and there ain't no Jews in Texas," he said, invoking Epstein's Semitic heritage. With that, he grabbed a pen and crossed out the names, one by one. Epstein, a former fullback on the Cal football team, flew off his seat as if at a tackling dummy. Reggie had no chance. "This was not a typical baseball fight," recalled Ken Holtzman, who watched it go down from his nearby locker. "This was a *fight* fight."

Epstein threw Jackson to the floor, straddling him and peppering him with punches. When he grabbed Reggie by the throat and began choking him, traveling secretary Tom Corwin raced to get Dick Williams, and players jumped up to intercede. First to the fray was Gene Tenace, hardly a diminutive figure, who found himself entirely unable to budge the irate behemoth. "Reggie's eyes are spinning around in his head and I think, *this ain't working*," said Tenace, looking back. "I've got to get his hands off of Reggie. How am I going to do *that?*" Eventually the catcher wrapped his forearm around Epstein's windpipe and, with full force, pulled. Epstein fell backward onto Tenace, sending both men tumbling to the floor. With all three players on the ground, Williams burst into the room.

"When Dick came out, it must have looked like Mike and I were taking out Reggie," recalled Tenace. "Reggie's laying over there on the floor, and Mike is laying on my chest. I'm exhausted from pulling this stinking animal off of Reggie, and then all of a sudden here comes Dick, and Dick's screaming at me and Mike. I'm going, 'Why is he screaming at me?'"

Tenace's response — "Man, if I wasn't here you might not have a right fielder" — bought him little goodwill. Williams ordered all three players into his office. Reggie — "cross-eyed and half out of it," according to Tenace — took one of two chairs, Epstein the other. Tenace leaned against a wall. When Williams began to yell, the catcher piped up.

"Hey, Skip, wait a second," he said. "You've got this all wrong. First of all . . ."

Williams wanted no part of it. "Shut up!" he shouted. "I'll ask the questions!"

By that point the entire team had gathered outside the closed office door, trying to catch snippets of conversation. The manager's anger — a hail of proclamations, curses, and threats — was directed primarily at Tenace and Epstein, until Epstein interrupted. "Gene is right," he said. "He's the one who got me off of Reggie. He wasn't even involved."

Williams eyed Tenace warily. "Get your ass out of here, Geno," he spat.

Never one to miss an opening, Tenace piped up. "You sure you want me to leave you in here with these two guys?" he grinned.

"Get your ass out of here, Geno!" Williams screamed.

When Tenace opened the office door, he found himself nose to nose with half the roster. "Screw it," he thought to himself. "If something else goes down, *they'll* take care of it."

Eventually, Williams talked Epstein and Jackson into agreeing that they could hate each other without killing each other. Clubhouse opinion, meanwhile, was divided. Those who came up with Jackson understood the delicacy of his personality, but some of the younger players were less forgiving. As Hunter walked by the whirlpool later in the day, rookie George Hendrick, having a soak, called him over. "Who the hell grabbed Epstein and broke up the fight?" he asked, angry at the intervention. "I wanted to see Epstein kick the shit out of Reggie."

Drama or no, upon leaving Texas, Oakland won nine of ten games. If anything, the fight solidified their ability to derive strength from strife, and served to illustrate that no matter how much the players might loathe one another, there was always one guy in the equation they loathed even more. Enter Finley.

The Owner had engaged Reggie in repeated battles of will ever since the slugger reached the big leagues in 1967. Now, however, he surprised many by taking Jackson's side. Maybe it was that despite Reggie's faults he was still Finley's guy—drafted and raised and nurtured into stardom by the Owner—while Epstein was an outsider. Or maybe Finley simply wanted to break somebody new. Before the following day's game he got Epstein on the phone and cut to the chase. "Who the fuck do you think you are, beating up my star player?" he shouted.

"Excuse me?" said Epstein.

"I *traded* for you," Finley said. "You're not one of *my* players. I could get you back to Washington just as fast as a phone call. You're the apple that's going to spoil the bunch. You're ruining this team!"

Epstein was uncowed. "You've got it reversed," he said. "The guy who's the problem is the guy that I knocked out on the floor. I did you a favor." Then he cut to his own chase: "Why don't you just trade me now?" he asked.

Finley was angry, but he was not stupid. Epstein was a key cog. A trade could wait until after the season, Finley told the first baseman, at which point he'd be good as gone.

After the season, he was.

By the middle of the 1972 season the A's were in first place and Dick Williams was in full bristle at the relentless nature of Finley's phone calls. The Owner found him in the dugout. He found him in his office before games. The phone was already ringing when Williams reached the clubhouse after games. Finley sought explanations for every bit of strategy, even when the team won, including situations that had little to do with the outcome. On the road, Finley placed the manager in a two-bedroom suite with traveling secretary Tom Corwin to ensure that somebody was always on hand to answer the phone. He found him at home, during Williams's family time. The calls came five, six, seven a day, "any time from eight in the morning until midnight," said Corwin. (Finley took to calling his employees so much, said farm director John Claiborne, that they bestowed radio call letters—KCOF—on his phone line.) Williams didn't complain about it much within earshot of the media, but around the team he began to openly wonder how much he could tolerate. Once, when Finley called the dugout from his stadium box in the middle of a game, Williams instructed trainer Joe Romo to answer the phone and "tell him I'm not here."*

The Owner also took his role as general manager seriously — perhaps too seriously — making deals at such a frenetic pace that Williams's best method for finding out who was on his roster at any given moment was to walk into the clubhouse and see who showed up. Finley made 62 deals over the course of the 1972 season, twice counting Brant Alyea and Larry Haney, each of whom was traded and then reacquired. In May alone Finley traded outfielder Reggie Sanders to Detroit for Mike Kilkenny; signed free-agent pitcher Gary Waslewski; sold Bobby Brooks to Detroit; traded infielder Dwain Anderson to the Cardinals for reliever Don Shaw; traded backup catcher Curt Blefary and Kilkenny to San Diego for Ollie Brown, whom he waived the following month; released Ron Klimkowski; traded Alyea to St. Louis for Marty Martinez; and sold Haney to the Padres. Eight deals, 13 players. Uniform number 4 was worn by three players in 1972, a total that would have been more impressive had not three other numbers — 11, 24, and 33 — been used with equal frequency. The remaining team members erected a makeshift tote board on the clubhouse wall commemorating their departed comrades. As writer Ron Bergman suggested in *The Sporting News,* "Once an Athletic, always an Athletic . . . or if not once an Athletic, then eventually an Athletic."

The genius to Finley's madness was that he left his core players alone. His was a tinkering at the edges.

Still, when the A's headed into the summer months they began to lose, less a straight tumble than a steady decline toward the mean. They dropped as many as four games in a row only once during July and August, but had four separate three-game losing streaks without an extended run of success to mitigate them. Every regular but Joe Rudi slumped. Jackson went on the 15-day disabled list in mid-August with a rib injury, and hit only two homers in his final 88 at-bats after returning. In late July,

---

* The best Finley-calling-the-dugout story happened in Kansas City in 1973, shortly after outfielder Jay Johnstone was recalled from Triple-A Tucson. About 15 minutes after the game began, the player fielded an unexpected phone call. "How do the shoes fit?" asked the Owner, following up on Johnstone's new pair of white spikes. As Johnstone attempted to answer him, the roar of the crowd led Finley to ask what was happening. "Uhhh, we're in the first inning, Mr. Finley," Johnstone said. The Owner thought the game was slated for 8:00 P.M., not 7:30, and had missed his mark. "Well, I'm glad the shoes fit," he said hurriedly. "If you have any other problems, just call old Charlie and let me know."

the A's were leading the division by eight and a half games, but only a month later had fallen a game and a half behind Chicago. Rumors spread that Finley would fire Williams in September following a four-game series against the White Sox at the Coliseum.

What saved the A's was their starting pitching—particularly Hunter (9-3, 1.68 ERA over July and August) and Odom (7-2, 2.01 during that span). The only member of the rotation to truly misfire was the guy for whom hopes had been highest at the beginning of the year. Vida Blue could still pitch—his fastball occasionally popped as it had in 1971—but he showed only intermittent command of his breaking ball and had difficulty sustaining momentum. By the end of June his record sat at 1-4, despite a 2.91 ERA. "Vida was still real good," reflected Bando, "but there was a difference."

When the team flew east in July, Vida remained in Oakland to fulfill Army Reserve obligations, then showed up at Yankee Stadium a day later than he'd been allowed. "Evidently he's not interested," snorted a furious Williams as he skipped Blue's spot in the rotation. It appeared to be true. Blue kept his ERA respectable through the summer, but that was mostly a function of brilliant games mixed with disasters. By the end of August he was 5-7. At the same point a year earlier he had been 23-6.

Off the field, Vida was sour. He stopped answering fan mail. (One guess pegged the number of letters collecting in a huge wooden box near his locker at upwards of 7,000.) Opponents theorized that he lost confidence. At the very least, his focus was divided. When Blue shagged balls during batting practice, he took to numbering each one sequentially with a marker, then tossed them into the stands—an angry response to Finley's fanatical parsimony when it came to office supplies, including baseballs. Blue stopped the practice after about 400 balls, when coach Vern Hoscheit—tasked by Finley with keeping a precise accounting of every ball used in practice—began to draw heat. "Shit, I would've hit 2,000 if I kept it up," Vida said later.* It did little to help his pitching.

Blue began to talk about baseball as employment, no different than had

---

* Also missing were uniforms. In those days players' togs were recycled—first among big leaguers, with numbers and nameplates interchanged depending on who was on the roster, and then they were sent to the minor leagues. Vida's uniforms, however, rarely made it that far. "Charlie would see the bill and ask why we had to order so many new uniforms," said clubhouse manager Steve Vucinich. "Well, Vida would always steal his. It was another of his anti-Charlie things."

he been working in an office at the Dura Steel Products Company. "Hey, man, I just throw the ball," he said. "They hit it or they don't. Nothing I can do about it. I play the game and pick up my pay. Just doing a job." In the clubhouse he sulked. "Yes, I'm bitter," he said when asked if he was bitter. Teammates implored him to pull it together. "I sat next to Vida every time we were on the bench, and I talked to him until I was tired of talking, but I don't think he listened . . . ," said Jackson. "I said, fuck Finley, you're not doing this thing for him, you're doing it for you. I told him he wasn't being Vida Blue. He wasn't bearing down. He wasn't concentrating. He didn't give a damn whether he won or lost."

Vida's friend and ex-teammate Mudcat Grant put it a different way. "His soul is broken," he said. "His heart just isn't in it anymore."

On September 5, at the Olympic Village in Munich, Germany, eight Palestinian terrorists breached lax perimeter security and broke into two apartments being used by the Israeli Olympic team. They captured, held hostage, and eventually killed 11 athletes and coaches in what came to be known as the Black September attack, after the faction of the Palestinian Liberation Organization that carried out the act. The news was met with horror around the world.

The A's were in Chicago in advance of a series against the White Sox when the news reached them. With a rare night off, the team's two Jewish players, Ken Holtzman and Mike Epstein, found themselves independently pacing their rooms at the Ambassador Hotel, unable to sit still. The information filled the space around them, drawing the walls in close. Neither man had been to Israel, but both felt a visceral connection to the events. Beyond even the religious connection, Epstein had participated in the Tokyo Olympics in 1964, when baseball was a demonstration sport, and couldn't stop thinking about how proud he had been as "The Star-Spangled Banner" was played at Meiji Jingu Stadium. For such terror to happen to people representing their country, as he had, who had been bursting with pride, as he had been, was beyond his ability to reconcile. Unable to stand his solitude, Epstein went to the lobby seeking . . . something. There he found Holtzman, who had descended from his room for the very same reason.

When Holtzman joined the team at the beginning of the season, he approached his Jewishness as a trait about which undue public attention was hardly merited. Teammates nicknamed him and Epstein "Jew" and "Super Jew," respectively, a lighthearted homage to their heritage and respective bulk. (Rollie Fingers, Holtzman's roommate and close friend, took to calling him "Regular Jew" to lend some heft to the nickname.) Holtzman's wife, Michelle, was all too happy to play it up. When the *Oakland Tribune* contacted her for a profile of her husband shortly after he was acquired, she cut right to the chase. "Is Ken a big eater?" she said. "Well, no more so than any other Jewish boy. Do you want me to go through the whole ethnic bit? You know, the chicken soup, the matzo balls and the rest? Yes. He loves chicken soup. Yes, I cook it all the time for him. No, it doesn't help him win games. When I married him, Ken was tall and rangy. But after feeding him for the past nine months, he's now short and fat."

Things hadn't been so different for Epstein, who upon reaching the big leagues was labeled "a kosher Lou Gehrig" by one writer and "Mickey Mantle bred on blintzes and gefilte fish" by another.

This, though, was different. Holtzman never sought to play up the differences between his own heritage and those of his teammates, but at that moment he wanted nothing more than the companionship of somebody who understood who he was. When he saw Epstein enter the lobby, neither of them had to say a thing; within moments they were out the front door, walking the streets of Chicago. "We just wanted to be with each other and bond," said Epstein. "We tried to understand what it was all about. What did those athletes do? What is it they did that was wrong?" The ballplayers paced off block after block, hour after hour, hands dug deep into jacket pockets in the September chill. They weren't just Jews but Jewish athletes, going about their professional lives in a strange city, as the Israelis had been doing a day earlier. They were down, and they wanted explanations they knew would never come. In that moment each was all the other had.

It was one thing to be quietly Jewish inside a major league clubhouse, but some moments called for more. Something like the decision by Detroit Tigers Hall of Famer Hank Greenberg not to play in a tight pennant race in 1934 on the most important day on the Jewish calendar, Yom Kippur. Like Sandy Koufax doing the same thing 31 years later, only this time in the World Series. It was easy to avoid identifying as Jewish within the context of baseball . . . right up until it wasn't. "This is who I am," said Epstein. "I put on tefillin at different shuls in different cities. I was Bar Mitzvahed. I can read Hebrew. I'm a Jew."

The walk helped, but it wasn't enough. Both men wanted to make a deeper statement — to themselves, to each other, and, as athletes, to the world. Much of it was personal, but part of it wasn't; at the time there was no way to be sure that the atrocity in Munich was even an isolated incident. "Believe it or not, some people thought that the ramifications were that other Jewish athletes could be at risk," said Holtzman. "Who's to say it won't happen to Jewish athletes in the United States, or that me or Mike wouldn't become targets? We just didn't know." The players wanted a physical manifestation of their feelings. As they walked they hit upon the idea of armbands, black armbands, to wear in remembrance of the deceased and to acknowledge the terror. Upon returning to the hotel, they tracked down clubhouse manager Frank Ciensczyk to see if anything could be done. He said he'd get right on it.

At the ballpark the following day Epstein and Holtzman arrived to find black strips of fabric already attached to the sleeves of their uniform jerseys. They also learned that they had a partner in their endeavor. Reggie Jackson had heard about the plan and asked Ciensczyk to make him one too. The action precipitated deeply held and wildly divergent feelings from the Jewish duo about the team's most mercurial player.

"Reggie had no business putting it on," said Epstein, whose issues with Jackson had culminated with Reggie's "no Jews in Texas" comment that led to their fistfight in May. "It had nothing to do with him. It called attention. He wanted to be known, he wanted to be seen. Kenny and I had a bond, and he was not part of that. But would we expect anything else?"

Holtzman disagreed. "Everybody recognized that for me and Mike it was kind of a special situation," he said, looking back. "And Reggie just chose to . . . it's funny about Reggie." With that, the pitcher launched into a story about Jackson's father, Martinez, a tailor from the predominantly Jewish township of Wyncotte, Pennsylvania. Holtzman's own father, Henry — who, like his father before him, dealt in industrial machinery — sat next to Martinez Jackson while watching several of their sons' games, and the two became friendly. "Mr. Jackson knew some Hebrew and Yiddish words because he had a largely Jewish clientele, so Reggie must have been exposed to that," said Holtzman. "He had contact with Jewish people growing up and was not entirely unaware of Jewish cultural characteristics. So when I saw Reggie with that armband, I felt that he was understanding what me and Mike were going through. He didn't have anything to do with being Jewish, but felt it appropriate to show solidarity not only with his own teammates, but with the fact that athletes were getting killed. Reggie is often accused by other players of grandstanding, of showboating, of trying to be the center of attention. Call it whatever you want, but Reggie's a lot deeper than that, okay? A *lot* deeper than that."

The press immediately latched on, racing to each man for comment. Beyond statements of solidarity with the Israelis, none of them took a firm stance. This was not a political statement, they said, but a personal one. "It was sorrowful," said Holtzman. "That's what it was."

Four days after the tragedy, Epstein was faced with a choice similar to those encountered by Koufax and Greenberg generations earlier. Jewish holidays begin and end at sundown, and that Friday night was the beginning of Rosh Hashanah, the Jewish new year, second only to Yom Kippur in terms of importance. Holtzman, not scheduled to pitch, was excused from the ballpark. Epstein, however, opted to play and went 4-for-5 with a home run and four RBIs. With Saturday's game scheduled at night, both men could attend synagogue in the morning, Epstein returning to the ballpark in time for the game. The armbands stayed on their uniforms all week . . . and through the next . . . and right on into the playoffs. They came off for the World Series, but by then the statement had been made. "It was an emotional period," said Epstein, looking back. "I'm just glad we did something."

As the A's slumped through the dog days, their most noteworthy weak link was the play at second base. Longtime starter Dick Green slipped a disc ten days into the season—possibly the result of his off-season job lifting heavy boxes for his family's moving company in South Dakota—mandating surgery that knocked him out for nearly four months. As the team's backups faltered, Finley schemed. The plan he dreamed up was enacted when Green returned in mid-August.

With their erstwhile starter back in the fold, the A's had four second basemen, and at the Owner's suggestion, Williams took to using all of them, every game, pinch hitting for each one when his spot in the batting order came up. Utility man Dal Maxvill made five straight starts without seeing the batter's box. Tim Cullen played in 18 games in September and batted seven times. Green, trying to play himself back into shape, batted only 21 times in 19 games, collecting four singles and lamenting later that "it sure did affect my confidence at the plate." The team ended up using 11 men at second base on the season, pinch hitting for them at such a clip that three catchers—Gene Tenace, Larry Haney, and Curt Blefary—as well as third baseman Sal Bando spent time covering the position in the late innings of games. Still, any at-bat his second basemen didn't have to take was an at-bat well spent in Finley's mind, and hell if he wasn't bold enough to at least see whether the plan could work.

The other position Williams maximized was relief pitcher. In the era before fully defined closers, when multiple innings to finish games was the norm and huge save numbers were not yet at a premium, the manager leveraged every reliever he had in every way he could. Rollie Fingers's 21 saves were good for third in the league, but Bob Locker and Darold Knowles also reached double digits in the category. Fingers, Locker, Knowles, and middleman Joe Horlen accounted for 92 percent of the team's relief appearances all season.

Fingers's emergence was a bit of a surprise, considering his reputation as a nervous and distracted starter. The right-hander opened the 1971 season as the number-two guy in the rotation, but after eight feckless starts Williams decided that he'd be better in relief. It wasn't a compliment. "Back then, bullpen pitchers were has-been starters," said Fingers. "The last place you wanted to be was in the bullpen." Fingers had a 7-15 record and 4.45 ERA during starts over his first three seasons, averaging about five innings per outing, yet managers kept running him out there even as they bemoaned the results.

The right-hander grew up in Steubenville, Ohio, learning baseball from his father, George Fingers, a short-time pitcher who as a 19-year-old in his lone minor league season, with the Class-D Williamson Colts of the Mountain State League, roomed with a 17-year-old Stan Musial.

When Rollie was a teenager, George Fingers, having long since given up his baseball dreams, moved the family to Rancho Cucamonga, California, just east of Los Angeles. Rollie leveraged his teenage success (he was named the American Legion Player of the Year in 1964 after leading his team, Post 73, to the national championship) into a $20,000 bonus offer from the Dodgers. It seemed like a no-brainer, but Fingers's path was blocked by the team's two Hall of Famers, Sandy Koufax and Don Drysdale, both still in their twenties. When the A's offered $13,000, he saw it less in terms of money than as an express train to the big leagues. In that he was correct.

Fingers made his Oakland debut in 1968, but it wasn't until Williams came along that he saw bullpen work as liberating. As a starter, he would dread assignments for days beforehand, but relieving allowed him to stay relaxed. "I was on my way to Sakizukiland, and that move kept me in the big leagues," he said, looking back. "I was going to the minor leagues if I didn't get the job done in relief."*

From the bullpen, the right-hander could go all out for a few innings rather than pace himself for nine. The additional velocity enabled him to augment a natural sinker with a hard slider that quickly became his out pitch. The remaining factor in Fingers's success, said second baseman Dick Green, was a simple lack of fear. "He just threw the ball, and they hit it and we caught it," the infielder said. "He really didn't think out there."

Actually, not thinking was something for which Fingers became known. A teammate once described him as having "a rubber arm and a rubber head," and stories abounded about his wandering mind. Walking to the plate but forgetting his bat. Being so lost in thought during the National Anthem that he remained standing on the baseline, cap over his heart, long after his teammates had returned to the dugout. It was said that Fingers once won $1,000 at a Phoenix dog track after he thought he put his money on a different dog.†

"All relief pitchers have a reputation for being a little bit spacey," said Holtzman. "It's just that Rollie has it in spades."

"He was pitching to Brooks Robinson one time, and afterwards he was saying things about it that made you realize he thought it was Frank Robinson," said Reggie Jackson, speaking of Baltimore's white Hall of Fame third baseman and black Hall of Fame outfielder, respectively. "It don't make no difference to Fingers, they're all the same to him. There's no point in his going to the meetings when they go over the hitters, because he doesn't know who the hell is hitting anyway. We call him 'buzzard' because he's off in his own world."

Setting it all into place, of course, was the guy's mustache, the ends

---

* Sakizukiland: a fictional place of banishment entirely of Fingers's own design.

† Hogwash, retorted Fingers. He was accustomed to the bat rack at the A's spring training ballpark in Mesa, which was located outside the dugout, and during a game in Salt Lake City had merely gone out to pick up a bat without considering where he was. As for the dog track . . . well, it was complicated. During an outing in 1971, Fingers correctly picked a quinella — the first- and second-place finishers of a race — but didn't realize that he accidentally bought a ticket for something called a "Big Q," which necessitated hitting two quinellas in a row. Unprepared, he quickly picked dogs number 3 and 4 in the second race, long shots that corresponded with his uniform number. When they won, he ended up with $1,250 on a $2 ticket. "Shit, I didn't even know anything about dogs," he said, looking back. "That was a month's salary."

slathered with wax to form gravity-defying curlicues that quickly became his trademark. The fact that he was the only player in baseball with such a look — the only player, probably, since the early 1900s — and that his name was *Fingers*, for crying out loud, was enough to spur the public's imagination. "It's my identity now," he said after a couple of years with the thing. "If I took it off, I would be just another Rollie Fingers."*

The turning point in Oakland's 1972 season came on August 27, three days after the A's coughed up the division lead to Chicago. Finley, wheels perpetually in motion, acquired 33-year-old Matty Alou from the Cardinals, who saw his $100,000 salary as an unnecessary expenditure for a team going nowhere. The trade showed Finley at his hungriest; the A's had benefited greatly in 1970 from the services of Matty's older brother, Felipe, and the Owner was sparing no expense in the quest for his first title. The acquisition solved multiple problems. Alou, a former National League batting champion, was a tonic for Oakland's slumping offense, and Williams immediately slotted him into right field and the third spot in the batting order. Reggie Jackson slid over to center, and Angel Mangual — perpetually in the doghouse for mental mistakes like forgetting the number of outs, dropping catchable fly balls, and failing to hit the cutoff man — went to the bench.

The other notable change to the lineup was less splashy but equally effective. Catcher Dave Duncan had hit ten home runs over the season's first six weeks, relegating Gene Tenace to late-inning replacement duty. By August, however, the ongoing pounding that Duncan absorbed from catching Oakland's sinker ballers had taken a toll, injuries to his left hand reducing him to a .163 batting average for the month. When Duncan missed four games for Marine Corps Reserve duty at the end of August, Tenace went 4-for-11 in his absence and seized the starting job.

It helped make for a glorious stretch run. A one-and-a-half-game deficit turned into a four-game lead over the course of ten games. Alou made himself at home, knocking in the go-ahead run in four straight victories. The bullpen was all but untouchable. Catfish Hunter won his 21st on Sep-

---

* Fingers grew so attached to his mustache that at the end of his career in 1985 he chose to retire rather than sign with Cincinnati after team owner Marge Schott insisted that he adhere to the Reds' clean-face policy. "There was no way I was shaving my mustache for her, just to be in the big leagues," he said, looking back. "She had more facial hair than I did."

tember 21 with ten innings of 11-strikeout, no-walk, one-run ball against the Twins and ended the year at 21-7, with a 2.04 ERA and 16 complete games. Holtzman finished with 19 wins, while Blue Moon Odom punctuated a remarkable comeback with a 15-6 record. Even Vida Blue, despite a 6-10 record, put up a 2.80 ERA and struck out more than twice as many as he walked. The A's clinched the division with about a week to play.

Because this was the A's, it was impossible for a team with obvious momentum to simply cruise into the playoffs. In August, *Oakland Tribune* beat writer Ron Bergman, listening to the team's radio broadcast during a day off of work, counted eight mentions of Finley's name over the course of a single inning. Bergman noted this in a column for *The Sporting News*, writing that "listening to the A's play-by-play announcers [Monte Moore, Jim Woods, and Jimmy Piersall], you get the impression that they're in some sort of contest to see which one can make the most complimentary remarks about owner Charlie Finley."

When Finley saw it, he called Bergman and profanely informed him that broadcasters' on-air dialogue was never dictated from the executive suite — *never* — and that Bergman made his crew "look like prostitutes." Then he debarred him.

Finley couldn't pull the reporter's press credential — Bergman was the primary contributor of A's news for the team's hometown paper — but he could make things difficult. In the Owner's reality, the print media, like the A's own broadcasters, were there to work for him, and if they weren't working for him, he sure as hell wasn't going to work for them. At the time it was standard procedure for teams to book flights and hotels for the traveling press, with newspapers paying the bills. When Bergman called ahead to the team hotel in Minneapolis, however, he was told that Finley had personally canceled his reservation. He also learned that traveling secretary Tom Corwin had been ordered to physically remove him from any team flight on which he was brazen enough to appear.

It was the latest example in a long history of antagonism between Finley and the press. Back in the 1960s, ballclubs made reservations for the media *and* footed the bill — a practice that the Owner discontinued upon moving to Oakland. It was, he proclaimed, the price of getting to cover the A's on the road. In response, most Bay Area papers simply chose to ignore the team outside of Oakland. The afternoon *San Francisco Examiner* sent reporters on the occasional trip, but the morning *San Francisco*

Chronicle — the paper that Finley should have been trying hardest to woo — based its accounts of road games on radio broadcasts and day-late rewrites of Bergman's *Tribune* dispatches. The Giants, meanwhile, with owner Horace Stoneham slathering expense accounts upon the local media, received far more attention in quantity and quality both. (When the *San Jose Mercury* pulled its A's road coverage in 1974, things grew desolate. "We would go into a city like New York, where they'd have eight or nine writers," said Jon Miller, one of the team's broadcasters that season, "and they'd come on the press box PA and say, 'We want to welcome the Oakland press corps: Ron Bergman.' He was it.")

It was all based on Finley's lack of respect for the news media. In 1971, after the Owner's PR director called *Time* magazine in New York trying to get a cover story written about Vida Blue — and succeeded — Finley not only failed to praise his ingenuity but complained about the telephone bill. He didn't want the players promoted, he said — he wanted Finley promoted.

The duplicity of the situation was that the Owner was frequently friendly to reporters, especially on the road, where he would buy them drinks while enjoying his life as a traveling baseball man. When working hours came around, however, newsmen who thought they might encounter the affable gent from the bar a night earlier were frequently mistaken. Finley regularly dialed area newsrooms to critique coverage. "He'd call Twombly in the office," said the *Examiner's* Glenn Schwarz, talking about his colleague — columnist, muckraker, and, like Finley, daytime drinker — Wells Twombly. "He wanted to bitch about something Wells had written, and they would spar back and forth. You'd hear Twombly laughing and yelling at Charlie, telling him how full of shit he was." So dogged was the Owner in this regard that he once managed to track down Schwarz at a girlfriend's apartment, using a phone number the reporter had given to few people, including his own editors. "To this day I have no idea how he found me, but he did," reflected the newsman years later.

That was the Owner's relationship with reporters *outside* the ballpark. Within the confines of the Coliseum, Finley tried to control them in every way possible. He could not have people physically removed from the press box — control of the space belonged to the Baseball Writers' Association of America — so he took other tacks. When Finley, decrying the abundance of freeloaders among the media ranks, cut the number of pressroom meals to 50, working reporters — the guys who had to be on the field before a game to cover the team — were inevitably shut out. "Before his first World Series," Twombly said, "Charlie announced he was going to have lobster flown in fresh from Maine every day for the press. I asked him if that was still the first 50. He said it was. Still, that was 50 lobsters, and some of us got there early to get ours. Only they were all gone. No matter how early we got there, they were always all gone. We got there when the room opened and they were still all gone. I asked Charlie where they were, and he said we just got there too late. It turns out he was feeding the lobsters to his friends and family first, before the room opened, and there were never any for the press."

The problem wasn't that Finley was feeding his friends before the media, it was that he set expectations without having any intention of fulfilling them. "I've tried to tell him there's no better way to make an enemy out of a writer than to take his free food from him," said Twombly, "but Charlie could care less." The second part of the lesson was that there's no better way to turn public sentiment against you than to piss off the guys who cover your team.

Actually, Finley enjoyed that part. In 1968, Bergman broke news of some drama surrounding a thumb injury suffered by Reggie Jackson, writing that just hours after team physician Dr. Harry Walker indicated the outfielder needed several days' rest, Finley phoned the dugout with a mandate that the slugger play that night. Prior to the following day's game, the Owner burst into the press box, nostrils flaring, and stood over Bergman. "You lying little fucker, you, how can you print that shit?" he screamed. "It's a lie. I *never* phoned the dugout." The reporter was unsure how to respond to this. He hadn't been in the dugout to hear it firsthand, of course; he'd been tipped by a player. But when he asked around after the game, he heard the same thing, from more than one source: Finley had indeed called. "It wasn't until the end of the season that I found out it wasn't Charlie who called the dugout that day, but that it was Dr. Walker," said Bergman. "That Charlie had made Dr. Walker call." For the Owner, semantics frequently sufficed.

"The reason Finley got a lot of bad press," said Dick Green, "was because he treated the press terribly."

After Bergman was kicked off the team charter, he consulted with the Commissioner's office, which advised him to call Finley and straighten things out. He did, and for his trouble got an earful of invective and a demand for an apology, which the newsman told him was neither merited nor forthcoming. Like many of the Owner's crusades, this one petered out in accordance with Finley's waning interest in the subject, and Bergman was eventually allowed back on team flights. Once Finley cooled down, he even went so far as to note that the entire affair was "probably beneath my dignity."

Heading into the playoffs, Oakland had plenty of reasons to feel good. Campy Campaneris stole two bases on the season's final day, giving him a league-leading 52 on the year — the sixth time he paced the circuit in the category. Epstein led the club with 26 homers, one more than Jackson in 44 fewer at-bats. The A's lacked a player with superstar numbers on offense, but they were deep. Bando led the team with only 77 RBIs, but three others also topped 70. Five players collected double-digit homers, enough for Oakland to lead the league.

In the AL East, the Detroit Tigers had overcome a one-and-a-half-game deficit with five games to go to overtake the Red Sox. The Tigers, led by 37-year-olds Al Kaline and Norm Cash, were the team that Oakland seemed to fight with most, a decidedly unstrategic development for the A's considering that Detroit fielded the most physically intimidating roster in baseball. Six Tigers were at least six-foot-two and 200 pounds, plus the likes of Willie Horton and Gates Brown, who made up in bulk whatever they lacked in height. "Man, Gates was like one of those guys out of prison — which he had been in prison, anyway," said Odom. (Brown had been scouted and signed by the Tigers at the Ohio State Reformatory in Mansfield, Ohio, where he was serving time for burglary.) "Oooh, god-dang, they had a team you really didn't want to fight. But you had to. You figured you're going to get your butt whooped, but you got to let them know you've been there."*

The most giant Tiger of all, acquired just after the cutoff for postseason eligibility, was six-foot-seven, 270-pound Frank Howard. Quipped Tigers

---

* The bad blood started in 1967, when Detroit second baseman Dick McAuliffe capped a robust inning against Odom by racing home with Detroit's sixth run of the frame on the front end of a double steal. Odom, put off by the tactic, brushed back McAuliffe during his next at-bat, then drilled Jim Northrup. The teams fought. In 1968, A's reliever Jim Nash hit Northrup in the head, sparking another brawl. Odom, who wasn't even playing, got tossed for repeatedly kicking McAuliffe, who was caught at the bottom of the dogpile. "I cracked his ribs," Odom said later. "Willie Horton said he was never right since then."

manager Billy Martin about his plans for his new titan: "I'm going to use him in fights. Otherwise: bodyguard."

The teams' latest dustup had come that August, only weeks before they met in the playoffs. With the A's holding a 6–2 lead in Tiger Stadium, Odom tried to steal third with one out in the seventh inning on a pitch that was fouled off by Angel Mangual. Such tactics with a four-run lead riled Tigers manager Billy Martin, who shouted instruction to pitcher Bill Slayback: "Knock him on his ass!" Slayback heard him. So did Mangual. The right-hander's next offering, however, sailed ten feet over Mangual's head, over the catcher, and to the backstop. Slayback sprang from the mound to cover the plate, as he was supposed to do, but all Mangual saw was a six-foot-four 200-pounder with an Old English "D" on his cap racing at him after failing to complete Martin's directive. Mangual threw down his bat and put up his fists. The ball was live. From the third-base coach's box Irv Noren shouted, "Angel, no, *no, NO!*" Within moments a free-for-all had broken out in the infield. Dave Duncan wrestled with Norm Cash, then got beat from behind by Ike Brown. Martin tried to punch Mangual, but couldn't reach him through the scrum. "I was right in the middle of the fight," said Darold Knowles, an off-season hunting buddy of Martin's. "I was trying to pull people off when Willie Horton grabbed me and threw me like a pretzel, six feet. I wound up on Epstein's pile."

The next day Martin ran out a lineup to the umpires featuring his starters listed as usual. Under the "Available" column, however, he listed 17 boxers, including Sugar Ray Robinson, Max Baer, Jack Johnson, and Rocky Marciano.

Now it was playoff time. Bring on Detroit.

5

Teetering in Tiger Town

Every time Billy Martin battles the A's it becomes more than
a game. The A's have accused Billy of ordering his pitchers
to throw at them. Martin, of course, denies the accusation.

—*Oakland Tribune,* October 3, 1972, five days before the
start of the American League Championship Series

The more time Dick Williams spent on his playoff roster, the clearer it became that there was little space in the rotation for Vida Blue. The short right field at Tiger Stadium cried out for left-handers, making righties Catfish Hunter and Blue Moon Odom no-brainers for the opening games at home, so southpaw Ken Holtzman could start Game 3 in Detroit. At that point Hunter would be rested and ready for Game 4, and there was scant chance that Williams would bypass his ace, no matter which arm he threw with.

It was easy to rationalize. Blue's moments of dominance were simply too streaky for comfort. Additionally, the day before the A's clinched, their primary bullpen lefty, Darold Knowles, broke his thumb in an awkward fall while running out a grounder. With Vida pitching in relief, Knowles's roster spot could go to pinch-hitter extraordinaire Gonzalo Marquez.

The strategy took precisely three hours to pay dividends. With some 20,000 empty seats at the Coliseum for Game 1 buttressing the impression that fans in Oakland simply didn't care in numbers big enough to matter, the A's and Tigers ended regulation tied 1–1. Hunter was dominant for Oakland, giving up one run over eight innings, but had long since been removed when Detroit took the lead in the top of the 11th, 2–1, on Al Kaline's solo homer against Fingers. The A's hadn't scored since the third against dominant lefty Mickey Lolich, mustering only seven hits through ten innings of play.

Bando's single leading off the bottom half of the 11th provided Oakland's first sense of hope in what seemed like hours. Epstein's following single was enough to chase Lolich, and the energy in the Coliseum grew palpable. On the bench, Marquez turned to Campaneris. "If I get to pinch-hit," he said, "I'll win the game."

Marquez, 26, spent the entire 1971 season on his family farm in Venezuela, caring for his ailing mother, and had accumulated only 26 at-bats since making his big league debut that August, all but three as a pinch hitter. That was why he was not on the original list of players Oakland submitted for postseason eligibility. The fact that Marquez went 7-for-his-last-15 was a big reason why, following Knowles's injury, Williams had him rejoin the club.

After Gene Tenace bunted into an out at third base against reliever Chuck Seelbach, Marquez got his chance, pinch-hitting for Dal Maxvill, Oakland's third second baseman of the night. He came through as promised, drilling a single to right field that brought home the runner from second. With no chance for a play at the plate, right fielder Kaline tried to nail Tenace at third, but his throw bounded away from third baseman Aurelio Rodriguez. Shocking everybody, Tenace scampered home for an improbable 3–2 victory. "I felt fast as Campaneris," said the grinning catcher afterward. Tenace didn't know it at the time, but that phrase — "fast as Campaneris" — would soon become a series theme.

Campaneris had been a quiet 0-for-4 in the opener, but in Game 2 he put on full display exactly what kind of havoc he could wreak. Wearing Oakland's all-white Sunday-special uniform in front of only 31,000 fans at the Coliseum, Campy led off the game with a base hit, stole second, stole third, then scored on Joe Rudi's single. He singled again in the third, and then again in the fifth, after which he stole two bases and scored once more, pushing Oakland's lead to 3–0.

By the seventh inning, when Campaneris was coming up for his fourth at-bat, the A's led 5–0 and Billy Martin was fed up. Odom had allowed only three hits, while Detroit was on its fourth pitcher of the day, six-foot-five, 220-pound Lerrin LaGrow. The 23-year-old rookie right-hander made his intentions immediately obvious, throwing a first-pitch fastball directly into Campaneris's left ankle. The shortstop collapsed on impact. This kind of thing was an established tactic for Martin, whose methods of operation did not come as a surprise.

Campy's did.

The shortstop jumped up as if to fight, then paused for a moment as he considered through the pain that he'd be giving up seven inches and 50 pounds to his opponent. Instead of charging, he did the unexpected, rearing back and sidearming his bat toward the mound. The lumber flew on a surprisingly accurate line toward the pitcher, helicoptering parallel to the ground. LaGrow ducked as the bat spun overhead, inches above the crown of his cap. "It was so different, so sudden," recalled Holtzman, who gaped from the dugout in horror. This was exactly the type of thing for which Martin thirsted. Hell, the man so loved to fight that Jim Murray once wrote in the *Los Angeles Times* that Martin didn't have a chip on his shoulder but "a whole lumberyard."

The manager's goal had been to slow Campaneris down. To judge by the shortstop's swollen ankle and frazzled mien, he accomplished much more than that.

Among the core group of Athletics, only Dick Green was older and had been around longer than Campy. Now 30 and in his ninth big league season, the shortstop was a two-time All-Star and had stolen more bases since 1965 than every player but Lou Brock. Known for his terrible hands on defense when he first came up, Campaneris had since become among the most capable fielders in the game.

Dagoberto Blanco Campaneris, known to many as "Bert" but referred to more frequently as "Campy," grew up in a village in northeastern Cuba called Pueblo Nuevo, where his father made lariats in a rope factory. Campy was ropy himself, at five-foot-ten and a diminutive 142 pounds, when he was discovered by A's scout Felix Delgado. The kid's athleticism, however, was off the charts. He was ambidextrous and motivated enough to play catcher, like his semipro father, despite his lack of bulk. Finley secured him in 1962 with a signing bonus of $500 and a ticket on a U.S.-bound airplane.

That Campaneris was miniature did not hinder his prospects. In his first minor league stop, at Daytona Beach, he even pitched in three games — using both hands — and notched a 3.00 ERA. Upon being called up as a 22-year-old in 1964, Campy blasted the first pitch he ever saw, from

Twins lefty Jim Kaat, 365 feet over the left-field fence at Metropolitan Stadium, his first of two homers in the game.*

Campy took over as the team's primary shortstop the following season, but his 35 errors (five as an outfielder) were second in all of baseball. Balls bounced off his glove so frequently that teammates nicknamed him "Iron Hands." Various changes — switching from an outfielder's glove to an infielder's glove, knocking off his chain-smoking — plus copious practice helped him steadily improve. The only thing that remained stifled, it seemed, was Campy's English, which was of little consequence since he was rarely inclined to utilize the parts of the language he commanded. Even the team's Spanish speakers found him to be introverted. So guarded was Campaneris that in the early 1970s, when A's reliever Darold Knowles unwittingly invested in a controlling interest in the shortstop's hometown bank in Missouri, Campy withdrew his money, telling his teammate, "I don't want you to know how much I have." Reported *The Sporting News* in 1970: "There is something withdrawn about him, an expressionless quiet best seen in the clubhouse after a game when he sits motionless on his stool in front of his dressing stall. It doesn't look as if he is thinking about anything."

Because Campy constantly stifled newsmen with his linguistic reticence, they stopped seeking him out. Headlines went to others, and the shortstop's legacy drew short shrift, even as he became the primary facilitator of a championship offense.

Billy Martin, however, knew precisely what kind of damage the guy could inflict. As Campaneris darted toward the safety of the A's dugout following his bat fling — one of the smartest moves of his career, said Williams later — Martin stormed the field in an effort to take out the shortstop himself, only to be restrained, screaming and gesturing, by three umpires. Shockingly, two teams that reveled in beating each other up over the years did not throw a single punch at this greatest of provocations.

In the aftermath, the A's were hardly confrontational. For one thing, it

---

* Upon arriving at the A's clubhouse for the first time, the rookie Campaneris, having no idea what to do, stood around quietly until equipment manager Al Zych spotted him. Then he stood around some more while people tried to convince Zych that the little guy was there to play ball. By game's end, Campy's line — 3-for-4, including the two homers — made Zych and everybody else in the organization aware of exactly who Bert Campaneris was.

was their guy who committed the unspeakable act. For another, they were trying to salt away their second victory in as many games and had little to gain from additional distraction. Apart from Martin, the Tigers' most aggressive stance came from Ike Brown, who smashed the offending bat into pieces against the ground.

After Martin was escorted back to his dugout, plate ump Nestor Chylak ejected Campaneris (obviously) and LaGrow (to "prevent further riot, mayhem or whatnot," Chylak explained later). If Martin truly had his druthers, he might have ordered a pitcher to take out Blue Moon Odom as well. Having allowed three hits and no walks over seven shutout innings prior to the Campaneris incident, the right-hander set down the final six Tigers he faced afterward to seal a 5–0 victory that gave Oakland a two-games-to-none lead in the best-of-five series.

In the postgame clubhouse, Martin held nothing back. "[Campaneris] has got to be suspended from further series games," he shouted at reporters. "That was the dirtiest thing I ever saw in my entire life in baseball." This was saying something, coming from a man who as a player once threw his own bat toward the mound, then coldcocked the unsuspecting pitcher, Jim Brewer, on his way to retrieve it. Martin also denied having ordered the pitch, just as LaGrow denied intent, which did little to sway the A's. "It was deliberate as hell," said Sal Bando, speaking for most of his teammates. "He threw it right at his ankles. That's how Billy Martin manages."

Some in Detroit's clubhouse were bold enough to agree. "What do you think?" said bullpen coach Charlie Silvera, answering a question years later about Martin's intentions. "Think about Billy and his background. Billy wanted to get Campaneris out of the lineup, and he got him out of the lineup." Detroit's backup catcher, Duke Sims, was even more direct. "The plan was to actually hit him in the leg," he said. "It turned out that [Lerrin] was good at it."

None of that mattered now, of course. Campy's bat toss was far more serious than the act that inspired it and was certain to draw considerable rebuke. Nobody knew it at the moment, but American League president Joe Cronin, sitting in the stands, decided almost immediately to fine Campaneris $500 and suspend him for the remainder of the ALCS. All that prevented him from announcing it immediately was his insistence on informing the shortstop first. Cronin handed a letter detailing his decision to MLB PR man Tom Monahan, with instructions to personally deliver it to Campaneris. This became problematic when Campy was taken away for X-rays before the game ended. Monahan headed to Merritt Hospital, but by that point the player had already departed, so Monahan returned to the Coliseum. Campy wasn't there either. People began to wonder whether the shortstop might be hiding out in an effort to avoid the inevitable discipline.

Had anybody thought to check the airport, they would have found an answer. Campaneris went directly from the hospital to Oakland International, where he spent an hour on the team's chartered World Airways jet waiting for everybody else to show up. Then he spent another hour in the terminal, along with his teammates, while authorities investigated a bomb scare.*

When the plane — decorated with giant portraits of the Owner and his mule on the fuselage, a green-and-gold color scheme inside, and boarding-ramp steps covered in a tiger-skin rug — finally took off, Campaneris sat quietly by himself, his tightly wrapped ankle propped on an adjacent seat. The shortstop's somber bearing was in stark contrast to the chipper mood of the Owner, who treated the flight like a victory party. Tuxedo-clad waiters circulated with trays of hors d'oeuvres. Guests included nine of Finley's family members, assorted pals from Indiana, and the team's two teenage ball girls. ("He told us to call him dad if we wanted to," said one of them, Mary Barry.) Hostesses in A's caps served an eight-course filet mignon dinner. As World Airways president Ed Daly, part of the Owner's entourage, introduced Finley over the intercom, a player hollered, "He's too drunk to talk!" It was a joke, of course; talking was what Finley did best, even while drinking. Especially while drinking. "In a few days," proclaimed the Owner, "we will all be world champions!" The sentiment was brash, premature, and wholly Finley.

Also on board was the Coliseum's five-piece Dixieland band, dubbed "The Swingers" by broadcaster Monte Moore, who at the Owner's direction played an extended loop of his favorite number, "Sugartime," made popular in the 1950s by the McGuire Sisters. In a state nearing rapture, Finley retook the intercom to sing the refrain: "Sugar in the morning / Sugar in the evening / Sugar at supper time / Put your arms around

---

* The plane was eventually towed several hundred yards so that authorities might examine the cargo hold without endangering the terminal. Coach Vern Hoscheit, one of the few to have boarded at that point, was using the restroom when the plane was evacuated, and ended up trapped inside as it was hauled away.

me / I love you all the time." As the liquor caught up to him, he eventually changed the last two lines to ". . . put your *legs* around me and love me all the time," all but daring the passengers to challenge his stature as the sky king of dirty old men.

It was after midnight when the plane landed and players settled into the Detroit Hilton. Monahan, too, had traveled to Detroit, Cronin's letter for Campaneris still in his coat pocket. He would wait until morning to resume the task of delivering it. That the Commissioner's office slept, of course, placed Charlie Finley under no such obligation.

Just before 2:00 A.M., A's traveling secretary Tom Corwin placed a call to the Lindell A.C., a favorite bar for visiting writers.* It was time for an impromptu press conference, and Corwin knew just where to find his target audience. Within minutes the four-man Bay Area media contingent — Ron Bergman (*Oakland Tribune*), Herb Michelson (*Sacramento Bee*), Glenn Schwarz (*San Francisco Examiner*), and Jim Street (*San Jose Mercury News*) — was hustling to the Hilton. There, in Williams's room, they found the manager, Finley, and Campaneris, the last of whom sat silently for the duration. By the time the Owner began speaking it was close to 3:00 A.M. and, damn the late hour, he did not stop for 90 minutes. He told the assemblage that Campy's ankle was in such sorry shape that he was being sent home for further tests. He proclaimed hope that treatment would get the player ready for the World Series should the A's make it that far. He talked about how he'd been trying to reach Cronin to tell him this news. If Finley had been informed about his shortstop's impending suspension, he did not let on. He proclaimed hope that Commissioner Bowie Kuhn would opt against extending Cronin's punishment, whatever it might be. Every so often he would turn to Williams and say, "Isn't that right, Dick?" and be met by a mute nod.

Finally, at 4:30 A.M., attendees were allowed to straggle off to bed. Monahan tracked down Campaneris about three and a half hours later, just before the shortstop was scheduled to depart for Oakland, and passed along Cronin's letter. At last, the suspension could be announced.

By the time it was, Campy was soaring over the Midwest, and his teammates were preparing to enter hostile territory in Detroit for Game 3.

---

* The Lindell A.C. was the place where Billy Martin decked his own pitcher, Dave Boswell, under extremely suspicious circumstances in 1969, leading to his dismissal from his first managerial post, in Minnesota.

This was more than an elimination game for the Tigers and their fans — it was a chance for retribution, a response to injustice served. "If there's a fight on the field tomorrow it could develop into a riot," warned Catfish Hunter. "Last time we had a beef here, I walked back to the bullpen and, *smack*, I got beer tossed in my eyes. I'm not going to that Detroit bullpen if trouble starts. They have just one little exit there. Those booin' fans could storm the bullpen and tear us apart."

The A's needed only one victory to clinch, and had three opportunities to get it. The first disappeared quickly as Tigers pitcher Joe Coleman struck out an American League playoff record 14 in Game 3, en route to a 3–0 victory. The game's biggest development as far as the A's were concerned was Williams's decision to not start Vida Blue in Game 4 — an eventuality that became obvious when the left-hander was called in from the bullpen to face a single batter, Norm Cash, in the sixth inning. The manager had said that he'd turn to Hunter only if the A's were trailing in the series, but here they were, leading two games to one, and he was skipping Blue for Hunter anyway.

Blue let fly a season's worth of frustration after the game. He blasted Finley for presumably ordering Williams to keep him out of the rotation, and he blasted the manager for a lack of communication. "The only way I find out what the club has in mind for me," he groused, "is by reading the papers."

One thing Blue couldn't argue with was Hunter's performance. The right-hander dominated early in Game 4, limiting the Tigers to five hits and a run heading into the eighth. Detroit starter Mickey Lolich was just as good, ceding only a solo homer to Mike Epstein. Rollie Fingers took over when Catfish tired, and Williams put to rest any lingering questions about Blue taking the start in a possible Game 5 by having him pitch the ninth. Vida responded with two strikeouts in a scoreless inning. The teams went into extras tied, 1–1.

In the top of the tenth, Oakland broke it open against Detroit's bullpen, with RBIs from Matty Alou and Ted Kubiak building a 3–1 lead. The pennant all but belonged to the A's.

Having burned through Hunter, Fingers, and Blue, Williams turned to Bob Locker to shut the door, but the right-hander lasted only two batters, giving up singles to Dick McAuliffe and Al Kaline. Williams called in another righty, Joe Horlen, who wild-pitched the runners over, then walked pinch hitter Gates Brown to load the bases with nobody out.

The outstanding detail that would come to color all of this was that Williams had emptied his carousel of second basemen — a simple matter, really, considering that three of them, Maxvill, Cullen, and Kubiak, were covering for Campaneris's absence at shortstop while being pinch-hit for as usual. As a result, catcher Gene Tenace had been manning second base since the seventh inning for only the third time in his big league career. Still, one of those games was the previous day, and it worked out fine, Tenace even serving as the middleman on a double play. Game 4 would be different.

With all three runners taking their leads, the inning's fourth batter, Bill Freehan, bounced a shot to the left of third base, an easy play for the shuffle-stepping Sal Bando. Upon gloving it, he had his choice of catchers to throw to — Duncan at the plate, or Tenace at second base. With his momentum carrying him toward the middle of the diamond, Bando opted for second. The A's had a run to give and going for the double play was the right move . . . or would have been with a capable fielder at the keystone. Bando's throw sailed to the center-field side of the bag, about knee-high. Dick Green might have been able to do something with it, but he'd long since been removed. Tenace could *feel* Gates Brown pounding down the base path. He braced for impact instead of stretching for the throw, then lost the ball, making Brown's ensuing barrel roll wholly unnecessary. Everybody was safe, McAuliffe scoring to close the gap to 3–2. There was still nobody out.

Williams called on rookie left-hander Dave Hamilton to face Norm Cash. Hamilton thought he struck the batter out looking at a 2-2 pitch, but plate ump Don Denkinger disagreed. With his next offering, Hamilton walked in the tying run.

Inside the clubhouse, seven A's — a mixture of players who had already been removed from the game and starting pitchers who would not be used — sat on the floor against a row of lockers and watched on television. "Isn't that something?" said a dazed Rollie Fingers as Kaline crossed the plate. Blue Moon Odom, less reticent, leaped to his feet. "Damn!" he shouted, hurling a small trunk across the room. Only moments earlier Thursday looked like an off day, but now they were on the verge of a deciding Game 5, with a trip to the World Series in the balance and Odom tabbed as the man to get them there. Unable to handle the pressure of so much as watching it unfold, the pitcher retreated to the trainer's room, and stayed there as clubhouse man Frank Ciensczyk dragged away the champagne that had been icing in a nearby trash can.

The next batter, Jim Northrup, soared a fly ball over the head of drawn-in right fielder Matty Alou, and Gates Brown trotted home for an improbable, momentum-shifting, 4–3 Tigers victory. The series was tied, with the deciding Game 5 to be played the next day.

An hour later, Tenace, the inadvertent goat, hadn't moved from in front of his locker. "I feel sick," he said, effectively speaking for everybody in the room.

The players filtered back to the Hilton in something approaching a daze. They were professionals, knew the platitudes about not letting their emotions get too high or too low, but Detroit's gut punch, sending them from World Series certainty to the verge of elimination, was unlike any defeat they had to that point suffered. Team members returned to their rooms for hours of nervous anticipation. Bando, Tenace, and backup first baseman Mike Hegan sought temporary refuge at a local theater, taking in a screening of Deliverance.

Reggie Jackson had other things in mind. At the hotel he sought out Rudi and Duncan, his best friends on the team since they played together at Single-A Modesto back in 1966. The trio had dinner plans, but sat for a while first, bouncing ideas around, building each other's confidence about doing something none of them had yet done: win a pennant. Then they took their message to the masses. Room by room, player by player, the three A's checked in on much of the roster, together and individually, making sure everybody's head was straight and that there were no lingering effects from Game 4. "It was like a pep talk," said Duncan. "We made sure that people were where they needed to be mentally."

If it seems like rah-rah schoolkid stuff to pull with a bunch of professional athletes, it was. And it was perfect. The bulk of the team's players were between 25 and 28 years old, and few had performed on so large a stage. The message had impact.

"Reggie came around and told us not to get down on ourselves or anybody else on the team," recalled reliever Bob Locker. "He told us to think about the other guy, and that we would be all right. I guess anybody on this team could have knocked on the doors and it would have helped. Only Jackson did it."

Among the stops was the room of the following day's starter, Blue Moon Odom. Odom's jitters were legendary, and while he had come through in many big games, he had never before faced this kind of pressure. None of the pitchers had. To mitigate the possibility that the right-hander would overthink things, teammates like Rudi, Reggie, Bando, and Tenace sat up with him at various points of the evening, coming, going, drinking a beer or two. Jazz singer Nancy Wilson, in town to perform the National Anthem prior to Game 5, stopped by. The scene was loose and breezy, and lasted into the late hours. "We just wanted to keep him relaxed, be with him so he wasn't fidgeting by himself," said Rudi. "When you're by yourself, you're always worrying about the next day, and Moony was very high-strung. He got worked up about games, and a lot of times he was a nervous wreck by the time they started."

Odom's nerves, however, were rarely evident once he took the field. John Odom grew up in Macon, Georgia, raised by a single mother, Florence Odom, after his father died when the lad was five years old. People came to attribute his nickname, "Blue Moon," to Finley, but it was actually coined during a fifth-grade football practice, when a bullying teammate teased the round-faced Odom with the epithet "Moon Head." That soon morphed into "Yellow Moon," then "Black Moon," neither of which sounded quite right, so "Blue Moon" it became. (It may have been bullying, but it wasn't racism — the guy who nicknamed Odom was also black. So, for that matter, was everybody else. "I didn't go to school with no white guys," said the pitcher.)

Odom gained notoriety as a prep, going 42-2 with eight no-hitters over four years and leading Ballard Hudson High School to back-to-back Georgia state championships. Eighteen of baseball's 20 teams sent representatives to Macon, with Charlie Finley himself making an appearance at the teenager's house, showing up in a rented cargo truck with mountains of produce from a local farmers' market, enough to feed the neighborhood. He passed out Kansas City A's jackets to the kids on the block, then blew into the Odoms' kitchen to help Florence whip up a Southern dinner of fried chicken, black-eyed peas, and collard greens. Then he stunned the young pitcher with a $75,000 bonus offer and told Odom to report straightaway to Double-A Birmingham.

The right-hander made his big league debut later in that 1964 season, only three months out of high school, but it wasn't until the A's moved to Oakland in '68 that he was able to consistently harness his greatest weapon: an explosive fastball with natural sink that opponents described as feeling like a rock when they hit it. The results were stunning: a team-leading 16 wins, a 2.45 ERA, and two scoreless innings in the All-Star Game. In 1969 he was 15-6 and again an All-Star. Odom was hindered by elbow issues for the better part of the next two seasons, but was among the team's most ferocious competitors, the only guy in the rotation who would try to retire hitters when pitching batting practice. If anyone was capable of making a comeback, it was him. He had proved it beyond doubt earlier in 1972, in an incident that had nothing to do with baseball.

That January, some nine months before taking the mound for Game 5 of the ALCS, Odom was in Macon, working an off-season job as a liquor store clerk, when his wife called to report some people casing the house next door. The pitcher raced home, grabbing his .38 caliber pistol, a Saturday night special, from the glove box of his car. There he found two young men in leather jackets trying to jimmy open his neighbor's window. From about 15 feet away, he called out, "What are you doing? I want to talk to you." One of the men pulled out his own .38 and shot Odom in the neck and chest. When Odom returned fire, the intruders fled.

Somehow both bullets exited the pitcher's body with minimal damage, missing bones and organs. Within an hour of arriving at the hospital Odom was providing health updates for Finley over the phone, and within three days he was back at home. He showed up to spring training precisely on time, with a burnished reputation for toughness.

Odom's 2.50 ERA in 1972 was second only to Hunter's among Oakland starters, and his 15-6 record was good for the second-best winning percentage in the American League. It was a resounding return to form. "Maybe the shooting is what I needed to turn my luck around," he theorized. Maybe it was, but Odom's teammates were taking no chances. On the pressure-packed night prior to Game 5, they did whatever they could to bolster his emotional well-being.

While the players handled their business with Odom, the Owner conducted some of his own. He had recalled Campaneris to Detroit following the Game 4 loss as a measure of moral support for the team but was shocked when Cronin declared the player ineligible even to sit on the bench. Finley stewed about it all evening, then responded as he responded best: by expounding at length about the injustice of it all. The first thing he needed was an audience. At about midnight Finley knocked on Williams's door, which was answered by the manager's wife, Norma, wearing a leopard-print robe. She had just arrived in town, having served as Campaneris's cross-country chaperone, and was asleep next to her husband when Finley began to bang. The Owner peered over her shoulder into the darkened room. Williams, trying to pretend this wasn't happening, was stunned to hear an order issued from the doorway: "Tell Norma to get rid of those pajamas."

As the manager considered punching his boss right there in the hall, Finley stammered a follow-up about tiger stripes being bad luck. Williams's patience was at an end. "What the hell do you want?" he snapped. The Owner answered directly: "Time for a press conference."

In front of 16 reporters from around the country (summoned, as usual, from the Lindell A.C.), and flanked by Williams and Campaneris, Finley talked about how remorseful his shortstop was. He tore into Cronin for his decision to bar Campy from the dugout and for the delay in telling Campaneris of his suspension. He even berated the AL president for his lack of action four years earlier when a Tigers pitcher threw a ball into the Coliseum stands, hitting a woman. Then he turned on Billy Martin, accusing the manager of intentionally injuring Campy—"I say with all sincerity that Mr. Martin instructed . . . no, *demanded* . . . that his pitcher throw at this young, great star"—and claimed to have "read a note" by Martin indicating that "the way to stop the A's was to throw at Campaneris' legs." Finley went into detail about how he tried to hire Martin in August 1970 but had been double-crossed after a verbal agreement.* This was Charlie O. at the peak of his powers, grandstanding as only he could. The media, most of whom had never experienced anything like it, lapped it up like the beers they left unfinished back at the bar.

The Owner proclaimed that Campaneris, barred from the dugout by

---

* Martin later enthusiastically refuted every point. His version held that in August 1970, as Finley considered firing manager John McNamara, he called the unemployed Martin to his Chicago office. According to Martin, the Owner offered him Oakland's managerial position on the spot, and the two shook on it. "I was to take over the A's just as soon as I got a better line on the players," he said. "I asked Charlie for all the data and film of the players in action. I waited one week for the stuff. Then another week went by. Still no word from Finley. Finally, I phoned him and he wasn't in. He never returned my call. Then I sent him a letter and told him the deal is off. A month later I was hired by the Tigers." Neither man discussed it publicly, but the reality was that the A's kept neither film nor data in any type of abundance. Perhaps this deficiency was what prevented the Owner from following up with Martin.

Cronin, would instead spend the game in the seat previously occupied by the Owner's wife, Shirley. A reporter suggested that planting the hot-button player amid angry Tigers fans might not be a great idea. Acknowledging the point, Finley re-declared that Campy would instead watch the game on TV from inside the clubhouse. Campaneris sat silently and listened. When asked for his thoughts, he said only, "I'm sorry."

At that point the Owner, court held, dropped his coup de grâce. At 10:00 P.M. that very evening, he recounted, he, Williams, Campaneris, Corwin, and the two eldest Finley sons had gone to Cronin's hotel room in a last-ditch effort to convince the league president to allow Campy into the dugout. "Cronin was sleeping, God bless him," Finley said. "He sleeps a lot." The crux of the Owner's story was not that Cronin slept, but *how* he slept — in an old-timey nightgown and cap. The hat on the Hall of Famer's head — fuzzy trim beneath a floppy cone, topped by a puffball — made a particular impression upon the men gathered at his door.

Finley spun the story with a smile that was either too powerful to suppress or entirely contrived. Even though he was asked about it directly, Finley did not divulge the color of the cap, perhaps figuring that imagination was inevitably more damaging than reality. "You could be damn sure it wasn't Finley green and gold," he said, beaming. Knowing that Campaneris would now have company in the following day's news, the Owner finally bade the gathered a good night.

It was 50 degrees at Tiger Stadium for Game 5, with a gusting wind that made it feel a dozen degrees colder. If anything, the weather rendered the packed house louder and angrier than usual. Odom started shakily, allowing a first-inning run on a single, a passed ball, and an infield out, spurring fans in the upper deck to launch a celebratory fusillade of toilet paper that rolled slowly across the diamond — the first of a half-dozen such volleys the game would see.

The top of the second was where everything changed. With the A's trailing, 1–0, Reggie Jackson led off with a walk, stole second, and moved to third on Sal Bando's fly ball to right field. A year earlier, Jackson had lain weeping across the dugout steps after the A's lost to Baltimore; he kept a photograph of the moment in his desk to serve as a reminder of his dejection. Now he stood at third base and considered his options. Reggie was not yet Mr. October, if only because he hadn't played deep into the postseason, but it was inside him, he was sure. This wasn't some symbolic home run he was expected to hit, no pitcher trying to stifle his glory —there was nothing between him and home plate but 90 feet of empty baseline. In the dugout, Dick Williams read his mind. When Dick Green stepped to the plate three batters later, Epstein having joined Jackson on the base paths after being hit by a pitch, there were two outs—but the manager didn't call for a pinch hitter for his second baseman. He called for a double steal.

On a pitch that tailed low and inside, Epstein took off for second. The moment catcher Bill Freehan unloaded his throw, Jackson broke for the plate. One stride, then two. Reggie was one of Oakland's strongest players, and also one of the fastest. His burst was right where he wanted it to be, his steps compact and powerful. He was flying.

Halfway home, his left leg twinged. Hamstring. Reggie tried to shake it off, took another step. Twenty feet from the plate the muscle tore. A step more and it ruptured completely. Jackson later likened it to somebody reaching into his leg and ripping muscle off the bone.

Second baseman Tony Taylor fielded the throw in front of the bag for a quick relay home. Freehan had the base path completely blocked. No longer possessing the ability to alter his momentum, Jackson barreled directly into the catcher with an awkward two-legged slide, both feet out front, heels kicking up dust. He arrived at the plate just after the ball, screaming. The throw came in high, and the catcher's swipe tag arrived too late. Reggie had tied the game.

As the A's celebrated the run in their dugout, Jackson rolled onto his belly, clutching behind him. It took only a moment for his teammates to recognize the severity of the situation. Green raced over, bat still in hand, as the writhing ballplayer flipped onto his back. Odom arrived, then Williams and trainer Joe Romo. Gingerly, they all but carried Reggie from the field. Now the A's faced a new reality: if they were to win the game, it would be without their best player.

George Hendrick replaced Jackson in center field, and in the fourth inning helped his team take the lead, reaching on an error, advancing on a sacrifice, and scoring on Tenace's single. Now it was 2–1, and the A's had only to hold on.

To do this they needed two outstanding pitching performances. One was from Odom, who for all his nerves was dominant. He allowed only one hit after the first inning, his massive sinker inducing ground ball after ground ball. When the right-hander returned to the dugout after shutting down the Tigers in the fifth, however, he began to cough so badly that he staggered toward the clubhouse for some water. He didn't make it. As the A's took their turn at bat, Blue Moon began to dry-heave right there in the dugout. He described it as feeling like vomiting, with nothing coming out.

"I was hot and my stomach was rolling and jumping," he recounted after the game. "I couldn't catch my breath. . . . I never had that happen to me before. I've never had as much pressure on me in my life. I hope I never again have that much pressure."

Odom had several things working against him when it came to teammate perception. One was that greenies — speed capsules used by ballplayers to get amped up for games — were prevalent around the league, and legal to purchase in the form of diet pills. Another was that Odom's natural nervousness led to the easy impression that he was strung out in one way or another, even when he was not. The third was his habit of drinking during games. "He was drunk," proclaimed one teammate, looking back with certainty. "He would go back to the clubhouse between every inning and drink a bunch of beer."

Odom did, in fact, make a practice of retiring to the clubhouse for beer during his starts, but said that he limited it to just one, after the fifth inning, as a means of hydration. On this day he didn't last even that long. Something else had gotten to him, and he wasn't sure what. The divergence between the cause of his intestinal distress and how his teammates viewed it is worth noting for what came later.

When Williams approached the heaving pitcher in the tunnel, Odom insisted that he could still pitch. He'd been brilliant to that point, but the outcome rested on this decision. The A's led by one run in hostile territory with four frames to go. Williams opted for keeping the door shut, and told Odom to take a seat. He called for Vida.

This was the moment upon which the season hinged. Blue, wunderkind award-winner-turned-underachieving-outcast, a guy who prior to the 1972 postseason had made all of two appearances out of a big league bullpen, was saddled with protecting Oakland's future. Said reliever Darold Knowles: "I'd never felt pressure like that, and I wasn't even in the game."

Vida was unperturbed. A blue glove on his right hand, he began with a fastball and ended with a fastball and threw nothing but fastballs in between, allowing only three hits over four innings, striking out the side in the seventh, walking nobody at all, and allowing no Tiger past first base. Never had a one-run game been more of a blowout. "I don't care what Vida's record was that season, and I don't care about his postseason record," reflected Holtzman. "For me, those four innings were the most important four innings of any we played while I was in Oakland. They turned the tide of our entire dynasty. And Vida came through."

Midway through the ninth inning a fan threw a beer at Hendrick in center field; the preternaturally cool player caught it on the fly. Moments later he caught Tony Taylor's fly ball for the game's final out, sealing the A's first trip to the World Series since 1931.

The visitors' clubhouse quickly filled with delirious players and a horde of nearly 100 newsmen. The room was tiny even by ballpark standards when it was built in 1912, and further cramped by the platforms set up at either end, one for the trophy presentation, the other for a TV camera. On the wooden floor in between was something approaching chaos. Champagne flew, players hollered, and reporters tried desperately to elicit publishable comments. TV people scrambled to set up equipment. Reggie was there, on crutches, saying that if he was at even 50 percent he'd participate in the World Series. Players started a cry of "De-*fense!* De-*fense!*" in honor of starting second baseman Dick Green's having accumulated four at-bats in the game — an event that occurred only three times all season. Finley circulated, offering congratulations and a target upon which to dump bubbly.

The trouble began when Odom was talking to reporters, about Billy Martin of all things. Vida, the cocky kid who saved the day, sidled up. "Why didn't you go nine?" he needled. Odom looked sheepishly at his teammate. "I was gagging," he said. "I was ready to throw up. The tension got to me. I wanted to throw up, but I couldn't." Odom clearly wanted commiseration from a friend. He didn't get it.

"Oh man, I know why you didn't go nine," Vida mocked. He put his hands up to his throat in the universal *choke* gesture. Blue was not making this up on the spot. The wisecracks had begun even as the pitcher found his way back to the clubhouse after being removed. "I bet Blue Moon shit his pants!" cracked one player on the bench. "Those weren't the dry heaves, they were the dry chokes!" said another.

Odom was humiliated. That his nerves forced him from a game he did not want to leave was embarrassing enough. He'd pitched 14 innings during the series and given up a single run — and even *that* was unearned. Odom was the winning pitcher in two of Oakland's three victories, for crying out loud. Had an MVP been named for the series, it probably would have been him. Wasn't that worth something? Heck, even the perpetually collected Hunter called the series "one of the most draining, emotionally exhausting experiences of my life," and he'd sat out the clincher. Choking was clearly *not* what Odom had done, at least not metaphorically. Unfortunately for his ego, choking was precisely what he did from a physiological standpoint. He expected this sort of treatment from some of his teammates, but viewed Blue as a source of safety in the clubhouse, someone who would not tear him down in a vulnerable moment. Odom had taken Vida in when the young lefty arrived in Oakland as a 19-year-old in 1969, offering homespun hospitality, one Southern black guy to another. Odom's wife cooked meals for Vida in the couple's San Leandro home. The older pitcher took the younger one out on the town, two ballplayers relaxing over drinks, shooting pool, going for drives. And now *this?* Already known for having the quickest temper on the club, Odom snapped.

"That shit burns me," he yelled as he stormed to his locker. Turning his back on the party, Odom set to punching and violently shaking the steel partition, making enough noise to draw attention from around the room. The pitcher faced the clubhouse wall, chest heaving, palms against the tile as if preparing to be frisked. Joe Rudi approached to calm him down, playfully hugging him as if he were going to pick him up. It didn't work. Odom wheeled out of Rudi's grasp and toward Blue, standing in front of his own locker. The air was thick with champagne and mayhem, and it was not immediately clear what was happening, whether the combatants were laughing together or crying. Nearby players knew the drill, however, and moved in quickly to pull the men apart before blows could be thrown.

Thoroughly shaken, Odom retreated to the shower room as Blue hammed it up for stunned witnesses. "Hey man," he said about the choke sign he gave, "I was only scratching my chin." Watching from across the room, clubhouse attendant Steve Vucinich marveled at the spectacle. "We won the motherfucking playoffs, we're going to the World Series, and we have two players fighting," he thought. "How about that?" Nearby, Dick Williams had a thought of his own: "We have to get to the World Series before we kill ourselves."

The more Blue thought it over, the more he realized that he had been looking for trouble, and soon his conscience got the better of him. After a few minutes he approached Odom to make peace, and the two hugged it out. "I'm sorry," Blue told him gently. "I'm sorry. I was just putting you on."

"Don't you ever say that," responded Odom, his voice cracking. "Don't you ever say that."

Decades later Odom remembered the moment vividly. "I'm still pissed," he said. "I hadn't given up a run in over 14 innings. A person doesn't choke when he doesn't give up any runs. He could've just said to reporters, 'He wasn't feeling good after the fifth inning, and Dick Williams had me go out and finish the game.' But he used the word *choked*."

"John is a very sensitive guy," reflected Blue. "I was just pulling his chain. It became an issue. We should have been celebrating." Vida quieted as he remembered the moment, a sliver of regret from a career full of it.*
"I was glad for him, really," he continued. "He got the win, I got the save. I didn't yell across the room, 'Hey, you choked!' Still, I should've been more respectful of him. He treated me like an uncle would. It didn't come out wrong, he just took it wrong."

In that, anyway, Odom was in the mainstream of Oakland's clubhouse culture. The A's thrived on grinding each other's gears through incessant needling, poking holes in whatever foibles any of them might have displayed, on the field or off, until business was handled accordingly. Even when things came out correctly they were sometimes taken wrong. It was part of what made the A's angry, and much of what made them good. And now they were World Series–bound.

---

* Blue's regrets run deep. He was introduced to recreational drugs after he moved away from inner-city Oakland to the tony Alameda Beach and Tennis Club west of the Coliseum. Drugs became an increasing presence in his life, culminating in his participation in a cocaine scandal as a member of the Kansas City Royals in the 1980s, for which he was banned for the 1984 season and served 81 days in prison. Vida came back to play two more seasons with the San Francisco Giants before retiring prior to the 1987 season amid reports of additional failed drug tests.

6

World Series, 1972

I really would have liked to play the Tigers. They're much
more predictable. Gee whiz, you don't know what these A's
are going to do.

— Reds manager Sparky Anderson

The charter flight from Detroit to Cincinnati was another air circus, complete with clowns, musicians, and, of course, the ringmaster. Finley strutted the aisles of the Boeing 707, directing the Swingers through ever more rounds of "Sugartime." In the rear of the plane, however, Reggie Jackson didn't much feel like partying. He had been in the trainer's room when the A's clinched the pennant, too distraught to so much as hobble to the clubhouse for the celebration's early stages. Duncan eventually tracked him down, a bottle of champagne in each fist. When he spied Jackson's crutches, the situation became all too clear. Duncan began to cry — for Jackson, his friend since the low minor leagues, and for himself, his starting job snatched away in the season's late stages. They had traveled all this distance together, he and Reggie, had finally reached the World Series, and were now staring at the possibility that neither of them would even play. "This should have been our greatest day," said Jackson, looking back, "and now the World Series was going to go on without us."

In place of Jackson, Oakland was left with injury-replacement outfielder Allan Lewis, whose primary value was stoking Finley's obsession with speed. Nicknamed the "Panamanian Express," after his home country, Lewis made a 12-year career out of pinch running with the A's, the great bulk of it in the minor leagues. George Hendrick would take Jackson's spot in center, with Mike Epstein moving up to fourth in the batting order.

Another issue was Campaneris, who had healed sufficiently to play, but whose availability for the World Series was up to Bowie Kuhn. It was tricky territory. The Commissioner's relationship with Finley was openly acrimonious, and an excessive penalty would undoubtedly be linked in at least some quarters — well, in at least *one* quarter, on South Michigan Avenue — to simple dislike of the guy. One of Kuhn's options was to do nothing and allow Campy to return, but that seemed too lenient. On the other hand, forcing him out of the Series, especially now that the A's would be without Reggie, seemed too severe.

After digging through 30 years of history, Kuhn unearthed a precedent: In 1942, American League president Will Harridge suspended Yankees shortstop Frankie Crosetti for 30 days for shoving an umpire during Game 3 of the World Series. Commissioner Kenesaw Mountain Landis, feeling a World Series suspension would be unfair to the Yankees and their fans, commuted the sentence until the following season. In this, Kuhn saw numerous parallels. Two days before the start of the World Series he ruled that Campy would be suspended for seven games without pay (coming to about $3,000, in addition to the $500 he'd already been fined), but not until the start of the 1973 season. Dick Williams had his leadoff hitter back, and that, anyway, gave him a shot.

One thing working in the A's favor was the sense of unity built around their collective shag.

Baseball was a clean-cut sport in the early 1970s, and had been for the better part of a century. While ballplayers were known to grow mustaches over the winter months, they'd invariably shave them prior to the season, frequently as a rite of spring training. In 1972, however, Reggie Jackson did no such thing. When his lip hair remained in place through the duration of the Arizona exhibition schedule, his teammates took notice.

Whisker prohibition hadn't always been enforced. Abner Doubleday himself wore a mustache in the 1830s. A photographic portrait of the first professional team, the Cincinnati Red Stockings of 1869, depicts eight of nine members sporting facial hair. But ballplayers of the early 1900s were seen as ruffians, low-ranking members of society whose reputations hindered the marketing of the sport; clean-shaved faces were part of reversing that image. In 1914, A's catcher Wally Schang became the last major league regular to wear a mustache. Until Reggie.

"Reggie was being his basic hot dog self, wanting to do whatever he wanted to do, and no one was going to tell Reggie what to do," said Rollie Fingers, who, along with most of his teammates, was appalled by Jackson's new look. Understanding their inability to sway the superstar, Fingers, Catfish Hunter, Darold Knowles, and Bob Locker took a different tack, theorizing that growing their own mustaches would draw a blanket rebuke from Finley, who would in turn command every player, including Jackson, to shave.

The Owner learned about it on the team plane. There was Jackson, mustache in place, and the quartet of pitchers, similarly adorned. Instead of getting angry, however, Finley was thunderstruck. Always on the make for unique promotional opportunities, he let it be known: any player or staff member who grew a mustache by June 18, the date of the team photo, would receive a $300 bonus. He decreed it Mustache Day, with mustachioed fans admitted to the game free of charge. Most players jumped right on board. "For $300," said Ken Holtzman, "I would grow hair on my feet." Only three players — Sal Bando, Mike Hegan, and Larry Brown — remained reticent and clean-faced. During an ensuing conversation with the Owner, Bando soon found out exactly where he stood on the subject. "Mr. Bando," Finley said to him, "I would like you to grow your mustache. We want to do it as a team, and we all are the same." With that, the holdout players acceded. (Finley himself did not grow one, of course. He never for a moment viewed himself as being on the same level as his players.)

By June 18, not only was Finley's own squad fully 'stached, but six members of the visiting Cleveland Indians grew out mustaches of their own, despite threats of fines from manager Ken Aspromonte if they didn't shave after the series finale. Finley presented gold mustache spoons, with attached covers for eating soup, to players, staff, and the participating members of the Indians. At the Coliseum, 7,607 men got in free with the promotion. Plate umpire Marty Springstead took one look at third-base coach Irv Noren before the game and said, "Jesus, Irv, when are you going to shave that off?" Noren didn't hesitate. "As soon as the goddamn check clears," he said.

This stood in contrast to their World Series opponent — a Reds team so clean-cut that in 1968 the club removed the handlebar mustache from its longtime mascot, Mr. Red. In opposition to Oakland's technicolor wardrobe, Cincinnati's color scheme had barely changed over the decades. Manager Sparky Anderson, a conservative South Dakotan, and GM Bob Howsam, a former Navy pilot, were unequivocal about their expectations both sartorially and attitudinally. Hair to be clipped above the ears. No high socks on uniforms. Shoes of pure black. Coats and ties mandatory on the road. Pete Rose couldn't help but have fun with it. "Do you think Jesus Christ could hit a curveball?" he once asked Anderson. The religious manager allowed that although hitting a curveball would not rank among the litany of Christ's miracles, he could accomplish it if he so chose. Rose jumped all over him, yelping, "Not for the Cincinnati Reds he couldn't — not with that beard!"

Anderson was utterly puzzled by the hobo affect of the opposition, asking a newsman, "How can a baseball team permit anybody to look like that?"* The media dubbed the series "The Hairs vs. the Squares," gleefully branding the A's as underdog outlaws. The role suited them nicely.

If only it was accurate. It was actually the Reds who played the wilder brand of baseball, capitalizing on base-path aggression to score their runs. Hell, the A's were so absorbed with battling Detroit that they hadn't fully considered the quality of their World Series opponent, and there was plenty to consider. The Reds, a nascent version of the vaunted Big Red Machine that would win back-to-back titles in 1975 and 1976, had appeared in the World Series only two seasons earlier and boasted a lineup of future Hall of Famers: Pete Rose, Joe Morgan, Johnny Bench, Tony Perez. Five of the top 20 players in MVP voting were Reds (including the winner, Johnny Bench), as were two of the top five Cy Young finalists. Hell, in Bench and Morgan, Cincinnati had *two* players who would one day be widely considered the best ever to play their positions. The more the A's thought about it, the more nervous they became.

"We just didn't think we could beat them," said Dick Green.

"We were going to get our asses killed," added Fingers.

Riverfront Stadium itself presented unique challenges. After 58 years at tiny Crosley Field, the Reds moved into the monolith on the banks of

---

* Anderson and Dick Williams were teammates at Fort Worth of the Texas League in 1955 and in Montreal in 1956. The Reds manager went even further back with A's third-base coach Irv Noren, having served as a teenage batboy for Noren's Hollywood Stars team that won the 1949 Pacific Coast League championship. "Hey," Noren gleefully shouted when Anderson showed up for Friday's workout, "get my bat!"

the Ohio River in 1970. Riverfront was the third of the National League's multipurpose concrete bowls that would define the era as blander than it needed to be, and the first with a playing surface made entirely of Astro-turf (save for the pitcher's mound and cutouts around the bases). The A's had little idea what to expect when it came to defensive positioning. "I had double-play balls hit to me that we couldn't turn because I was play-ing 15 steps back from where I should have been," Green admitted later.

One aspect in which Oakland was confident was the advance scout-ing report provided by Al Hollingsworth, a middling southpaw in the 1930s and '40s who had been tasked by Charlie Finley to follow the Reds through the final month of the regular season. Hollingsworth delivered a passel of detailed notes, handwritten on everything from Western Union copy paper to unopened mail. "It was," said Finley with only mild hyper-bole, "one of the most amazing scouting jobs in baseball history."

Dick Williams referred to the notes constantly, even atop the mound during mid-inning conferences with his pitchers. Pitch Pete Rose down and in with hard sliders, the pages told him, with A's second basemen staying ready to move to their right on ground balls. Low and away to Joe Morgan, with right-handers feeding him a diet of curveballs across the outside corner. Bobby Tolan: high fastballs and low curves on the outer part of the plate. None of the three, noted Hollingsworth, handled the changeup particularly well. Tease Johnny Bench with the fastball, he said, but pummel him with hard sliders away while positioning the right fielder slightly toward center. "Our scouting report was so good it was like we had played them all year," said infielder Ted Kubiak.

A's pitchers followed Hollingsworth's recommendations to the letter — and as the Reds would soon find out, A's pitchers would be the difference in the series. Well, A's pitchers and one guy without much name recogni-tion who hailed from about 100 miles down the Ohio River. But at that point nobody had yet pegged Gene Tenace as hero material.

Befitting a future athlete, Gene Tenace's given name was *Fury*, after his father's more Italian *Fiore*. The name's forceful bearing stood in stark con-trast to the pliability of Gene, taken from his middle name, *Gino*. Then again, even Tenace's family name had been softened from *Teh-NAH-chee* when his paternal grandfather, Pietro, arrived in Russelton, Pennsylvania, from northern Italy. Upon hearing enough of his colleagues in the local coal mines mangle the pronunciation, Pietro allowed the robust Italian to be pounded into American submission, where it would forevermore be verbally confused with the racquet sport.

Fiore moved his family to farm country outside Lucasville, Ohio, where his son eventually helped tiny Valley High to the Southern Ohio Conference championship in football. As a shortstop, however, Gene was too slow to draw much professional interest, which is why he was available in the 20th round of the first-ever player draft in 1965, 398 selections after the A's chose Rick Monday with the top overall pick. The team shifted him to the outfield, then to catcher, where he was lucky enough to apprentice under minor league managers John McNamara, Gus Niarhos, and Sherm Lollar — accomplished catchers all.

Tenace's studious improvement gave Dick Williams something to think about. Dave Duncan was among the league's best backstops, an outstanding handler of pitchers whose expertise and thoughtful approach would one day make him the sport's premier pitching coach.* The fact that he could also hit — 15 homers and an All-Star berth in 1971 — relegated Tenace to the bench, where in '72 he was able to scavenge only about 20 at-bats per month. In mid-August, Tenace was hitting only .189. He didn't know it at the time, but his best hope was Uncle Sam.

Duncan enlisted with the Marine Corps Reserve in 1965 and by '72 was obligated to show up for regular, weekend-long meetings (for which he had to miss Friday and Monday games to travel), plus annual two-week stints. It was during one of those weekends that Tenace made his mark, batting .333 while the A's went 4-0. The team that staggered through July and August at a barely better than .500 clip regained its footing on Tenace's watch, inspiring Williams to hand him the starting job in September and then stick with him even as he went hitless through the first four games of the ALCS. That was how the man who batted .225 with five homers during the regular season was out there for the deciding Game 5 in Detroit, in a position to drive in the winning run with what would be his only hit in 17 series at-bats. Now, here he was again, four days past his 26th birthday, starting Game 1 of the World Series only miles from his hometown and wide-eyed at the spectacle of it all.

· · ·

---

* Of the 32 years Duncan spent as a pitching coach, 29 were under the managerial leadership of former A's teammate Tony La Russa.

Jackie Robinson earned significant notice with his pregame speech prior to Game 2, delivered as part of the commemoration of the 25th anniversary of his breaking baseball's color barrier. Slender, white-haired, and nearly blind from diabetes, Robinson dug in, addressing the crowd with urgency rather than sentimentality. "I'm extremely pleased and proud to be here this afternoon," he said in his familiar, high-pitched intonation, "but must admit that I'm going to be more pleased and more proud when I look at that third-base coaching line one day and see a black face managing in baseball." Moments later he threw the ceremonial first pitch.

It was prior to Game 1, however, that Robinson made a close-up impression on the A's. Well, one A, anyway. With the rest of the team on the field for opening-game introductions, Ken Holtzman, Oakland's starting pitcher, had retreated to the clubhouse to change his undershirt, which is how he came to unexpectedly encounter a living legend. Robinson, on the field before the game, was being led upstairs via the visitors' locker room. He paused for a moment upon passing the pitcher. "Nervous?" he asked. "Yes sir, a little bit," replied the lefty. The two made a bit of small talk—one platitude that stuck with Holtzman was Robinson's instruction to "keep your hopes up and the ball down"—and the old baseball player shuffled off.*

"I was probably the last major leaguer to talk to Jackie Robinson," said Holtzman, looking back. Nine days later, at his home in Stamford, Connecticut, Robinson was felled by his second heart attack in four years and died at age 53. The ceremony at Riverfront Stadium was his final public appearance.

As George Hendrick batted in the second inning of a scoreless game, Gene Tenace knelt in the on-deck circle and scanned the ballpark, memories flooding back. He had followed the Reds as a kid, and the combination of bygone youth, personal evolution, and hometown pride grew jumbled in his brain, emerging in what, as best he could figure, was a sense of awe. He also took note of one thing more: he could see Hendrick

---

* When speaking to reporters, Robinson was asked whether the iconoclastic Charlie Finley might be the man to hire baseball's first black manager. His answer was curt. "No," he said. "I have no respect for Charlie Finley for what he did to Vida Blue. He tried to break him" (Associated Press, Oct. 16, 1972).

at the plate, but could not hear a thing. Fifty-three thousand screaming fans surrounded him — 15 of them Tenace's own relatives — and it was as if he was in a library. "That's odd," he realized. "It's like I've gone deaf." It would be his last thought before Hendrick drew a two-out walk.

As Tenace approached the batter's box, he gave a nod to Reds catcher Johnny Bench and umpire Chris Pelekoudas. He settled in, took a deep breath, adjusted his helmet. Reds starter Gary Nolan had cruised up to that point, but his first pitch, an outside fastball, looked to Tenace like it all but floated to the plate. His only explanation for so tepid an offering was that Nolan must have hurt his arm on the delivery. Tenace waited for Bench to go out and check on the pitcher, but the catcher only offered up another sign.

To Tenace's surprise, Nolan followed the first floater with a second one, too fat for belief but so slow it threw off his timing. Tenace pulled the ball sharply foul. This was confusing. Nolan was a hard thrower, so why was nobody on the Reds reacting to these meatballs?

Nolan's fourth pitch, a fastball down the middle, was equally languid. This time Tenace pounced. What his line drive lacked in height it made up in velocity; clearing the padded fence in left by some five feet, it fell just short of the elevated bleachers ringing the outfield. "I didn't even feel the ball hit my bat," he said, looking back. "It looked like a batting practice fastball."

As Tenace rounded first he didn't feel his foot hit the base and peeked back to make sure his steps lined up. When he looked toward the A's dugout, he saw his teammates on their feet, and behind them Oakland's rooting section. Everybody was going wild, only in complete silence. "How strange," he thought. "How strange." Hendrick scored in front of him, and the A's led, 2–0.

Cincinnati roared back against Holtzman in the second, loading the bases with nobody out. If there was a moment for the pitcher to submit to popular sentiment about which team was destined to win, this was it. But the left-hander had some history at Riverfront Stadium; his previous start there, as a member of the Cubs in 1971, resulted in his second big league no-hitter. Now, with more than a dozen members of his family, plus his coaches from high school and college, having driven east from St. Louis to watch him pitch, Holtzman called upon some of his old lightning. He lured Cesar Geronimo into a pop-up to second. He induced Dave Concepcion to ground out to shortstop, Bench scoring on the play. He finished things off by striking out Nolan. Threat over, lead intact: 2–1, A's.

As Tenace watched the Reds run the bases, he noted that catching felt normal. He could hear the crowd and the umpire now, and feel the ground firm beneath his feet. He found this to be reassuring, even when the Reds tied the game in the fourth on a walk, a single, and an infield out. When it was time for Tenace's second at-bat, however, it came upon him again —the silence, the slowing of time. His mind emptied until it was just him, his bat, and the game. The count didn't matter. The pitcher didn't matter. Every ball looked as fat as a cantaloupe, like it was sitting on a tee. Pressure from the game's biggest stage did not increase Tenace's load, it lightened it. If there is such a thing as baseball Zen, he had achieved it.

If Tenace thought that Nolan's first-inning fastballs had been slow, he was amazed by the glacial nature of the curveball the right-hander fed him. He judged it intently as it lolled toward the plate, and when it hung just enough to catch the strike zone, he reacted. His stride was long, left heel digging into the ground in front of him, right toes pivoting as hips, then waist, then torso, torqued toward the pitcher. Tenace's bat flashed, sending the ball crashing on an arc down the left-field line. Everything his first homer lacked in height this one offered in spades, finally coming to settle in the second deck. Tenace stood, transfixed. His first homer made him the 19th player to leave the yard in his first-ever World Series at-bat. With this one, he became the only man to do it in his first two.

"It never dawned on me at the time what I was experiencing," said Tenace, looking back. "No player ever said to me, 'Hey man, you're in the zone.' I didn't even know what a zone was —I'd have thought it was a time zone or something. But then I heard Michael Jordan talk about how in one of his NBA championships with the Bulls everything just kind of slowed down when he shot that winning basket. He said he could see everything so clearly, how everybody looked like they were moving in slow motion. I'm listening to this guy talk and thinking, *Man, I experienced that same thing. I went through every bit of that.*"

Tenace's blast regained the lead for the A's, 3–2. Holtzman held it through five innings, which was all Dick Williams wanted. When Johnny Bench led off the sixth with a double, the manager called for his closer.

Unlike the list of Hall of Famers in Cincinnati's dugout, Rollie Fingers, who was inducted into Cooperstown in 1992, was less a born superstar than a reclamation project. Only a season earlier he had washed out completely from Oakland's starting rotation, but here he was, one of the team's most vital members. The right-hander struck out the first two hitters he faced, Tony Perez and Denis Menke, then got Cesar Geronimo to line out to Rudi in left field. Bench never left second base. Vida Blue came on to face the left-handed Joe Morgan in the seventh, and dominated Cincinnati over the final two and a third innings to close out the 3–2 victory.

The win was more important to the A's than the loss was to Cincinnati.* Prior to the game, Oakland might have believed the hype about the Reds, but now the clubhouse was alive with surprised possibility. "We were looking around like, 'Oh, you mean they're not supermen?'" said Holtzman. "We're supposed to be the underdogs, but we just had a guy take their best pitcher deep, twice. We saw that we could play with these guys."

In the A's clubhouse, reporters crowded around Tenace, looking for the game's star to make sense of his performance. From the back of the scrum, a balding man with a thinning shock of salt-white hair pushed his way through the mass, his Kelly green jacket standing out even among the colorful uniforms of the players. Charlie Finley wanted a word with the man of the hour and had no use for waiting. Upon reaching his target, he grabbed the catcher's head with both hands and whispered into his ear. A smile lifted Tenace's face. Cameras clicked. A reporter asked the Owner what he had said.

"You have to ask Gene."

What did he tell you, Gene?

"You have to ask Mr. Finley."

Finley wanted Tenace to provide the details—other people complimenting your generosity has more impact than doing so yourself—but with the ball back in his court, the Owner played it. "He will get a substantial raise, retroactive to the start of the season," he said, beaming. The amount was $5,000. With the crowd keyed to the conversation, Tenace tried to lead it further. "Is that for the first homer?" he daringly asked.

"All right," said Finley. "We'll make it $5,000.05. The five cents is for the second home run."

Although Finley defined his largesse for the press as a retroactive raise, he presented it to the Commissioner's office as a straight bonus—the for-

---

* It was the fifth straight loss for the Reds in the opening game of a World Series. In fact, they'd won their last Game 1 because the other team had been paid to lose it, during the Black Sox scandal of 1919.

mer being allowable under Major League rules, the latter not. It would serve as the basis for the first of Bowie Kuhn's World Series fines against Finley . . . but hardly the last.

In Game 2 the following day the Reds put their leadoff man aboard in four of the first six innings. Twice they had men at second and third, once with nobody out. Catfish Hunter held them off the scoreboard each time. Twenty-six times he started Reds hitters off with strikes, pitching for contact and daring Cincinnati to get the best of him. The Reds did not get the best of him.

Nineteen-seventy-two was the year that Catfish Hunter came into his own. His 21-7 record tied with Cincinnati's Gary Nolan for the best winning percentage in the majors, at .750, and helped him notch the first of what would be four straight top-five finishes in American League Cy Young voting. The right-hander had no overpowering fastball, no knee-buckling curve. He won with control and guile. When Catfish was on, his opponent invariably had little idea what hit him. The right-hander didn't just fool his opponents, he teased them.

Granted a 2–0 lead courtesy of his own RBI single and a Joe Rudi homer, Hunter pitched shutout ball into the ninth, putting Cincinnati on the precipice of the unthinkable: losing two at home to the underdog A's. Tony Perez, however, led off the final frame with his team's fifth hit, a sharp single to left. That brought up third baseman Denis Menke, all but camouflaged amid the powerful Reds offense, as the tying run. Hunter should have paid closer attention.

Menke turned sharply on the righty's first pitch, blasting the ball on a high arc toward the 12-foot-high wall in left field. It was without question his team's best-struck ball of the night. Joe Rudi, playing in, spun and sprinted directly toward the fence, back to the infield. He tracked the ball over his right shoulder, battling the sun, as broadcaster Curt Gowdy called it on NBC's broadcast: "There's a long drive to left. That ball is going, going . . ."

It wasn't so different, really, from the March day four years earlier in Mesa when Rudi, then a 21-year-old first baseman, was trying desperately to make the A's big league roster out of spring training as an outfielder. New manager Bob Kennedy, sizing him up as a personal project, drilled him incessantly in the Arizona sunshine of 1968, shooting balls out of an air cannon toward left field, horsehide mortar fire that gained elevation so quickly Rudi could barely track it. Luckily for him, there was somebody nearby to urge him along, offering instruction every step of the way. As it happened, that person knew a thing or two.

"Go back on that one . . . *back!*" Joe DiMaggio yelled as Rudi broke the wrong way, then failed to compensate for lost ground. "Turn the other way . . . *turn the other way!*"

Over and over they ran the drill, Rudi sprinting backward toward balls angled behind him, DiMaggio — in his first of two seasons spent as a de facto coach in Oakland — steps away from the awestruck kid, telling him exactly what to do.

"Adjust your stride at the warning track," DiMaggio was saying. "Feel for the fence." His instruction was incessant, as was the drill, which occurred daily through the end of spring training, and again when Rudi was called up to Oakland that May. Every day for the rest of the 1968 season the three men arrived at the ballpark early for a half-hour of instruction, Kennedy hitting, Rudi chasing baseballs, and the smoothest center fielder in the history of the sport trying to coax the youngster into becoming better at his job.

DiMaggio's lessons began to take. Balls that at first landed 50 feet away from Rudi were less distant, and then were within arm's reach, and then were inside his glove.

By 1972 he'd built himself into an All-Star defender — the best, said many, in all the sport. And now here he was again, chasing another ball hit over his head. This time it was off the bat of Denis Menke, into the far reaches of Riverfront Stadium. DiMaggio wasn't even in the building.

When Menke made contact, the 53,244 fans in attendance exploded, but Rudi didn't notice. He was running calculations in his head, tracking the hook just like he'd been taught. He spun right, ran like hell, then turned again the other way. He flipped down his sunglasses, made a late adjustment to his angle without breaking stride, and stuck out his hand to feel for the wall, exactly as DiMaggio had showed him. He waited a beat, then put everything he had into his leap, extending his long body as far as it could stretch, back arched, legs curving behind him, reaching up backhanded . . .

On the mound, Hunter thought the ball was gone. In the bullpen, Rollie Fingers thought the ball was gone. Throughout the grandstand, throngs of Reds fans vociferously agreed. "Oh no," Bando thought as the ball was hit. "Oh yes!" he cried as he saw what Rudi was doing.

The outfielder slammed his six-foot-two frame vertically against the wall, legs splayed, the numbers on his back square to home plate. At the apex of his leap the ball settled into his glove, which he closed tight and yanked away from the padding just before impact to protect against unnecessary jarring. Rudi bounced off the wall, landed on his feet, and instinctively held his trophy aloft. It was the only part of the play he'd later want back, because there was still action in front of him. If not for that momentary delay, Campaneris's relay to first might have arrived in time to double off Perez, who'd already rounded second when the ball was caught and had a long trip back. Instead, the runner's desperation dive returned him to the bag with a heartbeat to spare. Still, an out was recorded. The Reds could not help but collectively wonder if their best chance had just been stolen from them. One down, two to go.

The next hitter, Cesar Geronimo, scalded a Hunter fastball on an angry, low line above the Astroturf. It appeared ticketed for right field, but first baseman Mike Hegan, who had entered the game in the sixth inning and was himself among the game's best defenders, snatched it from the air with a dive. Perez, having already broken toward second, was caught cold; he would literally have to run over the fielder to return to first. As Hegan landed, however, his glove smacked the ground and the ball trickled away. The fielder pounced upon it, then crawled six feet toward first, finishing the play by lunging from his knees to tag base with ball for a spectacular putout. Perez took second, but now there were two down. One to go.

With his final pitch of the game, Hunter gave up a single to pinch hitter Hal McRae — the fourth straight sharply struck ball he'd allowed — bringing Perez home and slicing Oakland's lead to 2–1. Williams called upon Fingers, who needed all of four pitches to dispatch pinch hitter Julian Javier on a soft pop-up to Hegan. Somehow the little team that could had stolen two straight on the road from the mighty Reds.

In the giddy postgame clubhouse, as the A's packed their gear for the long flight back to Oakland, a stunned Dick Williams called Rudi's play "the best catch I've ever seen." Finley showed up to revisit his previous day's generosity, bestowing upon Rudi his own $5,000 retroactive bonus.

In the Reds clubhouse, the questions were pointed. Had Cincinnati learned any lessons about underestimating their opponents? Cincinnati had not.

"[Hunter] is a good pitcher, but hell, I'm not going to make him out to be a super pitcher, because he's not," said Pete Rose. "He reminds me of Rick Wise. That's about how hard he throws, or maybe like Jim McAndrew." Wise and McAndrew were fine National League pitchers, but not Cy Young material. Hunter was, and had held Rose, Cincinnati's lead-off batter, to one hit. Rose — who after Cincinnati's first loss had said, "They're one game ahead and that makes us even" — was now batting .125 over two games and was hardly alone in his struggles. During the regular season he, Morgan, and Tolan — the first three hitters in the Reds lineup — had combined for 317 runs, but now they were a collective 2-for-23 and had yet to cross the plate. Meanwhile, Bench, Cincinnati's MVP, was scalding the ball at a .500 clip, but six of his eight plate appearances had come leading off an inning. Numerous Reds complained that a taut NLCS against Pittsburgh left them drained. None thought to mention that Oakland went through its own tense five-game series.

"I'm not going to panic yet," said Anderson in the manager's office. "I'm close to it . . . but not quite." No team had ever lost the first two World Series games at home and come back to win.

The unexpected two-game lead made for a happy flight home . . . for most of the A's. Mike Epstein, however, was angry. Shortly after takeoff, he was also drunk. And the more he drank, the angrier he became. Williams had removed Epstein for a pinch runner in the sixth inning of Game 2, partly to insert Mike Hegan's superior glove at first base with a late lead. The massive slugger's team-leading 26 homers had gone a long way toward saving Oakland's season, but he cooled over the schedule's final six weeks, then went 3-for-16 (with a homer) in the playoffs against Detroit. Now, elevated to the cleanup spot in Jackson's absence, he was hitless in two games against the Reds. His outrage soared. "I could have done the same thing if I had been on first base," Epstein told a newsman in the postgame clubhouse, referring to Hegan's defensive heroics. "I might have even held onto the ball for a double play."

By the time the flight crossed the Rocky Mountains, Epstein had had his fill of scotch and Dick Williams both. He hulked up the aisle toward the manager's seat in the airplane's front row. "I feel you don't appreciate me," he shouted at the startled skipper. "I've been busting my ass all season long, and you take me out of a fucking World Series game, and I don't appreciate it. I don't want this to happen again!"

Unfortunately for Epstein, Williams had also been drinking and was in no mood for discourse. The manager shot to his feet. "I'll do whatever I want," he proclaimed, pointing a finger. Epstein was a fine fielder, but he was no Mike Hegan. Few were. "You don't like my kind of baseball?" Williams spat. "You don't know what my kind of baseball really is!"

After Epstein stormed off to the rear of the aircraft, Williams turned to Ed Levitt, a columnist for the *Oakland Tribune* who was sitting across the aisle. "Mr. Levitt, you can print that," he said. Levitt did. Years later Williams looked back on the incident and said, "Here we are, two wins from a world title and the manager wants to kick the shit out of his first baseman and vice versa? We didn't fight, because even this team was not that crazy."

In the short term, holding a grudge was in nobody's best interests. The following day the manager, eyes firmly on the Reds, walked back his previous sentiments. "I can't blame a ballplayer for feeling bad about coming out," he told the press, confirming that Epstein would be in the starting lineup for Game 3, again batting cleanup. "If he feels bad about coming out, that shows that he wants to play. And don't forget, I had five or six scotches at the time." It was Williams at his best. He needed Epstein's focus in Game 3; sacrificing himself on a public pyre was a small price to pay for it.

The other piece of business to occur on the flight was Finley's announcement that he had torn up the contract Williams signed back in August and replaced it with a new two-year deal, pay bump included. Success, it seemed, was enough to settle even the antsiest of owners. (Technically, Finley had presented the deal to Williams in the afterglow of the playoff victory over Detroit, but the manager was too modest to say anything about it himself.)

The plane set down in Oakland at 8:23 P.M. to a throng of some 8,000 flag-waving fans, many of whom had been waiting four and a half hours for their heroes since shortly after Game 2 ended. Handmade signs dotted the perimeter of the terminal, people pressing shoulder to shoulder, belly to back. The overflow spilled onto surrounding sidewalks and through the building's ticketing area, bringing the airport to a virtual standstill — a wild departure from the regularly empty stands at the Coliseum. Finley, delighted, instructed his players to work the crowd. An audience like this must be satisfied.

A PA was set up on a stage in the lobby, and the Owner eagerly seized the microphone. "Dick Williams and his players are going to do it," he rasped, sweat trickling down his face. "We're going to win the World Series!" The players were physically and emotionally exhausted and hadn't been home in a week. Still, they carried on as best they could, save for a few — prominently, Vida Blue, who slunk home instead of joining the festivities. Finley noticed, of course. Finley always noticed. Afterward, as the A's bused from the airport to the team's unofficial headquarters at the nearby Edgewater Hyatt, the Owner stormed the aisle, venting to the heavens about the emotional weakness of those who skipped the proceedings. He hemmed until his already hoarse voice gave out, at which point he got on the intercom and kept right on going. Perhaps it meant little that now, in the midst of what should have been one of the happiest days of his life, Charlie Finley raged endlessly at some perceived slight. Or maybe it meant everything, a central churn that would eventually inform his every success and greatly hasten his ultimate collapse.

Tuesday, game day in Oakland, saw relentless evening rain. A propane truck overturned about five miles up the rain-slicked Interstate 880 from the Coliseum, slushing combustible liquid across both directions of lanes. The highway patrol shut down a ten-mile stretch all the way up to the Bay Bridge for seven hours, until well past midnight. It was the worst traffic jam in East Bay history.

The collective angst that built up through untold hours of gridlock was nothing compared to that of Charlie Finley when Bowie Kuhn informed him that Game 3 would be postponed. The Owner, after all, was the driving force behind the idea of starting World Series games at night — the better to serve the working man, he said — and so had nobody but himself to blame when, with a scheduled 5:15 P.M. start time, the sky turned into a sluice box at precisely 5:15.* Kuhn called off the game a half-hour later.

As it turned out, the rain-out was only the first opportunity for Finley to be shot by his own late-start-time bullet. Wednesday provided the second. Without rain clouds, the twilight beginning of the rescheduled third game left the sun sinking low behind the western rim of the Coliseum,

---

* It was the ninth consecutive day of rain, but only the second time since 1889 that the Bay Area had experienced precipitation in October. Ironically, the previous time was a decade earlier, in 1962, when rain had caused three consecutive rain-outs during the Giants' only World Series appearance since moving west from New York. Several players in the A's clubhouse remembered it well; Matty Alou was on that Giants team, and Joe Rudi had been a high schooler in Modesto, about 100 miles east of Candlestick Park, where both Series teams traveled to work out while the Bay Area dried off. Rudi still carried a grudge against the players who didn't pause to sign autographs on their way into or out of the minor league ballpark. "I won't mention any of their names," he said in the middle of the '72 Series, "because some of those guys are still playing across the Bay."

behind the plate, as Blue Moon Odom threw the first pitch. The long shadows it cast played havoc with hitters, and the blinding white light on the bleachers made pitchers' release points all but impossible to pick up.

This was how Game 3 came to feature 21 strikeouts and only seven hits between the two clubs. Odom whiffed 11 over seven innings and remained sour years later that he wasn't left in to strike out more. Reds starter Jack Billingham, a distant cousin of Christy Mathewson, notched seven strikeouts of his own over eight innings of work, holding the A's to just three infield hits — evidence that overly soggy turf from the previous day's deluge was all but swallowing batted balls. People recalled Catfish Hunter's perfect game four autumns earlier, which started on the same field at nearly the same time. "In the crepuscular light, the batters were hitting by braille," wrote Jim Murray in his syndicated column. "They were like guys crouching in a dark room and swinging at sounds." At least the game was a sellout.

Odom allowed only three singles, but two of them came within the span of three batters in the seventh inning and proved to be his undoing. It started when Tony Perez led off the frame with a hit to left and was sacrificed to second by Menke. Then things got weird.

With the game still scoreless, Cesar Geronimo fisted a ball into the center-field marshland. Hendrick chased after it in deliberate fashion, owing to the treacherous footing and the fact that Perez should have scored easily from second. But a waterlogged field that giveth can also taketh away. Lumbering around third, Perez lost his footing on a patch of mud and ended up sprawled in foul territory. By that point, however, Hendrick's relay was already in the air, and the guy preparing to catch it, Campaneris, had his back to the plate and didn't see a thing.

Other players did, of course — Odom hit the ground to avoid Campy's would-be relay home, and on-deck hitter Darrel Chaney frantically signaled for Perez to slide. But the increasingly urgent cries from Bando and Tenace were drowned out by 49,410 roaring fans. Campaneris did not turn around until Perez had righted himself and was crossing the plate with the game's first run, giving Cincinnati its first lead of the series.[*]

---

[*] The partisan Oakland crowd grew downright surly when Cincinnati took the lead, hurling eggs and oranges at Pete Rose in left field. Cincinnati's captain took it in stride. "I'm not sore," he said afterward. "Oakland fans can throw at me as much as they want, as long as they miss. One guy kept bombarding me with oranges. He must've had a crate of them. He also had a terrible arm. He never even came close to hitting me. . . . Let them have their fun."

As the innings wore on, Dick Williams unloaded virtually his entire clip in service of freezing the deficit. In the eighth inning Blue came on in relief, all but assuring that he would not start Game 4 (or, likely, Game 5). When the lefty put runners at the corners with one out and the right-handed-hitting Bench at the plate, Williams summoned Fingers.

Things did not go as planned. A slider squirted away from Tenace, allowing Bobby Tolan to advance from first to second, giving the Reds two runners in scoring position. Fingers augmented the drama by running the count full to Bench, at which point Williams tapped third-base coach Irv Noren on the rump and said, "Watch this." Then he ambled to the mound, where he was joined in short order by Bando and Tenace.

The manager gestured dramatically while talking to his pitcher, pointing toward first base, then at Bench. The message was clear: with first base open, he wanted an intentional walk to load the bases and set up the double play. What Williams was saying, however, did not sync with his actions. He was looking at Fingers, but he was talking to Tenace.

"Gene, I want you to stand up and call for an intentional ball," he said. "Rollie, I want you to throw a breaking ball, because if it's a fastball and somebody figures out what we're doing, Bench can hit the shit out of it. Geno, after you jump outside the plate for the intentional walk signal, don't jump back behind the plate so quick. Wait until Rollie picks up his leg. Do you understand?"

The audacity was ludicrous — it was a playground move that wasn't even used on playgrounds. Williams remembered Billy Southworth doing something similar while managing the Cardinals in the 1940s. He also knew that Fingers could throw sliders on the black all day long and didn't need a catcher to frame them. Bench was without question the greatest threat in Cincinnati's lineup, but Williams wasn't much for caving.

"What is this, Little League?" thought Fingers. "You don't do this in a World Series game." He had never even faced Bench before. All he could say — all any of them could say — was "Yes, sir."

"I had never seen that play, never heard of that play," said Tenace, looking back. "That play was never discussed, never even brought up as a remote possibility that it could ever come up in a game, *ever*. Dick Williams should have won a flipping Academy Award for what he did out there."

The plan's flaw was that infielders tend to stand around during intentional walks, but this time every Oakland player was at the ready, poised for a ball to be hit. Fingers had just started his delivery when he heard Morgan yell, "Be alive! They're going to pitch to you!" Reds third-base coach Alex Grammas also called for urgency. On the national TV broadcast, Tony Kubek said, "He's not going to walk him. He's going to throw a strike."

They were correct. Fingers unleashed an unhittable slider over the outer part of the plate, and Tenace slid into place to catch it. The pitch was perfect. A perfect pitch. A pitch-perfect perfect pitch. Fingers called it "the best slider I ever threw." Bando said that "Bench might not have hit it even if he was trying to hit it." Stunned, the Reds catcher watched helplessly as the ball sailed past for strike three. It was the third time he'd struck out looking on the day. "Man," he said to Tenace, "you guys made me look like a goat."

Now there were two outs, and Williams called for a legitimate intentional walk to Perez to load the bases. The next batter, Menke, popped up to Green to end the inning.

It was the final high point of the game for the A's. None of their six remaining hitters — the first three against Billingham, the last three against closer Clay Carroll — could get a ball out of the infield, and Cincinnati sealed its first victory of the series, 1-0. Afterward the main story lines were new life for the Reds and Bench's full-count slider. "He called it the best one he ever threw?" the mortified catcher said. "Great. Why did he have to do it to *me?*" Bench also confirmed Williams's theory that had he somehow anticipated such madness, he would have been looking for a fastball. The manager's genius in the moment was not that he had the guts to call a small-time play on a big-time stage, but that he was willing to go with a lower-percentage pitch in order to achieve a higher-percentage result. It was exactly the kind of tactic his team needed to continue executing if it was going to beat the Reds over the long haul.

The A's proved to be effective front-runners over the Series' first two games, taking early leads, then hanging on for dear life. Holding a two-games-to-one advantage heading into Game 4, they showed that they could also play pretty good catch-up. Holtzman was fantastic in his second Series start, allowing only four hits through seven shutout innings, but when he put runners at the corners with one out, Williams summoned Blue. It was the left-hander's sixth appearance in seven games over the course of nine days—an astonishing schedule for somebody not used to relief work. Vida walked Morgan to load the bases, and Bobby Tolan drove in Cincinnati's first two runs with a double to right.

The A's had taken a 1–0 lead back in the fifth thanks to another Tenace homer, but now they trailed 2–1—a score that held into the bottom of the ninth. The prospect of a knotted-up series looked likely, right up until Dick Williams put on his witch's hat.

After Mike Hegan led off against right-handed reliever Pedro Borbon by grounding out to third, the manager called upon lefty Gonzalo Marquez to hit for Hendrick. The rookie topped a ball into center field for his fourth pinch-hit of the postseason. As Allan Lewis, the Panamanian Express, came in to run, Sparky Anderson signaled for closer Clay Carroll.

The next batter, Tenace, connected for a single—his fourth hit of the Series, and the first that did not clear the fence—sending Lewis to second. Williams went to his bench again, this time tabbing lefty Don Mincher to hit for Green. Mincher had led the A's in home runs as recently as 1970, but at age 35, times had changed. Finley banished him to Washington in the 1971 trade that netted Epstein and Knowles, then reacquired him 14 months later. In spot duty over the 1972 season, Mincher batted only .148. An out would bring Oakland to the precipice of defeat, and a double play would push them over it. "Go up swinging," Williams ordered.

Mincher did as instructed, smacking Carroll's second-pitch fastball on a bounce into right-center field, bringing home Lewis with the tying run, and advancing Tenace to third. Improbably, the score was knotted, 2–2.

Williams then called on Angel Mangual—his third M following Marquez and Mincher—to pinch-hit for Fingers. With that, every seat in the Coliseum went empty, nearly 50,000 fans entering delirium. "All you could hear," wrote Bob Stevens in the *San Francisco Chronicle*, "was noise." Of all the wildly flapping pennants, none were wilder or more flappy than the one waved by the bald-headed chap wearing a yellow blazer in the front row.

Williams prolonged the pandemonium when, with Mangual having already approached the plate, he ambled from the dugout to whisper some strategy into the hitter's ear. Taking no chances with signals from the dugout, he then approached Irv Noren in the third-base coaching box for a conversation that lasted a full 15 seconds. The Reds had to be thinking about the possibility of a suicide squeeze. Instead of returning to the dugout, however, Williams walked down the third-base line while giving a series of hand signals to first-base coach Jerry Adair — at which point he decided to replace Mincher at first base with pinch runner Blue Moon Odom. When Odom emerged from the dugout, the manager hugged him sidelong, offering protracted instructions directly into his ear. Williams had already established a relentless regimen of visiting his pitchers through the Series (by the time it was over he'd gone to the mound an astounding 55 times), and this spate of on-field dialogue fit the pattern nicely.

Having conversed with Mangual, Noren, and now Odom, the manager appeared to be talked out. He patted the runner on the shoulder and turned toward the dugout . . . then reconsidered and called him back, Odom backpedaling as if on an elastic string. The pair's second conversation lasted even longer than the first, taking so much time that the hitter, Mangual, wandered to the on-deck circle for a couple of practice swings. In all, more than 90 seconds elapsed between Mincher's single and Mangual finally settling into the batter's box. Carroll could do nothing but wait.

With runners at the corners and one out, Anderson played his infield in. Every member of the A's was perched on the dugout's top step, watching intently as Mangual slapped Carroll's first pitch on the ground to the right side. Reds second baseman Joe Morgan, stationed 20 feet closer to the plate than usual, had no time to react. The ball shot by him and Tenace raced home with the winning run as gleeful Athletics streamed from their dugout to mob Mangual near first base while fireworks erupted overhead. Oakland's 3–2 victory was the fourth one-run margin in as many games, and brought the A's to within a win of the championship.

"It's unbelievable," exulted Reggie Jackson in the postgame clubhouse. "I looked at that big Oakland crowd, with all those happy faces. Then I looked at the Cincinnati players, with all those sad expressions. Here the Reds had it won, and then it eluded them. We've beaten a lot of teams who thought they had it won."

The regular-season scoring total of either Rose or Morgan would have led the American League, but neither had yet crossed the plate against Oakland. Reds pitchers allowed only eight runs through four games, but it was the A's who were on the cusp of a title. Even better, Oakland still had another game at home, with their ace, Catfish Hunter, on the mound.

If only things were ever that easy.

· · ·

Catfish Hunter's prime weakness as a pitcher was a susceptibility to long-balls, the right-hander finishing in the AL's top five in homers allowed six times. In Game 5, Cincinnati's offense against him consisted of exactly that. Pete Rose deposited Hunter's first pitch of the game into the Coliseum's right-center-field bleachers, and Denis Menke — hitter of nine homers during the season — slugged another in the fourth.

The blows helped the Reds carry a 5–4 lead into the bottom of the ninth, despite a three-run homer by Gene Tenace in the second inning — his fourth in five games, one fewer than his regular-season total. Facing an unwanted Game 6, that homer was on the A's mind when Tenace led off the final frame, but Sparky Anderson, not about to let Oakland's hottest hitter tie things up, had reliever Ross Grimsley pitch around him. Ted Kubiak, attempting to bunt Tenace over, popped into the inning's first out, so Williams — having already used Allan Lewis — inserted Blue Moon Odom as a pinch runner, a move that paid off when the pitcher motored to third on Dave Duncan's single. With one out, the A's needed only a medium-deep fly ball to tie the score. The next hitter, Campaneris, gave it to them. Sort of.

What he actually hit was a foul pop-up, just beyond first base. It was hardly deep, but it presented second baseman Joe Morgan, in pursuit, a lot of ground to cover. Morgan was an Oakland native, still lived just off 98th Avenue, about two miles east of where he was desperately pursuing a vital out. He caught up to the ball in foul ground, but in putting it away slipped on the turf. Odom saw this as providence.

It might seem crazy, tagging up on a fly ball that barely breached the outfield grass, but it was precisely what the game plan called for. The A's knew that Morgan had accuracy trouble when moving to his left; as recently as Game 2 he sailed a cross-body throw wide of its mark. Third-base coach Irv Noren had just reminded Odom of this very thing, reinforcing the runner's green light if Morgan ended up making a play anywhere close to first base.

Well, Morgan *had* moved left, but the play didn't look quite like it was drawn up, mostly because the fielder was stationary by the time he released the ball. Morgan recovered quickly from his stumble, regained his footing, and threw a bullet to Bench — "Son of a bitch if Morgan didn't make a perfect throw," Williams said later — who put down a one-handed swipe tag for the game's final out.

Oakland's chance to win the title at home had passed. In another hour both clubs were headed for the airport and flights back to Cincinnati.

Travel did the teams no favors. Because Tuesday's rain-out had eaten the schedule's off day, Game 5 in Oakland and Game 6 in Cincinnati were played back to back. NBC had a contract to fulfill for a Saturday night game, awkward logistics be damned.

In transit, Williams rejiggered his pitching plan. The loss of the off day eliminated his original starter for Game 6, Blue Moon Odom, who had pitched only two days earlier. In fact, there was only one viable starter available, and even that was up for interpretation. Vida Blue hadn't started a game since the postseason began, but he relieved in four of the five play-off games against Detroit, and three of the five thus far against Cincinnati. That was seven games in 14 days for a guy who was used to pitching once every four. "For a man who throws as hard as Vida, well, that's too damn much for Vida Blue's own good," posited Sparky Anderson, noting that Blue was not nearly as sharp in the World Series as he had been against Detroit. "He can't be the same," Anderson said. "No young man who fires them like Vida, with his whole body behind every pitch, can keep it up day after day." Still, Blue was Oakland's best bet.

The A's didn't land in Ohio until nearly 3:00 A.M., with a ballpark call time only a few hours off. Vida, exhausted under every definition of the word, ended up pitching capably, giving up two runs—highlighted by a solo homer by Johnny Bench—through five.

After Tolan hit a two-out double in the sixth, however, Williams finally acknowledged the left-hander's overuse and, with the Reds leading 2–1, went to his bullpen. It didn't go well. Cincinnati's powerhouse offense, stifled through five games, burst open with one in the sixth and five in the seventh, and what had been a close game ended with an 8–1 score. It was the Series' only contest to be decided by more than one run, and it locked things up at three games apiece. Sunday's Game 7 would be winner-take-all.

Afterward, talk in the A's clubhouse focused on some glaring issues. One was the nearly unimpeded ability of Cincinnati's runners to steal bases, their three thefts in Game 6 bringing their Series total to 11 in 13 tries. Tenace's bat may have been vital to Oakland's success, but there was no hiding that his arm did not measure up.

The second issue was cleanup hitter Mike Epstein, who without Reggie in the lineup had fallen into a nasty tailspin, going hitless in 21 World Series at-bats.*

Those were the easy problems. The big one presented itself fully on Saturday, although its genesis had come six days earlier, prior to the second game in Cincinnati. That was when a woman in a Riverfront Stadium concession line overheard a stranger say, "If Tenace hits another homer, I'm going to shoot him." It could have been an off-color joke from a bitter Reds fan, but the woman was concerned enough to alert the police, who found an open bottle of whiskey and a loaded handgun on the man. The FBI was summoned.

The A's departure from the ballpark directly to the airport and the safety of California tempered concerns somewhat, but returning to Ohio for Game 6 presented logistical considerations. The possibility that the arrested man was not working alone led the feds to sequester Tenace in plain sight. Instead of taking the team bus, he was chauffeured to Riverfront Stadium in a bulletproof town car, accompanied by a trio of armed guards. He entered and exited the team's downtown hotel, Stouffer's Inn, via back entrances and service elevators, and agents were stationed outside his door. His room-service food was checked, and the waiters frisked. "I'm not going to lie," said Tenace, looking back. "It was kind of cool."†

As Sunday morning broke with drizzles, Gene Tenace arrived at the ballpark hours earlier than his teammates. His reason for doing so had nothing to do with death threats and everything to do with Dick Williams's frantic search for solutions.

Since turning pro in 1965, Tenace had appeared in 785 games, majors and minors combined, and played first base in seven of them. Williams had woken him up the previous night with the news that he wanted num-

---

* When Brooklyn's Gil Hodges was en route to going oh-for-the 1952 World Series, he called on his parish priest to pray for "one base hit, anyhow." That avenue of slump-busting held negligible interest for the Jewish Epstein.

† Ten years later, in 1982, when Tenace was in his second-to-last-year as a big leaguer, he returned to the World Series with the St. Louis Cardinals and got an unusual piece of fan mail before one of the games. "It was from him, from *that guy*," he said. "The same guy who said he was going to shoot me wrote me a letter and apologized for what he did in Cincinnati. He did his time, they put him in jail. He said he was sorry and hoped I accepted it. I just kept thinking it was kind of strange, this guy 10 years later picking up on me again in the World Series."

ber eight. The move would solve two problems at once — replacing Tenace's ineffective arm behind the plate with Dave Duncan's cannon, and removing Mike Epstein's ice-cold bat from the lineup. The manager may have been crazy enough to expect a novice fielder to handle a foreign position in the season's biggest game, but he wasn't crazy enough to have him do it cold.

Tenace (and his FBI escorts) rolled into the clubhouse at 8:00 A.M. to find Williams, backup first baseman Mike Hegan, and coach Vern Hoscheit. Every bit of furniture had been pushed against the walls, leaving a long swath of carpet down the middle. At the far end sat a base. The Reds had refused Williams's request to use the infield at so early an hour, so the manager improvised. He had time at his disposal and was determined to put it to use.

Tenace couldn't have asked for a better crash-course instructor than Hegan, among the game's best defenders, who dissected for him the position's finer points, going over footwork, where to stand, and how to keep from getting spiked by runners. Tenace did his best to absorb it. Then Williams asked Hoscheit to hit him some grounders.

The coach's first offering came in at full speed, a carpet-hopping smash that picked up velocity as it skipped across the concrete substrate and rocketed into Tenace's chest, knocking him to a knee. "What in the hell are you doing?" Williams screamed at the coach as Tenace tried to catch his breath. Hoscheit muttered a sheepish "Sorry, Geno," and dialed things down. It didn't much matter; Tenace, half blinded by the room's fluorescent lights, could barely see the ball anyway. There was no getting around the fact that they were taking infield in a locker room.

With Jackson injured and Epstein on the bench, Oakland's Game 7 lineup featured eight right-handed bats against Cincinnati right-hander Jack Billingham, a deficiency that Williams mitigated by elevating Tenace from seventh in the order to cleanup. Angel Mangual, who didn't make so much as a pinch-hitting appearance until Game 4, was tabbed to start in center field over the slumping Hendrick. Joining the players in the dugout were Tenace's FBI escorts, wearing their standard dark suits and sunglasses.

Williams's decision to bat Tenace fourth paid quick dividends when the freshly minted star came to the plate with two outs in the first inning and Mangual on third. Thoroughly confounded by a Billingham sinker, Tenace topped an easy two-hopper to Menke at third base to end the inning . . . or at least it would have had Tenace not been touched by the Baseball Gods.

On its second hop the ball hit a seam in the plastic turf and shot high into the air, just beyond Menke's desperation stab, allowing Mangual to scamper home. "Gosh doggit, that ball looked like it disappeared on me," said Tenace, looking back. "I mean, Jiminy Christmas, I don't even know how I *hit* that ball, how I even made contact. When I got to first is when I really knew I was having a heck of a series. Oh shit, you got to be kidding me — that should have been an easy grounder and out of the inning."

Williams's other move looked brilliant in the fourth, when Joe Morgan walked and immediately took off for second. He'd stolen 58 bases during the regular season, but this wasn't Tenace he was testing. Duncan whipped a bullet to Campaneris that easily beat the runner. It was the last time the Reds would test the catcher's arm.*

Odom, pitching on three days' rest, was electric through four, but in the fifth he began to falter. With one out and the A's leading, 1–0, the right-hander put runners on first and second, then ran the count to 2-1 on Dave Concepcion. Wanting to risk nothing, Williams turned to the bullpen and the best pitcher on his staff, Catfish Hunter, who had started Game 5 only two days earlier.

At first the move did not appear to pay off. Hunter finished the walk to Concepcion, at which point it was Sparky Anderson's turn to be aggressive. His starting pitcher, Jack Billingham, had allowed only two hits over five innings, but the bases were loaded with one out, and the Reds were trailing. He sent in Hal McRae to bat for the pitcher.

The switch looked like a winner when McRae drove a fastball toward deepest center field. Activity in both dugouts froze. A grand slam was the killer blow the Reds had been seeking all series long but could not find.

---

* Williams, who had multiple run-ins with first-base umpire Jim Honochick during the regular season, twice went out to argue calls at first base in the early innings. "It's a known fact that the best teams are in the World Series," he screamed at the hectored ump. "Why can't we get the best umpires in the World Series?" The manager was relentless. When the A's batted in the top of the fourth, it was Williams, not regular first-base coach Jerry Adair, in the coaching box. The manager's motive was immediately evident — he kept his back toward the plate through the entire inning as he focused on new ways to berate the umpire. Bolstered by Bowie Kuhn's edict that the NBC telecast not be deprived of key field personnel, Williams undertook an extended balancing act. "He didn't even know where the hitter was," said Tenace. "If a guy hit a ball down there, it'd have killed him. He sat there and ragged that stinking ump through the whole inning until they got us out." Afterward, the phone rang in the visitors' dugout. It was Kuhn, calling from his stadium box to warn the manager against repeating his display at the risk of a heavy fine. Adair returned to his post the next inning, and Williams was fined $200 regardless.

The heavy Ohio air, however, stifled the blast, and the ball settled into Mangual's glove at the base of the wall. It wasn't Cincinnati's preferred outcome, but it was enough to score Perez from third to tie the game, 1–1.

Anderson's strategy paid short-term dividends, but Cincinnati's bullpen proved to be no match for Oakland's hottest player. In the sixth inning, the clock still ticking on his man-of-the-hour status, Tenace smoked a double to left to score Campy and give the A's a 2–1 lead, which they extended moments later when Sal Bando doubled off the center-field wall to drive in pinch runner Allan Lewis.* Now it was 3–1, and the A's only job was to hold on.

It did not come easy. The eighth inning necessitated three pitchers — Hunter, Holtzman (Williams's third starter of the night), and Fingers — but the A's escaped with one man in, the tying run at third, and the winning run at second. It would be Cincinnati's last, best chance.

His team holding a 3–2 lead, Rollie Fingers rolled through the first two hitters in the bottom of the ninth, needing only to retire pinch hitter Darrel Chaney — 0-for-7 in the Series and literally the last man on the Reds bench — to end it. As a light rain began to fall over Riverfront Stadium Fingers's task was clear: put the ball over the plate, a point that Williams reinforced when he offered explicit direction during a mound visit: "Three fastballs, game's over, we win." Inexplicably, Fingers's first pitch was a tailing slider, which hit Chaney on the shin. "I thought he would be looking fastball," the closer explained when an exasperated Williams asked later what the hell he'd been thinking.

Now Fingers had to deal with the .307-hitting Pete Rose as the Series-clinching run. Williams returned to the mound so angry that he had already decided to pull Fingers in favor of Vida Blue. Duncan, however, lobbied for status quo. "I know what you're going to do," he said. "Don't do it. Rollie is throwing as good as I've ever seen. He can get Rose." Williams glanced at Fingers, considered the possibility, wondered if he was making the biggest mistake of his career, and left the right-hander in.

---

* The following inning, as the A's congregated on the bench, Bando and Rudi asked Tenace how he managed to hit that pitch for a double. Tenace had no idea what they were talking about. Bando asked if he even knew where it was located. "Right down the middle," Tenace said. Rudi and Bando looked at one another in disbelief. "Geno," said Rudi softly, "that ball was off the plate, down and away, knee high. You had no business pulling it down the line." They walked away, heads shaking. "Gosh," thought the man lost in a hitting zone for his seventh straight game, "it sure looked down the middle of the plate to me."

Fingers's first pitch was a low, tailing fastball, which Rose slapped on a line to left-center. The ball was well struck but did not get down quickly enough, Rudi cutting in front of Mangual to catch it even as his teammates swarmed to the mound to celebrate the franchise's first championship since 1930. "If it's not against the boards I'm going to catch it," Rudi said moments later in the victorious clubhouse. "If it is, I'm going through the wall to get it."

Some 2,500 miles away, the Oakland Coliseum, filled to capacity with fans awaiting the start of the Raiders-Broncos game, burst into applause as transistor radios broadcast the final out. On the field in Cincinnati, Charlie Finley stood atop the roof of the visitors' dugout and grabbed his wife, Shirley, in a deep embrace. With typical Finley exuberance, he later called it "the greatest kiss of them all." The Owner, green blazer shocking the eye amid a sea of red, beckoned Dick and Norma Williams alongside. Each couple hugged in the drizzle.

Oakland's three starters, plus Blue as a swingman and Fingers out of the bullpen, had carried virtually the entire load for Oakland. The A's held Cincinnati to two runs or fewer in five of the seven games. Even with their eight-run outburst in Game 6, the Reds still averaged only three per contest, in contrast to 4.59 over the regular season. That Oakland batted only .209 as a team was mitigated entirely by the fact that Cincinnati, despite a superior offense, hit at precisely the same clip. "As good as their hitters were," said Bando, "our pitchers were better."

A less obvious factor was the reserves. "The A's have a great bench," wrote Ron Bergman in the *Oakland Tribune*. "Theirs is lowercase. The Reds' Bench is tremendous. The Reds' bench is underwhelming." Even the capital-B Johnny Bench had been limited, less by his .261 Series batting average than the fact that there was rarely anybody on base when he hit. The catcher's solo homer in Game 6 accounted for his only RBI of the Series.

When Finley arrived in the victorious clubhouse, he took one look at the World Series trophy and brashly proclaimed that every one of his players would receive a full-size replica — an unprecedented and not inexpensive bit of whimsy. Rudi returned the favor by giving the Owner the ball he caught for the final out, poo-pooing Finley's initial refusal with logic that nobody in the room wanted to refute. "It's just the first one," he said. "We'll get plenty more."

Flanked by sons Martin, 17, and Luke, 15, Finley told writers that "money, sweat and sacrifice really have paid off." When reporters directed questions toward the boys, Finley, playing the wary father, shushed them and answered himself. Less supervised was Dick Williams's 16-year-old son, Rick, who, encouraged to drink by Catfish Hunter, went quickly overboard. "He got so looped I had to stand him in a cold shower and dress him myself before heading to the airport," the pitcher said later.

Tenace was named World Series MVP, having batted .348 and driven in nine of Oakland's 16 runs. (Nobody else on the team had more than one RBI.) His slugging percentage of .913 broke Babe Ruth's World Series mark of .900, set back in 1926. Said Epstein: "It's one thing to be pitched to, but it's another to be man enough to do something about it." Added Rudi: "The equation was simple: if Geno doesn't get hot, we don't win."

As Commissioner Kuhn presented the MVP trophy — an award accompanied by a new Dodge Charger — the catcalls began. Players joked that Cincinnati ran so freely against Tenace that he should drive the car away before a Reds player stole it. "How the hell can you win a car, Geno?" ribbed Knowles, referencing Tenace's removal for a pinch runner in the sixth inning. "You can't even go nine."

The clubhouse wasn't the only place for mad celebration. Just outside the door, players' wives congregated with a stash of champagne. ("They couldn't drink it all," wrote Ron Bergman. "They tried.") "We're number one! We're number one!" the women chanted, shouting for their husbands to join them. Williams, the first to emerge, was mobbed. Others followed — Tenace, Duncan, Rudi — and received similar treatment. Finley made his way to the middle of the horde, holding a magnum of champagne he had promised to Green if the A's won. The second baseman appeared, the cork was popped, and consumption continued. This type of celebration was by then old hat to the players, but their wives were new to it all. Spurred by a quick-strike overdose of adrenaline and alcohol, one of them fainted and was tended to by trainer Joe Romo. Mike Epstein's wife, Barbara, found her way into lip-lock with Dave Duncan, then passed out in the arms of Catfish Hunter. (When the catcher saw Epstein the next day, all he could say about the situation was, "God, your wife can kiss.")

As things wound down, Campy Campaneris, Dick Green, Joe Horlen, and Don Mincher warbled through a rendition of the National Anthem while fully clothed underneath a flowing showerhead, led by a stark-naked Vida Blue. In a room so thick with champagne that it bordered on precipitation, six players shot a hair-spray commercial touting follicular resiliency. What better subjects, after all, than the Hairs, baseball's shaggiest bunch? "I don't even know [what I was plugging]," said a giddy Fingers afterward. "I just held up the can and smiled in front of the camera. It sure pays to be a winner in the World Series."*

The party eventually transitioned onto the team plane. Those who felt while sober that four hours of airborne Dixieland music was disturbing were now certain of it. So fervent was the celebration that Vida Blue even joined the Owner in a sing-along. Players who maintained consciousness gorged themselves on steak, lamb chops, and butterscotch sundaes, augmented by a free-flowing supply of wine.

Finley strolled the length of the plane, offering nonstop congratulations. Upon seeing an open seat next to Duncan, he plopped down and asked in slapdash fashion, "Who do we have here? Oh yes, here we have Dave Duncan. I know you, Dave Duncan."

The catcher was in no mood. Things had been tense between him and the Owner since 1970, when Duncan publicly proclaimed that "there's only one man who manages this club, Charlie Finley, and we will never win as long as he manages." Finley responded days later by firing manager John McNamara and hitting coach Charley Lau, then pinning his decision — despite having already settled on both moves beforehand — on the catcher's outspokenness.† From that point forward, Duncan lost all tolerance for the Owner. "Oh fuck, you don't know me, Charlie," he spat back.

---

* In actuality, A's players would find that their phones were as silent after the championship as they had been beforehand, the provinciality of Oakland scaring off sponsors in ways that players in places like New York and Los Angeles never understood. Things grew so bad that two seasons later Tenace and Bando pounced on one of the few opportunities that came their way, from a toupee shop in Manhattan — their primary payment being free replacement hair. The player to profit most from the team's success was Joe Rudi, mainly because he operated an off-season insurance business out of his home and was prescient enough to advertise in the World Series program, which gave him more work than he could handle.

† During the press conference at which Finley fired McNamara and Lau, things got downright bizarre when the Owner suggested a homoerotic relationship between Duncan and Lau — the man who, in reshaping the swings of Duncan and Joe Rudi, was as responsible as anybody for turning the players into future All-Stars. The Owner's exact words: "One day I found out that Duncan was sleeping with coach Charley Lau." Pause. "By that I mean they were rooming together, sharing expenses. When I found out about this, I called it to their attention, asked them to break it up immediately, because as we all know, in the Army troops don't fraternize with officers." At least some of what he said was true, anyway. Duncan and Lau, both recently separated from their wives, had decided to share a roof to pare expenses. And the criticism was valid — Duncan said as much later himself. But Finley's word selection — he was a master salesman, after all, prone to choosing his verbiage carefully — left a decidedly different impression.

Finley looked quizzically at the glowering player for a moment. Somewhere, a needle scratched across a jukebox record, but Finley did his best to roll with it. "Oh, no," he persisted. "I *do* know you, Dave Duncan."

"Bullshit," the catcher shouted. "You've never taken the time to know me. You don't know any of us. You don't care about us. You only care about what we can do for you."

With that sentiment, Duncan did what few people over the years had been able to do—he left Charlie Finley speechless. The Owner got up and tottered down the aisle, his gait giving away hours of giddy exertion, at which point a fully disgusted Duncan said, "I would like to open the bomb bay doors and drop this whole thing on Bad Breath, Montana. Not that I have anything against the people there."

Looking back years later, the catcher's perspective was less caustic but just as firm. "Finley was trying to be friendly," he said, "but for me his friendliness was so phony that it kind of made me sick. He'd say and do anything he had to to get what he wanted. No sincerity, no honesty. You couldn't trust that he was speaking the truth, kind of like a used car salesman. That was his nature." Duncan would be traded five months later, ostensibly the victim of a contract dispute but more likely the result of an aggrieved owner who no longer wanted anything to do with him.

Later in the flight, Mike Epstein had his own showdown with Finley. Summoned to the front of the plane, Epstein stood in the aisle as the Owner berated him at something approaching top volume. Not only had the first baseman gone oh-for–the World Series, but his shouting match with Williams following Game 2 did little to endear him to management. Finley got on him for his hitting. He got on him for his defense. He got on him for his attitude. He got on him because he didn't play in Game 7. He got on him because he did play in the other games. The kicker for Epstein was that it was mostly true. The player was so shaken that he could do little more than stand there and take it, up to and including Finley's promise that he would soon be traded. "I had been of no help to the team during the World Series," said the disbelieving first baseman later. "My ego was hurting, and there was Charlie, yelling at me in the aisle. That's just how things went around there." It hadn't yet been codified, but Game 6 would be Epstein's final appearance in an Oakland uniform.

When the jet set down in Oakland, players found an airport mob scene that made previous receptions look downright quaint. Police began setting up at the airport at 1:00 P.M., about ten minutes after the game's final out, and by 6:30 had to close Hegenberger Road, the main access thoroughfare, after 30,000 people packed the terminal to celebrate the Bay Area's first championship in any sport. Throngs crushed into the airport's side hallways and stairwells, seizing every available crevice. The press of bodies heated the terminal to more than 100 degrees. People fainted. About 2,000 of them managed to storm the tarmac, forcing the team plane to park a half-mile away. There was little mistake about where the players were headed, though. Finley would have it no other way.

Team wives boarded a bus that bypassed the terminal entirely, heading instead to the Edgewater Hyatt to await delivery of their luggage. Vida Blue, knowing an opportunity when he saw one, joined them. "I just can't stand scenes like this," he said, crouching low in the back to avoid detection. (Blue's absence was quickly noted, what with the crowd chanting "We want Vida! We want Vida!" and no Vida to step up.)

"It was a madhouse," said Bando of the airport display. "You couldn't walk through the place. The fans were hysterical. We wondered where they came from, because they'd never been at the ballpark."*

Players slowly made their way to the podium that had been erected for the event, Bando and Hunter carrying the World Series trophy between them while Finley held aloft a Reds batting helmet, spoils of the defeated. "Let's keep this trophy for 10 years," Epstein shouted to the crowd. Duncan read a poem he had written for the occasion: "We worked as one / And all had fun / We're world champs now / And as you can see / We're as happy as can be." Delighted as they were, the exhausted players made beelines for home as quickly as they could.

Blue was also a no-show for the next day's victory parade, and absent later at the team party. "Season's over and I had enough," he said, looking

---

* Finley ordered a podium erected in the terminal upon which to introduce the players, the image of a lord ministering over his court playing no small part in his fantasy of civic ascension. The reality, though, was unsustainable. People were actually spilling *out* of the terminal, pushing into the players who were trying to get in. It was a wild throng, intent on touching its heroes, tactile affirmation of their success. The pandemonium was so fierce that the Oakland police chief, noting assistant Jimmy Piersall's efforts at orchestration, pulled him aside. "You better get [the players] all out of here or we'll have a riot," he ordered. "Take them back the way they came." Everybody was sent back to the buses even as Finley reached the podium and wondered where the hell everybody was. Said Piersall, "[Finley] came running down from his platform, down the stairs, and caught up to me outside. He was ranting and screaming. 'Who the hell told you to let the players go back? Who did this? Who did this to me?'" Eventually, players were escorted back in and festivities commenced.

back years later. "It was my way of getting back at Charlie." As he reflected, Vida fiddled with his shirtsleeve and disappointment filled his voice. "Now I wish I'd celebrated those things. I was still pissed off about stuff all the time, but I was the one who ended up being the big loser." Shockingly, Finley didn't hold it against him. When the Owner's hometown of La Porte, Indiana, honored him with a civic banquet over the winter, he asked four players to appear. The first to accept his invitation was Blue. In front of 800 banquet attendees and another 1,600 in the bleachers, the mercurial left-hander, the man who once said that Charlie Finley had soured his stomach for baseball, stood up and proclaimed the Owner to be "baseball's executive of the year." Success, it turns out, can mend fences after all.

7

Springtime For Champions

Charlie Finley thinks he invented baseball.

> — Dodgers owner Walter O'Malley, after Finley spent the
> duration of an awards-ceremony acceptance speech
> lobbying for interleague play, orange baseballs, and
> Saturday starts for playoff series, with an increasingly
> uncomfortable O'Malley sitting alongside him on the dais

Charlie Finley had finally given the Bay Area a World Series title, but to merely bask in the afterglow would involve neither sweat nor sacrifice. The Owner had a roster to tend to and pieces to move. First up: vendettas. Mike Epstein may have led the A's in home runs, but he was a nuisance — and a slumping one at that. A .094 postseason batting average could be overlooked for the right guy, but to the Owner, Epstein was not that guy. He had blown up at Williams on the flight home from Cincinnati. He had beaten Jackson half to death. He had made a stink over the June acquisition of Orlando Cepeda, seeing it as a threat to his playing time, despite the clearly hobbled Cepeda collecting only three at-bats with Oakland before being disabled for the season. Worst of all, earlier in the year Epstein had refused a dinner invitation directly from Finley himself, without so much as a valid excuse. Admitted the slugger later: "I just couldn't see sitting through a meal and listening to him talk." Damned if the Owner was going to abide that.

Ultimately, Epstein served as the latest example of Finley's willingness to shoot himself in the foot for the sake of making a point. With no apparent memory of what he lost when he petulantly released Ken Harrelson in 1967, the Owner shipped Epstein to the Rangers in November for pennies on the dollar, getting right-hander Horacio Pina, a middling reliever who had just gone 2-7 for Texas, in return. It was a full-fledged excommunication. With Tenace taking over at first base full-time, Epstein was all but erased from the team annals, his 1972 statistics deleted from the '73 press guide save for two lines: his .188 batting average against the Tigers in the ALCS, and his .000 batting average against the Reds in the World Series. Finley took additional delight in sending the first baseman to the worst possible location; the Rangers had just completed their first season in Texas by losing 100 games while discovering the brutality of summertime in Arlington. "Sometimes," said Epstein upon hearing the news, "there just isn't any justice in life."

Finley's second significant off-season move had more lasting repercussions. The Owner desperately sought somebody to lock down center field, allowing Jackson to slide back to his natural position in right. He got his guy on November 21, sending reliever Bob Locker to the Cubs in exchange for a fleet-footed 24-year-old, Billy North. As far as Williams was concerned, any equation that put Angel Mangual on the bench was okay by him.

The additional depth allowed Finley to divest himself of expensive role players. Cepeda, whose exorbitant contract had been acquired from Atlanta in exchange for the similarly expensive Denny McLain, was released. Matty Alou was sent to the Yankees for spare parts. Don Mincher retired. With some of the savings, Finley reacquired lefty reliever Paul Lindblad (mostly for cash), whom he had been coveting since trading him away to Texas in 1971.[*]

In December, *The Sporting News* named the Owner its Sportsman of

---

[*] Another part of Finley's savings went directly to the Commissioner's office. Bowie Kuhn fined him $2,500 for the "bonuses" he paid to Tenace and Rudi following their World Series heroics, claiming violation of rule 40-6(a) prohibiting performance-based stipends. The Commissioner was unmoved by Finley's insistence that the money was disbursed by way of retroactive raises. Curiously, the $5,000 Finley gave to Mike Hegan as a regular-season bonus went unmentioned. Being fined, however, wasn't even the biggest indignity Finley suffered at Kuhn's hands. The Owner couldn't wait for the official World Series film to be released, then was aghast to see that his name wasn't even mentioned during its 37-minute run time. It wasn't until the recap of Game 4 that Finley's image even appeared, and then for only a moment. The Owner countered by producing his own historical document, a promotional LP featuring audio highlights of the season. It was obvious from its title — *Finley's Heroes* — who was behind it. Every player was given a copy.

the Year, trumpeting his innovative bent for increasing baseball's appeal.*
It took winning a World Series to do it, but Finley's ideas were finally
gaining traction. Within three years, 18 of baseball's 24 teams had adopted colorful pullover tops, recalling Finley's implorations back in 1963
that "there was a time when most of the cars were black, but in modern
times, cars are red and blue and green and gold . . . bright and attractive."
Baseball, he followed, had to keep up with trends, "even if a fellow has to
force it."

Finley had been championing nighttime World Series games and Saturday openers for some time, and he used his newfound championship
juice to push the rest of his modernize-or-get-left-behind agenda with
renewed vigor. Shockingly, baseball's power brokers actually agreed with
him on certain points. They may have found him intolerable, but there
was no debating that the man had ideas.

It began in mid-December, when one of Finley's pet projects served
as the centerpiece of the plan adopted by American League owners for
the following season. The year 1973 would see the first use of designated
pinch hitters for pitchers, a position that was quickly truncated to "designated hitter." At baseball's winter convention in Hawaii, the American
League approved the DH by an 8–4 vote. The idea was hardly the Owner's
alone — it had been banging about for more than a century — but his was
unequivocally the loudest voice in the room.

The new rule began serving its purpose immediately. Before a bat
could be swung, the American League was more relevant than during
any off-season in memory. In Oakland, it made the release of Orlando
Cepeda (not to mention Tommy Davis the previous season) all the more
perplexing. Finley among all owners should have recognized Cepeda as
the prototype designated hitter — 35 years old and, with shredded knees,
too injured to play the field, but still only two seasons removed from a
34-homer campaign.

Not so blinded was Red Sox GM Dick O'Connell, who snapped up
Cepeda on a one-year deal, making him the first player signed specifically

---

* A's players were not similarly honored. Adding insult to ignorance, Oakland failed to land any
of the ten first-team berths on the Associated Press's postseason All-Star team — the Cubs boasted
three — and only Joe Rudi landed on *The Sporting News*'s roster. Widespread sentiment proclaimed
the A's championship to be little more than a temporary stroke of good fortune. George Vass of
Baseball Digest was representative when he wrote, "With all credit to the A's pitching staff, their victory was a fluke. It was the biggest surprise of 1972."

as a DH. Not until the slugger began powering home runs over the Green Monster at a regular clip would the Owner realize his mistake.[*]

Some of Finley's other ideas were met with less enthusiasm. In recent years the Owner had frequently bandied around the idea of three-ball walks as a means of creating additional offense. Such was Finley's fervor that in 1971 he convinced American League president Joe Cronin to sign off on a spring training experiment wherein the A's and the Brewers played an exhibition game under the rule. Finley was right about the extra baserunners, but 19 walks and six home runs later, there wasn't much clamor for a repeat performance.

Uncowed, the Owner claimed additional permission from Bowie Kuhn to implement the three-ball walk format in additional spring training games that year — never mind that baseball's rules committee denied his request before it ever reached the Commissioner. Thus was Angels manager Lefty Phillips surprised upon showing up in Mesa and being informed that three-ball walks were in effect for that day's game. The A's director of minor league operations, Phil Seghi, handled his end of the bargain by greeting the arriving umpires in the stadium parking lot while waving around a piece of paper that he described as official consent to use the three-ball format. (It was actually just an A's press release describing the plan.) When the umpires were unable to confirm Seghi's claim with league officials, they called Finley himself. Of course it's legit, he told them, and furthermore, we don't need approval from the visiting club. With no further information upon which to base their decision, the umps relented. Three balls it was.

Angels general manager Dick Walsh called Finley to straighten things out, but the conversation lasted only moments. Before anyone around Walsh knew what was happening, he hung up the phone in shock and proclaimed, "He called me a fucking idiot." ("I did not call Mr. Walsh a

---

[*] When people suggested that Finley goofed in letting Cepeda go, he responded in full bluster. "Our team physician [Dr. Harry Walker], who performed the operation [on Cepeda's knees], said that all of the cartilage in his knee was gone — that it was almost bone on top of bone," he explained. "Dr. Walker advised me that it was very, very questionable whether he could hold up. And even if he does hold up, if he gets on base you sure as hell have to put a pinch-runner in for him. That's two players used up right there. Now you need another designated pinch-hitter. That's three players used up with one move." This from the guy who invented the second-base rotation and who would never stop advocating for the designated runner.

fucking idiot," Finley later clarified. "I told him to quit *acting* like a fucking idiot.") Walsh nearly packed his team back onto the bus, but the possibility of being liable for ticket refunds swayed his decision to stay. The game featured 16 bases on balls, and the experiment was officially killed shortly thereafter.

By 1973, Finley's cause du jour was "alert orange" — the color of the baseballs he trumpeted as a replacement for the drab old white ones in use since forever. The fans will love it, he gushed, and hitters would be better able to pick up the ball out of the pitcher's hand. "More offense," he said in a familiar refrain, "that's what baseball needs and the public wants." As in '71, the Owner received official approval to test his theories, this time in an exhibition game against Cleveland.

Just as the three-ball walk didn't turn out quite like the Owner had anticipated, the debut of the Day-Glo ball offered similarly varied results. "I don't know how to say this without it sounding like a lot of bull, but it's a little hard to pick up the spin on the baseball," said the since-traded George Hendrick. And that was *after* he hit three homers on the day.

One problem was that because the balls, made by Spalding, were dyed, not tanned, they could not be rubbed up with tacky Delaware River mud, as was standard practice in Major League Baseball. Instead, a resin was applied that made them unusually slippery and caused the covers to crack upon impact. The Commissioner went out of his way to note that the flaws were correctable and that mass production would help refine the manufacturing process. It made no difference. The balls were used only once more, on April 2, against the Angels in Palm Springs, after which California outfielder Bob Oliver spoke for the majority when he said, "They should take the orange baseball, wrap it in a blue blanket and drop it in the Red Sea."

When spring training opened in 1973, the story around Oakland's camp was holdouts. Dick Green stayed at home in South Dakota, threatening for the second straight season to work for his family's moving business full-time unless a substantial raise was in the offing. Dave Duncan was back in Oakland, demanding $50,000 — ten grand more than the Owner offered, which was itself a substantial raise over the $30,000 Duncan made in 1972. Most notably, Vida Blue was again nowhere to be found.

Nobody — not the Owner, not Vida, not the fans — wanted a repeat of the previous spring's acrimony, but Finley seemed physiologically incapable of caving to players' contract demands. He opened negotiations at $50,000 — the base portion of the $63,000 he paid Blue in 1972 — then, anticipating a holdout, began talking openly about how Vida was no longer untouchable when it came to potential trades. That seemed to do the trick. Vida began negotiating on his own, not through attorney Bob Gerst, a development greeted joyfully by the Owner. "Vida called me on my birthday [February 22]," Finley proclaimed to the press in victorious tones. "He asked me to turn my recording machine on. I asked him for what. He said just turn it on. I turned it on and he was very kind to sing for me a happy birthday song, which I appreciated very much." See? Things between them were peachy.

Still, rumors of Finley sending Blue to the Rangers for pitcher Pete Broberg and cash grew so serious that on March 17 the *Oakland Tribune* announced it as a done deal. The newspaper was wrong, of course; when talks fell through, Finley, as he was entitled to do under baseball's reserve clause, unilaterally renewed the contracts of both Blue and Duncan at their previous salaries. "In spite of [Blue] reporting late last year, and in spite of his 6-10 record, I have not cut him a penny," said Finley. "Here again, I feel I'm being extremely generous."*

The Owner's real goal was to gird for salary battles to come. The 1974 season would be the first with new arbitration rules under which players could submit salary proposals, owners could counter, and an outside mediator would select one or the other. Had Finley given Vida or Duncan the raises for which they'd clamored, he said, it could be used as leverage against him in the future. He was right.

The Owner's negotiations with Duncan held none of the feel-good promise of his talks with Blue. The catcher had borne animosity toward Finley ever since signing with the A's as a 17-year-old in 1963, when Duncan — whose divorced father had long since moved away — requested that an adult advocate on his behalf during contract negotiations. (Such was player representation then that the adult Duncan chose, the father of a girl he was dating, was a dentist.) Finley refused. He offered $45,000, then told Duncan that if he didn't accept the terms immediately, the of-

---

* There was also the notion of World Series bonus money, which came directly from postseason gate receipts and related income, not from owners' pockets. It was a dividend for winning, but until the day Charlie Finley died he failed to see those checks as anything but generous salary boosts, no different from any raise he himself might provide.

fer would be withdrawn and "you will never hear from us again." It was considerable pressure to put on a teenager, especially one who had been refused the services of an adviser. "I didn't think a lot of it at the time," said Duncan, looking back, "but I eventually realized how shitty it was." He signed, but soon thereafter learned that other teams had authorized as much as $100,000 for his services. "I was bullied into signing the contract because I didn't know any better, and I was scared," he said in March 1973, tying his first negotiation to his current holdout. "Every year it's been the same thing. It's boiled down to *Sign the contract or you won't play*. I've had it. I've had it."

The catcher eventually went to camp anyway, to avoid falling behind on conditioning. He was in the clubhouse following a morning workout when Finley called from Chicago, repeating the same $45,000 offer he'd made all winter long. For Duncan, it was about money and pride, but it was also about short-circuiting the one-sided negotiation process with which Finley perpetually bludgeoned his employees. The catcher didn't want to be talked *at*, he wanted to be talked *to*. Again, he refused.

"What will you do if you don't have a contract when the season starts?" Finley asked.

"I guess I'll make that decision when the time comes," Duncan replied. "I might not play at all."

"I'll call you back in an hour," said Finley. "If you're not ready to sign, I'm going to trade you."

Click.

When Finley called back, he didn't say much. When Duncan again refused his terms, the phrase "You've been traded to Cleveland" conveyed every sentiment necessary.

Duncan's ten-year anniversary with the A's had fallen only days earlier. The news hit just before a Cactus League game against the Cubs and affected nobody more than Reggie Jackson. The catcher was his best friend on the team — had been since they met as farmhands in Modesto in 1966. Jackson shouted at reporters about the inequity of it all, then, announcing he would not play that day, stomped off to take a shower. He ended up being counseled and calmed by Duncan himself.

As Duncan packed his gear he made sure that reporters heard every one of his thoughts on the matter. "I am a human being with an identity of my own," he told them, speaking frankly as always, "and I think this is something [Finley] tries to take away from everyone around him." For the

Owner, this was the kind of statement that made Duncan an easy player to relinquish.

Included in the trade was George Hendrick, who, faced with the likelihood of returning to Triple A to start the season, asked out. (The 23-year-old eventually made four All-Star teams over an 18-year career.) In return, the A's got Ray Fosse, an All-Star catcher in 1970 and '71 whose career was derailed by a broken shoulder suffered in a violent collision with Pete Rose in the 1970 All-Star Game. The injury diminished Fosse's offense — he hit only .241 with ten homers in 1972 — but he provided expert defense and was lauded for his ability to handle a pitching staff. Of benefit to Finley was that Fosse earned $40,500 — about the same as he had offered Duncan.

Among the first to greet Fosse upon his arrival was Dick Green, who had been lured back from the Plains by a generous salary bump from Finley — proof that players who didn't need the Owner for matters of survival actually had a fighting chance in negotiations. At almost the same time another round of Vida-to-the-Rangers news broke, this time with Blue being as good as gone so long as Texas was willing to part with $300,000, plus Broberg, Dick Bosman, and Mike Epstein, of all people. Perhaps the Owner was having seller's remorse, belatedly realizing Epstein's potential as a DH.

It didn't matter. Rangers owner Bob Short offered Broberg *or* Epstein, not both, and talks petered out. The discussion served, however, to illustrate Blue's expendability. Placing renewed value on his comfort in Oakland, the left-hander agreed to a deal worth about $56,000. It wasn't the $63,000 he sought, but it was more than his base salary in 1972. Even more important for Vida was that this more amicable negotiation actually extracted a concession from Finley in the form of a slight pay bump — something the pitcher had been entirely unable to do a year earlier.

As much as anything, a ring ceremony was the baseball moment about which the Owner had always dreamed. The March 1 proceedings were pure Finley, the man in charge giving glory to his ranks. It was he who assembled this crew, and he who took care of them as no owner in the game's storied history had ever taken care of his players.

Champions had never seen such hardware. Major League Baseball allotted a $300-per-ring budget, which Finley spent and much more, believably claiming that his rings cost $1,500 apiece. (When Bando had his appraised for insurance purposes, its value was placed at $3,500.) The Owner didn't stop there, commissioning full-size replica trophies for each of his players, as promised, and presenting their wives with $600 charm bracelets featuring half-carat diamonds. Said Finley with a wink, "Nothing ever has been given to the wives as nice as my charms."

All told, the Owner laid out some $100,000 in a spectacular show of grandiosity. In a burst of enthusiasm that would come back to haunt him the following season, he concluded by promising more and better. If the A's repeated in 1973, he told the players, "I'm going to make that [ring] look like a dime store model."

Would he do it? Of course not. Times were soon to change, and so was Charlie Finley.

A man and his mule. Charles Finley and Charlie O before a game at the Coliseum. The mascot, said the Owner, was the result of "the greatest mule search in history."

In Kansas City, Finley's ideas for improving the fan experience flew rapid-fire, including a petting zoo beyond the outfield fence, interior dugout lighting so that fans might better see the action therein, and an automated ball-retrieval system, which he dubbed Harvey the Rabbit, for the umpires. The contraption so impressed him, in fact, that he brought Harvey (shown here in 1969, with Sal Bando in the background) to Oakland when the team moved.

Catfish Hunter was Finley's first homegrown star, having jumped straight to the big leagues out of high school as a bonus baby in 1965. Hunter helped christen the Oakland Coliseum in 1968, throwing a perfect game in the team's eleventh game at their new home.

Vida Blue pitches to one of the 1,207 batters he faced across 312 innings in 1971. His 24 wins, 1.82 ERA, and 301 strikeouts led to his becoming the youngest player ever to win Cy Young or MVP awards, let alone both in the same season.

Blue's spectacular success in 1971 resulted in relentless attention from fans and media. Here, he sorts through mail on the clubhouse floor of the Oakland Coliseum.

It took months for Vida to recognize Charlie Finley's complete unwillingness to bend when it came to contract negotiations. By the time he finally agreed to sign his contract in May 1972 (shown here, at Boston's Fenway Park), the principals were all too aggravated to demonstrate much joy.

With a man aboard in the ninth inning and Oakland gripping a 2-0 lead in Game 2, Joe Rudi makes the defensive play of the 1972 World Series, flying into the right-field wall to rob Cincinnati's Denis Menke of extra bases.

In a moment that shocked everybody in the stadium — nobody more than his own teammates — Campy Campaneris reacts to getting plunked in the ankle during Game 2 of the 1972 ALCS by hurling his bat at Tigers pitcher Lerrin LaGrow. The act would earn him a suspension for the remainder of the playoff series and the first seven games of the 1973 season, although Campaneris was allowed to play in the World Series.

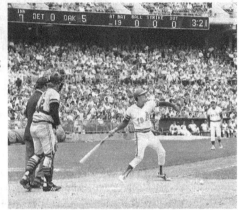

Gene Tenace is best remembered for his MVP-worthy offensive output in the 1972 World Series, but here he puts the tag on Cincinnati shortstop Dave Concepcion, fielding the throw from right fielder Matty Alou for Oakland's final putout in the Reds' Game 5 victory.

Sal Bando crashes the party between Rollie Fingers and Dave Duncan after the A's record the final out of the 1972 World Series.

1972: In the middle of a madcap celebration, manager Dick Williams and coach Vern Hoscheit soak Blue Moon Odom — who went 2-0 with a 0.00 ERA over two starts in the ALCS, then gave up only two runs over 11⅓ World Series innings — with champagne.

Happiest of all in the 1972 Series aftermath was Charlie Finley himself. Here, the Owner soaks in adoration from a crush of team wives gathered outside the A's clubhouse.

Never mind the season-long grudge Vida Blue held against Charlie Finley in 1972; championships mend fences. Here, Vida (left) and Blue Moon Odom join the Owner in an airborne singalong en route from Cincinnati to Oakland following Game 7 of the World Series.

The party continued even after the team set down in Oakland, with Sandy Bando, wife of Sal, leading the team on the bus back to headquarters at the Edgewater Hyatt. In the foreground is Catfish Hunter (wearing a tie). Across from Sandy Bando is Campy Campaneris. Looking on with delight in the rear is her husband.

Billy North stretches for first against the Red Sox in 1973. He broke out in his first year as a full-time starter, finishing second in the American League with 53 stolen bases. North would lead the league in the category in two of the next three seasons.

When Reggie Jackson — never one for partial effort when it came to swinging a bat — connected with a baseball, it went a long way. When he missed, however, it looked like this.

In 1970, Reggie Jackson broke out of a protracted slump with his first-ever grand slam, then — fed up with season-long interference from Charlie Finley — made an obscene gesture (the moment shown here) toward the Owner's box. His standing with Finley would deteriorate quickly from there.

Catfish Hunter (far left) at the Coliseum playing Flip, a cross between pepper and dodgeball, which resulted in a fracture to his left thumb in 1973. (For more details, see the footnote on page 131.) It's difficult to tell from a black-and-white reproduction, but the A's are wearing their vibrant, all-yellow uniforms.

In a representative moment from 1973, Campy Campaneris lays down a bunt against the Orioles in a nearly empty Oakland Coliseum. In another representative moment, he reached on a single, stole second, and then scored on an error.

Sal Bando emphatically agrees with the call of umpire Don Denkinger as Reggie Jackson beats catcher Steve Yeager to the plate in Game 4 of the 1974 World Series. Both men scored on Jim Holt's one-out single to give the A's a 4-2 lead over Los Angeles in a game they'd eventually win 5-2.

Reggie Jackson spins Billy North as the A's celebrate following the World Series–clinching Game 5 at the Coliseum, pushing aside what had been season-long acrimony between them.

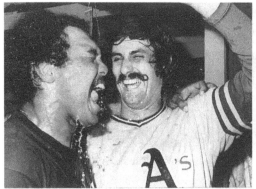

In what would be a final hurrah, Reggie Jackson and Rollie Fingers celebrate Oakland's playoff-clinching victory over the White Sox on September 24, 1975. It would be one of the final games of Jackson's career in green-and-gold, and the beginning of a freefall that would see the A's in last place only two seasons later.

For a brief moment, Joe Rudi (left) and Rollie Fingers were full-fledged members of the Boston Red Sox, going so far as to put on uniforms in the visitors' clubhouse at the Oakland Coliseum. Commissioner Bowie Kuhn quickly overturned Charlie Finley's attempt to sell the duo. After significant drama, they returned to the A's.

The Owner.

Defending Your Flag

> People expect more of us now, and other teams are definitely using us as something to shoot at. Like it means something now to beat Oakland. I don't think we were really prepared for that at the beginning of the season. We were just out playing our game. Well, it doesn't work that way anymore. We've found that out.
>
> —Reggie Jackson, May 1973

The A's were on a bus. The bus was barreling toward a hotel in Chicago, the first stop on the team's initial road trip of 1973. Oakland was already 0-3 after a dispiriting series against the Twins at the Coliseum, during which they committed five errors and failed to make a litany of plays that Dick Williams felt should have been made.* The manager was not happy.

As the bus motored away from O'Hare Field, new acquisition Billy North began feuding with Blue Moon Odom in the rear seats, the type of verbal needling with which the team was so familiar. As their digs grew increasingly antagonistic the rest of the A's began hooting at the spectacle, egging them on. Williams considered the possibility that his team would have its first fight of the season before its first victory, and turned around in his seat. "Are you guys 3-0 or 0-3?" he barked.

Instantly, the row died down. Odom was the only one bold enough to answer. "We're 0-3," he said.

"Well, you'd better start busting your rears," Williams shouted. "You

---

* Opening day at the Coliseum drew only 38,207, well short of a sellout for the defending champions, but still the second-largest opening day crowd in Oakland's six-year history. In the season's second game, attendance was 7,246, and Finley's million-dollar scoreboard, which had barely functioned in the opener, crapped out altogether.

better pray for a rainout tomorrow . . . and for a room check tonight." The message — *freedom is earned* — took time to sink in. The A's didn't win a series until beating Cleveland on April 26, by which point they were 7-10 and in fifth place in the six-team American League West. "If it keeps up," reasoned Williams, running his fingers across his mustache, "this is going to turn awfully white."

Everyone was off. Numerous regulars, including Bando, Rudi, Campaneris, and North, were hitting in the low .200s. Hunter didn't win a game until his sixth start, while Blue turned in three middling outings, then missed two weeks with a knee injury. Even Reggie closed April with a 12-game homerless stretch during which he batted .178. One of the few regulars doing anything, newly acquired center fielder Billy Conigliaro, was hitting .300 . . . until he injured his knee sliding into second base, had surgery, and missed 70 of the next 73 games.

Worst of all was Odom, who didn't make it out of the first inning in two of his first three starts, lost his first five decisions, and was 1-8 with a 6.75 ERA when the calendar turned to June, at which point he was summarily yanked from the rotation. Nobody could explain it. "I just feel like I want to die," lamented the bewildered pitcher.

Of particular concern for Oakland was the gaping hole at designated hitter, where over the season's first month six players combined for a paltry six RBIs even as the competition blossomed at the position. The A's watched Twins DH Tony Oliva, an All-Star in eight of the previous nine seasons, homer off Hunter in his first at-bat of the year. Frank Robinson went deep twice in his first three games at DH for the Angels. By the end of the month Tommy Davis was batting .342 for Baltimore and Carlos May .328 for the White Sox. Most painful of all, Orlando Cepeda, the man Finley only recently spurned, crushed five homers in his first ten games with Boston and ended April batting .333. "We're being out-designated so far," sighed Williams.

Finley's solution was another reclamation project. Deron Johnson first joined the Athletics as a 22-year-old back in 1961 but was traded a season later. Since then he'd blossomed into one of the league's better power hitters, topping 20 homers five times and 30 homers twice. Now, however, he was 34 and coming off an injury-marred 1972 with Philadelphia. His future, if he had one, was in the American League; Finley got him in early May for nearly nothing.

Johnson took immediately to DH-ing, singling in two runs in his first Oakland at-bat as part of a 3-for-5, four-RBI performance. After a week he was batting .406 with three homers and nine RBIs, almost single-handedly saving the A's from a freefall in the standings. As it was, Oakland entered May at 24-24 and in fifth place, six games back of the division-leading White Sox. The more the players examined it, the more it became clear that the season's opening months had been a coast job by every measure, the team sliding through its schedule in whichever way gravity dictated. Their recent championship seemed to weigh on them.

The A's needed something to shake them up beyond their manager yelling at them, their owner lording over them, and their fans ignoring them. So they turned to totems. After beating Detroit while wearing all-green uniforms, they donned them again a day later — and after another win, the day after that. Following a loss, they changed into an all-yellow combo and won another three straight. Joe Rudi and Dick Green shaved their mustaches. Bando switched to a heavier bat. Blue changed his uniform number from 35 to 14, which he had worn as a high schooler in Mansfield. If it seemed odd for defending champions to hunt so desperately for success . . . well, it was. The season was nearly half over, and seven American League clubs had better records. What Oakland really needed was something organic, a jolt of energy to bring the whole, hulking corpse back to life. They got it courtesy of Reggie Jackson — though hardly in optimal fashion.

On June 6 against Milwaukee, Jackson misplayed two fly balls into doubles, and another into a triple. With a man on third, he hung back passively on defense as a catchable pop-up dropped in front of him, allowing the runner to score. Never mind that Reggie also homered and doubled, or that the A's won, 11–1; when Jackson had the temerity during his postgame comments to lodge a complaint about playing time, Williams sizzled. "When your name's on the lineup card," the manager told him through gritted teeth, "go out and play."

The tension was undeniable — and it was the stuff that powered the A's, who ran off four straight series victories, climbing from fifth place to first in the process. As if to ensure against a relapse, Reggie doubled down at the end of the month.

On June 30 he got caught 20 feet off first base in such a state of puzzlement that Royals catcher Fran Healy was able to run the ball from behind the plate and tag Jackson himself. The Coliseum fans — all 5,565 of them — booed. Williams was so upset that he barred the press from the clubhouse after the game and vigorously lit into the player. Ever sensitive, Reggie's performance tumbled, and he batted only .115 over the next week. On the Fourth of July he dropped a fly ball for an error. Later in the game, having lost track of the count, he had to be reminded by plate umpire Ron Luciano that four balls meant he could take first base. The A's lost to the Angels, 3–1, and afterward, as fireworks crackled above the Coliseum, Jackson burst. He was talking to reporters in typically confident tones when third-base coach Irv Noren passed by and muttered, "Reggie, if you played defense like you play offense we would have won the game." A glower crossed Jackson's face. When newsmen asked what was wrong, he all but shouted, "I can't play here and be happy."

Come again?

"Make a mistake, and the manager and coaches are on you," he proclaimed. "Don't drive in a run and coaches stand in the dugout and complain, kick the water cooler, go into the bathroom and holler. It's nothing they say to you directly. They must think they were Babe Ruth or something when they played. They weren't that good. It's not just me. They're on Fosse and Green and other players. It's not good for morale."[*] Despite having specifically called out one of Williams's traits — responding to mistakes in the field by closing himself in the dugout bathroom and ranting at top volume — Reggie later clarified that the subject of his diatribe was Noren.

The team left for Baltimore the next day. Williams was already seated in the front of the airplane when Reggie boarded and, without looking up from his newspaper, muttered, "Superstar, my ass," as the player walked past. It was the only button that needed pushing. Jackson wheeled. "Hey, man," he snapped. "Who the fuck are you to be talking to me like that? I followed the damn game my whole life, and I remember when you played, and you didn't do shit. So don't lay any of your sarcastic superstar shit on me. You just leave me alone from now on. You write my name down on the lineup card and leave my ass alone."

Reggie stomped down the aisle before the manager could respond, then continued his invective for reporters in the back of the plane. "We

---

[*] Inadvertently delighted by all of this was Sal Bando, whose seventh-inning error led to every one of the Angels' runs. He woke up the next morning expecting to see headlines ripping his performance, but the bulk of the news was about Jackson's outburst. "I couldn't believe I got off the hook like that," he said later. "When I left the clubhouse I didn't even know Reggie had done that."

just don't get along and never will," he explained. "I'm not one of their favorites because I'm too cocky. . . . I've been playing with it all year. I'm not talking crazy. I'm telling it like it is. I'm not the only one. They do it to others." The "others" Jackson mentioned during his earlier tirade, Green and Fosse, steered as far from the drama as possible, Green announcing that he was too wrapped up in his bridge game to give it any thought, while Fosse pleaded ignorance, claiming, "I just work here."

During what Williams described as a "tension-filled flight," the manager huddled with Noren and his other coaches, making sure he had the facts straight. Then he publicly gave Noren his full backing.* Hours later Finley did the same, renewing the coaches' contracts for the following season, complete with raises, and extending Williams's contract by a year, through 1975. It was a quick-strike response on the Owner's part, impetuous and effective. At the price of a few bucks' worth of contract extensions, Finley was able to put Reggie in his place as publicly as possible while looking like a good guy in the process.

Still, the manager was a pragmatist and knew that the A's needed Jackson at his best to repeat. The following day Williams called him into his office in the visitors' clubhouse at Memorial Stadium, and the two reconciled. Williams understood how Reggie worked: when the player felt valued, the player performed. It went off as planned: over the next three weeks Reggie hit eight homers, drove in 21 runs, walked 19 times, and stole four bases. In many ways Jackson *was* the A's, not only providing their loudest bat and strongest opinions but serving as a personal marker for their maturity as a team. Reggie's rookie season, 1968, was the A's first year in Oakland, and as he found his footing in the American League, so did they.

Reginald Martinez Jackson was raised in a family of limited means in the tony Philadelphia suburb of Wyncotte, Pennsylvania. His father, Martinez, was the son of a black father and Spanish mother and looked more Italian than anything, said his son. When Reggie was six, his mother left town with the boy's three siblings, but Reggie stayed behind, living with his father in an apartment above Martinez's tailor shop on Greenwood

---

* Williams and Noren grew up together in Pasadena and signed with the Brooklyn Dodgers within a year of each other. When Williams was assigned to Fort Worth of the Texas League in 1948, he moved into Noren's house. Upon being fired by the Red Sox in 1969, Williams promised his pal a spot on his next coaching staff. When he landed the gig in Oakland, Noren was among his first calls.

Avenue. Martinez was so no-nonsense that in 1973, when he caught a burglar prying open the skylight to his shop, he shot him twice, then twice again after the guy fell to the floor. (The wounds were not fatal.) Martinez earned additional income by running numbers (for which he served prison time in the 1940s) and bootlegging corn liquor (for which he was arrested during Reggie's senior year of high school). He was serving a six-month sentence for the latter when his son departed for a football scholarship with Frank Kush at Arizona State University.

It was with the ASU baseball team, however, that Jackson earned renown, culminating in his selection by the A's with the second overall pick in the 1966 amateur draft.* Jackson has long maintained that the Mets bypassed him with the top selection in favor of a catcher named Steve Chilcott because they disapproved of him dating a white woman (even though Jenny Campos was actually Hispanic). Reggie would marry her in 1968 and divorce her four years later.

Jackson flourished in his second full season, 1969, compiling an astounding 40 home runs by the end of July — a pace well ahead of Babe Ruth's 60 and Roger Maris's 61. So frequent were his longballs that Reggie's word for them, "taters," entered the popular lexicon.†

It wasn't just the quantity of his homers that impressed but the quality. In June, Jackson hit a ball off the top of the scoreboard at Kansas City's Municipal Stadium. He hit one over the distant right-center-field fence in Fenway Park so hard on a line that Dick Green swore he saw the second baseman jump for it. In Minneapolis, he hit a titanic 450-foot shot that touched 55 feet up the Metropolitan Stadium scoreboard. He became the first player to reach the second deck of his home ballpark in Oakland. Jackson's teammates took to calling him "Buck" in deference to his admiration for the similarly nicknamed Willie Mays, and it seemed to fit better every day.

The more homers Reggie hit in 1969, however, the more reporters descended. The 23-year-old did hundreds of interviews over the course of several weeks, plus a shirtless beefcake photo session for *Sports Illustrated*.

---

* Jackson demanded a $100,000 signing bonus from Finley, but the Owner refused to budge past $95,000, a difference that was financially inconsequential but symbolically profound: *never forget the distinction between who grants wishes around here and who gets wishes granted.*

† Back at Single-A Modesto, Jackson and Duncan had begun referring to homers as "long potatoes," which was subsequently shortened to "taters" by Milwaukee slugger George Scott.

He began to press, going homerless for 11 games in early August. The pressure led to a rash so severe that it required hospitalization, costing him ten games in early September. Jackson hit only six home runs over the season's final two months, finishing with 47, while his batting average fell nearly 25 points. All but a lock to win the AL MVP two months earlier, Reggie placed a distant fifth, failing to secure even a single first-place vote. Never had a dominant season felt so disappointing.

Still, it was revelatory. Reggie became the bright young star sought not just by Finley but by baseball at large, a player people would pay money to see. This did not go unnoticed in Jackson's camp. If he was going to be a national cover boy, he wanted a taste of the action. In a precursor to what Vida Blue would go through two seasons later, Jackson requested a $75,000 salary for the 1970 season, then boycotted spring training until he got it.

The problem, as Vida would come to learn, was that Reggie was still only 24 years old and had been a full-time big leaguer for all of two seasons. Finley was willing to pay for veteran status, but Jackson did not have that. The Owner offered $45,000, then watched Reggie steadily bend, reducing his demand several thousand dollars at a time until he finally arrived at the face-saving contrivance of $47,000 — or $1,000 per home run he hit in 1969. It was the perfect solution, allowing Finley to accommodate him with a middling two grand extra.

This was the lesson Reggie learned: $2,000 might as well have been $10 million in the eyes of the guy holding the checkbook. Finley was the one who decided what was fair, and damned if he could be budged from that spot. Finally, with ten days left in the Cactus League schedule, Reggie accepted the Owner's terms.* Like Blue two years later, he began the 1970 season woefully out of baseball shape, going 3-for-his-first-38 while striking out 14 times. He could not breathe. Coliseum crowds, rapturous a season earlier, turned on him.

By late May that season Reggie still hadn't cracked .200 and began to sit — first against lefties, then against righties too. On June 3, then-man-

---

* Jackson's one demand to which Finley agreed (because it could not be counted as part of his contract during future negotiations) was that the Owner pay his rent in Oakland during the season. Finley figured the amount would come to about $2,000. Jackson then moved into a penthouse apartment just across Lake Merritt from Finley's own residence at a rate of $750 a month, an exorbitant cost that infuriated the Owner.

ager John McNamara floated the idea of Jackson reporting to Triple-A Iowa for a couple of weeks to straighten himself out. (Bowie Kuhn, in his first year as baseball commissioner, reprimanded Finley for using the minor leagues as a threat rather than as a development tool.) Reggie refused. "That big asshole," he said of the Owner. "If he would've signed me, I would've been ready." It became a rallying cry, Jackson pinning his troubles on Finley's lack of negotiating foresight.

Reggie found himself benched shortly before the All-Star Game, and again thereafter. When he did play, he took bad breaks on fly balls and threw to the wrong bases. The A's played 25 games between August 9 and September 5, 1970. Reggie started five of them and totaled eight at-bats in the others. In the 19th game he did something unusual and magnificent. At the Coliseum, with the bases loaded and two outs in the eighth inning against the Royals, Reggie powered his first grand slam as a big leaguer. Nearly 10,000 fans leaped to their feet in celebration. In the owner's box, Finley sat stock still.

Upon crossing home plate, Jackson removed his batting helmet, glowered toward Finley, shook his fist, and shouted something that nobody could hear above the din. Slowly, the Owner stood. Then he clapped. Then he leaned over the railing like a kid about to spit off a bridge, and thrust his hands over his head. In the game's immediate aftermath, Finley seemed to delight in Jackson's attention. "It inflated my ego," he reasoned. "He could have been saying a number of things. He could've been saying, 'There, I showed you I still can do it. I've had it in me all the time.'"

When a reporter in the postgame clubhouse asked Reggie what he'd uttered, his only reply was, "You can't print it."

The home run was a cathartic break for Reggie and the A's. The following day Jackson went 2-for-3 and homered again. The day after that, Labor Day, he went 4-for-7 in a doubleheader in Chicago, which the A's swept for their seventh and eighth wins in a row. Reggie was finally approaching the place he wanted to be, just as Oakland — the nascent 1970 version of what would become a championship squad — was entering the point of the season where they needed him most. Heading to Minneapolis for a vital three-game series, the team packed its bags with confidence.

When they reached Minnesota, Finley, who had already arrived, summoned Jackson to McNamara's hotel suite. Reggie anticipated a let-by-gones-be-bygones meeting that might even lead to some genuine goodwill. He had dinner plans at 9:00 P.M., but that was more than an hour away. He didn't even bother to inform his companions.

That was a mistake. Reggie was greeted at the door by the manager, and entered to find Finley, the coaching staff, and Sal Bando, beckoned in his role as team captain. Nobody was smiling. The Owner showed Reggie a days-old newspaper clipping that contained his "You can't print it" comment.

"What you think of this?" Finley asked him.

"I'm proud of it," said Jackson.

"It's a disgrace to baseball," Finley said. "Why'd you do it?"

Reggie had held back when delivering the quote, but he did not hold back now. "Because I hate the way you treat me," he yelled. "The way you treat people."

Reggie knew he was right, and he knew that everyone in the room save for the Owner knew it too. Instead of jumping up to back him, however, his would-be compatriots took an immediate and abiding interest in their shoetops. Finley was on the hunt, and speaking up on Reggie's behalf was a dangerous proposition.

Finley presented Jackson with a sheet of paper bearing two typewritten sentences: "Last Saturday, I made gestures and comments I wish I never made. I would like to apologize to the fans, my teammates, John McNamara, and Mr. Finley." The Owner demanded Reggie's signature at the bottom. Reggie refused. Finley said that if he didn't sign, he would be fined $5,000 and American League president Joe Cronin would suspend him for the rest of the season. It was nonsense, of course, but Jackson didn't know that at the time.

Later, Reggie would liken the process to being interrogated at police headquarters, then whipped. "I'd never been so alone, so alienated from people who I thought were my friends," he said. The Owner harangued him mercilessly for hour upon hour, until Jackson could see no other options. Finally, he promised to sign the page and stumbled from the room, eyes red. It was almost 2:00 A.M.

Thoroughly demoralized, the outfielder went 0-for-9 with five strikeouts in the make-or-break series against the Twins. The A's were swept, and the 1970 playoff race was essentially over. Even more shocking was that to Finley what happened on the field seemed entirely ancillary. The Owner had two primary goals in his debasement of Jackson, neither of which had to do with winning ball games: controlling the player and setting an example for the rest of the team. He succeeded on both counts. Reggie lost all interest in outside attention, at least for a while. "I don't want any more big years," he said sadly. "All I want is a lot of years. All I want is to maybe hit .300, maybe thirty homers, maybe drive in ninety runs every year, be a part of the team, contribute to the team every year, get a little raise every year. I don't want to be a big star anymore."

So hurt was the player that over the winter he visited Finley's Chicago office with the goal of forcing a trade. Reggie spent 30 minutes railing about the injustices he suffered and how things could have been different with even an iota of understanding from the Owner. He was angry, bursting with things to say. Finley, having already won the battle, was not. After a time he cut the rambling player off and offered the sort of platitudes for which Jackson had thirsted several months earlier, before he'd been so thoroughly broken. "You've talked for a half-hour," Finley said. "I listened to everything you had to say. Now I'm going to talk for 30 seconds. Number one, I love you. Number two, I'm not going to trade you. Number three, let's go to lunch." Which they did. Jackson — knowing now that money lost was no impediment to the Owner — settled quickly for $45,000 for the 1971 season, almost the same as he made in 1970. Which may have been Finley's endgame all along.

"It was just another indication of the type of guy Finley was," said Bando, looking back. "An owner shouldn't have been doing the things he did to his best player like that. You build him up, you don't tear him down. That was in the back of our minds: if he can do it to Reggie, he can do it to any of us. And he eventually did."

Now Finley had again put Jackson in his place, this time by siding with Dick Williams and the coaching staff. How he did it, with new contracts and lavish bonuses, may have come as a surprise, but there was no mistaking whose boot heel Reggie — or any of the A's — was playing under.

In July, Dick Williams underwent an emergency appendectomy at Merritt Hospital in Oakland. Fortuitously, it happened just before the All-Star break. Less fortuitous was that, as manager of the defending champions, Williams was slated to helm the American League squad in Kansas City. Five days after the operation, he piled himself onto an airplane to fulfill his obligation.

Catfish Hunter started for the American League and in the second inning instinctively tried to field Billy Williams's one-hop smash up the middle with his bare hand. Williams ended up with a single, and Hunter with a broken thumb. For those in Oakland the rest of the game — the American League's tenth loss in 11 years — was an afterthought.

What wasn't known at the time was that Hunter had already fractured his other thumb, the one on his glove hand, back in May while horsing around with teammates, and had been playing through pain ever since.* At least the time off would leave him strong for August and September, he theorized as his digit was being fitted for a splint. The right-hander missed four weeks and a day, and the A's staggered through a succession of fill-ins, watching their two-and-a-half-game pre–All-Star lead disappear. On July 30, they fell into a virtual tie with Kansas City when Rangers right-hander Jim Bibby no-hit them at the Coliseum. ("The A's 104-game hitting streak came to an end last night," quipped former traveling secretary Tom Corwin, who had resigned days earlier after Finley saddled him with additional full-time roles as the team's PR man and statistician.)

The struggles reached beyond the pitchers. Jackson and Bando stopped hitting. North and Campy stopped running. Fosse didn't homer until mid-September. Rudi contracted Stevens-Johnson syndrome, which left his throat so swollen that he could barely breathe, and had to spend a week in the hospital. Billy Conigliaro returned from surgery for the first eight games of Rudi's absence and batted .179 without an extra-base hit.

This was where the Owner's essential nature paid the best kinds of dividends. Why monkey around with ineffective players, he figured, when others were available? On July 31, Finley sent $25,000 to Houston for his third Alou brother in as many seasons, Jesus, the baby of the bunch, who was immediately inserted into an outfield platoon with Vic Davalillo, purchased from Pittsburgh that same day.

Because Oakland's second basemen were also struggling, Finley ac-

---

* The injuries were sustained during pregame warm-ups in a game called Flip, a cross between pepper and dodgeball that was played mostly by pitchers in the time following batting practice. A ball is hit toward a line of players, one of whom fields it and flips it with his glove at another player in the line. That player in turn slaps it with an open glove, sometimes worn a bit off the hand to increase torque, at someone else. The point is to make somebody drop the ball. Guys would play balls off their bodies, legs, whatever kept the thing from hitting the turf. The game inspired rabid betting (and a few angry confrontations) among the A's. It was not unusual for several pitchers to gang up on one unfortunate member of their ranks, whacking ball after ball at him as hard as they could — hard enough, even, to break the occasional thumb.

quired one of Williams's favorite players from his Boston days, Mike Andrews, who had just been released by the White Sox. Andrews, 30, was a scrapper, Williams's type of guy, even though he had some trouble in the field. The second baseman had ranked among the American League leaders in errors at his position for six straight seasons, and that was before a string of shoulder injuries curtailed his ability to throw the ball effectively. Williams urged Finley to pick him up strictly for pinch-hitting duty.

The sentiment was soon put to the test. With Dick Green and Ted Kubiak mired in slumps, Andrews started three games at second base in a four-day span. He bounced a would-be double-play relay against Detroit and later missed first base entirely with a throw, allowing another run to score. Williams cared less about the mistakes than the lifelessness on the lobs. After that, Andrews was used almost exclusively as a pinch hitter.

On August 7, Charlie Finley had a heart attack. Nobody knew what to make of it. He was in Chicago and the A's were in Detroit and most of the reporters covering the team were back in Oakland. It was first reported as merely chest pains, then as a mild coronary occlusion. The details told a different story.

Finley spent nearly two weeks at Chicago's Northwestern Memorial Hospital, followed by a month of convalescence at his farm in La Porte. (A year earlier, chest discomfort had sent him to Oakland's Merritt Hospital for three days.) Doctors ordered the Owner away from business dealings, which meant no telephone time, but this was Charlie Finley, serial salesman. He snuck out to a hospital pay phone to maintain regular contact with Dick Williams, albeit with far less frequency than usual. Williams enjoyed this stretch of the schedule more than any other, partly because of his newfound freedom, partly because Finley's absence coincided with a late-season surge.

Blue tossed six complete games in a nine-start span. Hunter came back on August 19, and Oakland won his first three starts. Even Blue Moon Odom, resurrected from the bullpen through sheer necessity, began to pitch well. On offense, Rudi returned following a 23-game absence and retook his spot in left field. Jackson blasted seven homers in 12 games, leaping into the league lead. It was the kind of championship play — finally — that was expected from the outset. Before anybody knew what was happening, the A's won 13 of 14 and turned a two-game deficit into an eight-game lead.

Still, Finley was antsy. On September 18, he sold Jose Morales — a 28-year-old catcher who had appeared in only six games with Oakland after a decade in the minors — to Montreal in order to create space on the 25-man postseason roster for pinch runner Allan Lewis. The move was little more than semantic roster mumbling by the Owner, a means of allowing his team to carry a pinch runner instead of a pinch hitter. It would have attracted little notice had Billy North not nearly ripped his ankle in half.

North was by that time ensconced atop the A's lineup, his base-path acumen having long since earned him a starting role and relegated Bert Campaneris to the second slot in the order. On defense, North ran down fly balls that A's center fielders of years past wouldn't have come close to touching. For all the stability he provided in center field and atop the lineup, the Seattle native's most notable quality was his fiery attitude. Frequently, this was an attribute. Sometimes it was not.

North's teammates had been introduced to that aspect of his personality some months earlier. After becoming the starting center fielder in late April, North sizzled through the end of May with a .324 average and ten stolen bases. In a May 18 game against the Royals at the Coliseum, however, he let slip his bat on a swing against reliever Doug Bird, the lumber sailing harmlessly between the mound and third base. While going to retrieve it, however, North took an unexpected right turn and pounced upon the unsuspecting pitcher, peppering him with as many punches as he could land before being tackled away by players from both teams. The only guy in the building who wasn't confused as hell was the guy swinging his fists.

The feud dated back to 1970, when North played for the Quincy (Illinois) Cubs of the Single-A Midwest League. Bird, pitching for Waterloo (Iowa), had given up homers to the two players preceding North in the lineup, and responded (in North's opinion) by brushing the hitter back. "Hey, man, I didn't hit those homers," he snapped at the catcher before settling back into the box. The next pitch, a fastball, hit him in the head with such velocity that North required hospitalization.

He'd been keenly waiting for revenge ever since, paying close attention to the transaction wire for the moment Bird was called up from the minors. The fight occurred during the pitcher's fourth major league appearance. "I don't think I could live with myself and not challenge that dude," North said afterward.

Such certainty did not grip his teammates. "We were all looking at each other, going, 'What the hell is happening?'" said Rudi. Added Fosse, "We're trying to win a championship, and when we found out this guy's doing something to redress a problem from the minor leagues, we couldn't believe it." Joe Cronin suspended North three games and fined him $100.

Four months later, in the midst of the September stretch run, North stole his league-leading 52nd and 53rd bases during the first game of a doubleheader against Minnesota. In the nightcap, however, he landed awkwardly on first base while legging out an infield grounder and violently turned his ankle. It was in many ways worse than a break, and cost North the final nine games of the regular season.[*]

Jose Morales had been shipped to the Expos two days earlier. Even as North returned to the Bay Area for treatment, Finley desperately tried to reacquire the catcher, who, because he had been with Oakland on August 31, was eligible for the postseason roster. Morales, however, did not clear National League waivers, spurring the Owner to petition for the activation of Rico Carty, whom he'd purchased from the Cubs on September 11 — too late for playoff eligibility. When that was refused, he requested second baseman Manny Trillo, who, while not on the big league roster at the September 1 postseason deadline, had at least been with the organization at Triple-A Tucson. With the approval of the Baltimore Orioles — who secured the American League East and would face Oakland in the playoffs — Trillo was allowed.

The A's clinched with a week left and ended the season six games ahead of Kansas City. The final tally had Jackson with 32 homers and 117 RBIs, both totals tops in the American League, which bore their own story of internal turmoil among the A's. Jackson had been chasing Pittsburgh's Willie Stargell for the major league RBI lead when he was sidelined by a strained hamstring in early September, and was desperate to get back.

The Owner didn't like it. Williams suggested letting Reggie work his way into form at DH, but Finley insisted that if Jackson was not healthy enough to play the field, he was not healthy enough to hit. The mandate was ostensibly made to protect the player, but it wasn't difficult to wonder whether the Owner also wanted to diminish in some small way the

---

[*] As if North's injury didn't hurt enough, Boston's Tommy Harper stole 17 bases over the season's final 21 games — including seven after North went down on September 20 — to lead the league with 54, one more than North.

incandescence from the only man on the roster whose star power rivaled his own.

To prevent a blowup on the cusp of the playoffs—and to make sure that Jackson understood precisely where things stood—Williams invited the player to dinner at his Fremont apartment. This type of meeting was rare, and it showed Reggie just how serious his manager was. After nearly three full seasons of meddling, all-hours phone calls, and general despotism from the Owner, Williams had just about reached his limit. Jackson already had dinner plans with Rudi, and brought him along. The players sat in disbelief as Williams opened up. "Reggie, I can't play you," he said disconsolately. "If I play you, you'll have a new manager by next week." He raised his hand to his forehead, as if saluting, and added, "I'm fed up, up to here." Jackson wondered whether Williams might quit there on the spot. By the time Finley finally allowed Williams to reinsert Reggie into the lineup, the division was all but decided.

The rest of the team stepped up in Jackson's absence. Bando drove in 34 runs over the season's final 31 games for a total of 98 and finished fourth in the league with 29 homers. Tenace's 24 homers tied for ninth. Despite missing a month of action, Catfish Hunter (21-5) topped 20 wins for the third straight season and was joined by Holtzman (21-13) and Blue (20-9) for the franchise's first 20-win triumvirate since Lefty Grove, George Earnshaw, and Rube Walberg in 1931.* When the A's clinched the American League West with a victory over Chicago at White Sox Park, their celebration bore little resemblance to the bacchanalia that had taken place a season earlier. Most of the players sat quietly on their stools in the clubhouse, "stolidly drinking like customers in a blue-collar bar," wrote Ron Bergman in the *Oakland Tribune*. The lone exception was Fosse, who in a career spent with Cleveland had never experienced so much as a winning record. Alone in his excitement, the catcher tilted back his head and sprayed champagne into the air, consuming it like a fountain.

Hovering around the periphery was Finley, who had mostly laid low since his heart attack in August. He was at the ballpark when the A's

---

* "[Vida] has really dominated the game like he did in '71," enthused Bando. In some ways he was even better, thanks in part to pitching coach Wes Stock, who had been after the lefty all year to make better use of his breaking ball. Blue ramped it up during the stretch run in terms of speed, accuracy, and frequency, refining it to the point where catcher Ray Fosse developed separate signs for Vida's hard curve and the regular one. All of it served to keep hitters off balance for the fastball, which on occasion still showed its old heat.

clinched, primarily to test his ability to withstand the rigors of spectatorship, and on doctor's orders didn't even go into the clubhouse. The Owner was thin, pale, and frequently wheelchair-bound. Trying to walk even short distances proved challenging; in the coming days he would lose his balance several times, once falling down a short staircase and bloodying his nose. His in-game regimen included between-innings pulse checks by his personal cardiologist.

Attendance at the final home game of the regular season was announced as 7,422. Those on hand knew immediately that the number was cooked; there were no more than a couple thousand fans scattered around the Coliseum. The reason for the trickery was obvious: the tally — the most recent in a long line of phantom attendance — finally pushed the season total above Finley's long-coveted 1 million mark. (The team finished at 1,000,761.) For all the hopes that a winning product would inspire Oakland's fan base to actually attend some games, it was now clear that such was not the case. Apart from giveaway days, the A's rarely drew even five figures and frequently attracted fewer than 4,000 fans. Sal Bando took to calling the ballpark the "Oakland Mausoleum" — a moniker that was quickly adopted by his teammates — and asked how Finley could expect to draw a crowd with "no staff, no marketing, and [when] you're constantly ripping your own team."

Also keeping fans away was Finley's nearly complete inattention to the Coliseum's ancillary services. His publicity was shoddy (the Owner served as his own marketing director, which took a distant backseat to his duties as general manager), so advance sales suffered. Walk-up patrons were forced to suffer minimally staffed ticket booths, occasionally waiting in lines so long that they didn't gain admittance until the middle innings. Once inside the ballpark, lines at the few concessions that were open were equally outrageous. None of this encouraged repeat business. "The ballpark was horrible, in a bad part of town," said Fingers, listing off additional reasons for the Coliseum's perpetually desolate grandstand. "It was cold at night, and the fans sat so far back from the field."

Upon moving to Oakland in 1968, Finley had predicted 1.5 million fans, but attendance barely topped 800,000. He attributed the tiny numbers to having no superstar on the roster to attract attention. The following season Reggie Jackson burst into national prominence, and attendance dropped below 780,000. "When we have a winner, we will win fans as well as games," Finley explained. In 1971 the A's won 101 games and the American League West, and boasted baseball's biggest draw in Vida Blue. They still finished seventh out of 12 American League teams in attendance, 85,000 short of a million. In 1972 they won the World Series and *still* could not crack seven figures.

"With the mustaches, the characters, the long hair, and all the other stuff, if you put us in Chicago, New York, Boston, anywhere, they would have had us walking on water," reflected Joe Rudi. "In Oakland, they barely knew we existed."

Then there was Finley himself. The Owner's refusal to relocate his personal life to Oakland, or even to visit very often, did little to ingratiate him to the fans, no matter how many games his team won. Oakland loved its Raiders, embracing the NFL's bad boys as their own because that team's owner, Al Davis, embedded his franchise — and himself — deep within the community. Finley, meanwhile, couldn't even shake the perpetual rumors about wanting to move the A's someplace else.

The saving grace for overall attendance — the difference between ridiculously low numbers and historically low numbers — were half-price Family Nights, held on Mondays, which Finley expanded from seven dates in 1972 to 12 in '73. It was an awkward admission, but one that seemed to pay dividends: people in Oakland simply did not attend baseball games without a bargain to be had. All told, half-price Mondays represented only one-seventh of the home schedule but drew more than one-third of the Coliseum's overall attendance.

By enacting such a policy, of course, Finley was cannibalizing his own product, giving sporadic attendees an incentive to stay home Tuesday through Sunday in favor of getting the same experience at a reduced rate on Monday nights. "That's it, *that's* a promotion?" asked Jon Miller, who watched his share of half-price drama as one of the team's broadcasters in 1974. "If you're going to bring your kids to any game that week, you're going on half-price night. It was just stupid."

Still, Monday attendance finally provided Finley with his long-desired attendance total. When the message "Thanks a Million" flashed on the scoreboard during the season's final game, players in the dugout, all of whom knew better, erupted in laughter.

9

Beating the Birds

If everything the press says about us playing best when we're mad is true, we got this thing wrapped up. I've already ordered me a new Rolls-Royce.

— Reggie Jackson, October 1973

One could forgive Vida Blue for feeling some whiplash, what with the breakneck speed of his turning fortunes. Back in 1971, Blue was baseball's end-all, a horsehide-hurling Hercules who led his team into postseason battle with a playoff-opening assignment against the self-same Orioles that Oakland was again preparing to face. The first time around he stunningly was blown out of the box with a four-run seventh, and the A's went on to lose game and series alike. Then Blue held out, suffered through a miserable 1972, and opened '73 by winning three games over the season's first two months while his ERA hovered around 5.00. It appeared as if his pan had flashed, possibly for good.

By October, though, Blue was beautiful again, going 13-4 over his final 18 starts of the season, including nine complete games, with an ERA of 2.77. It allowed him to come full circle and once again draw the opening playoff assignment against Baltimore, in Memorial Stadium.

Any hope Vida had of proving the permanency of his comeback, however, came crashing apart with the very first pitch he threw. The lefty was a fastball pitcher — he started nearly every hitter off with a heater — but he'd become so recently enamored of his curveball that he opened the game with one. Merv Rettenmund cracked it between Campaneris and Bando for a single. Before anybody knew what was happening, Vida wild-pitched Rettenmund to second, walked Paul Blair on four pitches, and allowed a one-out RBI double to Tommy Davis. Don Baylor walked, and one out later Earl Williams connected for a two-run single. The Orioles led, 3–0, and Dick Williams found himself trudging to the mound in disbelief. Vida had a history of overcoming slow starts to find his middle-innings groove, but this would not be among those times. The manager signaled for right-hander Horacio Pina. Blue was finished after two-thirds of an inning. (Pina immediately hit a batter and gave up an RBI single, the run charged to Blue.)

The Orioles won 97 games, three more than the A's, though they were a far cry from the team that beat Oakland in '71. Frank Robinson was gone, replaced in right field by the comparatively punchless Rettenmund. Earl Williams was the only player on the team to hit more than 12 homers. Of the four 20-game winners from '71, only Jim Palmer's stats were comparable to what they had been. None of it seemed to matter. The Orioles' new formula was working.

The four runs Baltimore scored in the first were three more than Palmer needed. The right-hander, who would win the Cy Young Award a month later, looked every bit the part, tossing a complete-game five-hitter while fanning 12 in a 6–0 victory. The A's never stood a chance. "Man throws like that," said Jackson afterward, "he don't lose no games." The A's may have been defending champions, but Baltimore hadn't lost a playoff game since the format was adopted in 1968. Now the O's were back where they expected to be, dominating in October, their aura of invincibility firmly intact.

Sunday's Game 2 was better for the defending champs, thanks primarily to Sal Bando. In the third inning, he blasted a would-be three-run homer that Al Bumbry somehow caught at full extension two feet above the seven-foot fence in left field. Upon returning to the dugout, Bando loudly proclaimed that his next time up he would "hit one [Bumbry] won't be able to catch" — and then he did, going back-to-back with Joe Rudi in the sixth. Two innings later he did it again, blasting a two-run shot with Campaneris aboard.

Equally vital was Bando's presence in the field. Prior to the series, Bowie Kuhn issued an edict aimed squarely at Dick Williams, banning a repeat of the manager's roadshow to and from the mound for incessant conferences during the '72 World Series. Barred from more than one visit per inning at the cost of having to remove his pitcher, Williams turned to his third baseman. Bando was the clubhouse's *capo di tutti capi*, a guy who then-manager Hank Bauer initially named captain in 1969 for the simple reason that "he was doing the job anyway." Bando visited the mound multiple times throughout Game 2 to work his magic on Catfish Hunter, reminding the right-hander about things like concentrating on the first pitch of an at-bat, not being afraid to waste a pitch, maintaining his arm slot, watching his mechanics, or just focusing, goddammit. Hunter listened.

Before coming to Oakland, Salvatore Leonard Bando was Cleveland, through and through. The offspring of native-son parents who each had ten siblings, he was the oldest of three by more than a decade. (His youngest brother, Chris, 12 years Sal's junior, went on to a big league career of his own.) Bando's father, Ben, was a carpenter and raised his family in homes he built around town. During the summer months Sal would show up at a job site for a few hours' work, then spend his afternoons on the local diamonds. That was where he met Rich Liskovec, the sponsor of a semipro team for which Bando ended up playing. Liskovec was also a math professor at Arizona State University, where he recommended Bando for a scholarship under head coach Bobby Winkles. The third baseman ended up as the MVP of the 1965 College World Series and shortly thereafter was selected by Oakland in the sixth round of the first-ever player draft.

It didn't take long for Bando to become the glue that kept the A's together under occasionally trying circumstances. "Take him away and that team was nothing," said Jim Bank, Oakland's traveling secretary in 1973. Pitching coach Wes Stock agreed. "If there was one guy who made a difference," he said, "there's no doubt in my mind it was Sal Bando."

Even Jackson admitted as much. After *Time* referred to Reggie as the leader of "the Wild Bunch," he confessed that "we all knew that Sal was the leader." Now Bando had not only driven in three of his team's six runs against Baltimore but goaded Hunter into the eighth inning of a 6–3 victory that evened the playoff series at a game apiece. The teams headed back to Oakland, tied.

The A's arrived in California amid a deluge, and though skies had cleared by the following morning, American League president Joe Cronin deemed the field too wet to play Game 3. It was 12:15 P.M. on a Monday, a quarter-hour before the scheduled start, and considering that weather reports called for another squall within the hour, Cronin had plenty of justification. Charlie Finley, however, wanted no part of the news. Upon being informed of the cancellation, he raced downstairs, his mending heart drawing strength from the anger in his veins. Finding Cronin in front of the home clubhouse, the Owner held nothing back, screaming bloody murder right there in the hallway. "I've got a big Columbus Day crowd here," he blustered, thinking about the 30,000 advance-sale tickets he'd have to refund, plus the holiday gate being difficult to replicate the following day, on a Tuesday afternoon.

Cronin replied that he wanted to see a complete game, not one that would be called after only a few innings. "Can you expect to play a game under these conditions?" he asked.

"You sanctimonious little shit," Finley shrieked. Cronin cut him off. "I don't think we should be discussing this here," he said, trying to transition the conversation away from public view. "Why don't we . . ."

"I don't give a fuck what you think!" the Owner interrupted. Dick Williams stood nearby, embarrassed but unwilling to risk insubordination by walking away. Still, he wrote later in his autobiography about the moment: "I started thinking that maybe life wouldn't be so bad if I did just that. Walk away. At least I'd be able to keep my self-respect."

There is no record of Finley apologizing to Cronin, even after the rain came as predicted and continued throughout the day. Fortuitously for the Owner, league policy prohibited refunds. Game 3 tickets were good for Game 3, whenever it was played, and nothing more. Thus, Tuesday's nonholiday crowd was a robust (for Oakland) 34,367.

Finally, something that didn't give Finley fits.

In 1971 a rain-out of the first game of the A's playoff series against Baltimore proved fatal, exposing Oakland's two-deep starting rotation. Of course, that was before the A's acquired Ken Holtzman, the man who in 1973 started more games than any pitcher on their staff (40), tied Catfish Hunter for the team lead in victories (21), and led the club's starters in ERA (2.97) by a wide margin.

Nearly as important was his workmanlike approach in a volatile clubhouse. The lefty was fond of intoning how he didn't need the game, how he wouldn't hang on too long, and how he'd happily transition to the private sector whenever it suited him. Holtzman had a college degree in business administration from the University of Illinois and spent off-seasons working as a Series 7–licensed stockbroker in his native St. Louis, setting up in another industry in which his competitive instincts would prove a boon once his baseball career ended.*

When Holtzman came up with the Cubs in 1966, being left-handed and Jewish led to inevitable Sandy Koufax comparisons. As luck would have it, in his first appearance of the season during his first April as a big leaguer, he squared off against the Dodgers great for two innings of relief work. Afterward, as Koufax iced his arm following six shutout innings, Holtzman approached to timidly ask for an autograph . . . for his mother. Jackie Holtzman wouldn't let her son into the house without it. "She doesn't care what *I* do," Holtzman said later, "just as long as she's up to date on *him*." The pitchers met again that September, with Koufax pitching a complete game and allowing only two runs. Holtzman, however, held the Dodgers to one, sticking the legendary lefty with the final loss of his career. When Koufax retired weeks later, Holtzman proudly proclaimed, "I am now the best lefthanded Jewish pitcher in the world."†

The next season Holtzman made a bid to become the best left-hander, period. Despite spending much of his season on duty with the Illinois National Guard, he went 9-0 for Chicago, with a 2.53 ERA in 12 starts. Over the coming years he would be a staple of the Cubs staff, throwing two no-hitters, but mandatory meetings with his military unit prevented him from finding a consistent rhythm. The lefty was good, but people had forecast greatness. The next Koufax? Expectations can be a bitch. Combined with an overt willingness to speak his mind—a trait he would share with many of his teammates in Oakland but that did not sit well in Chicago—it was enough to sour the pitcher in the eyes of manager Leo Durocher.

---

* During the season Holtzman funneled much of his nonbaseball energy toward another competitive pursuit: bridge. A *lot* of bridge. He subscribed to revolutionary theories on precision bidding and, upon forming a four-man clubhouse game with Dick Green, Darold Knowles, and Rollie Fingers, brought his comrades up to speed. The cadre came to include *Oakland Tribune* reporter Ron Bergman, and their small faction of the clubhouse grew obsessed. They played in airplanes and hotel rooms. Holtzman scanned newspapers to find the local bridge club in a given city where he, Fingers, and Bergman would go for games. "We'd be the only three guys there, major leaguers playing against 85-year-old women," Holtzman said. Added Fingers, "It was all gray-haired old ladies. We'd beat them during the afternoon, and then we'd go to the ballpark and beat a baseball team."
† In 1972 Finley purchased outfielder Art Shamsky from the Cubs, giving Oakland a full 60 percent of the five Jews in the major leagues. "I hear rumbles that Finley is going to draft Golda Meir," responded Holtzman. The triumvirate, including Mike Epstein, lasted three weeks until Shamsky was released.

By 1971 Holtzman's record had slipped to 9-15 and his ERA to 4.48, and he was shipped to the A's in exchange for Rick Monday. It was the perfect move. The lefty thrived under Dick Williams's loose leash, his success predicated almost entirely on a fastball that he threw up to 90 percent of the time. "I've never seen a pitcher throw as fast as he does who has his control," gushed pitching coach Wes Stock.

Now Holtzman was facing the Orioles. Clubhouse consensus held that Game 3 was vital — "more important even than starting the first game of the World Series against Cincinnati," said the lefty, who had done that very thing. "If we don't get this one," he admitted, "we probably don't get in."

The comment was valid, except that Holtzman made it *after* throwing 11 innings of three-hit ball, earning a 2-1 victory over Baltimore's Mike Cuellar on a day when Cuellar — who went 10 innings himself — should not have lost. Holtzman gave up a solo homer to Earl Williams in the second inning, then retired 14 straight Orioles. When Williams considered a pitching change before the 11th, Holtzman addressed him directly. "If you pull me out, I'll kill you," he said. "I don't give a shit if this game goes forty innings, I'm not leaving." Then he set Baltimore down in order.

Cuellar could not match him. Joe Rudi singled home a run in the eighth, Campaneris led off the 11th with his second homer in as many games, and A's fans went home happy, their team holding a two-games-to-one advantage with a chance to clinch the following day. Game 4 would be a rematch of Game 1, Palmer versus Blue. As reporters milled about the postgame clubhouse, somebody asked Vida if he would be "revenging himself" for his opening loss.

"Revenging myself?" asked the pitcher. "You mean 'redeeming.' Redeeming myself." Hanging curveballs were tolerable. Bad grammar was not.

Before Game 4 of the ALCS even started, the Mets became the National League's representatives in the World Series. New York ace Tom Seaver overwhelmed the highly favored Cincinnati Reds in the deciding Game 5 at Shea Stadium, his 7-2 victory serving as the finishing touch on a dominant pitching performance by the entire Mets staff. Fans ripped the field to ribbons in celebration.

Across the country in Oakland, Blue — well rested after his abbreviated Game 1 outing — had a fastball every bit as good as his English and held the Orioles to two hits through six. As for his counterpart, it was quickly clear that Palmer did not possess the same stuff he had in the opener. In the second inning he allowed three runs on three doubles, a single, and a walk, retiring only Deron Johnson before being yanked by manager Earl Weaver. The right-hander had notched 27 outs in his previous start, but this time could get only four.

By the sixth inning the A's led 4–0, and Blue was nine outs from accomplishing something that had evaded him through three starts and seven relief appearances in postseason play: winning a game. Then, in the seventh, Earl Williams drew a one-out walk, and back-to-back singles by Don Baylor and Brooks Robinson produced Baltimore's first run. Before Dick Williams had time to consider what was happening, Andy Etchebarren — with four homers to his name over the previous two seasons combined — hit only the second curveball Vida threw all day over the 375-foot marker in left-center field for a three-run homer. Blue's implosion was as close to instantaneous as baseball allows. The game was tied, and Vida, having followed six innings of shutout pitching with four runs over the span of four batters, hit the showers.

Rollie Fingers was mostly dynamite in relief, giving up only a leadoff homer to Bobby Grich in the eighth, but that was all Baltimore needed. The Orioles, all but dead two innings earlier, held on for a 5–4 victory, forcing a winner-take-all Game 5 the following afternoon.

As the A's sat in their clubhouse amid cases of still-boxed victory champagne, Fingers lamented. "We had them by the nostrils and we let them get away from us," he said to nobody in particular — even as his gaze fell upon Blue. Vida was too shell-shocked to even consider a response, but Blue Moon Odom wasn't. "You shouldn't be talking," he cried at Fingers, leaping from his stool. "If you don't give up that homer, we don't lose." Then the mercurial Georgian, jiber of jibes, fighter of fights, stepped toward the closer. Fingers responded in kind. Watching the would-be combatants approach each other from across the room, Dick Williams gave a frantic nod to Jackson, who stepped between them, managing to talk down a fight that seemed all but certain. Later Reggie went so far as to label the confrontation a positive for the team. "Heck," he said afterward, "we'll probably score twenty-five runs tomorrow. You know us."

Vida had his world-class fastball. Holtzman was the type of dominant left-hander for whom every team thirsts. In his day Odom had the wondrous sinker and the don't-fuck-with-me attitude that largely kept opponents from fucking with him. But the unquestioned leader of the pitching staff was Catfish Hunter. He didn't throw the hardest, and he wasn't the loudest or the biggest or the smartest. Really, Hunter had only four things working in his favor: an ability to remove speed from his fastball, control over his breaking pitches, a wild competitive streak, and absolute fearlessness. "Winning isn't everything," he once said, "but wanting to win is."

When Hunter missed a month between July and August after injuring his thumb, he anticipated that the rest would make him strong for the stretch run. Now he was putting theory to test as Oakland's starter in Game 5 at the Coliseum. Oakland sure was a long way from Hertford.

Hertford, North Carolina, is the oldest town in the nation's 12th-oldest state, about 60 miles southeast of Norfolk, Virginia, inland down the Perquimans River from Albemarle Sound. Its forests are pine, and its cropland yields rich harvests of cotton, corn, and soybeans. This was where James Augustus Hunter was born, the youngest of Abbott and Lillie Hunter's eight children. Abbott was a tenant farmer and part-time logger who raised his boys to farm, hunt, fish, and play ball. Jimmy Hunter would rise early to handle his chores, leaving his afternoons free for baseball. In high school he became a genuine phenom, winning 26 of 28 games while pitching five no-hitters.

In 1963, on Thanksgiving Day of his senior year, Jimmy went hunting with two brothers and a cousin in the woods near the family farm. The boys were traversing a drainage canal at Bear Point, about a half-mile from the Hunter home, when his brother Pete's gun unexpectedly went off, sending buckshot into Jimmy's right foot.

Hunter's pinkie toe was blown off, and the nerves in the toe next to it were severed. Doctors located 45 embedded shotgun pellets (they would later find many more) but were able to dislodge only a dozen. Jimmy figured his athletic career was finished, but the feeling lasted only a few months; when springtime arrived with the whiff of baseball, he could not help himself. If he could walk, Hunter figured, he could pitch. He cut a foam-rubber cushion to fit his cleat, then carved out indentations to accommodate the pressure from the remaining pellets. By season's end he was 14-1, and the Perquimans High School Pirates were North Carolina's Class-AA champs.

Some scouts were scared off by the diminished velocity of Hunter's fastball (which he never recovered) and the fear that changing his motion to compensate for the injury would lead to arm issues down the road. One scout, however — a fellow North Carolinian named Clyde Kluttz, a former big league catcher now in the employ of Charlie Finley — stuck around. Kluttz endeared himself to the Hunter family by checking in on the youngster's progress through every step of rehab. He continued to drop by the farm even when it looked like Jimmy would never pitch again, his attention so thorough that it "almost earned him a spot in the family portrait," Hunter said later.

Finley himself flew in for Hunter's final prep game. His first stop was the farm, where, from the window of his limousine, he gazed in awe. The house had a tin roof, and a peanut patch off to one side, where Lillie Hunter, bonnet on her head, hoed crops. Abbott Hunter was preparing ham in the smokehouse. Water came from a long-handled well pump.

Finley spent most of his time in town passing out warm-up jackets (green), bats (also green), and baseballs (orange, of course) before taking in the state championship game. When he eventually called to negotiate, Hunter opened at $50,000. No problem, said the Owner. Hunter tacked on $25,000 to cover college in case baseball didn't pan out. Of course, said Finley. Also a new car, said the pitcher. There was a pause on the phone line. Then, *No way*.

It would represent only a small increase in the overall package — the car Finley included in Rick Monday's deal the following year cost $4,000 — but the Owner had reached his perimeter and would not be pushed from that point. Hunter was adamant. They went back and forth for four hours, discussing the merits of Hunter's pitching versus the limits of Finley's generosity. Finally, Hunter asked for a break to canvass other scouts and see what else might be on the table. Not a chance, said Finley. Accept my offer right now or it will disappear.

Never mind the effort that Finley had already put in; his threat was believable because it was true. Hunter accepted.

Finley quickly added two caveats to the arrangement. One was that Hunter go to the Mayo Clinic in Rochester, Minnesota, to have his foot examined by the country's best surgeons.* The second was less formal. "Do you have a nickname?" Finley asked.

"No, sir," replied the newly minted pro.

---

* Doctors ended up removing 45 more pellets from Hunter's foot, leaving 15 they couldn't effectively reach. The pitcher missed the entire 1964 season recuperating from the procedure.

"Well," said the Owner, "to play baseball, you've got to have a nickname. What do you like to do?"

"Hunt and fish," said Hunter, who liked to hunt and fish.

Finley thought for a moment, then spun a yarn. "When you were six years old, you ran away from home and went fishing," he informed the startled teenager. "Your mom and dad had been looking for you all day. When they finally found you, about, ah, four o'clock in the afternoon, you'd caught two big fish — catfish — and were reeling in the third. And that's how you got your nickname. Okay?"

"Yes, sir, Mr. Finley," said Hunter, thinking more about the money he had coming than the story he was hearing. He figured the conversation would be forgotten by morning.

"Good," said Finley. "Now repeat it back to me."

From that moment on, Jim Hunter was all but extinguished from baseball's annals, replaced by a man named Catfish. The pitcher spent the next several years appeasing the Owner by halfheartedly confirming his story, but Hunter's mother would have none of it. "I raised eight children, and not a single one ever ran away from home," Lillie proclaimed to the local press. "I don't understand why Mr. Finley made up that name and that story. I have never, never, never, ever called Jim 'Catfish,' and I never will. I don't like 'Catfish.' Jim's a lot prettier."

Now it was Catfish's job to pitch his team into the 1973 World Series.

Spectacular weather in Oakland on Thursday, 68 degrees and sunny, was insufficient to inspire the masses. The Coliseum crowd, which had been only 27,500 for Game 4, was an even scrawnier 24,265 for the clincher. Charlie Finley was the kind of guy who saw the stadium as half empty, but on this day it was true.

Hunter's performance was typical. The guy hardly looked dominant, striking out only one hitter and retiring the side in order only once. But the Orioles didn't get a hit until the fifth, never put multiple runners on base, and couldn't get anybody past second. When the A's scraped together three runs against right-hander Doyle Alexander by the fourth inning, things were all but over. Almost.

Leading 3–0 with two outs in the ninth and nobody on base — one out away from the World Series — Catfish could not slam the door. Brooks Robinson doubled, and Hunter grew nervous. He was tiring, having trouble locating his pitches. A first-pitch ball to the next hitter, Bobby Grich, confirmed his fears. A walk would bring the tying run to the plate, and given Hunter's propensity for surrendering homers, he felt certain that this was more than a passing terror. He threw another ball. Tension cascaded through the Coliseum.

Then fans broke the outfield fence.

A crowd had surged to the railing, poised to storm the field when the game ended, and managed to dislodge a piece of the wall's wooden paneling. With time called for emergency repairs, Williams visited his pitcher and informed him that he would finish the game, win or lose. "Don't walk him," Williams said. "Don't try to strike him out. Just let him hit it. If you have to, lob the ball up there."

Hunter did exactly that. Grich hit his next pitch on the ground to shortstop, and Campaneris relayed it to Tenace at first for the final out. As fans spilled onto the field, A's players, concerned for their safety, sprinted for the clubhouse tunnel behind home plate — no small trek for the far-flung outfielders. Fans grabbed players' caps from their heads, made attempts at their gloves, and were summarily beaten back. One person tried to leap on Hunter's back. An Orioles coach was knocked to the ground. An usher trying to control the crowd ended up with a black eye and a split lip. Still, said Jackson later, "I felt so great [after the final out], all I wanted to do was be a fan, run wild out there with all those other people and scream and yell." Reggie, having missed the previous season's World Series, was particularly happy. "Fabulous," he said again and again in the postgame clubhouse. "Fabulous, fabulous, fabulous."*

In the celebratory clubhouse, where the air was tactile with the stickiness of champagne spray, Hunter was backed into his locker by a mass of vora-

---

* Jackson's evening was just beginning. Following the clubhouse party, he and a lady friend took his 1941 Chevrolet coupe to San Francisco. There, traveling along Broadway Avenue, they got stuck behind two motorcycle patrolmen driving exceedingly slowly. From the passenger seat, Jackson opted against common sense and reached over to lean on the horn. The policemen pulled the car over, at which point Jackson told them he was carrying no ID. They quickly discovered Reggie's bevy of outstanding traffic warrants for things like speeding, and dragged the increasingly obstinate outfielder to be booked at a nearby station. Jackson staunchly refused to post bail and turned down an offer by his date to do so on his behalf. He was transferred to the city prison, where three hours later and against his own explicit directions bail bondsman Al Graff cited him as "a special case" and plunked down $82 for his release. The next morning, when the A's gathered for a pre–World Series meeting at the Edgewater Hyatt, Reggie was needled mercilessly, Billy North going so far as to face a wall and demonstrate the finer points of a police-ordered spread eagle.

cious newsmen. Before a question could be asked, from out of the crowd came the annoyed shout, "Hey, who the hell is pushing?"

Who the hell indeed. Charlie Finley himself, Kelly green blazer standing out in any crowd, even this one, was pushing his way to the front of the pack. He yanked an obviously embarrassed Hunter into an awkward embrace. The media would have to wait. While the pitcher was otherwise occupied, a reporter on the scrum's fringe asked one of Catfish's teammates about Oakland's prospects of beating the Mets. The player turned his glance toward Finley and minced no words. "It's him we have to beat, not them," he said coldly. "He is our obstacle. He is our handicap, the burden we have to bear. The Mets are easy. Charlie is something else. You have to wonder what the hell he will do next."

If only he knew. If only any of them knew.

10

Scapegoat Nation

We had to get Charlie off our asses as soon as possible.

—Dick Williams, explaining his motivation for ending postseason series prior to the maximum number of games

Mike Andrews wasn't out to make history. He harbored no grand illu-
sions of heroics. The guy had been with the A's for ten weeks, started three
games at second base, pinch-hit 12 times, and accumulated all of four
hits. Still, only two years earlier he'd been an All-Star–caliber player, so it
was hardly fantasy to picture him contributing to Oakland's postseason
cause. Had somebody informed Andrews that he would receive multiple
standing ovations in the World Series against the Mets, he'd have had little
choice but to imagine that things went well.

But only if he wasn't told the reasons why.

Those, of course, had to do with Charlie Finley and a fresh round of
controversy. Controversy was nothing new, of course; these A's were accustomed to the stuff, absorbing it and processing it and using it for fuel.
Players didn't seek it out, but neither did the idea that their ballclub perpetually danced on the edge of disaster seem to bother them. Andrews
was as tough as any of them in that regard, only less practiced. Most of
his teammates had spent their careers suffering Finley, and, much as they
despised his treatment, were at least familiar with the guy's twisted brand
of motivation. They'd watched helplessly as a parade of managers were
ignominiously fired before Dick Williams came along. They'd seen the
suffering heaped upon Reggie Jackson after the young star argued in favor of receiving fair market value following the 1969 season. They'd seen
the mental ruination of Vida Blue for similar reasons in '72. They had

absorbed the banishments of Dave Duncan and Mike Epstein, and the one-man jihad against Tommy Davis.

Andrews heard the stories about the raving Owner, saw reaction to him on the faces of teammates, but he had not yet felt — truly *felt* — the old-growth antipathy toward the man that coursed through the clubhouse. Finley's most recent heart attack may have left him diminished, physically shriveled and wheelchair-bound, but before the World Series was over the man would have his team in a state approaching open revolt. For Andrews, it was a crash course. For his teammates, it would take everything they had to simply drown out the white noise and remember that they were in Oakland to do only one thing: play baseball.

On August 26 the Mets were in last place, a dozen games under .500, and just breaking even by season's end seemed wildly ambitious. Then something crazy happened: They started to win. A lot. They closed August by taking nine of 13, then went 20-8 over the season's final month. Their final record, 82-79, would have put them in a statistical tie for fourth place in the National League West, but the Mets played in the moribund East, where they emerged as the only team with a winning mark. New York's offense finished next-to-last in batting average, home runs, stolen bases, and runs scored, but their pitching was sublime. Tom Seaver would be the runaway Cy Young Award winner, with 19 victories and a league-leading 2.08 ERA, 251 strikeouts, and 18 complete games. He, 23-year-old John Matlack, and longtime stalwart Jerry Koosman were key to New York's playoff victory over the Reds, between them throwing three complete games, plus eight dominant innings from Seaver in the clincher.

The Mets also had an effective counter to Rollie Fingers. Like his team, closer Tug McGraw was a second-half supernova, going 5-0 with 12 saves and a 0.88 ERA over the season's final six weeks. He was also New York's emotional leader, coining the club's rallying cry, "You gotta believe!" — a phrase that became ubiquitous across Queens through the late summer months.

Still, New York's winning percentage was the lowest ever for a Series team, and no club since the 1918 Red Sox (who played 36 fewer games than the Mets) had reached the Fall Classic with so few victories. Oakland's three 20-game winners were three more than played at Shea Stadium. The A's boasted more power (131 homers to 85) and stunningly more speed (128 stolen bases to 27). "The Mets got no business being in this thing," snorted Reggie Jackson just before the Series began.

Mets manager Yogi Berra raised the ire of second-guessers (otherwise known as New York sports fans) by holding Seaver, the ace of his or any staff, until Tuesday's Game 3 rather than push him up a day to start Sunday's Game 2. The strategy set Seaver up to pitch a potential Game 7, should the Series last that long.

Rising above the conversation was Willie Mays. The superest of superstars had been forged in New York during six seasons with the Giants before he moved with them to San Francisco for the next 14. Mays's trade to the Mets in 1972 brought him full circle, but at age 43 there was not much kid left in the Say Hey Kid. Having already announced that he would retire after the season, he'd accumulated only six at-bats in September as New York steamrolled all comers. October, however, would be different, since a shoulder injury suffered by star right fielder Rusty Staub in the NLCS opened a spot in New York's outfield. This was how Mays came to open the World Series in center field for the Mets. It made for a fabulous homecoming to a Bay Area fan base that never stopped loving him.

To judge by the state of the Coliseum, however, the 1973 World Series could not match the caliber of the previous season's party. To start, there were no programs, owing to Finley's reluctance to pay the printing company in a timely fashion. There was no sign of the ubiquitous red-white-and-blue postseason bunting; the previous stuff had been torn away by souvenir-hungry fans after the playoff clincher and was never replaced. With the Owner's convalescence forestalling his usually manic levels of energy, everything around him ground to a halt. Even the ceremonial first pitch prior to Game 1 was delayed, owing to the refusal of A's coach Vern Hoscheit — Finley's Keeper of the Baseballs — to relinquish one without the Owner's tacit approval.

Finley, looking to maximize profits, sold tickets for seats in the centerfield bleachers that, because they were directly in hitters' sight lines, were ordinarily used only for football games. The decision was particularly startling since some 5,000 seats remained empty in the upper deck. The inability to sell out the opening game of the World Series was a low point even for A's supporters, who had long since proved their willingness to stay home.

But was it the fans' fault? Joe Rudi didn't think so. He recalled a visit to the team's ticket office just prior to the Series. "There were these great big desks, business desks, in the ticket room, piled high with envelopes," he said. "Finley didn't hire enough people to answer the requests for tickets. There were thousands of checks sitting there for people wanting tickets to the World Series, which were not filled. Finley was just too cheap."

As for the playing of baseball, Game 1 featured a bona-fide pitching duel: Ken Holtzman versus Jon Matlack. Holtzman did more than throw four-hit ball through five: he overtly embraced the lack of a DH in the Fall Classic by smacking a third-inning double, then scored the game's first run one batter later when Campy Campaneris's grounder rolled through the legs of usually sure-handed Mets second baseman Felix Milan.

Milan's error was New York's first of the inning. The next one came moments later when Matlack had Campy picked off cleanly but fired the ball high and wide to first baseman John Milner, allowing the runner to advance. Joe Rudi brought Campaneris home with a single, increasing the A's lead to 2–0.

It was all they would get against Matlack. It was also all they would need.

Holtzman tweaked his knee sliding into second on his double and left after the fifth, handing a 2–1 lead to Rollie Fingers. The closer toiled for three and a third innings, none of them easy. Williams made angry trips to the mound each inning, between which he yelled at his pitcher from the dugout. "You've heard the expression in baseball that some guys you have to pat on the back, others you have to kick in the butt?" the manager explained after the game. "Fingers is a kickee."

Still, the closer held the Mets in unsteady check through 14 batters, highlighted by his eighth-inning confrontation with Mays. Fingers had gone to high school in Upland, California, east of Los Angeles, and as a teenager once sprinted the length of the Dodger Stadium parking lot after a game to have the departing Mays autograph a Dodgers cap. Eleven years later at the Coliseum, he uncorked a two-strike sinker that, when Mays watched it pass, made Fingers the final man ever to strike out the Hall of Famer.

Left-hander Darold Knowles came on to secure the final two outs of Oakland's 2–1 victory. Nobody knew it yet, but it would be the last time for a long time that the primary discussion topic of the World Series would be the playing of baseball.

Game 2 featured a couple of old standbys: a less-than-sold-out Coliseum (with a crowd of 49,151) and a mediocre Vida Blue postseason start. The southpaw surrendered a home run to Cleon Jones in the second, a home run to Wayne Garrett in the third, and two baserunners in the sixth who were allowed to score by reliever Horacio Pina. Luckily for the A's, New York starter Jerry Koosman was even worse, giving up a triple, two doubles, and two walks in the first and another triple in the second, then loading the bases with one out in the third. At that point, somehow having surrendered only three runs for all that damage, he was pulled.

It was a long day for pitchers, six men logging time for the A's, five for the Mets. Knowles thought he'd wear goat horns when, after relieving Pina in the sixth, he awkwardly tumbled down the mound while fielding a bases-loaded comebacker, tossing what should have been an easy flip to Fosse all the way to the backstop and allowing two runs to score. The error capped a rally that turned Oakland's 3–2 lead into a 6–3 deficit.

The play would have been momentous had the game ended there, but in the aftermath of what followed it was barely remembered. Things started small. As the A's prepared to bat in the bottom of the ninth having pulled to within two on Reggie Jackson's seventh-inning RBI double, Willie Mays trotted out to right field for New York. He'd entered the game as a pinch runner in the top half of the frame, and seeing him play anyplace but center was shocking to the eye. Even as the press corps was being informed that it would be Mays's first appearance at the position all season (and only the 13th of his long career), he talked center fielder Don Hahn into swapping spots. The aging star was immediately tested when Deron Johnson led off against closer Tug McGraw with a soaring fly ball that Mays lost in the high sun, stumbling after it, then watching it fall to his right for a double. That the sun had been giving outfielders fits all day mattered little; the play undeservedly became the epitomic example of a ballplayer who hung around too long.

Still, the Mets led 6–4, and McGraw kept things neatly under control by retiring the next two batters. One out from victory, however, the left-hander walked Bando, then allowed a single to Jackson, scoring Allan Lewis, who was pinch-running for Johnson. The A's, all but finished moments earlier, had new life. Gene Tenace capitalized, driving in Bando with a game-tying single to right field. Remarkably, the game went into extras, tied 6–6.

The Mets thought they took the lead in the tenth against Rollie Fingers when, with one out, Bud Harrelson tagged up from third on Felix Milan's medium-deep fly ball to left field. Joe Rudi's throw tailed up the third-base line, forcing Ray Fosse into foul territory to field it. The catcher offered a desperation backward swipe with the ball as Harrelson streaked past, but the runner was clearly safe . . . to everybody in the ballpark save plate ump Augie Donatelli, who emphatically thumbed him out, ending the inning. Harrelson hopped up screaming, while Yogi Berra and a coterie of Mets streamed from the dugout. In a lasting image, a capless Mays dropped to his knees to futilely plead New York's case.

By that point day had turned to evening, and Charlie Finley ordered the Coliseum lights turned on. By rule, however, illumination could only be activated by order of the chief umpire, and only at the start of an inning, to avoid the sort of imbalance that might be created by, say, firing up the lights *after* the Mets batted. Bowie Kuhn, seated along the third-base line, had them turned off again. It was dramatic. It was also window dressing for what came in the 12th.

With the game still knotted at six, Fingers, in his third inning of work, put runners on the corners with two outs. That brought up Mays, only days from retirement, who had already wobbled through the outfield after Johnson's ninth-inning fly ball. Mays may have been old, but his superstar status was based upon more than physical gifts. As he stepped into the box the future Hall of Famer recalled that the Montreal teams for which Dick Williams coached consistently fed him a steady diet of fastballs, alternating from inside corner to outside edge. And so Mays waited for a heater on the outside, which Fingers delivered with his second pitch. Mays drilled it into center field to score Harrelson with the Mets' seventh run. It was the final hit of his storied career.

Cleon Jones followed with another single to load the bases, at which point Williams brought in southpaw Paul Lindblad to face the lefty-swinging Milner. It was the correct move. Lindblad induced a soft three-hopper to second base for what should have been the inning's final out, but just as Milan had done a day earlier, Mike Andrews, having entered the game as a pinch hitter in the eighth inning, let the ball bounce through his legs. Two runs scored, expanding the Mets' lead to 9–6.

That Andrews was in the field at all was a matter of some controversy. On October 3, three days before the start of the ALCS, Finley had petitioned Bowie Kuhn to include Manny Trillo, his 22-year-old second baseman of the future, on Oakland's World Series roster as a replacement for the injured Billy North. (Trillo's participation in the ALCS had been contingent upon quid-pro-quo agreement from Baltimore, which allowed it in exchange for catcher Sergio Robles being able to replace the injured Elrod Hendricks.) An hour before Game 1 of the World Series, however, the Mets officially refused the Owner's request, saying that they would accept only Allan Lewis as a replacement — an outfielder for an outfielder.* That left Andrews as Williams's late-inning guy at second.

Then things got worse. Lindblad got the very next hitter, Jerry Grote, to top another ball to second. Andrews, charging hard, fielded this one cleanly, but his cross-body throw sailed just wide of first, up the line toward right field. Tenace stretched, back to the plate, to make the catch, but first-base umpire Jerry Neudecker ruled that in so doing he pulled his foot from the bag. Another run scored and another error was charged to Andrews's ledger, even though numerous Oakland players later called it Tenace's fault. In reality, there should have been no error at all; replays showed Tenace's foot planted firmly on the base ten feet ahead of the charging runner. It made no difference. What would have been a three-run deficit was now four, Mets 10, A's 6. Andrews sheepishly kicked at the dirt in front of second. His long-standing shoulder injury was a known quantity when Oakland picked him up in July, and the primary reason he had played only a handful of innings in the field. Now he was expected to come in cold and almost completely unpracticed. It didn't seem fair.

The A's battled in the bottom of the 12th, loading the bases with one out and a run in before Mets reliever George Stone closed the door. All told, New York's 10–7 victory took four hours and 13 minutes, a taut marathon that left players drooping. Afterward, Andrews sat at his locker, head down, mumbling "my fault" again and again. Williams, passing by, gave the player a reassuring pat on the back. "Remember what I've said about physical mistakes," he said, trying to console the inconsolable. "They happen to everybody. It wasn't your fault. You're human." When

* Finley later claimed that New York GM Bob Scheffing told him it was not the Mets who objected, but National League president Chub Feeney. The Owner, freshly irate and ever obstinate, protested by playing the World Series with only 24 players instead of the full complement of 25 — yet another example of his willingness to scuttle his best chances in favor of making a point. To the clubhouse majority who did not consider pinch runner Allan Lewis a full-fledged player, the team was down to 23. Finley threatened to announce the snub over the ballpark PA, an action that Kuhn aide Johnny Johnson expressly forbade. The Owner did it anyway, an act that the Commissioner saw as a deliberate attempt to simultaneously embarrass him and fire up the fans — which it was, and which it did.

newsmen approached, Andrews was straightforward. "I have no excuse for what happened," he said. "I should be able to catch the ball and throw it. Injured? No, my shoulder bothered me last year, but it's been fine this year. . . . I'm not going to die tomorrow just because I made two errors today."

With the A's leaving directly for the airport and a New York–bound charter, Andrews began to pack as soon as the media were finished with him. He was interrupted, however, by a message that his presence was requested in the trainer's room — something about an examination. Waiting for him there was the team orthopedist, Dr. Harry Walker, who proceeded to lay hands upon Andrews's right arm, poking and prodding the shoulder and bicep. "Do you feel any pain?" he asked as he tweaked. "No," said Andrews each time. "No."

Walker was ambiguous when Andrews asked the reasons for the exam, which lasted less than ten minutes. The doctor knew exactly what was happening, of course. He wasn't saying because he wasn't sure how Andrews would handle the idea that he was about to become the first player to be fired in the middle of a World Series.

Upstairs, Finley was meeting with farm director John Claiborne. It didn't make a bit of difference to him that Oakland was trailing 7–6 at the time of Andrews's miscues, or that as a team the A's committed five errors on the day, or that Andrews's arm was healthy enough to throw batting practice that very morning. The Owner outlined to his deputy the idea of disabling Andrews in order to activate Trillo — a tenable scheme, he felt, since both players were second basemen. Ever the pragmatist, Claiborne responded directly. "The Commissioner is going to ask what type of garbage you're trying to pull," he told Finley. "They're not going to let you do it." He suggested that a modicum of proof might be beneficial, and that while a letter from the doctor would be good, a letter from Andrews himself would be better. Finley had his secretary type one up while he headed downstairs.

Williams was in his clubhouse office, pondering how the game's exhausting outcome would affect his team. The tiny space, only about 15 feet along each wall, was nearly empty, adorned only by a locker and some scattered chairs. Williams was startled when the Owner fairly flew into the room, Claiborne on his heels, and slammed the door. "Dick," Finley said, his voice crackling with anticipatory energy, "we're putting Andrews on the disabled list and activating Manny Trillo."

This made no sense to the manager. "What happened?" he asked. "I didn't see Andrews get hurt."

"Oh yes he did, that son of a bitch," replied Finley. "He got hurt real bad."

This was when Williams became fully aware of the depths to which Charlie Finley would sink in order to get his way. Unable to tolerate Andrews's errors and insufficiently sophisticated to recognize their scope within the greater scheme, Finley wanted action, and he wanted it now.

"Charlie, you can't do this!" the manager shouted. Williams was already aware of the treatment suffered by A's employees at the hands of a megalomaniacal boss who consistently put his own needs in front of theirs. What he was about to experience, however, was something new — not in tone but in depth.

The Owner waved around Dr. Walker's notes. "It says here Andrews has a bad shoulder, so the hell I can't do it," he snapped. As Finley sent for Andrews, the manager did what he could to staunch the tide.

"Charlie, you are wrong — you are dead damn wrong!" he shouted. "You're getting rid of a man because of physical errors, which means you're getting rid of him because he's a human being!" The Owner was just beginning to dismiss his concerns when Andrews walked in the door. "Mike," said Williams quickly, "I've got nothing to do with this."

For Andrews, things just kept getting weirder. First was the doctor's examination for an injury suffered years earlier, which had been well documented when he signed with Oakland and had grown no worse in the interim. Now he found himself in a room with the upper echelon of team brass instead of preparing for the trip to New York. The moment Andrews arrived Finley's demeanor changed. He stopped shouting at Williams about how the player was off the club. Now he was a sweet-talking salesman, trying to convince his mark to buy whatever he had to peddle.

Finley expressed sympathy for Andrews's shoulder issues. He said that he understood how hard it must be for an athlete to perform at diminished capacity. He spun 180 degrees from his actual feelings, claiming compassion instead of rancor. "You had to be hurt to make those plays," he cooed. At that point the Owner told Andrews about the statement he was having composed upstairs and requested his signature at the bottom of it. It would be the right thing to do, he insisted, allowing the younger, more capable Trillo to take Andrews's spot on the roster. Andrews was a team player, wasn't he? Did he not want to help the ballclub? "Not in this way," answered the despondent player. Andrews said the story wasn't right, that he wasn't hurt. He allowed that he screwed up, but told Finley that he was in no pain and sought no excuses. When he refused to sign, the Owner's cool waned. "Fine," he snapped. "We'll get through it without you."

Finley was irate, but he was also canny, and quickly composed himself. He hadn't landed the American Medical Association account, after all, by giving up at the first rejection. The four men had been in Williams's office for more than a half-hour by that point, but the Owner wasn't finished. He considerately inquired as to whether Andrews would be amenable to heading to the team offices to review his freshly drafted memo in person. Grudgingly, the player agreed. There, Finley produced a sheet of paper bearing the date Sunday, October 14.* It read:

> To whom it may concern:
> At the request of the Oakland A's, I examined Mike Andrews, second baseman, today. He has a history of cronic [sic] shoulder disability. He attempted to play, but was unable physically to play his position because of a bicep groove tenosynovitis in the right shoulder. It is my opinion he is disabled for the rest of the year.
> Sincerely,
> Harry R. Walker, M.D.

In the lower left-hand corner was the sentence "I agree to the above," with a space for Andrews's signature.

The Owner doubled down on his previous approach, trying again to convince Andrews that signing the statement was best for the team. He spun gold. Finley had acquired Andrews for pinch-hitting purposes, he said, but now the team was stacked with right-handed hitters and in desperate need of a middle infielder. He asked again whether Andrews wanted to help the ballclub. The player wondered aloud what effect his signature would have on his return to the A's in 1974, to which Finley replied that he could guarantee only that Andrews would receive the best medical care available. Signing would be the selfless thing to do, he stressed, the ultimate act of sacrifice.

---

* The original date of the memo was incorrectly typed as October 15. The number was subsequently crossed out and corrected by hand.

Still, Andrews was unsold. He wanted to talk to Williams once more, he said, and returned downstairs to the manager's office. Williams, aghast from the outset, was trapped. He could not strongly counsel the player against Finley's wishes, but neither could he in good conscience endorse them. "Do what you feel is best for yourself," he told Andrews. But Andrews had no idea what was best. He knew the truth, and he knew that he was probably finished with the A's no matter what happened. What he didn't know was how agreeing to Finley's ludicrous plan might affect his livelihood. Would prospective teams be scared off by such a statement, or could it provide leverage, institutional evidence that his failure was healable, like his shoulder, over time?

With that, almost an hour after the screws started to tighten, Andrews cracked. He went back upstairs. He took the paper. He signed it.

By this time the clubhouse was empty. The rest of the team had showered, changed, and packed, and they were sitting in a bus that, for reasons none of the players could fathom, was not moving. Slowly, rumors began to build that Finley was trying to take Andrews off the roster. Reggie, Vida, Bill North, and Dick Green had all been in or near the trainer's room at some point during Andrews's examination, and as they sat immobile on the bus they pieced together details. Neither Andrews nor Williams was among their ranks. The one thing players agreed upon was that nobody knew anything, and that made them nervous. The longer they waited, the more agitated they became, at one point even working themselves into a chant: "We want Mike! We want Mike!" When Andrews went back upstairs to Finley, Williams boarded the bus and grudgingly convinced them to relax.

Inside, Andrews told the Owner that he'd rather go home than accompany the team to New York. "That's a great idea," enthused Finley. "With you not with us, it will make it look more like you're hurt, and we're not going to use you anyway." The player went to the parking lot to retrieve his luggage, but, not up to facing his teammates, sneaked into the cargo hold of the bus. That's where Williams, having disembarked to seek answers over the continued delay, found him. The last thing the manager had seen was Andrews refusing Finley's overtures, but now here he was, in tears, unloading a suitcase. "It finished him . . ." wrote Williams in his autobiography, *No More Mr. Nice Guy*. "He had been torn from the inside out."

The bus left soon thereafter, and by the time it reached Oakland International players were peppering Williams with questions. That's when they heard about the statement Finley wanted Andrews to sign, and the temperature began to broil. The next five airborne hours included an ongoing number of conferences between shifting groups of players, all of whom tried to make sense of things. Firing a player? Turning a team doctor against somebody he was ostensibly hired to serve? The mood at the back of the plane quickly spun toward rage. Finley sat up front, at his usual remove from the rabble. When pressed by newsmen to explain why his players were turning the airplane's rear rows into the USS *Caine*, the Owner pulled Dick Williams into an impromptu half-hour meeting, then pointed all queries the manager's way. This was when the press first saw a copy of Dr. Walker's letter — which, soon enough, would be printed in newspapers coast to coast.

Unlike the previous season, when the effervescent Owner led sing-alongs over the airplane PA, Finley remained rooted in his seat for the duration of the trip. He did not interact with those in steerage class and kept a bounty of bodies — his entourage and assorted hangers-on — as a buffer. He never bothered to explain his rationale, made no effort to mollify an increasingly explosive situation — probably because he had no clue just how explosive it had become.

"Believe me, that was the wrong bunch to get pissed off," said Holtzman, looking back. "I said, 'That son of a bitch. If he could do it to him, he could do it to all of us. If he doesn't like our performance on the field, he can get rid of us in a minute.' And we knew that it was true."

"Everybody was pissed," said Fingers. "I mean, *everybody* was pissed. We talked about it all the way from Oakland to New York. Everybody got upset. And when we got to New York, we went to bed upset."

The news of Finley's decision broke even before the plane landed. Most of the writers were traveling on the team charter and had to depart the clubhouse along with the players before Andrews emerged from his meeting with the Owner. Only one man, John Lindblom of the *San Jose Mercury News*, a columnist who was not traveling to New York, managed to get the seeds of the story, by chance, from Vida Blue — late as usual — on a ballpark elevator. "I can't believe what I just saw!" Vida proclaimed when Lindblom stepped inside. Lindblom's account was the first to hit the streets.

It had been a seditious night for the A's roster, but players grew even more upset in the morning. One after another, they went downstairs to the lobby of the Americana Hotel and saw the lone set of unclaimed luggage remaining from their late-night check-in. Chained to the bell captain's desk like some unwanted prisoners of war, the three suitcases — ones the second baseman did not rescue from the bus back in Oakland — bore Andrews's name tags for all to see. It wasn't until the media caught wind of it and began to treat the bags like roadside memorial markers that traveling secretary Jim Bank had them moved to a storage room.

By the time the players reached the ballpark for Monday's off-day workout and media session, their anger had settled into something resolute, a hard-pitted fury that threatened to overwhelm the idea of even playing the games. Inside the clubhouse they openly discussed revolt, entertaining the notion of boycotting the World Series until justice was served. Bando spoke, Jackson spoke, even Williams spoke, saying, "This is chickenshit. I just want you to know I'll back you guys whatever you want to do."

When the clubhouse doors were unlocked following the meeting, the national media virtually tumbled into the room. "I never saw so much press in my life," said Holtzman. Among their ranks was Major League Baseball's media liaison, Joe Reichler, who, upon learning of the boycott talk, predictably flipped out. The very possibility of such a scenario was enough to throw every level of the operation — from NBC's telecast all the way up to the Commissioner's office — into a state of panic. Reichler raced around the clubhouse yelling at the players, "Are you nuts? You can't boycott the World Series! You can't just say, 'I'm not going to play.'" He was right, and the players knew it — had already known it — but they sure as hell weren't willing to hear it from a member of baseball's establishment. They ran Reichler from the room.

"This thing is a real embarrassment and a disappointment," said Jackson afterward. "A team is a team. Finley doesn't seem to understand that. He spent yesterday getting his friends and freeloaders on the plane and a player off it. Well, the other players won't stand for it. We won't just take it and shut up. This team has endured a lot of incidents from Finley, but this may be the last straw. I've never seen the mood of the team so mean."

By the time the A's took the field for their workout, many of them bore Andrews's uniform number, 17, on their sleeves, made from athletic tape stuck there by Dick Green. "Remember," the second baseman told a line of players awaiting his services, "if you make an error, you can't go back to Oakland." Green started the taping in jest, but before long players were asking in as a matter of individual protest, their numbers limited only because trainer Joe Romo ran out of tape. Feelings ran particularly hot among the remainder of the team's second-base corps: Green, Ted Kubiak, and Manny Trillo — the guy for whom the entire affair was orchestrated, who was in uniform (pending Bowie Kuhn's decision about allowing him onto the roster) as insurance in case of further injury. There was talk of fabricating black armbands to wear during Game 3 the following night. "The press ate it up," said Fingers. "In New York they love that kind of stuff."

The workout was lackluster, players' focus diffused from late-night travel and too much chatter, their hostility toward Finley undercutting any desire to take wholehearted swings in the cage. With the media stirred into a tumult, they had plenty of opportunities to unburden themselves. Reporters staked out their hotel lobby and took to knocking on doors in a frantic quest for comment. Players did not hold back, their quotes hitting Finley hard. Inside the Owner's operation the only opinions that counted were his own, but now he was in the country's biggest city, on the sport's biggest stage, and much as he wanted to ignore the chorus of dissenting voices, the media simply would not allow it.

So Finley called a midnight press conference in the media room at the Americana, where he laid out his own version of events in a long-winded oratory. He labeled the players' decision to wear Andrews's number 17 on their sleeves "horseshit" and informed the press that the only reason anybody on the roster was upset was because they lacked vital information. Williams would be calling a clubhouse meeting before Tuesday's Game 3, he said, "to give the players all the facts."

As for the infamous "I agree to the above" letter, Finley explained it straightaway, saying, "You must have a letter from the doctor, and Mike Andrews' signature just adds credence." He added that Andrews attempted to horse-trade his complicity in exchange for a contract in 1974, an allegation that Andrews later vehemently denied. The Owner was asked whether the player's shoulder was injured when he signed with the team, and didn't answer. When the question was repeated, he stood up. "Gentlemen," he said curtly, "this press conference has ended."

On Tuesday, Bowie Kuhn took action on two fronts. His first step was to deny the Owner's request to add Trillo to the roster. His second was to order Andrews's immediate reinstatement. The Commissioner sided unequivocally with the players, writing to Finley in a publicly released letter that "the handling of this matter by the Oakland club has had the unfortunate effect of unfairly embarrassing a player who has given many years of able service to professional baseball."

Andrews was at home in Peabody, Massachusetts, when Finley — accurately divining that Andrews would refuse his phone calls — sent him a telegram informing him of the Commissioner's reinstatement and ordering him to New York immediately.* The player, however, was reticent. His name was headline fodder across the country for reasons that shamed him; the last place he wanted to be was back in the spotlight. Before he agreed to anything, Andrews wanted to check in with the only people whose opinions mattered to him. About two and a half hours before Game 3, he called the visitors' clubhouse at Shea Stadium.

First he spoke to Jackson, telling him that he had signed Finley's statement under duress and that Finley had threatened to "destroy" him. He talked to Dick Williams about the tenor of the team, asking how the players felt about both him and the situation at large. He asked Catfish Hunter to pass along his thanks to the club for backing him in so public a fashion.

Jackson told Andrews that the response in the room was not something to worry about, and that "sometimes all of us have to be men and stand up to Finley." Hunter said that the players were on Andrews's side and were counting on welcoming him back. Williams added regret over what had happened. By the time the call ended two things had developed: the players, particularly Jackson, were angrier than ever, and Andrews agreed to return.

He had a caveat, however: he wanted a platform from which to tell his side of the story and assurances that the Owner would not stand in his way. Finley, back pressed firmly against the wall, assented.

It was shortly after Andrews's phone call that Williams, as Finley prom-

---

* Finding Andrews was not easy. Finley said that Andrews's wife, Marilyn, told him that her husband was on a hunting trip someplace in Northern California. (Probably not, countered the rest of the A's — the guy didn't hunt.) Suddenly, it was all hands on deck in Oakland's front office. Even clubhouse assistant Steve Vucinich, left at home while the team was in New York, got a call from Finley's secretary, Carolyn Coffin. "Where do you think Mike Andrews is right now?" she asked. Vucinich knew that Andrews grew up in Southern California, so he found some phone books and, along with Coffin and the small handful of people they could round up at the Coliseum, made calls until the player was tracked down.

ised, called a clubhouse meeting to explain the Owner's side of the issue to the team. Players sat on stools as the manager told them that Finley's action was not personal against Andrews, that he wanted only to stack the roster with the best talent available. The speech was brief and passionless. Williams later called it the hardest thing he'd ever been forced to say, adding that "to give even a quick and superficial account of Charlie's reasons made me feel cheap and dirty." The players saw right through it. Williams told them that he was on their side. Then he said something else — something that nobody expected.

"I get a lot of satisfaction out of this game, because as far as I'm concerned, you guys are one of the greatest teams that ever played," he told the assembly. "And I get a lot of satisfaction being your manager. But I'm not taking this shit anymore." Williams began to get emotional. "This is the hardest thing I've ever done," he said, "but somebody has to stand up to this man, and it's going to be me." With that, he dropped the bombshell: "I'm going to deny this if it leaks out from this room, but I'm resigning at the end of this World Series, win, lose or draw." Then he turned, retreated to his office, and closed the door.

His players were staggered. "It was pure quiet," said Bando, looking back. "It's like, *Really? Why now?*"

Williams would be giving up two years at $70,000 per, more money than he had ever made. His intent was to let his players know that while he loved them, his situation was no longer tolerable. He had their respect; now he wanted their understanding. To a number of men in the room, however, it was the height of selfishness.

"Dick said he didn't really give a shit if we won, that he wasn't coming back to manage the club next year," said Tenace, looking back. "We couldn't believe the manager just jumped ship on us, didn't care if we won or lost. Oh wow, we'd never heard that one before. You don't have to have a meeting and say *that*. He could have said anything but *that*."

Never mind that Williams neither said nor intimated that he didn't care about winning the World Series. Such was the timing of the message amid an already exhausting whorl of emotions that Tenace's interpretation was entirely understandable.

It was a microcosm of the A's most essential fabric, unspooling right there in the visitors' clubhouse at Shea Stadium. Angry players who felt abused, and a manager who could take no more. Hard feelings around the room about the way Williams handled his business. The confusion of sorting out feelings while dealing with a World Series game that was due to begin in less than an hour. Above it all was one constant, something that had tethered the club together through long years of hardship, internecine squabbling, and now postseason distraction: blinding hot hatred for the man at the top, from whose twisted mind every bit of this drama originated. Once again, Finley, despite his best intentions, had kept his team from splintering.

The circumstances were unique, but the dance was familiar. Finley acts, players react, nothing changes. This, though, was different. The Commissioner had stepped in to stifle the Owner's despotic turn, called out the lack of integrity in his scheming. At least Finley could dismiss that much out of hand; Kuhn hated the Owner, after all, just as much as the Owner hated Kuhn. What really got to Finley — maybe not immediately, but inexorably, over time — was the fact that his players, his *people*, turned on him too. Oh, they had always been fond of bitching about him, taking shots at his crackpot ways, and bristling under what even he admitted was a heavy hand. But they had also seen him as something of a benevolent dictator, of this he was certain. He took care of their needs as they arose, showered them with gifts and bonuses and fancy World Series trophies, invested their money for them without thought of taking any for himself. Sure, they complained about things, but they never really *hated* him.

Did they?

This was the point at which everything changed, when Finley, the self-proclaimed man of the people, saw the true surface of the landscape he had created. This was when the guy who thought that sporadic gestures of largesse were sufficient to ensure loyalty and trust — never mind that they always came on his own terms, every time — finally opened his eyes. Finley never banked on his players liking him, but now, finally, he understood that they didn't even respect him. His manager, whom he had showered with faith and bonuses, the only guy he hadn't fired in fewer than two years, the man with whom he had so publicly sided in his dispute with Reggie Jackson only months earlier, had rejected him more overtly than any manager ever rejected an owner. Williams was walking away from what stood to be a two-time championship team *because he couldn't stand the owner*. And everybody knew it. Finley's players lounged about the stadium below him, in the clubhouse and on the field, showering the media with quote after quote, explaining in every way possible not just how wrong the Owner was but how rotten, how down-to-the-core ruined. Not one of them had his back, even now in his diminished, post–heart attack state. Finley had to be escorted everywhere for fear of falling, was frequently in a wheelchair, and had never felt worse. Where was the freaking sympathy?

The Owner finally saw that these weren't his children but his indentured servants, who tolerated his presence only because they had no choice in the matter. It was Tuesday, October 16, and Finley's players — the men he'd brought up from boys — would soon take the field, not to please him and not even to spite him, but to try to scrape the very idea of him from their collective consciousness. Charles Finley had taught himself to thrive on being argued with, but he was entirely unused to being ignored. For the first time since rising from his sickbed at Parramore Sanatorium all those years ago, the Owner felt . . . irrelevant. And he didn't have a single idea what to do about it.

The weather at Shea Stadium for the first nighttime World Series game ever played in New York was biting — 48 degrees with a 20-mile-per-hour wind howling off of Flushing Bay. "If it gets this cold in Puerto Rico," said Felix Milan, "everybody dies." The weather was a trifle, however, compared with what else the A's faced.

It made no difference that Oakland's starting pitcher was Catfish Hunter, the least perturbable man on the staff. In his head, thoughts about Finley, Andrews, and Williams elbowed aside consideration of New York's leadoff hitter, Wayne Garrett. With his second pitch of the game, the right-hander fed a low fastball to a low fastball hitter, and Garrett pummeled it above the auxiliary scoreboard in right field, ten rows into the second deck. The next batter, Milan, stroked a clean single to left. New York's number-three hitter, Rusty Staub, slapped a hit-and-run single through the left side, sending Milan to third. Ten pitches in and Hunter was on the precipice of disaster. Williams visited the mound and tried desperately to calm his pitcher, even as Blue Moon Odom began warming up in the bullpen.

Hunter's second pitch to the next hitter, Cleon Jones, bounced off Fosse's shin guard and into Oakland's dugout, allowing Milan to skip home with the Mets' second run. One out later, John Milner bounced a soft comebacker to the right of the mound, but Catfish — averaging less than an error a season over the previous five years — dropped it. That put runners on first and second with one out and two runs already in.

The Shea Stadium crowd was in a frenzy. "I had a little bit on my mind," Hunter admitted after the game.

From that point on, however, the right-hander let baseball trump both anger and nerves, shutting out New York until being removed for a pinch hitter in the seventh. It was necessary: Mets manager Yogi Berra had reserved Tom Seaver until Game 3 to allow him full rest, and the All-Star didn't disappoint, striking out five straight batters across the first two innings and nine over the first five. "Blind people come to the park to hear him pitch," said an awestruck Reggie Jackson afterward.

Seaver's only early hiccup involved sixth-inning doubles by Bando and Tenace that scored a run and cut New York's lead in half. Still, the right-hander allowed only five hits and struck out 11 through the first seven innings. In the eighth, though, he surrendered a leadoff single to Campaneris, who promptly stole second. Joe Rudi then slapped a single into right field, where Rusty Staub — returned from his NLCS shoulder injury before he had fully healed — could put hardly anything on his throw. Campy scored easily to tie the game, 2–2. That was where it stayed into the 11th, when Mets reliever Harry Parker allowed a run on a walk, a passed ball, and another single from Campaneris. Nobody could figure out how it happened, but despite Seaver's dominance and Oakland's litany of distractions and the fact that the A's were playing with 23 men against New York's 25, Oakland held on for a 3–2 victory and a two-games-to-one series lead.

The postgame clubhouse did not feel victorious. As adrenaline waned, a pall settled over what should have otherwise been a giddy group. "Dissension does it again," sighed Odom.

Down the hall, Berra sat in his office and openly wondered whether the A's system might be worth emulating. "Maybe we could use a good fight now," he quipped. "Could be we're all too happy on this club. Heck, the A's fight just deciding what to eat." Moments later, a newsman raced in. "There's another fight among the A's," he yelped. "Reggie Jackson just told Charlie Finley off. Reggie says the A's win despite Finley." Yogi listened with bemusement. "You know," he said, "it's about time we started a little fuss of our own."

On Wednesday, Andrews's primary condition for returning was met. In a ballroom at the Americana, sitting beside his Boston-based attorney, Harold Meizler, he told a packed-in press corps his version of what went down. He wore the same suit in which he left Oakland on Sunday. He was emotional.

Andrews did not come off like a man with a vendetta. Refusing to paint the Owner in an unusually harsh light, he even went out of his way to soften some of the blows, which lent additional weight to his words.[*] No matter how he phrased it, of course, Andrews's testimony was damning. "Mr. Finley never threatened me," he said. "I never demanded a contract for next year. I figured I'd be finished in baseball if I didn't sign. I figured we didn't need another ballplayer, and the least I could do was sign." By the time he reached the phrase "I'm sorry I signed it," Andrews's eyes were welling with tears and he could talk no more.

The player shuffled quietly up to his room, where he waited until it was time for the bus to leave for Shea Stadium. He had not yet seen his teammates. Andrews and Dick Williams were the first to board, Andrews grabbing a window seat toward the rear. Players greeted him as they got on, some with genuine delight, others with mock indignation. Vida Blue did an exaggerated double-take as he walked by, shouting, "Hey, man, where's my five?" Andrews extended his hand to slap palms with the pitcher, but Vida informed him with a smile that he was talking about a football bet that Andrews had yet to pay off. Darold Knowles joked that it was a shame Andrews came back because "we already voted to split up your Series share between the rest of us." Fosse suggested that, once the team took the field for pregame warm-ups, Andrews throw some balls to the plate from center field and "really stretch out that old shoulder." If needling was how the A's drew each other close, Andrews had never been more a part of the team.

"Seeing him was like an energy," said Bando, looking back. "It's probably like what soldiers feel in combat — he's back, he's okay, it's good." Knowles said that Andrews was "like a hero, like a king, partly because it was great to have him back, partly because it meant that Finley didn't get his way."

The repartee was lighthearted. It felt good. Andrews was actually beginning to enjoy himself as the bus headed east across Manhattan and through the Midtown Tunnel toward Queens . . . right up until it pulled into the Shea Stadium parking lot. Already emotionally drained from his

---

[*] It may even have been part of a broader strategy: Meizler went so far as to refer to Finley's actions as "friendly persuasion."

press conference, he wondered if he could muster the strength to face it all again on an even bigger stage. Andrews stayed in his seat while others disembarked, delaying the inevitable. Catfish stayed with him, and they got off together, the final two, Hunter serving as impromptu bodyguard for his suddenly more famous pal.

When the players took the field for warm-ups, there was only one guy whom everybody wanted to talk to, but Andrews was talked out. He'd said everything he had to say at his press conference. Then a reporter posed a question that the player could not help but answer: "Were those errors your worst moment?"

"No," Andrews sighed. "Signing that piece of paper was."

Game 4 turned out to be what Game 3 should have been: a distraction-filled mess for the A's. During Tuesday's game the players were numb, too struck by the newness of it all to have fully absorbed everything. Now the bewilderment they'd overcome only a day earlier seemed to be all there was.

"None of this baseball stuff really seems too important anymore," Ken Holtzman had said on Tuesday. "It is just very, very hard for me to care about playing in the World Series." On Wednesday he pitched like it. The left-hander's first inning went: single, single, home run (an opposite-field shot by Staub), groundout, walk, single. Three runs in, two runners on, one out in the first inning — and that was it. The lefty had barely broken a sweat when Williams sent him to the showers.

For the A's, the game's primary moment of note came in the top of the eighth, by which point they trailed 6-1. Mike Andrews was in the bullpen warming up relievers when Williams called. The skipper wanted him to bat for the inning's first hitter, pitcher Horacio Pina. There was little strategy behind it. Better options were available, and Williams was under direct orders from Finley to keep the controversial player as far from the field as possible. Which was precisely the point. "He'll probably get fired for this," said somebody in the dugout as Andrews approached the bat rack. By then, of course, it didn't matter — Williams was quitting anyway.

As Andrews emerged from the dugout — the guy wearing a real number 17, not some tape facsimile — his teammates stood and applauded. A moment later, as he made a slow walk to the plate, so did the crowd at Shea. Mets fans held no particular love for Mike Andrews, but they sure as hell hated Charlie Finley by now, and knew exactly what to do when presented an opportunity to express it. The roar started with the fans nearest the dugout and quickly spread as realization settled around the stadium. As Andrews stepped into the batter's box, the nearly 55,000 people around him who jumped to their feet became conspicuous for the few who didn't: alongside the A's dugout the Owner and his traveling party remained seated and stone-faced. As the ovation persisted, Finley — wearing a green blazer, white shirt, bow tie, and, notably, a black hat — lamely flapped his A's pennant over his head in a token show of support for his own team. He never did stand. A number of players peeked out of the dugout to see his reaction. Some of them heard Williams mutter, "Take that, you son of a bitch." After grounding out, Andrews received a second ovation on his return trip to the dugout.

"I played with great players, Hall of Famers, but I have never seen anybody get a standing ovation like that," said Tenace, looking back. "I thought Mickey Mantle was pinch-hitting. I got goose bumps. You're talking about a *reception*." Added Knowles: "I started falling in love with Mets fans."

New York's 6–1 win tied the Series at two games apiece and added ac- tual baseball concerns to Dick Williams's litany of off-field drama, which now included a string of rumors tying the manager to the Yankees. The reports, which had surfaced weeks earlier, had gone largely unnoticed in the heat of the pennant race but found new life when, as Williams guessed it would, news of his resignation leaked almost immediately. As prom- ised, Williams denied it.

More pressingly, the A's — who during the season hit more home runs than all but five teams in baseball — had yet to leave the yard during the World Series. Meanwhile, the Mets, who had finished second to last in that category, 62 behind Oakland, bashed four homers in four games. Williams's starting pitchers were knocked out by the sixth inning three times, including Holtzman's first-inning disaster in Game 4. If a turn- around was to happen, it had to happen fast.

The A's wanted no more drama for Game 5. To make something of this World Series they'd have to pack away their abundant agitation. Then the game began, and not much changed.

New York starter Jerry Koosman shut out Oakland on three hits into the seventh inning, after which Tug McGraw tossed two and two-thirds hitless frames of his own. Vida Blue pitched commendably if unspectacularly, allowing two runs over five and two-thirds innings, a performance that on many nights would have been enough but on this night wasn't even close. The final score was only 2–0, but it felt like a rout. As the A's filtered off the field the Shea Stadium crowd sang a coda to its Game 4 ovation for Andrews: "Goodbye Charlie / Goodbye Charlie / Goodbye Charlie / We hate to see you go."

The A's were a hot mess. They still hadn't homered, and now they'd stopped scoring altogether, held to eight hits and one run over their previous 18 innings. The same things Cincinnati had said a year earlier about Oakland were now applicable to New York: the Mets' pitching was spectacular, their offense was just good enough, and their defenders were consistently positioned wherever the A's hit the ball. Shortstop Bud Harrelson's glovework was so robust that Gene Tenace wondered whether New York was fielding two players at his position. "I wondered why the third-base coach was counting every time we took the field," quipped Harrelson in response.

The Mets needed to win only one of the two remaining games in Oakland, and Yogi Berra had his pitchers lined up perfectly. George Stone — a 26-year-old left-hander who went 12-3 on the season with a second-on-the-Mets 2.80 ERA — was primed for Game 6, setting up a fully rested Tom Seaver for Game 7, if it came to that. Dick Williams tried to comfort himself with the recollection that back in 1952 his Brooklyn Dodgers held a 3-games-to-2 lead over the Yankees, then lost two straight. Comebacks were possible. But those Dodgers did not have anybody like Tom Seaver to protect them.

The A's arrived at the Coliseum on Saturday morning, however, to some unexpected news: Stone was being bypassed in Game 6 in favor of Seaver on short rest. Second-guessers were ready to pounce no matter which move Berra made, but his decision both confounded and delighted Williams. Seaver had gone 13-6 with a 1.86 ERA during the regular season when granted his usual four days between starts, but was just 2-4, with an ERA a point and a half higher, at all other times. "Yogi played right into our hands," enthused the manager when he heard the news. It may have seemed like an odd stance considering that Williams's own starter, Catfish Hunter, was also working on three days' rest, but unlike Seaver, Hunter pitched in a four-man rotation.

The move looked bad for Berra from the outset. Oakland's second batter of the game, Joe Rudi, slapped an opposite-field single and one out later raced home on a double by Reggie Jackson for the A's first lead since Game 3. It was only the start for Reggie. While a slightly diminished Seaver proved more than capable of handling most of Oakland's lineup, in a determinant of greatness he was no match for Jackson, who doubled again in the third, scoring Bando for a 2–0 lead.

Hunter, Darold Knowles, and Rollie Fingers held the Mets to six hits and one run, making superfluous Jackson's third hit of the game, an eighth-inning single off of Tug McGraw. Shortly thereafter, Reggie scored the final run in Oakland's 3–1 victory, courtesy of a Jesus Alou sacrifice fly. Game 7 would be played the following day.

Afterward, clubhouse conversation turned to Seaver, who had pitched admirably with what everybody agreed was not anything close to his best stuff. Rudi talked about the right-hander's limited curveball. Bando said that Seaver had thrown harder at Shea. Reggie made it poetic, intoning that "he was Tom Seaver today only in heart and fortitude." Already people were shouting about how Berra should have held his ace another day, the better to complement his heart and fortitude with a fully rested right arm. Now Jon Matlack—in the middle of an astounding run of 26 straight innings without surrendering an earned run, but who himself would be pitching on short rest—was all that prevented the A's from becoming the first team in the 70-year history of the World Series to win two straight Game 7s.

Matching up against Matlack in Sunday's finale was Ken Holtzman, who, after being blasted out of the first inning in Game 4, had plenty in his tank. In bright sunshine at the Coliseum following a night of rain, the left-hander took care of business early, setting down the Mets in order over each of the first three frames. He also continued his one-man protest against the DH, slicing a third-inning double—his second two-bagger in as many Series at-bats—down the left-field line. Campaneris pounded Matlack's very next pitch, a curveball that came in flat, over the wall in right field. It took 52 innings and a guy who had gone deep only four times during the regular season, but the A's finally had their first World Series homer, and a 2–0 lead.

Oakland wasn't finished. After Rudi singled, Bando popped up for the inning's second out, bringing Jackson to the plate. People mostly attributed Reggie's slow start in the playoffs—he went 3-for-21 against Baltimore, then struggled through three of the first four World Series games—to a late-season hamstring twinge. Few knew the rest of the story, which had started back in September when Reggie received the team's second death threat in as many seasons. A group calling itself "The Weathermen" — whether they were connected with the outfit of the same name that had been tied to numerous assassinations was unclear — portended via a letter sent to broadcaster Monte Moore that any postseason appearance by the outfielder would be the last thing he ever did. "The kook said he had a high-powered rifle with a long-range sight, and he'd pop me from the stands," Jackson said later. In addition to the FBI agents assigned to shadow him, Reggie enlisted one of his largest friends, six-foot-five, 290-pound auto restorer Tony Del Rio, to serve as his bodyguard.

Death threat or no, hamstring or no, slump or no, Reggie was feeling it. He hit Matlack's first pitch, another hanging curve, so hard that he didn't hesitate after contact, not so much dropping his bat as flinging it underhand at the plate. The ball disappeared some 25 feet beyond the 375-foot marker in right-center field, and Reggie literally skipped with joy as he rounded the bases, hands clapping out a celebratory rhythm. Upon reaching the plate he leaped high into the air, drawing knees to chest before landing with a two-footed stomp. The A's were up, 4–0, and Berra had little choice but to remove his beleaguered starter. "You can't expect to have any kind of fastball with only three days' rest," said a disconsolate Matlack afterward.

With that, Holtzman set his jaw and began to throw as hard as he could, confident that his bullpen would back him up when he ran out of gas. Williams agreed; the moment that Holtzman faltered, giving up back-to-back doubles in the sixth for New York's first run, the manager called for Fingers, who got out of the inning and then breezed through the seventh and eighth.

By the ninth inning, Oakland led 5–1 and appeared to have things fully in hand, even after New York scored a run and put runners at the corners with two outs. That was when pinch-hitter Ed Kranepool hit what should have been a Series-ending grounder to first, but Tenace, ready to celebrate, kicked it. Milner scored on the error, making it 5–2 and bringing up the lefty-swinging Wayne Garrett, second on the Mets with 16 home runs during the season, as the tying run. Garrett was also the 16th batter that Fingers — who by that point led the staff in World Series innings — had faced. So Williams brought in southpaw Darold Knowles, making him the first pitcher to appear seven times in a World Series. Knowles hardly cherished the distinction. "I didn't want to come in at all," he confessed afterward. "My knees were shaking in the bullpen as it was."

In right field, a fan jumped onto the outfield grass and grabbed Jackson's cap. When Reggie dropped his glove and gave chase, another fan scrambled from the bleachers and tried to make off with *that*. Jackson corralled both items with the help of umpire Harry Wendelstedt, but he wasn't the only one chasing headwear. Knowles's hat had been stolen minutes earlier in the bullpen by fans prematurely storming the field when Kranepool's grounder found its way to Tenace for the presumptive final out. With few options available when he was called into the game, the lefty grabbed the one from Hunter's head — never mind that Knowles wore a $7^5/_8$ and Hunter a $7^1/_4$. The thing was green and had an "A" on it, and Knowles pulled it tight.

Garrett flared the reliever's second pitch into short left field, an easy play for the backpedaling Campaneris, and the A's became baseball's first back-to-back champions since the New York Yankees of 1961–1962.

As players dogpiled Knowles atop the mound, fans stormed the field by the thousands in a reprisal of the team's playoff victory over Baltimore. Somebody swiped Knowles's backup cap, while four others jumped Holtzman, one of their fists connecting with his nose. The lefty returned fire, knocking one of them backward far enough to create an opening through which to escape. (Holtzman insisted afterward on getting credit for two hits on the day: one double and one fan.) Reggie avoided similar treatment thanks to the presence of Del Rio, who beat the rush of fans and literally carried the giddy player off the field.

The crowd demolished the diamond, stealing bases, flattening the mound, and ransacking the dugouts. Inside the clubhouse, the mass of media members, hangers-on, and party crashers pushed players against walls and into lockers. Every reporter wanted to know the same things. Either of the week's primary story lines — the Andrews situation and Williams's resignation — would have rated among the greatest distractions in World Series history, and the A's managed to overcome them both. How did it happen? How was it sitting? What did it all mean?

As questions flew, more news came down: based almost entirely on his performance during Games 6 and 7, *The Sporting News* named Jackson the World Series MVP. It was surprising inasmuch as Campaneris had been the odds-on favorite when the team left New York, and then went 3-for-8 with a homer, two RBIs, and two runs scored over the final two games. But putting Reggie in the spotlight guaranteed good copy, something the taciturn, Spanish-speaking Campaneris could not provide.

True to his reputation, Jackson entertained the largest scrum of reporters in the victorious clubhouse. He was giddy under the spotlight, but his mood visibly changed when Finley sidled up. "Thanks for all you did for the club," the Owner said, partly to Reggie and partly to the rolling cameras. Jackson looked at him blankly and offered no response. After a moment the player turned back to the press and asked, "Now where were we?"

Finley moved on to Hunter, who reminded him of his promise to outshine the previous season's rings, enthusing that "I'm looking for a great big diamond in the middle of mine this year." Finley turned toward reporters and took credit for the pitcher's success. "I'm standing next to the finest young man I know," he said. "We signed him when nobody else would because he had happened to get shot." It was a compliment, anyway, which Hunter appreciated. But the pitcher was serious about those rings.

Flying champagne lent trappings of celebration to the room, but the ennui was palpable, coating much of the joy that had driven the team's festivities a year earlier. When a reporter asked Jackson how much credit should go to Finley, he snapped, "Please don't give that man the credit. . . . He spoiled what should have been a beautiful thing." Reggie took a swig of champagne and spat it out, calling it lousy, cheap, and typical of the Owner. When Yogi Berra walked in minutes later to offer congratulations, he could hardly believe it, saying, "This doesn't look like a winning dressing room to me."

This was where Dick Williams made things official. He was so disgusted by Finley that he didn't even celebrate with the team on the field, instead offering a couple of perfunctory claps at the final out, then turning toward the clubhouse while everybody raced in the opposite direction. A year earlier Williams had kissed his wife alongside Charlie and Shirley Finley, but now the thought of elation from the Owner's box repulsed him. Williams's connection to the team had been severed, his ability to tap into the joy of his players all but vanished. He realized that regardless of everything the A's did to spite Finley, they had in fact done just the opposite. The Owner wasn't defeated. Thanks to Williams's own efforts and those of his players, Finley *won*. The manager grimaced.

Williams met with reporters in a hallway alongside the clubhouse and confirmed his open secret: he had managed his last game for the A's. When questions came up about the Yankees job, the manager stressed that he was now unemployed, with his only plan being to travel home to Riviera Beach, Florida. With TV cameras rolling, he took care to stay positive, spinning things so far as to appear suspicious. "This is a great day for me, but also a sad day," he said, "because I am leaving the A's for personal reasons, and not out of any dissatisfaction over my relations with Mr. Finley." Because Finley knew no other way, he jumped into the frame and hugged Williams. "You are a great manager and I will not stand in your way," he proclaimed. Soon Reggie was there too, grabbing Williams and speaking into the microphone. "I'm sorry, I'm sorry, I'm sorry," he said to the manager with whom he'd feuded more than any other. "I hate to see him go, but I understand." Responded Williams: "I am, too, Reggie, I really am."

All too aware of Finley's vindictive nature, Williams did everything he could to stay on the man's good side. He was still under contract and knew how difficult the Owner could be. Now, though, Finley had given his word—on national television no less—to avoid hindering his manager's future opportunities. Finley offered similar sentiments to assorted sportswriters around the room, saying things like, "I won't stand in his way if the Yankees approach me and ask for permission to talk to Dick Williams," and, "There's a certain amount of glamour to working in New York. Maybe this interests him." The manager was optimistic.[*]

After the trophy presentation, Williams visited the interview room, where he continued to heap praise upon Finley. He described their relationship as "exemplary," saying, "I have great regard for Charlie." As if to make sure sufficient tail was kissed, Williams went so far as to praise the Owner for his part in the Mike Andrews saga, noting that he was only trying to help the team. "Mike and I are very, very close friends,"

---

[*] "I would love to manage the Yankees if they'll have me," Williams said in the early going, "but I can honestly say that I haven't contacted anybody, and nobody's contacted me." That was technically true, but it didn't mean the parties were bereft of communication. Nat Tarnopol, the president of Brunswick Records—an R&B label best known for its work with singer Jackie Wilson—was a huge Yankees fan, with season tickets alongside the team's home dugout. He'd befriended Williams some years earlier (as he befriended many people in the game), going so far as to name the manager an honorary VP at Brunswick. When Yankees GM Gabe Paul wanted to reach out to Williams without violating tampering rules, Tarnopol was his guy. The record exec allowed the Yankees to maintain official distance, even while a mutual understanding was reached.

Williams said. "Mr. Finley and I are very, very close friends. The timing was just poor." His rationale for leaving, he explained, was to spend more time with his family, because he wanted to one day manage a team closer to home.

Finley's claims of ignorance about Williams's rumored departure were believable. The Owner's illness and the relentless turmoil surrounding Andrews had been enough to draw the entirety of his attention. Finley heard the gossip, of course, just like everybody else, but because the manager had not approached him directly, he had not paid it much heed. Williams's confirmation that it was true struck Finley numb. It was his farm director, John Claiborne, who woke him from his reverie, reminding him that Williams's contract, which ran through the 1975 season, made the manager a tangible commodity. If Williams was to work in baseball, it would either be for the A's or because Finley allowed it someplace else. Claiborne figured that the Owner's permission was worth something, and that the Yankees would agree. The two talked it over while walking back to the office from Finley's favorite fish market in downtown Chicago. The Owner, who in the glow of victory had so giddily proclaimed benevolence toward his manager, swallowed the idea whole.

The World Series ended on a Sunday. By Tuesday Finley was saying, "If anybody gets Williams from me he will have to pay through the nose." When Yankees GM Gabe Paul officially asked Finley's consent to speak to the manager, the Owner was touched. "It was the first time anyone asked my permission," he said. Then he turned him down.

Finley approached Sparky Anderson about jumping the Reds for the post in Oakland and was refuted. When the Orioles wouldn't let him talk to Earl Weaver, his resolve grew even stouter. "I never said I would not stand in the way of Williams going to manage another team," the Owner rationalized. "I said I would not stand in his way if he wanted to leave *our* team." He fabricated moral high ground about how he had never stolen another club's employee and concocted story lines about how his own hard work and emotional outlay were instrumental in Williams's development as a manager. If somebody else was to profit from Charlie Finley's investment, Charlie Finley said, then Charlie Finley should be compensated. He threatened a lawsuit if George Steinbrenner tried to sign Williams without permission.

He also said that he'd prefer to keep Williams, regardless of the manager's feelings about the situation. "Would I want a manager working for me who doesn't want to work for me?" the Owner asked. "That wouldn't bother me a bit."

Over the coming weeks he would use that detail to his great advantage.

Following Game 7, the A's held a victory celebration in an upper room at Vince's restaurant, just down the road from the Coliseum. Bando arranged it, inviting players and their wives to collectively appreciate their accomplishments and gain some perspective away from the usual distractions. No media to keep them on their toes, no drama on high from the Coliseum's executive suite. This was the A's at their most casual, goals fulfilled and free of expectations save for having a good time. Which they did, right up until Campaneris grabbed a table knife and went after Reggie.

As best as anyone could tell, the shortstop's bitterness over Jackson being awarded the World Series MVP was not constrained to the ballpark. The two never actually came into contact; Bando grabbed Campaneris, and Jackson remained unstabbed. Because no media was there to document it, the incident was quickly lost amid the annals of team drama. What really could be said? This, apparently, was how the A's relaxed.

22

Wherefore Williamʃ?

And Vida Blue and Blue Moon Odom always thought it was
them.

—Dick Williams, on Charlie Finley driving him to George Steinbrenner

Charles Finley spent the autumn of 1973 engaged in a game of player
roulette over long-distance phone lines to New York, using the Yankees
roster as chits. He wasn't crazy enough to think that any of his sky-high
proposals for relinquishing Dick Williams would fly, but the manager was
gone from the A's either way and the Owner had little to lose. In addition to cash, Finley started ticking off players for whom he would con-
cede Williams's contract, starting with New York's best, catcher Thurman
Munson. When the Yankees shot that idea down, the Owner proposed
All-Star outfielder Bobby Murcer instead.

New York GM Gabe Paul, meanwhile, was wondering about the eq-
uity of the system. He had lost his own manager on the season's final day
when Ralph Houk jumped ship to take over operations in Detroit. Like
Williams, Houk was under contract. If the Tigers could get their guy, why
couldn't he?* By this point, Williams had already agreed on terms with
the Yankees—a three-year deal for $90,000 per (down from $100,000,
owing to the possibility of court costs should Finley sue), and the only
thing standing in the way was an intransigent lout in a green blazer.

The two sides met during baseball's winter meetings at the Astro-
World Hotel in Houston. There Finley offered to relinquish Williams in

---

* Houk's move was ultimately allowed by league president Joe Cronin because New York never
lodged a formal objection to his departure.

exchange for Scott McGregor and Otto Velez, two of New York's most prized prospects. Paul rejected him outright, countering with washed-up second baseman Horace Clarke. Finley came back with McGregor *or* Velez, plus cash or another player. At times the Owner seemed to be in it primarily for the sporting nature of the process. Again New York demurred, offering $150,000 and a jumble of lesser players. "You can't play cash," reasoned the Owner in turning them down.

For a while, the Yankees kept a responsible distance from Williams. As Finley dragged things out, however, New York officials decided to expedite the process. In mid-December, notifying neither the A's nor the league office, they staged an extravagant press conference at their temporary headquarters at Shea Stadium. Beside a lavish shrimp buffet (cost: $1 per crustacean) they introduced Williams as their manager for 1974. By New York's estimation, Finley had, on the occasion of Oakland's Game 7 victory, repeatedly and publicly allowed Williams to leave his employ. "We have waited long enough," said Paul in a statement released by the team. "To wait further would jeopardize the Yankees' chances of success in 1974, and therefore would be unfair to our fans." With that, the GM fairly well dared Finley to act. It would have taken far less provocation.

That same day Finley filed suit in U.S. District Court in San Francisco to prevent Williams from managing any team but Oakland's for the two years remaining on his contract. In his claim, the Owner lavished praise upon Williams the likes of which he never would have uttered had the manager stuck around. Subverting his familiar I-built-him theme, Finley claimed that the A's success on the field and at the gate was due to Williams's "record of achievement, the style of play he has instilled in his teams, the level of performance he has developed from team personnel, his personal skills, and his popularity with baseball fans." He detailed how Williams's "special, exceptional, and unique" abilities would be detrimental to the team were they shared with a competitor. Most of all, he said, the manager's departure would result in "incalculable loss of revenue and goodwill." Never before (and never again) would the Owner not only share the credit for his team's success in such a manner but cede it entirely to one of his subordinates.

It worked. American League president Joe Cronin, no fan of this kind of politicking, had purposely been dragging his feet. His retirement was slated for December 31, less than two weeks away, and he was actively ignoring Bowie Kuhn's implorations to act, preferring instead to pass the whole mess off to his successor, Lee MacPhail. New York's decision to hire Williams, however, forced his hand.* On December 20, Cronin agreed with the Owner on all counts, dismissing the Yankees' claims that Finley's repeated public proclamations about not standing in Williams's way were proof of intent. "A man can't divorce his wife by making such a statement on television," he theorized. "He must go through the judicial process."

On January 3, 1974, the Yankees gave up and hired Bill Virdon as manager. (The announcement did not include a shrimp buffet.) Williams was stuck. Many wondered why he didn't just show up at A's camp, do something egregious, get fired, and move on with his career. The answer carried no flourishes; Williams simply could not tolerate the thought of putting his future into Finley's hands for even another minute. "I can get up tomorrow and look myself in the face when I shave," he said, so angry at this point as to avoid calling Finley by name, "and I don't think the man in Chicago can."

On January 10, at a press conference at the Colonnade Hotel in Williams's hometown of Riviera Beach, he announced that he had accepted a position as an assistant to his friend and neighbor, 76-year-old Florida billionaire John D. MacArthur. The deal was perfect: Williams would promote MacArthur's business interests while earning more money than Finley had paid him. When a suitable baseball position became available, MacArthur said, Williams was free to leave.

Williams even went so far as to retain celebrity attorney Edward Bennett Williams in a countersuit to Finley, but in February, U.S. District Court Judge Lloyd Burke ruled in the Owner's favor. Williams's decision to opt out of his contract, Burke said, "constitutes breaches, both actual and anticipatory." When Kuhn ruled that the Yankees could not pay Williams's legal fees, the manager aborted his plans to take the fight to court.

---

* The Yankees did themselves no favors. MacPhail had spent eight years as New York's general manager prior to Gabe Paul, and many years before that as a team executive. His father, Lee, had been part owner of the franchise. MacPhail said later that had Paul not jumped the gun with Williams's contract — had the decision been MacPhail's to make instead of Cronin's — Williams would have ended up managing the Yankees. Key to Cronin's decision was a precedent set in 1935, when the Senators received a quarter-million dollars from the Red Sox in exchange for their manager — Joe Cronin.

For the next two years his employment in baseball would be on the Owner's terms or not at all.

On October 26, five days after Oakland won the World Series, Bowie Kuhn fined Finley $7,000. The first $5,000, he said, was for the Owner's bungling of the Andrews affair. Another $1,000 was for announcing over the ballpark PA, against direct orders, that the Mets refused to allow Manny Trillo onto the postseason roster. The final $1,000 was for turning on the stadium lights during Game 2. Kuhn took the additional step of placing Finley on probation, with a warning that "further conduct not in the best interest of baseball may lead to disciplinary action against you as provided in Article 1 of the major-league agreement." This was the nuclear option. Article 1 allowed the Commissioner to remove any officer from any team should it be in baseball's best interests to do so, and nobody appreciated that particular turn of phrase more than Bowie Kuhn.

Finley remained uncowed, filing suit against Kuhn a month later regarding the Andrews incident. "The Commissioner is saying Finley is lying, the doctor is lying, and I am God looking down from my baseball heaven," he said. "I like to feel that right is right and wrong is wrong, and no one, even the Commissioner, can deal with you unfairly."* The Owner was limited physically, which made him angry. He had written a string of checks to Bowie Kuhn to cover fines he felt were unjust, which made him angry. He had been branded as a villain for his handling of Andrews, his own players had slagged him to the press, and his manager had run away from the best team in baseball.

The more Finley thought about it the angrier he got. His temper finally got the best of him at December's winter meetings in Houston, where outside his room at the AstroWorld he physically assaulted *San Jose Mercury News* reporter Jim Street. Street and Ron Bergman of the *Oakland Tribune* were there for a prearranged interview but had to wait several

---

* After the season Finley sent a registered letter to Andrews, per MLB policy, informing him of his unconditional release. Then he announced that the player could be had by any club for one dollar. Nobody bit. The standing ovation that Andrews received at Shea Stadium would be the coda to his major league career. He spent a year selling tires, then played the 1975 season in Japan. "I live with it every day, the jokes, the little rips," he said at the time. "No one ever tells me, 'You were a hell of a ballplayer.' I've been to a few banquets, and every time they introduce me they make jokes about the errors. When they pass me the bread, they say hand it to Andrews or else he might drop it."

long minutes before the Owner—wearing a knee-length raincoat and no pants—finally answered his door. "Why are you bothering me?" he screamed. "I'm sleeping! I'm a sick man!" The frenetic burst of energy inspired Bergman to instinctively retreat into the hallway, but Street was too slow. Finley swiped at the newsman's face, his fingernails opening cuts in three places. Perhaps he was disoriented after being awoken. He could have been thrown off kilter by medication for his heart condition, or by the painkillers he'd taken after suffering two cracked ribs in a recent fall.

Still, the realization of what he'd done seemed to snap the Owner out of his fugue state. Haltingly, he invited Street and Bergman inside, fetched a washcloth, and tended to Street's wounds, offering apologies all the while. Then he sat for a 45-minute interview. Afterward, Finley implored Street not to write about what had happened, mentioning that he was already under pressure from the Commissioner to avoid trouble. When Kuhn first put him on probation, the Owner publicly excoriated the vagueness of the term, but now he acted as if he knew precisely what was in store and wanted no part of it. Street never did report it, but Finley didn't speak to him for a month anyway.

Such abuse was not uncommon in the Owner's world. Only days earlier, Street got a preview of what was in store when he called Finley to ask about progress in negotiations with the Yankees regarding Dick Williams. Finley was in no mood. Street asked if the A's would have a manager soon. "None of your fucking business," the Owner told him.

Has the list of candidates been narrowed?

"None of your fucking business."

What kind of compensation are you seeking from New York?

"None of your fucking business."

Any possible trades on the horizon?

"None of your fucking business."

Here's a simple one, Charlie: are you going to the winter meetings in Houston?

"None of your fucking business."

Click.

The Owner never got physical with his players, but tales abound of him shoving subordinates. When Shirley Finley showed up on the team plane for the return flight to Oakland following the 1973 World Series, she sported oversized sunglasses—the better, said multiple eyewitnesses, to hide blackened eyes. Reports pegged the Owner as having slapped her around as far back as his TB sickbed at Parramore Sanatorium, with one nurse recalling the imprint of his hand on her face. Police were called to the farm in La Porte on several occasions, always for the same reason, said one local patrolman: "Him and her."

Rumor had it that by the time the calendar turned to 1974, Shirley Finley had hired a bodyguard to protect herself from her husband. Within months she filed for divorce. This was devastating to the Owner in numerous ways, but there was no mistaking that the world he built around himself, already focused on satisfying the needs of Charles O. Finley, would only become more self-centered — sometimes for better, and frequently for worse.

12

Another Run

Does not nature itself teach you that for a man to wear long hair is degrading to him?

—1 Corinthians 11:14

With February came chaos in Oakland. Spring training was only weeks away and the A's still had no manager. They also had neither radio nor TV affiliates to air their games. Charlie Finley was dealing with IRS claims that he owed nearly $550,000 in back taxes from the 1960s. There was fallout from the Mike Andrews and Dick Williams situations. Through it all the Owner was working at such diminished capacity following his heart attack that his doctors advised him to get out of sports altogether.

For Finley, it amounted to little more than surface tension. By far the biggest procedural item with which he had to contend was the implementation of salary arbitration in baseball, a structural revolution that would soon rock the sport to its core. At first Finley appeared to be the only owner to recognize this possibility, but as baseball's resident maverick he was accustomed to being dismissed by his colleagues. He would also become the first among them to see the ruination of his franchise as a result.

Arbitration came about in the wake of the 1972 strike, a response to Players Association executive director Marvin Miller's threat to go after the reserve clause — ownership's magic wand, which bound player to team for life (or until the team decided otherwise). Owners, fearful of a full-fledged push toward free agency, embraced arbitration as a compromise measure that would maintain the bulk of their existing leverage. Within the new system, any player with sufficient tenure who had not come to terms with his club could take his case to an outside mediator. The player would submit a salary figure, as would ownership. Each side could then present arguments about why its number was appropriate, with the presiding officer picking one without possibility of compromise. The decision was binding.

The owners liked it for two primary reasons. It solved the ongoing issue of player holdouts, making obsolete the type of months-long battle that cost Vida Blue the early months of the 1972 season. It would also stifle the increasingly emphatic noise coming from Miller.

By and large, owners had been fair with the salaries they handed out — the biggest of which were by then well into six figures — and so didn't feel that the opinion of an outsider would change much. They figured that while players would win some of the battles, they would lose just as many and the overall salary structure would be largely unaffected. Players liked it because finally, for the first time in the sport's history, somebody other than team owners would have a say in the way things played out contractually. Finley, never shy when it came to voicing his opinion, was among the proposition's loudest detractors. "We will be the nation's biggest assholes if we do this," he proclaimed. "You can't win. You will have guys with no baseball background setting salaries. You will have a system that drives up the average salary every year. Give them anything they want, but don't give them arbitration." Now, instead of unilaterally dictating terms each December, Finley would have to hold his nose and allow somebody else, somebody who didn't know his team — somebody who didn't know a goddamn thing about the Oakland A's — to have a say in how much he paid his employees. Despite the Owner's near-desperate efforts to drum up opposition to the proposal, it passed 22–2.[*]

Overlooked by owners was that arbitration finally brought ballplayer salaries into the open, providing a league-wide point of comparison. A's players had long guessed they were not receiving market value for their services, but they had no idea just how underpaid they actually were. "We learned that, wait a minute, these players on other teams were making two and three times what we were making, even though we were the best team and had similar statistics," said Ken Holtzman, exaggerating only a little. "Shit, that was eye-opening."

Better than that, as far as Miller was concerned, was that the system was not a step away from free agency — in which anybody playing out

---

[*] One vote was Finley's own. The other came from St. Louis's Dick Meyer.

his contract could make himself available to the highest bidder — but the first step toward it.

The initial hearings had been slated to take place in Los Angeles, with ensuing dates in Chicago and New York. The 11 participating A's players, however (three of whom settled with Finley beforehand), dwarfed the combined number of Dodgers and Angels, so the litigious mountain was brought to Mohammed. On February 12, at the Palace Hotel in San Francisco, things got underway.

The leadoff hitter in the opening frame of the process was Holtzman, and the drama began before the hearing room even opened. That morning's *San Francisco Chronicle* contained a story, bylined by Bob Stevens, in which Holtzman said that Finley "can go bleep himself," called him a "cheap son of a bitch," discounted Marvin Miller as "a phony," refuted the merits of the arbitration process as a whole, and went so far as to agitate for a trade to the last-place Rangers. If Finley wanted evidence of intransigence or emotional instability to back up his arguments against the pitcher, the area's biggest newspaper handed it to him on a platter.

The trouble for Holtzman and the *Chronicle* both was that the pitcher had said none of those things.

Stevens was the dean of Bay Area sportswriters, having started with the *Chronicle* in 1936, and the mistake was not his. It was made by reporter Jack Fiske, who after Stevens clocked out for the night tried to contact Holtzman for an additional quote for his colleague's story. Fiske found what he believed to be the pitcher's phone number on a scrap of paper atop Stevens's desk, but it actually belonged to Wells Twombly, a columnist for the rival *San Francisco Examiner*. When Twombly received a call from the *Chronicle* for Holtzman, he simply went along with what he presumed to be a gag (even though he never explained why he called his own news desk afterward and warned them against picking up the story the *Chronicle* was about to run).

Holtzman was livid when the paper hit the streets. He wanted to avoid unduly antagonizing Finley on the day of his historic hearing, and even more importantly he wanted to avoid antagonizing the arbitrator, Los Angeles attorney Howard S. Block. The pitcher went so far as to call a press conference across the hall from the arbitration room at the Palace Hotel, where, with the Owner in attendance, he debunked every aspect of the account. "Even if they're completely innocent," he said of the *Chronicle* reporters, "the best they could be is dumb." The following day's paper carried the Peace-in-Europe-sized, eight-column headline: "Holtzman Story Erroneous." By that time, of course, the hearing was already underway.

Holtzman was asking for $93,000, up from the $55,000 he earned in 1973. Finley, who would have laughed the proposal out of his office had the decision been up to him, countered with $80,000. The Owner had been thinking about the showdown for some time, going so far as to tell Holtzman after his stellar performance in Game 3 of that fall's ALCS, "I bet you mention this game in your arbitration hearing."

To help with the process, the pitcher enlisted agent Jerry Kapstein, who was already representing Rollie Fingers and Darold Knowles.* Only two years earlier, Charlie Finley had gone into near-hysterics when Vida Blue showed up with a lawyer, but from the moment Kapstein took the floor it was clear that this was what doing business now looked like.

The agent arrived at the hearings laden with statistics. Finley represented himself, relying primarily on the conversational acumen that brought him success as a salesman. Eschewing notes, the Owner offered slow, thoughtful statements, stretching out his points while pacing the floor, hands clasped behind his back like a trial attorney. His tone was casual, many of his musings theoretical. Holtzman, he said in one extended riff, was indebted to Finley for acquiring him, lest he still be toiling in the second division with the Cubs. "Now, Mr. Arbitrator, let me tell you something," the Owner added in another line of attack. "The only reason that he was so successful is because I've got the best relief pitcher in baseball saving these guys. Rollie Fingers is the only reason this man was so good."

It was an ironic claim, given that Fingers's hearing followed Holtzman's, and was where the Owner argued, in front of the same arbitrator, in precisely the opposite direction. "Mr. Arbitrator," he said, "Fingers here is a good enough reliever, but you must not be misled by all the saves he had. Without the great staff of starting pitchers I have, who day after day keep the runs scored against us down so that we remain ahead in the late innings, Mr. Fingers' saves total would be quite modest." Finley never mentioned how short he expected Block's memory to be.

"Charlie just tried to downgrade you," said Fingers. "He told Rudi,

---

* Before catching on to represent a number of players around the league, Kapstein, 30, had reached out to Bando, on the basis that the third baseman went to grade school with Kapstein's wife. Bando turned down his overture. Such was the landscape of baseball representation in 1974.

'Look, Vida is on the front page of this magazine, and you're on the back page.' That was actually one of his arguments. He would just think of anything he could to belittle you."

Kapstein helped all three of his clients — Holtzman, Fingers, and Knowles — win their cases, but players with less astute representation did not fare as well. Bando, Tenace, and Kubiak were represented by Oakland attorney Wayne Hooper, while Rudi enlisted a lawyer in his family. Neither counselor had experience with sports law. Finley, meanwhile, continued to counter his own arguments, alternately positing that Bando's good numbers in the field were due to Tenace's outstanding glovework at first base, and that the only thing making Tenace look halfway competent in the field was the great defense around him. "I had tears in my eyes," said Tenace. "Finley wore me out talking about all the things I couldn't do. I wanted to strangle him as he stood there, lying."

"Finley actually told the arbitrator that I didn't belong in the big leagues because I couldn't hit, I couldn't field, and, if it wasn't for him, I wouldn't be there at all," said Kubiak. "I was sitting right there, fuming. We went outside after it was over, and he came over and put his arm around my shoulder and said, 'Don't believe anything I said. It's just business.' He gave me a watch and something for my wife, and then said, 'I'll see you in a couple weeks, in spring training.' What was I going to say?"

Bando won his bid for $100,000. Rudi, Tenace, and Kubiak all lost.

The most newsworthy case was Jackson's. Since season's end, Reggie had added the regular-season MVP Award (based on his .293 batting average, 32 homers, and 117 RBIs) to his World Series MVP and was asking for $135,000 — nearly double the $75,000 he made in 1973. Finley's $100,000 counter virtually guaranteed Reggie victory, since Bando had already won $100,000 and Jackson was unequivocally the better player. Reggie came prepared with a package of stats and charts illustrating his importance to both team and sport. His reps procured endorsement letters from the likes of Frank Robinson and Jim Palmer. Dave Duncan was flown in for an in-person testimonial. Jackson contacted a passel of recent MVPs and found out what the award had been worth to them in terms of raises. Most beneficial of all, Reggie talked Marvin Miller into helping argue his case.

It was a direct counter to the preparations undertaken by the Owner, who, as always, relied more on his own ability to persuade than facts or figures.

"Mr. Reggie Jackson and his representative maintain that he deserves this princely salary," Finley told the room in a characteristic piece of discourse, "because he is" . . . pause for effect . . . "a superstar." He followed the pronouncement with a question: "Gentlemen, I ask you: What is a superstar?" It was the Owner at his most ludicrous, trying to counter the indisputable fact that Jackson was not only the best player on the two-time defending champions but, as evidenced by the recent MVP vote, the best player in the American League. The only reason Reggie was so honored, Finley argued, was that it had been a down year and "they had to give it to somebody." He called Jackson's season the worst of any MVP ever, but failed to show how that might be. He labeled Reggie a troublemaker and a slouch who never reached his potential. He went into detail about the player's injury history, never mind that Finley himself hadn't let Jackson return from the DL in a timely fashion earlier that very season. He offered that the biggest factor in Reggie Jackson's success was Charles O. Finley.

Miller's job had never been easier. He didn't even respond to the allegations, instead noting that in baseball the best players on the best teams always receive the highest salaries — *always* — so what did it say that these A's, at baseball's pinnacle, had the league's second-to-lowest payroll? As part of Finley's what-is-a-superstar routine, he had tried to unfavorably compare Jackson to some of the game's legends: "Babe Ruth" . . . pause . . . "was a superstar. Ty Cobb" . . . pause . . . "was a superstar. Mickey Mantle and Ted Williams" . . . pause . . . "were superstars. Is Reggie Jackson — *Mr. Reggie Jackson* — a superstar? Who knows what he'll be hitting 10 years from now? Who knows how many home runs he'll hit 10 years from now?" Miller pointed out that nowhere in the arbitration rules did it say that a player had to top Babe Ruth to receive $135,000, and that Reggie's performance a decade on had no bearing on what he should be paid for the 1974 season. The approach so disturbed the Owner that he tried to have Miller removed from the room. Ultimately, Finley came off as a bully, wielding his old-school mallet in the middle of the newest-school event the game had ever seen. Jackson won the biggest arbitration award of any player in baseball.

All told, Finley won three cases and lost five.* (Players from other teams won only eight of 33.) Five of the top six salaries awarded league-wide went to Oakland. Even more important was the players' realization that under this new system the Owner was, for the first time, vulnerable. "He likes to be the lord and master of everything," said Rudi at the time, "but arbitration has taken some of this power away from him."

Six years earlier, in 1967, the entire budget for A's clubhouse salaries — players, coaches, staff, and the manager — had been $443,000. Now Finley, the master of thrift, had four men on his roster — Jackson, Bando, Hunter, and Holtzman — combining to earn $428,000. Years later the Owner posited that during his two decades in baseball only two things hurt the sport. One was his longtime nemesis, Bowie Kuhn. "The other," he said, "was arbitration."

Arbitration proceedings ended just days before training camp opened in mid-February, at which point a number of loose ends dangled. The Owner neglected to promote the team during the off-season to a nearly complete degree, still had no radio or TV contracts, and hadn't filled the open seat in the broadcast booth after firing Monte Moore's partner, Jim Woods. More pressingly, as spring training bags were being unpacked in Mesa, coaches Irv Noren and Vern Hoscheit met to discuss what drills to lead on account of the team *having no manager.*

The Owner refused comment on the litany of names being bandied about for the job, but various criteria were assumed to be in play. The new manager had to be willing to retain the holdover coaches, on account of Finley's unwillingness to pay them off. He had to be able to withstand meddling to a degree beyond even the long-standing rumors. And he had to be willing to step aside at the last moment if for some reason Williams decided to return. People suggested that this might limit the candidate pool.

---

* Not every member of the A's participated. Catfish Hunter negotiated a two-year contract at $100,000 per season prior to his hearing (which would later present its own entanglements), and Campy Campaneris had signed a two-year pact following the 1972 campaign. Vida Blue signed his contract quickly in order to avoid the process altogether, feeling that he'd already absorbed enough abuse from Finley. Also, Vida was uncertain about his ability to adhere to conduct befitting a hearing. "I just knew had I gone to arbitration I was going to say motherfuck the arbitrator," he said. "I was going to say motherfuck Finley and his attorney. I might have motherfucked *my* attorney. I was going to motherfuck myself out of baseball."

Finally, three days before spring training, the Owner called a press conference at the Edgewater Hyatt. He did not specify the agenda, but it could
only be to introduce the team's new skipper. Finley, a sucker for drama,
played this one to the hilt. Upon taking the dais, he wasted no time in saying how proud he was to have hired the man he was about to introduce,
how much he was looking forward to seeing him in the full glory of per-
forming his job. Ladies and gentlemen, he said, I give you . . . *Jon Miller!*

The air left the room. Finley might have no radio station for his team's
broadcasts, but he did manage to find Moore's 12th boothmate in 13 years.
Miller, a 22-year-old broadcaster from the East Bay suburb of Hayward,
about 15 miles south of Oakland, was decidedly not the next A's manager.
It was his first play-by-play gig at any level.

The press conference had, in fact, been called to introduce Oakland's
next manager, but Finley wanted to tease it a bit. Miller, as eager as everybody to find out who was on deck, kept his remarks short.

Then the Owner finally called out the real man of the moment, and
Alvin Dark strolled into the room. The reaction was less amazement than
Are you putting us on? Dark had already managed the A's for a season
and a half before being fired in 1967 under dramatic circumstances, during which he refused to back Finley on a contrived fine for pitcher Lew
Krausse.* Even the newly hired Miller, standing next to Dark on the podium, couldn't help but wonder, *Alvin Dark? Again?*

Dark had been out of baseball for close to three years, since being fired
as Cleveland's manager during the 1971 campaign. He was 52 and by his
own account had been spending his time on Florida golf courses getting
fat. Dark proclaimed how pleased he was to be with the A's again, but
when he began naming the Oakland players with whom he was excited to
work, he grew flummoxed after only six. "Really, I haven't even looked at
the roster," he admitted. At least the coaching staff would be retained to
help him out, he said, as if Finley would have it any other way.

Questions arose about Dark's past, primarily his born-again Christian-
ity and overt devotion to the Baptist faith, and the incongruity of having
left his wife for another woman in the face of it all. More troubling for
many was the racial imbroglio that had engulfed him in 1964 while managing the San Francisco Giants, spurred by an interview he gave to *Newsday*. In the ensuing article, writer Stan Isaacs attributed to Dark three

---

* It was the same series of events that culminated in the release of Ken Harrelson.

sentences that would forever haunt him: "You can't make most Negro and Spanish players have the pride in their team that you can get from white players. And they just aren't as sharp mentally. They aren't able to adjust to situations because they don't have the mental alertness." The manager subsequently dug himself a deeper hole when, after admitting that Jackie Robinson and Willie Mays were not the types of Negro he was talking about, he said that "you couldn't name three colored players in our league who are always mentally alert to take advantage of situations." Dark spent the ensuing decades claiming to have been quoted out of context, and that his views could not be further from their portrayal by Isaacs. Still, there was obvious racial tension on his Giants teams. Dark forbade his Latin players from speaking Spanish in the clubhouse and continued into his second tenure with the A's to refer to African American players as "colored boys." Still, the *Newsday* remarks didn't reflect a hatred of other races and cultures so much as a nearly complete lack of curiosity when it came to understanding them. Dark was a Louisiana boy, raised in the deep South of the 1930s; these sorts of attitudes were to be expected — at least by many of those in Oakland who used his past to add context to his present.

Dark had done some thinking about how his religion would play with his new employer and in his new workplace. He had no plans to hide his devotion, he said, and moreover he viewed the Bay Area as a "mission field." Dark dropped Bible passages and praised the Lord at every opportunity, hoping that he wasn't coming off as too pious, but not caring enough to do anything about it. It wasn't that Dark *had* to quote Corinthians, it was that quoting Corinthians was the best means of communication he knew.

Reporters asked the Owner how he expected his new manager to handle extensive input from the executive suite. As was frequently the case when Finley explained one of his positions, it seemed to make sense. "For a team to be successful, the manager and the general manager have to work together," he said. "Since I'm the general manager of this club as well as the owner, I expect to be talking quite often with my manager. And I would hope he would call me when he feels the need. That's only normal, isn't it? Alvin had free reign before, and he will have free reign again. If I have any suggestions, such as putting my catcher, Ray Fosse, at shortstop, and Dark doesn't like it, then he'll explain to me why he doesn't, and if I say Fosse is at shortstop, then Fosse will be at shortstop."

Dark responded without hesitation. "I will call Mr. Finley many, many times for his opinion," he said. "If as owner and general manager Mr. Finley tells me to put Fosse at shortstop, then I will put Fosse at shortstop. If Mr. Finley says this will be done, it will be done. The Bible teaches this. I think respect should be paid to the men who pay your salary."

With that, playing Ray Fosse at shortstop became an enduring metaphor for Dark's tenure in Oakland. As he would display repeatedly over the coming months, the manager had perfected the act of supplication. Doing something ludicrous because Finley thought it a good idea would be the new order of things.

Their contract negotiations reflected as much. When Finley presented a one-year deal, Dark offered to "take a day-to-day if you want me to." When Finley asked how much money he wanted, Dark left it up to Finley. The Owner offered $50,000 plus bonuses for winning the pennant and World Series. Dark accepted.

The manager wrapped up his introductory press conference with a passage from Deuteronomy: "Be strong and of a good courage, fear not nor be afraid of them: for the Lord thy God, he it is that doth go with thee; he will not fail thee nor forsake thee." Whatever Dark hoped this might convey was more or less lost on the crowd.

It didn't take long for cracks to appear in the manager's refurbished veneer. A's players respected Dick Williams for bringing discipline to a talented club, but now they were two-time defending champs. They understood the drill and worried that somebody new might gum up the works. "When you have a championship club, you don't make many changes," opined Bando in a majority opinion. "I hope [Dark] doesn't have too many strict rules, because we haven't had many the past two years and we won."

When camp opened, Dark set to learning the lineup, and players set to learning Dark. During his first team meeting in Mesa, the manager addressed the reports about himself, claiming only somewhat contradictorily both to not have said the quotes in *Newsday* and to be a changed man. Some on the team were unsure how to approach these details. Reggie Jackson, whose African American and Latino heritages were each disparaged by the manager a decade earlier, decided to give him a chance, figuring that "Finley manages this team anyway." Vida Blue was not so open-minded. He spent his youth dealing with Bayou-bred rednecks and was reluctant to embrace another one.

The other rumor Dark was desperate to disprove concerned his temper. There was no denying his quickness to anger during previous managerial stints; he had the scars to prove it. In 1961, after his Giants left 12 men on base in a 1–0 loss to Philadelphia, Dark flung a metal stool against the clubhouse wall in a fit of pique, ripping the tip of his pinkie finger — which had inadvertently jammed into the V-shaped intersection of the support braces — from the bone. Of his proclamations of change, this was the most easily verifiable. Now, instead of acting impulsively during hard times, Dark meditated on scripture and emerged nearly as calm as he had been beforehand.

What really concerned the players, however — more than Dark's anger or religiosity, more even than his potential racism — was his willingness to stand up to the Owner. If he didn't, the players reasoned, things would not end well for anybody.*

Any good spirits that arrived with the opening of training camp lasted all of two weeks. On March 1, traveling secretary Jim Bank called the players together on the field at Rendezvous Park in Mesa to present their championship rings. Finley had personally conducted the ceremony a year earlier, reveling in the players' awe at the opulence of the jewelry and thoroughly enjoying the euphoria of the moment. So why was Bank in charge? The answer had to do with the Owner's year-old promise that the team's second championship ring would make the 1972 version "look silly."

Formality was disregarded entirely; Bank simply passed out boxes. As far overboard as Finley had gone in 1972, he went an equal distance in the opposite direction in '73. The new rings didn't feature a diamond, or any gemstone at all — only green glass where a jewel should have been.

"The new rings are horseshit," yelled Catfish Hunter, claiming the superiority of high school rings and calling Finley "a cheap so-and-so." Reggie Jackson spoke of fulfilling expectations — how he strived for it as a player and expected the same from his employer. Darold Knowles called the rings "the worst in World Series history." Players who were not around in '72 — guys like Ray Fosse, Billy North, and Deron Johnson —

---

* Early returns were not promising. At that first team meeting, Dark informed the players that Finley "will be calling me and telling me things he wants me to do. I will put up with the phone calls as long as I can, and I will do what he wants." When Jackson responded, "Fuck Charlie Finley, we'll win it again, anyway," the manager raised players' hopes by smiling, then dashed them by requesting that players refrain from profanity. Then he changed the subject.

were looked upon particularly sadly for having missed out on the good times while the good times were rolling.

Fosse spoke for everybody when he said, "I went on national television after the World Series and said money wasn't important, just give me that ring. People have been asking me about the World Series ring and when they could see it. Now I'm not so sure I'll show it to them." Holtzman took things a step further and said he'd use it as a fishing weight.

Sentiment held that it was Finley's way of getting back at the players for siding with Mike Andrews the previous October. That much seemed obvious, considering that a huge portion of Finley's generosity — sporadic bonuses for things like throwing a perfect game and World Series glory — had all but disappeared. Following the 1972 postseason, Joe Rudi gave Finley the bulk of his World Series share to invest; after the 1973 season, that option was no longer available.* "Finley changed," said Green. "He was somehow disgusted, even though we just won two World Series."

"He hated the ballplayers," added Fingers, looking back. "We were traveling shitty, staying in bad hotels. He was cutting corners because he was pissed off at us after the '73 season."

The Owner responded to the outcry with a sentiment that would prove to be his undoing as arbitration and free agency became the way of the sport. "Pigs get fat, hogs go to market," he said. "Modern professional athletes are like hogs. They're gluttons." What Finley failed to accept through his remaining years in baseball was that the owners who recognized the value of fat hogs were the ones who ended up gaming the system. Those who kept trying to take starving pigs to market were not long for the era.

On March 18, about two weeks before the start of the season, a new player walked into the A's camp with a guaranteed roster spot in his back pocket and turned things upside down. That he hadn't played a competitive baseball game since his sophomore year of high school made little difference, because Herb Washington was in Mesa for only one reason: the man could run.

Known as the "Chairman of the Boards" during his four years as a

---

* It wasn't until fresh blood came along later in the season in the person of Claudell Washington — who had not offended Finley's sensibilities the previous October on account of being an 18-year-old at Single-A Burlington at the time — that the Owner would again extend a bonus to the ranks of the A's.

sprinter for Michigan State University, Washington held world records in the 50- and 60-yard dashes (5 seconds flat and 5.8 seconds, respectively) and gave Charlie Finley what he always dreamed about with Allan Lewis but never quite achieved: somebody to set the base paths aflame. Of all Finley's screwball schemes, this may have been the screwballiest. Next to Washington, Lewis was a plodder. Next to Washington, Billy North was a plodder, and he'd nearly led the league in steals. Dark had seen the sprinter race on television, and Finley immediately embraced the manager's suggestion to sign him, no tryout necessary.

Washington's price tag — $42,500, nearly as much as Gene Tenace was making — would have elicited wild clubhouse dissension had anybody known about it, not to mention the $35,000 bonus Finley paid to trump the player's offer to become a wide receiver in the World Football League.* Even so, Washington's very presence in camp was enough to set his teammates off. "That's a joke," said Tenace. "This is going to cost somebody who should be in the major leagues a job."

At six-foot-one and 170 pounds, the 22-year-old Washington may have been a baseball rookie, but he boasted confidence born of world-class athletic triumph.† Finley encountered it during their very first telephone call

---

* Washington spent two years on the Michigan State football team, catching one pass for 41 yards. In 1972 he was selected by the Baltimore Colts in the 13th round of the NFL draft.

† Washington's confidence helped him survive an A's clubhouse culture that would have emotionally demolished a less-assured person. The sprinter's teammates may never have respected him as a ballplayer, but through sheer dint of personality he forced them to respect him as a man. When Bando said, "Herbie, you better be glad that we don't have to vote on your World Series share because you wouldn't get anything," Washington responded, "I wouldn't worry about it — if it was paid based upon batting average, I'll get more than you." Hunter was throwing batting practice one day and called out to Washington, "Herbie, if I see your ass in the batter's box, I'm going to throw like it's a game." Washington's response — "Hell, if you throw that shit up here like you did last night, I might take you deep" — won the verbal battle so decisively that Catfish brushed him back with his first pitch. The man who started out sitting in the front of the bus was quickly invited to the back with the veterans, where the barbs flew especially sharp. Such was Washington's verbal alacrity that Jackson actually pulled him aside and offered a pact, promising to not insult Washington in a group setting if Washington would return the favor. That lasted as long as the next bus trip. When zingers started to fly in his direction, Herb piped right up. "Fellas, I'm a rook, and I don't know the rules," he said. "I want to know how this thing works, because Reggie came to me and asked me not to talk about him and he won't talk about me. Is this how y'all play?" Instantly, the focus of derision shifted off of Washington and onto the team's best player. *Oh my God, Reggie, you did not go to that rookie and ask him to lay off you!* "It got crazy, just crazy," recalled Washington. "I couldn't wait to ask the question. Could not wait."

when, upon introducing himself as "Charlie Finley, owner of the world champion Oakland A's," Washington coolly responded: "Hello, Mr. Finley, this is Herb Washington, world's fastest human. How can I help you?"

The sprinter's wheels were unassailable, but his drawbacks were quickly obvious. He did not know how to take a lead. After a lifetime spent in starting blocks, he had to learn how to build momentum when facing 90 degrees from his destination. He did not know how to slide. He did not know how to round a base, how to read a pitcher's move, or how to anticipate a throw to first. And that was in his area of strength — running. When it came to other baseball skills, the man had even less of a clue. High school teams across the country had players who could hit, field, and throw better than he did. "He couldn't throw a baseball from here to that lamp, and putting him in a batting cage was a joke," said Fingers. Added Jackson, "He has as much business playing baseball as I have running the hundred-yard dash."

Washington backed away from pitches during batting practice. When shagging balls in the outfield, he went to lengths to be where the ball wasn't, heading to right field for right-handed hitters, then sprinting to the opposite side when a lefty came up. "There goes Herbie," said Tenace. "He got his running in as he was trying to get away from the baseball."*

Still, as training camp progressed, Dark held out hope, in his Louisiana good-ole-boy way. "Anyone who can start as fast as he can could steal bases," he said. "Black boys can instinctively learn because of their natural quickness in getting started."

Washington's limitations were so quickly apparent that within a week Finley hired Maury Wills to tutor his newest player in the finer arts of base thievery. Wills, who won the National League's MVP Award in 1962 based largely on his modern-era record 104 steals, had his work cut out for him. The pair spent six days in Mesa on base-path navigation, Wills demonstrating and Washington doing his best to follow along. The sprinter did so many sliding reps that the point of impact on his thigh grew covered in road rash. Trainer Joe Romo would tape it up, and the next day Washington would rip off the scabs with his very first slide. "I'd come back to the dugout and feel the dampness on the side of my leg and be like, 'Oh hell,

---

* Washington couldn't even grow the team's requisite mustache. That was how the guy who admitted that "I'd never shaved a day in my life" came to be in front of a clubhouse mirror on opening day, shading in his upper lip with an eyebrow pencil.

I did it again,'" he said. Washington's solution was to don a pair of trucker gloves and do his best approximation of a headfirst dive.[*]

"Herbie didn't know about baseball," said Tenace, "but he could stinking run. Oh my laundry, he could flat run."

When Sal Bando saw the lineup for the season opener against the Rangers, he began to rage. For some reason, Joe Rudi was listed in Bando's customary third spot, with the Captain dropped all the way down to sixth in the order. Dark's logic held that Rudi, a fastball hitter, would benefit from the frequency of heaters he'd see with North and Campaneris on base ahead of him, while Bando could protect Reggie and Tenace from the lower spot while seeing more of the breaking balls that he handled so well.

Bando — who had finished fourth in the league's MVP race a season earlier while batting third — stormed into Dark's office. As he unloaded the manager had to decide quickly: make an authoritarian stand or present himself as open to suggestion? He chose the latter, conceding the third spot to Bando with the rationale that "I think a happy ballplayer is going to make more good things happen for a club than an unhappy player." Dark ambled to the dugout and rearranged his previously posted lineup. Already seen by the press as spineless before Finley, Dark now also came off as weak-willed when handling his players.

The other news of opening day was Herb Washington's debut, running for Rudi in the seventh inning. The score was 7–0 — hardly a typical

---

[*] Phil Garner recalled a game against Minnesota: "Bando's at the plate, we're late in the game, Herb Washington's at first base. They throw over to first five or six times, and actually picked him off a couple of times, but the umpire called him safe. [Twins manager Frank Quilici is yelling now — he's got the gas. So we put on a hit-and-run and Herbie takes off. Bando hits a bullet to left field, but Herbie looks back toward home plate and gets totally lost. About five feet before second base he cuts toward shortstop, and doesn't hit the bag. He runs past second on the inside of the field, misses it by about five feet, and runs about ten feet past the bag. He looks up at the bench and everybody's yelling, 'Bag, bag, bag, bag!' Well, Herbie just turns around and takes off on a straight line across the grass back to first base. They appealed that he didn't touch second on the way back, but the umpire said, 'Well, he didn't touch it going out, so he didn't have to touch it going back.' Now Quilici is at wit's end, and on the very next play Herbie steals second and gets thrown out, but they called him safe. Quilici goes absolutely berserk and gets thrown out of the game. He throws all the helmets on the field, all the bats. And the next batter drives Herbie in. That's where they started calling him 'Herbie, the Cat with Nine Lives.'"

spot for a pinch runner — and Rudi, 3-for-3 and hoping for more, spiked his helmet in frustration in the dugout. "I want to play 162 games and nine innings of every game," he said afterward. "When you get taken out for a pinch-runner it makes you look like half a ballplayer." On orders from Finley, Washington was inserted into all three games of the season-opening series, but he didn't do anything of note until the third one . . . when he was picked off by Texas lefty Jim Merritt. "John McGraw must be turning over in his grave," sighed Rudi afterward.

By the end of the opener Rudi wasn't the only player ticked off at being removed too early. Dark yanked his starting pitcher, Catfish Hunter, with nobody out in the eighth after the right-hander gave up three straight hits and two runs. That they were Texas's only tallies of the night was unimportant to the manager, nor was the fact that Oakland led, 7–2. Hunter had faced only 28 batters and felt as strong as ever. Fingers closed out the game. Catfish was unhappy.

In the season's second game, Holtzman allowed five hits through four innings and was never in trouble. In the fifth, however, Jackson misplayed a fly ball into a leadoff double, and one out and two singles later the Rangers scored their first run. Again Dark dipped into his bullpen, and Paul Lindblad allowed another run on Holtzman's line. The A's lost, 2–0. Holtzman was unhappy.

In the third game, Vida gave up a hit an inning through four, and the A's led, 5–1, going into the fifth. When Texas opened the bottom half of the frame with two singles, Dark brought another early hook. Fingers allowed both of Blue's runners to score, then stayed in for the final five frames. Because Vida had not pitched the requisite five innings he was not credited with the victory, despite leaving with a lead his team never relinquished. Blue was not just unhappy, he was steaming.

As the team packed for a trip to Kansas City the starting pitchers' collective mood was so dour that pitching coach Wes Stock saw fit to call a clear-the-air meeting with the manager. Dark was three games into his tenure. In the manager's office at Royals Stadium he tried to explain his logic to the starters. None of them agreed.

Hunter told reporters that he'd lie down on the mound if Dark came out early again. Blue said that the only way to stay in a game with Dark in charge was to pitch a no-hitter. Holtzman groused that "the only twenty-game winners on this ballclub this year will be [relievers] Rollie Fingers and Darold Knowles." To make matters worse, the players suspected that the moves were ordered by the Owner. "I knew Alvin Dark was a religious man," said Blue, "but he's worshiping the wrong God — Charlie O. Finley."

From the moment the A's arrived in Oakland for their home opener on April 13, the Owner's lack of off-season promotion was impossible to miss. The nine-game homestand averaged about 7,000 fans, which would be the best turnout until June. The Coliseum itself did not appear ready, the turf having been grown out for football to the point, said Jackson, that it was fit for an Easter Egg hunt.* The tarps in the outfield appeared faded and filthy. The Owner canceled the fireworks used to celebrate home runs — to prevent neighborhood noise complaints, he said, while failing to mention that it saved him about $7,000 per game. Even the ball girls had disappeared.

To top things off the team didn't even have a championship banner to raise, the 1972 pennant serving as the Coliseum's only testament to victory. Finley lamely offered that the new one hadn't arrived.

Internally, the Owner ordered members of the front office to stop processing outgoing fan mail, putting the onus on players to handle postage costs when responding to requests for promotional photos. Also, the players were expected to pay for the photos. Finley finally reupped his radio deal with KEEN out of San Jose (which had aired the team's games since 1971), but decided that there would be no television broadcasts. (Meanwhile, the club's Triple-A affiliate was televising 15 games.)

None of it hurt the team on the field, of course — the A's had proved immune to far worse distractions — but it did set a tone. Even more worrisome was that things were still changing, and nobody yet knew how drastically.

Early on, wins did not come with a frequency befitting defending champions. It took 16 games for a starter other than Hunter to earn a victory. Vida Blue didn't win until May 8, at which point Oakland was 13-15.

In the bullpen, Finley's off-season trade of Horacio Pina for the much older Bob Locker blew up from the start when Locker suffered a sea-

---

* Later in the season local police went so far as to check out reports that the Coliseum outfield was festered with pot plants, the result of seeds scattered during various rock concerts at the venue. They found nothing.

son-ending elbow injury during spring training. To compensate, Fingers trod an increasingly familiar path from the bullpen, appearing in 11 of the team's 20 games in April. The abundance of his outings was less dramatic than their duration, which included stints of five, four, and three innings. By the end of the month Fingers had more victories (three) than Holtzman and Blue combined. Also, he was tired. And when Fingers was tired, his sinker tended to sail — a fact he detailed for reporters after getting battered by the Angels in late April. Afterward, Dark's postgame comments confirmed his lack of attunement. "I don't think Rollie is tired," he said. "He just got hit."

Across the room, Knowles tried to make sense of things. "I don't agree with the way, and how can I put this delicately, Alvin Dark is handling the pitchers as a whole," he told reporters, pointing out that Fingers was not the only bullpen option and that starters could occasionally pitch into the seventh. The sentiments led to an angry one-on-one meeting in Dark's office a day later, from which neither pitcher nor manager emerged satisfied. Meanwhile, Hunter took to sitting in the bullpen during games in which he was not pitching so as to freely berate Dark at top volume: "Hey, genius, Knowles is ready." "Hey, genius, what the fuck do you want to bring Fingers in for?" "Hey, genius, when are you going to take him out?" Over his first month on the job Dark received more public criticism from his players than Dick Williams had in three years.

It was also clear that the players did not trust the manager's instincts. In Boston, Dark instructed Blue — not through signs but face-to-face on the mound — to pitch Dwight Evans high and inside. Instead, Vida intentionally fed the hitter a low fastball, which Evans crushed into the right-field bleachers for a three-run homer. Five days later, on the mound at Yankee Stadium, as Fingers prepared to face Thurman Munson with a runner on third, Dark was explicit in his directions: don't walk him, even with first base open. As the manager talked, Bando, standing alongside, looked at .192-hitting Horace Clarke in the on-deck circle, then hung around after Dark departed. "Walk him," he ordered. Fingers did just that, acting as if he couldn't find the strike zone, then struck out Clarke to end the inning.*

---

* Everybody on the team knew that Bando told Fingers to walk Munson. Later, on the bus to the airport, somebody called out, "Hey, Bando, why'd you do it?" Rudi answered for him, saying, "Because he wants to be manager of the year." That was enough to crack everybody up. Even Dark.

When the calendar turned to May, the defending champs were under .500, and the players held a meeting — no coaches or management allowed — to figure out what the hell was going on. Reggie took the floor, then Bando, Hunter, Knowles, Blue, North, Odom . . . people couldn't wait to unload. Dark was the manager in name only, said one player. He was unwilling to get after them when they screwed up, said another, and accountability was failing. That's not it, said someone else, it was his bad decisions that did the team in. A fourth player cited Dark's habit of calling pitches and shifting fielders without consulting his coaches, an egregious decision given his general lack of familiarity with team and league.*

The players also said some constructive things. "So what if he brings in the wrong pitcher or puts the bat in the wrong guy's hands or puts the wrong man in the field?" offered Jackson. "If you're that man, you can still strike out the batter, hit a home run or make the catch, and the hell with management." Bando said that while Dark wouldn't be around long if he continued to bollix things up, every player in the room had more enduring hopes. "Accept his moves and do the best you can," he urged.

It didn't help. The A's dropped four of their next six, with Blue getting roughed up for seven runs over three and two-thirds innings against Cleveland, Odom getting knocked out in the fourth two days later, Lindblad not lasting the fifth, and Holtzman getting hammered for 11 hits and five runs in a horrid three-inning stint. No complaints about being yanked too soon there. And it wasn't just the pitching — the A's failed to score more than three runs in nine straight games. The problem was less about bearing down, said Jackson, than "overbearing down."

As players' poor performance stripped away their justification for being hard on the manager, the manager became hard on himself. "I'm not doing a good job yet," Dark admitted, suggesting that his blunders were all part of the learning experience. When it was mentioned that a number of players were openly agitating for more discipline, Dark demurred. "It won't work with these ballplayers who have won the past two years," he said. "They have too much pride over a long season. If I have something

---

* Dark tried to talk the team out of the meeting, not because he was afraid of what they might say but because he felt, said Jackson, that "if we were too hard on our teammates it would create hard feelings." It was another example of cluelessness from the embattled manager.

to say to a ballplayer, I'll say it to him in my office." As improbable as it seemed, the manager was sticking to his guns.[*]

In mid-May, the A's visited Chicago, and focus shifted to how Dark would handle the heat in Finley's hometown. The answer: not well. With the Owner in attendance for the series opener, Holtzman pitched poorly, giving up a two-out RBI single to Bill Melton in the third that put the White Sox up, 3–1. Dark visited the mound for what everyone assumed would be a pep talk, but instead he summoned Blue Moon Odom from the bullpen. Shocked, Holtzman did not pay his manager even the minimum respect of handing over the baseball, instead flipping it into the air as he departed. Dark let it fall to the ground.[†]

That only began the drama. Sal Bando had missed nearly three weeks with a severely bruised calf, and he asked Dark if he could work his way back into the lineup as designated hitter. Reggie Jackson, who had missed

---

[*] Some of Oakland's struggles were beyond the reach of anybody. Take second base. In early May, John Donaldson separated his right shoulder colliding with North in short center field and was placed on the disabled list. Donaldson had been filling in for Manny Trillo, who appeared in nine games before pulling his thigh muscle and being placed on the disabled list. Trillo had been filling in for Dick Green, who strained his instep four games into the season and was placed on the disabled list. Ted Kubiak could not fill in because he was already subbing for Sal Bando, who was limited to three pinch-hitting appearances over a span of 16 games after being hit in the calf by a pitch. Reacting to the carnage, the A's snapped up old friend Dal Maxvill, recently released by Pittsburgh, who lasted two days before getting spiked and going on the DL. The A's couldn't even call up their top prospect, Phil Garner, who was disabled with a bad back. Instead, Finley had to turn to Gaylen Pitts, a career minor leaguer who stanched the tide for five weeks before returning to Triple A in June after batting .244.

[†] Holtzman felt that he was yanked prematurely in his next start as well, and did not hold back in his postgame comments. "He's horseshit," the pitcher shouted about Dark to the gathered media. "And Finley's horseshit. Print that!" There would be no pinning these quotes on Wells Twombly. Holtzman didn't have a winning record until June 9, when he picked up his seventh victory against six losses, then promptly lost five of his next seven starts. The lefty felt that Dark was pulling him too early on an almost ceremonial basis, and had long since stopped trying to stifle his commentary about the manager. So deep was Holtzman's animosity that once, as he was throwing his final warm-up pitches to Fosse before a game at the Coliseum, he saw the catcher glance toward the dugout. Fosse was gazing wistfully at the nearby seats for which his recently deceased father-in-law had held season tickets, but Holtzman misread the gesture and thought the catcher was looking toward the bench. "Oh, no, you don't!" he yelled. Fosse was startled. "Don't what?" he asked. Holtzman screamed, "He's not calling pitches for me!" The pitcher thought that Fosse had been looking into the dugout for signs from Dark. The pitcher's record would not reach .500 again until the middle of August.

six games himself with a tender hamstring, was slotted to return as DH in the series' third game, but volunteered to retake right field so that Bando could hit. To everybody's surprise, Dark refused, saying that if the third baseman was not healthy enough to play the field, he would not play at all. The chance of aggravating his calf was too great. "Well, hell, Alvin, I'm coming back from an injury and you're using me as a designated hitter," reasoned Reggie. Dark pulled the outfielder aside. "Just between you and me," he said forthrightly, "we know black boys heal faster than white boys." It was Alvin in a nutshell. There was nothing malicious about the comment. He had even intended it as a compliment to Jackson. Reggie didn't even respond, realizing that if the decade since Dark's *Newsday* comments hadn't changed the manager, nothing he could say would either. "I'm not sure he knows he's a bigot," Jackson theorized later. "If he does harm, he doesn't mean to. He hurt me, but he didn't mean to. I can't respect him for it, but it's hard to hate him for it."

Jackson ended up going 1-for-2 with a walk, but when his fourth at-bat came against reliever Terry Forster, Dark had Jesus Alou pinch-hit for him. Reggie had been off to the best start of his career prior to the injury, batting .385 with 11 homers through 30 games, and the manager wanted to play it cautiously. Forster had a wild streak, Dark explained to the slugger, and any quick movement on Jackson's part to avoid a pitch might reinjure his leg. Reggie disagreed — he hadn't been pinch-hit for since Finley's attempts to embarrass him in 1970 — but at least he understood the logic. He decamped to the clubhouse without protest to shower and change.

The cost of the move became apparent with two outs in the ninth when, with the A's trailing 3–2 and the tying run at second, Jackson's spot in the order came up — only now it was filled by Alou, who popped up to end the game.

Afterward, players incorrectly pinned Dark's decision on Finley's meddling. Before Reggie could correct them, the Owner burst into the room and roared into the manager's office. With a slam of the door, he lit into Dark with neither reservation nor restriction. The thin clubhouse walls allowed players to hear everything as clearly as if Finley was yelling alongside them.

"I don't know what the fuck you're in this game for, but I'm in it to win!" he shrieked. "And if you don't get your fucking ass in gear, you're going to be gone! We won two straight without you and we can make it three without you, too. All you've got to do is write the fucking names down on a piece of paper and let them play. We've got the best goddamn team in baseball, goddammit, and if you can't win with the talent we've got, you can't win!" Finley was partial to finding scapegoats during tough times, and Dark, too reverent to talk back, was the perfect patsy.

Then the Owner turned his attack in a direction that surprised everybody. "You've got Washington on this ball club, and in the ninth you've got a chance to use him with a man on first and a run behind," he shouted. "You're the one that wanted him. I got him for you. I'm paying him 40 grand a year, and you don't use him. If you don't use him in a situation like that, what good is he?"

The information flew like daggers. Washington was *Dark's* idea? And he was making *how much?* Now players were really paying attention. The manager spoke softly in an effort to subtly influence the volume of Finley's harangue, clearly aware that their conversation was in no way private. Washington was shockingly raw, missing signs, hesitating when aggression was called for, and once even overlooking a direct verbal order from first-base coach Jerry Adair to take off for second. He'd attempted only four steals to that point and had been thrown out in three of them. Once, as Washington prepared to enter a game at first base, he asked Dark if he should steal early in the count. Probably not, the manager replied, what with a runner already at second. People began to think that the low bar for the sprinter's baseball instincts might actually have been set too high.

Dark tried to relay this to Finley but was met with further bluster. "He ain't ever going to learn if you don't use him!" the Owner yelled. "If you don't want to use him, get rid of him. And maybe you ought to get rid of about 25 pounds off that fat ass of yours and maybe you'll be able to think better!"

This was the moment at which players began to feel sorry for Alvin Dark. On the bright side, every ounce of energy devoted to pity was an ounce no longer earmarked for resentment. He still had to earn their respect, but being at the barrel end of Finley's scorn put him on equal footing with the rest of them.

After 20 minutes' worth of chastisement, Finley asked Dark if he had any final words. "Just sit down and relax, you're going to get sick," the manager replied calmly. Finley was unprepared for that type of response, and for the first time in the conversation he spoke in regular tones. "You're killing me with kindness," he conceded. "How about going out for a sandwich?"

The pair ended up at the Billy Goat Tavern* and talked until 1:30 in the morning. When they parted ways, Finley, temper cooled, told Dark to forget what he'd said earlier. It was a fine gesture, but the manager had little hope of following through; newspapers across the country spent the next several days recounting the explosion, thanks to players' re-creations of it for reporters. Dark limited his public response to another psalm, 119:165, which he repeated for newsmen the following day: "Great peace have they that love thy law, and nothing shall offend them."

Privately, though, the man was roiled. He didn't know what to make of Finley's anger, and didn't know how to reconcile it with the running of a team. Dark barely slept that night. He wasn't positive that his players had heard the tirade until the following day, when Tenace pulled him aside. "How do you stand it?" the first baseman asked. "How can you take all that?" Now Dark knew: the players had heard.

Changes were coming. They had to.

Jackson showed up at the Coliseum on June 2, his hamstring finally stable enough to eschew his DH duties for good. Stark naked, he walked into Dark's office and pounded his chest. "You see this?" he bellowed. "I've got a Cadillac body with Volkswagen wheels, but I'm ready to roar. I've got to get out and do my thing. You hear me? I got to play!" Reggie ran from the room, howling.

"When he begs like that, I know he's ready," Dark told a visiting reporter. That night Reggie hit his 14th and 15th homers, and the A's beat Milwaukee. The slugger was batting .399 through 50 games, with 42 RBIs. A 15-game hitting streak (and 28 out of 30) helped earn appearances on the covers of both *Sports Illustrated* (under the headline "Superduperstar") and *Time*. Most owners would have seen such acclaim as a positive development, but Charlie Finley was not most owners. So threatened was he by Jackson's celebrity that he refused to talk to the reporter from *Time*, and he barred the *Sports Illustrated* writer from a chartered A's flight that was otherwise open to the press.

The Owner needn't have worried about knocking Jackson off his ped-

---

* Three years later the Billy Goat Tavern would serve as the model for *Saturday Night Live*'s Olympia Cafe, in which John Belushi repeatedly called out orders of "cheezborger, cheezborger, cheezborger."

estal. The slugger was more than capable of doing it by himself, with an assist from Billy North.

The trouble started in early May, after the players-only meeting during which team leadership demanded accountability from the entire roster. The very next day North tapped a ball to second base and, giving deference to a lightly pulled groin muscle, opted against running it out. Reggie watched in disbelief. "Here we had just had a team meeting and agreed to bust our asses, and this guy is going bad and can't be bothered to give it his best," he said later.

Had Reggie thought about it, he'd have realized that calling out North in the dugout, in front of the entire team, would back his teammate into a corner, forcing him to either supplicate or strike back. There may have been players for whom this strategy was effective, but North was decidedly not among their ranks. Maybe Bando could have gotten away with it. He was the captain and the team's unquestioned leader, but this was not his moment and North was not his target.

Jackson, too, was a leader, but his own self-image in that regard was — like many aspects of his life — a greatly inflated version of how everybody else perceived him. Reggie brought things to a ball field that could be matched by few of his peers and none of his teammates, and that alone earned him cachet. The trick was that he was acutely aware of it, thirsted for the spotlight his talents brought, and misguidedly thought that because outsiders worshiped him for his baseball feats, the same would be true within clubhouse walls. Proclaiming oneself a leader does not necessarily make it so. When North returned to the dugout, Jackson asked if maybe his leg was hurt. North responded that his leg felt fine. "Then maybe your ears aren't working or something," Reggie said. "Maybe you didn't hear what we were talking about at the meeting last night."

"Who the fuck are you?" North shot back. "I've seen you loaf before."

"I'm the man who's telling you you had no business doggin' it on the play," spat Jackson, who indeed possessed a reputation for failing to run out grounders and infield pop-ups. "Look, we had a fucking meeting here yesterday just because we've been fucking around, and we made up our minds we were going to bust our butts on every ball. Then you come out here and the first thing you hit, you loaf on it. I want you to know if you're not going to do your job, we don't want you out there with us."

This was a break from routine. Jackson and North had spent much of the winter together, with Reggie traveling to Seattle to visit his teammate.

During spring training Jackson had gone so far as to cook breakfasts for two before they headed to the ballpark together. The dugout dustup, however, was indicative of an ongoing dialogue in which some African Americans on the A's felt that Reggie criticized black teammates far more frequently than whites — underneath which were veiled undertones that he cozied up to Caucasians at the expense of his other relationships.

Reggie did not entirely deny it. "I'm not afraid to tell a black player off, but I don't try that stuff on a white player," he theorized. "I leave that to other whites, so I guess the blacks believe I'm picking on them." It was true that his closest friends on the A's — Joe Rudi and the departed Dave Duncan — were white, but skin color had nothing to do with their closeness, he said, just as skin color had nothing to do with him spending so much time with North. At least Rudi looked out for him, once even telling his landlord at Double-A Birmingham in 1967 to shove off when threatened with eviction if Jackson — the black man staying in his guest bedroom — didn't leave.

Black players on the A's, however, seldom invited Reggie along when they went out. Having grown up black and Latino without incident in a largely Jewish neighborhood, Reggie was reluctant to acknowledge such racial divides, let alone buy into other people's perceptions of them. "I wouldn't know what color I was if whites didn't make me feel black and blacks didn't make me feel blacker," he said. This alone distinguished him from North, who while attending Central Washington University was president of the black student union — a role that in those days, he said, involved "taking over the president's office and issuing a list of ten demands."

Behind the Coliseum backstop during BP the following day, North laid out for Reggie just how hurt he was, and how he must have been mistaken in thinking that Jackson respected him. "Never speak to me again," he demanded, leaving no space for equivocation. In retrospect, Reggie would have been better off with silence. Before long, North began a stream of under-his-breath comments when Jackson was nearby, things like, "What motherfucker is managing this club anyway?"

"Reggie is a great player," North told one interviewer, "but off the field I don't have any use for him."

This was where the relationship stood for several weeks, until the team took off for a nine-game road trip in June. Jackson spent the afternoon of June 5 at a hotel in downtown Detroit with NBA players Archie Clark,

Charlie Scott, and Lucius Allen. There are at least two versions of what happened next. In one, a lady called for one of the basketball players, and when she found out that Reggie was there, asked to speak to him. She was North's girlfriend (or ex-girlfriend) who may or may not have been an airline stewardess and who, having heard that he and Reggie weren't getting along, took the opportunity to prod Jackson for details. In another version, the girl came on to Reggie at a bar some weeks earlier when North was not around, only to be rebuffed by the ballplayer. Both versions were told by Jackson at different times.

The way North reacted, there may well have been a third option.[*] He arrived at Tiger Stadium a bit later than the rest of the team, already afire. At that point the clubhouse — a tiny space, with lockers consisting of mesh metal frames sticking out at right angles from the white-tiled wall every three feet or so — was sedate. The scant area in the middle of the room contained a table where the team's regular bridge players — Holtzman, Fingers, Green, and Knowles — were midgame. Ray Fosse sat nearby, looking on. Reggie, naked save for a towel, entered the clubhouse from the adjacent trainer's room just as North arrived. The center fielder started in on him as soon as he walked through the doorway. "Superstar, my ass!" he shouted, striding toward Jackson. "You're a fucking jerk, you know that?" When North got close enough, he reared back and punched Reggie in the face, twice. Jackson was stunned, but absorbed the blows without falling. Then he lowered his shoulder and charged. "It was surreal, like, 'Is this shit really happening?'" said Herb Washington, who, having spent the afternoon with an increasingly agitated North, had a good idea of what was about to go down.

North and Jackson scuffled up one side of the room and down the other, ultimately falling hard to the concrete floor. The men playing bridge in the center of the room looked up disinterestedly and returned to their card game. "I had a slam bid I wanted to play, and damned if people were fighting," said Green. "I *still* played it." Fingers was even more blasé, saying, "They're just going to fight later anyway if we break it up now."

That meant that the only peacemakers on the scene were Blue Moon Odom and Vida Blue (the same Odom and Blue who nearly fought each other in the same clubhouse following a playoff game two seasons ear-

---

[*] North presently chooses to keep quiet on the matter, but teammates suggest that whatever Reggie said to the lady was unkind and that North took it exceptionally personally.

lier). With Blue scheduled to pitch that night, collateral damage became a real concern, so Fosse jumped up to help. By that time North was on top of Jackson. Blue pulled on North, Fosse pulled on Blue, and everybody fell backward, Fosse crashing into a locker divider on his way down.

Everything stopped. Fosse shakily picked himself up. Jackson and North scrambled to their feet, took some deep breaths, and eyed each other warily. The peace lasted about three minutes, until North began shouting (according to Reggie), "You know damn well what this is about! You're trying to steal my girl from me is what this is about!"

Jackson did his best to settle his teammate. "Hey man, I don't know what the hell you're talking about," he said. "I talked to a girl . . . that's all. I didn't ask her for a date. I didn't ask for anything. I don't want anything from her. I don't want your girl. I don't want anything from you."

The only reason Reggie didn't want her, taunted North, was because his sexual proclivities did not lean toward her gender. Jackson flashed and, still naked, went after him again. Again the pair stumbled across the floor. Reggie clipped a locker with his shoulder and fell awkwardly, and North leapt atop him and began swinging.

Across the room, Bando looked at Tenace. "What are you doing?" he said.

"What do you mean, what am I doing?" asked Tenace.

"Why are we letting it go on like this?" asked Bando.

"Did you see what happened to the last guy who tried to break it up?" said Tenace, referring to the still-woozy Fosse. "I ain't going to be a stinking statistic."

"Get over here," said Bando, pulling his teammate toward the players. Bando grabbed North, Tenace grabbed Reggie. Alou, Campaneris, and Washington raced in for damage control.

Once the fisticuffs ended, Jackson decamped to find ice for his aching shoulder and North stomped off to change into his uniform. Bando looked around and clapped his hands in mock satisfaction. "Well, that's it," he said. "We're definitely going to win big tonight."

He wasn't wrong. Blue allowed four hits over seven innings, and Tenace hit a grand slam in a 9–1 victory. This wasn't as simple, however, as the A's-will-be-A's narrative the players used to justify their infighting. Jackson's shoulder grew increasingly tender as the game went on, and he left midway through the sixth inning after going 0-for-4, then sat out the following day. Fosse, his own right shoulder barking after his fall, had increasing trouble throwing the ball and came out of the game in the seventh.

Within a day news outlets across the country were reporting on the latest dustup of the Swingin' A's and wondering whether they were winning despite it or because of it. "Being on this club is like having a ringside seat for the Mohammed Ali–Joe Frazier fight," said Fingers in a quote that found its way into virtually every account.[*]

The day after the fight the A's traveled to Milwaukee for a series with the Brewers. This was convenient for Charlie Finley, who had only to make a 90-minute drive north from Chicago to lay into his beleaguered players in person. Upon arrival at County Stadium, he called Jackson and North into the trainer's room. Dark followed. Unlike the last time the Owner did some clubhouse shouting, he didn't even bother to close the door. Finley, increasingly threatened by Jackson's recent spate of magazine covers, wasn't about to waste an opportunity to knock his superduperstar down a notch. All but ignoring North, he yelled about how there was no place on his team for egomaniacs and how he was not about to sit idle and let internal strife destroy that which he had sweated and sacrificed to build. Nobody else said a word. Finally, Finley sent Dark and North away. He wanted Reggie alone.

You are a troublemaker, he shouted. He had already traded one player because Jackson fought with him, Finley said, but he wasn't about to give North the Mike Epstein treatment — because, he added for no reason other than to get Reggie's goat, North was the team's best player.

Jackson had options. He could argue back. He could, as he said he felt like doing, "punch him in his damn mouth." Instead, head spinning, Reggie simply sat and took it. Jackson's equilibrium was thrown further out of kilter when, after ten minutes of harangue, the Owner stomped into the clubhouse and called the players to order.

There he repeated his diatribe for a team that had already heard it through the open door. Then he turned his focus on the room. "You're

---

[*] After the fight, Jackson tried to make sense of what went wrong between him and North. "It's very bad," he said. "I don't think it will ever be resolved, although I tried to make peace at least six times. Even when we got into the tussle I wasn't mad. I'm not angry now. I'm just embarrassed about it, no matter who was right and who was wrong." Even if Jackson's leadership wasn't quite as he envisioned it, he earned respect with his response in the fight's aftermath. "It's my fault," he said two days later. "I should know better. I'm older. I've been around. This whole thing is bad. Two black guys, two teammates. It shouldn't be like this."

world champions," he said. "Stop acting like a bunch of fucking kids." Finley threatened hellfire for whoever impeded the team's success, his eye on Jackson all the while. For an absentee owner with the need to assert control over everybody in his employ, this was a sterling opportunity. He talked down to his players, berating them, said Dark later, "as if they were ten-year-olds."

Apart from Fosse, the one to really suffer in the fight's aftermath was Jackson. Naturally prone toward internalization and acutely aware of how others perceived him — or at least how he wanted others to perceive him — Reggie began to wonder, to a degree he hadn't since 1970, what he was doing wrong. His former friend tried to kill him. The team owner wasn't far behind. Jackson's shaky self-esteem began to eat him alive. The A's lost 6–4 on the night Finley chewed him out, and when Reggie realized he didn't care, *that* shamed him. Two days later he got thrown out tagging up from first on a fly ball to right field — the result, he said, of having his mind on Finley and not the game. "For the first time in years I let him get to me," he said. Jackson was quickly becoming the world's least confident .400 hitter.

That night Reggie called the Owner from a phone in the trainer's room to discuss the incident. "I don't know why you don't like me, but I know you don't," he said when Finley came on the line. "I don't know if it dates back to my first holdout. I know a lot of people feel that you don't like anyone who takes the spotlight away from you. Whatever the reason, I am not going to be treated the way you treated me the other day. You don't have to like me, but you do have to treat me like a man. You did not treat me like a man the other day. You did not try to find out what had happened or why it had happened or who was to blame."

Then Jackson threw down the gauntlet. "You said if any player didn't want to play here, you would find some other place for him to play," he said. "Well, I'm telling you right now, I don't want to play here anymore." Jackson's love for his teammates, he said, was outstripped by his hatred for the Owner. He would not be taking absurd orders anymore, he said. He would refuse them, and Finley would look bad in the process. "You said that there were some bad guys on this ball club," he concluded, "but the worst one is you. If there's a horse's ass on this team, it's Charlie Finley!" The Owner hung up on him.

Jackson was certain that Finley would never trade him under these circumstances, if only because Reggie himself had requested it. He wasn't proud of a diatribe that he felt sank to Finley's level, but he felt justified in delivering it. Unlike the Owner, at least he said it in private. Because nobody else knew about it, Jackson figured — correctly — that Finley would simply act like it never happened.

What unburdening himself didn't do for Reggie was end his slump, which grew so pronounced that North approached him with an olive branch before the second-to-last game of the road trip. It wasn't that he had forgiven Reggie — only days earlier he responded to Jackson's dugout braggadocio by calling out, "Hey, Skip, you better tell that boy to shut up before I beat him again" — but nobody, he told Jackson, deserved the kind of abuse that Finley had laid on him. It served as a microcosm of the club's greater dynamic: stay at each other's throats, animosity held in check primarily by a mutual disregard for the man in charge. There was also the fact that North was hearing a faction of white players on the team pile on Reggie in racially insensitive terms. The only way to stop it, he realized, was for the combatants to make up. The following day at the ballpark North met with Jackson inside Dark's office. "The shit between me and you is over," he said. "I can't stand here and let these people do this to you." They might no longer share the same kind of friendship they once had, but at that moment Jackson learned unequivocally about where North's priorities lay. He was grateful for the overture and gladly accepted. "We need you," North said. "I'm not about to let these assholes get off on you anymore. Don't *you* let them get off on you anymore. If one of them wants to come around and say some more foolish shit and you rear up, I'm there with you." The two shook hands, and North drew Jackson close. "The next time anybody says anything like that to you," he said, his voice dropping nearly to a whisper, "you better get up."

People began to see two players who were freshly cordial to each other both on and off the field. Newsmen noticed North delivering Jackson's glove to him when Reggie was stranded on base at the end of an inning, and Jackson doing the same in return. Even an accidental outfield collision between them a few days later in which North was briefly knocked unconscious could not deter them. "I don't have to love or hate anybody," said North, delivering his new party line. "As long as I do my job, everything will be all right."

And it would. It just took some time for Jackson to get there. Still preoccupied with Finley, and now playing with a shoulder that required bandaging and sporadic cortisone injections, Reggie hit only .212 with two homers in June. "I can't control the bat," he lamented. "I can't hit anymore with two strikes. I can't hit the ball to left field. I can't seem to hit it to right, either. I haven't hit a ball out of the infield for a week." After he went 0-for-3 on August 1, Jackson's average was down to .307 — a drop of 84 points in the 50 games since the fight.*

Reggie's slump was nothing compared to what Ray Fosse endured. The catcher was diagnosed with a separated cervical disc and returned to Oakland, where he spent a week in traction at Merritt Hospital, 20 hours per day with a strap wrapped around his jaw and neck, pulling his head upward in an effort to alleviate pressure on his spine. Unfortunately, Fosse's injury wasn't to a disc but to his C6 and C7 vertebrae, with resulting detritus impacting a nerve in his throwing shoulder. This became apparent after he took six weeks off, then felt a stabbing pain in his shoulder the first time he tried to throw a ball, as if no time had passed. He immediately scheduled surgery at UCSF.

The A's had been playing well, going 19-7 since May 8 to turn a three-game deficit into a four-game lead, but with Gene Tenace taking over behind the plate they lost nine of 11. The streak was capped by an 11-inning, 2–1 loss to the Red Sox at the Coliseum on June 19, Bando grounding into the final out with the tying run on base. Across the country, Kansas City starter Steve Busby threw a no-hitter at Milwaukee to pull the Royals to within a half-game of Oakland in the standings.

So upset was the Captain by the loss that he stormed into the clubhouse and, passing a large rubber garbage can, kicked it as hard as he could. He was mad at himself for ending the game the way he did, and madder still at Dark for failing to bunt Campaneris into scoring position in the tenth. As the garbage can tumbled Bando hurled his glove after it and shouted, "He couldn't manage a fucking meat market!" At least Dark wasn't around to hear it.

Dark shouldn't have been around to hear it, anyway. The manager typ-

---

* So scattered was Reggie that on July 21, in the last game before the All-Star break, he was on first base when Joe Rudi hit a ball over the head of Cleveland right fielder Charlie Spikes. The main question was whether Jackson would be able to score, but for reasons that went against everything first-base coach Jerry Adair was screaming, he decided to tag up on the play. Rudi nearly passed him rounding first and was improbably held to the longest single of his career when Jackson made it only as far as second base. Rudi was chasing the league leaders in doubles and grew angry over the miscue. To make matters worse, Reggie would have been the tying run.

ically went straight to his office after games, but on this day he wanted to commiserate with Blue, who pitched ten and a third outstanding innings, then watched the bullpen cough up the lead. Dark was steps away when Bando cut loose and absorbed every word. So did the reporters milling nearby. The Captain's overt disrespect was certain to be public fodder the following day.

In this matter, anyway, Dark was decisive. When Bando realized that the manager had heard him, he walked quietly to his locker and sat, eyes downcast. Dark paced the room, staring daggers in Bando's direction. Upon receiving no response, he bade the player into his office.

"Did you mean that?" he asked once they were alone. Bando was mortified. He had been angry — at Dark, sure, but at a lot of other things too, notably himself. "Shit, I didn't mean it, Alvin," he said, apologizing for the outburst. The two got to talking, and Dark diverged into scriptural lessons about love and forgiveness, saying he had done similar things out of frustration during his own playing days. He told Bando that he appreciated the apology. "After that," said Bando, looking back, "we were fine."

The manager had said early on that he would handle sensitive matters in the privacy of his office, and he was true to his word. The players saw how he dealt with Bando, and when Bando himself admitted culpability, the moment of Dark's greatest public embarrassment at the hands of a player actually earned him a measure of confidence from the team. Even as the outside world drew obvious conclusions and "meat market" became a hot-button catchphrase, Dark's standing in the room incrementally improved. It was a seminal moment in the trajectory of the season, the point at which the manager began to exert more influence and subsequently garnered additional respect. The Captain himself kick-started the process by proclaiming on-the-record support. "He's still feeling his way around," Bando told newsmen. "He's had twenty-five different personalities to learn. We had only one. I know this: The players respect him."

How about Sal Bando, he was asked? "*Especially* Sal Bando," he said.*

Gene Tenace struggled into the dog days, carrying a .204 batting average into the middle of June. His slump bothered him, but what he found truly

---

* Along the way Bando received a telegram from a meatpackers' union. "It said, 'If you think running a meat market is easy, you don't know what you're talking about,'" Bando recalled. He received no free steaks for his trouble.

confounding was the lack of institutional attention it garnered. "I'm not a .200 hitter, yet there is not a guy on this club who's taken a genuine interest in my problem," he said, citing just the latest indication of the abandonment he and his teammates felt. "I go to batting practice and nobody watches me," he continued. "Nobody says anything. Nobody is telling me what I'm doing wrong. If we only had a hitting instructor, he could spot something. Even a guy with a camera taking film of my batting could help me. . . . I need help, but where am I going to get it?"

Bando seconded the catcher's opinion after he asked for extra batting practice and coach Vern Hoscheit — responsible to Finley for an exact accounting of practice balls — turned him down, decreeing that such activities necessitated prior approval from the Owner. The A's had lost four series in a row, were only three games over .500, and, as of the meat-market game, held a shrunken half-game lead over Kansas City. With nobody in management appearing sufficiently interested in righting the ship, Bando phoned Finley to complain.

The following day the clubhouse door bore a memo: "Attention: To All Players: If anyone desires to take batting practice at any time, all they have to do is request it and they will get it." It was signed, in red ink, "Al Dark." Players were delighted. Finally, somebody was looking out for them. (Hoscheit, less pleased by the development, grumbled something to Dark about being undermined, adding that if this was the way things were being run, it would be his last year with the team. Little did he know.)

It worked. The A's snapped their losing streak the next day, took three of four from Kansas City, then three straight from the Angels. Still, Finley wanted more. At the end of June he waived Deron Johnson, who had been hampered since ripping a thumb tendon from its sheath while diving into third base the previous August. The injury resulted in a miserable 10-for-84 slide to end the 1973 campaign — including 27 strikeouts and not a single home run — which was followed by 10 strikeouts and only four hits over 20 at-bats in the postseason. When a 3-for-32 spell dropped Johnson's 1974 average to .195, the Owner cut the cord.

To replace him, Finley called up a 19-year-old who'd been lighting up the Double-A Southern League with stats almost too good to believe: a .362 batting average with 11 homers, 23 doubles, 55 RBIs, and 34 stolen bases in only 73 games. The best part: Claudell Washington was a local kid — a Berkeley High School graduate — and a success story for part-time scout Jim Guinn, the Berkeley policeman who went on to sign

Rickey Henderson. Washington didn't even play for his high school base-ball team; Guinn found him via local legend. The kid could dunk two basketballs in one leap, it was said, and was rated among the fastest men in the East Bay based on a single season of prep track. As if to give himself a character quirk, the six-foot, 190-pound Washington swung a comically heavy 42-ounce bat; among big leaguers, only Dick Allen's had similar heft. "He's the best player for his age I've ever seen or known," admired Jackson upon taking a gander.

Washington's first start was not an enviable matchup. It pitted the A's against Cleveland's Gaylord Perry, who, after losing his first start of the season, had won every time since. The right-hander was 15-1, one victory away from the American League record of 16 straight. That and half-price Monday tickets produced the Coliseum's largest crowd of the season: 47,582.

Perry did not reach his mark. Vida Blue pitched ten innings of four-hit ball, and the A's new prodigy — who had until very recently never heard of Gaylord Perry — made a quick mark. Starting at DH, Washington's first major league hit was an eighth-inning triple. His second hit, a tenth-inning single off a still-strong Perry, drove in Blue Moon Odom to win the game, 4–3. The victory pushed Oakland's division lead to four and a half games and left Finley feeling so good about things that he fired Ho-scheit and third-base coach Irv Noren.

The move wasn't as impulsive as it may have seemed. Dark had been having problems with Noren since he arrived, and with Bando's batting practice incident having taken place only two days earlier, Finley includ-ed Hoscheit in his housecleaning. The moves barely affected Dark; Wes Stock was the only coach he talked to anyway.

"Nothing surprises me anymore," said Hunter when he found out. "If they told me half the team had been traded to Mexico — Jackson, Bando, Rudi, North — I'd believe it."

Replacement coaches were at the ready. Taking over for Noren was Bobby Winkles, the ex–Arizona State coach under whom Jackson, Bando, and Rick Monday had played as collegians, who had recently been fired as manager of the Angels. (Finley had a hand in that decision too, having just sold the rights to Dick Williams's contract to Angels owner Gene Au-try, one of the few owners with whom he had a cordial relationship. All it took to secure the manager was $100,000 and the promise of a last-place team for Williams to helm. The fact that the Yankees had offered more didn't bother Finley a bit; Williams wanted to be in New York, so to New York he would not go. Winkles was booted to make room for him.)*

To coach first, Dark brought in old pal Bobby Hofman, his teammate on the New York Giants in the 1950s. Hofman was already in the A's system, managing their rookie league club in Lewiston, Idaho. He'd also coached under Dark in the manager's first go-round with Finley and served as the A's first-base coach under John McNamara in 1970.

The players' wall of ex-employees now had two more names to add, a development that was hardly shocking. "What can you expect on this club?" asked Tenace. And the drama continued apace.

Clubhouse perceptions about Dark had already been shifting, but New York was where they began to settle in earnest. On July 13, Vida Blue gave up six earned runs, five of them in the fifth inning, but was hardly humbled. Like Holtzman before him, Blue refused to hand the ball over when Dark approached the mound, instead flipping it backward as he brushed past the manager. It was as insolent a move as could be imagined from a player whose teeth had just been kicked in.

In response, Dark called the team together prior to Sunday's doubleheader. It was precisely 100 days since the season opener, and the manager could take no more. Dark typically paced when addressing the group, but this time he stayed rooted in the center of the room. He did not shout or curse. Of even more impact was that, for the first time that anybody could remember, he did not quote the Bible. This was no time for preaching, for Alvin Dark was a baseball man.

"I've never been more disappointed in a group of young men in my life," he said, glancing from face to face. "I've never been more disappointed in a team of world champions. If being a world champion makes you act the way some of you are acting, no thank you. I don't care to be one."

His gaze turned toward Blue. "Vida, you and I are even now," he said. "I screwed you out of a game your first start of the season, and I was never more sorry in my life. But we're even now. I left you out there yesterday

---

* Williams quickly agreed to the richest managerial pact in baseball history, $300,000 through 1977, and took over on July 1 — by simple dumb luck in a game against Oakland. Williams still had an "A" on his cap, but this one had a halo over it; when he ran out the lineup card at Anaheim Stadium, his former players stood on the top step of the dugout and booed. (There was no hiding their smiles, though — they were merely giving the manager a hard time.) To Finley's delight, Williams's Angels lost all four games of the series, then another six after that, to start the manager's SoCal tenure at 0-10.

trying to get you a win, and I'm the one who suffers. You degraded the position of manager. Not me, the *position,* by acting like a bush kid." He fined Blue $250 and said that the next such incident would cost $500. The manager looked toward Holtzman. "There's a pitcher on this ball club who's a cancer," he said, his target obvious. "He affects the whole pitching staff with his attitude, and I'm fed up with it." Dark claimed that the incessant complaints from the two lefties were having a poisonous effect in the clubhouse, resulting in poor hitting and a lack of hustle throughout the roster.

He called out something Billy North did during the previous day's game, saying that "outfielders aren't paid to flip the ball back in to the pitcher after a base hit as if to say, 'When are you going to get somebody out?'" When North contested the point, Dark shot back: "If you want to be the manager, phone Charlie and ask for the job. Until you get it, don't manage for me and don't second-guess me."

It was one of numerous actions taken by players that the manager said would thereafter be seen as fineable offenses. Then Dark hit his ultimate point. When he was hired, he told the room, "You all said in the papers that I should just stay out of your way. That was your advice for me. You said that Dick Williams taught you how to win, and that this club manages itself. You hoped I wouldn't come in here and screw that up, and I took that to heart. That's exactly what I've been doing. I took you guys as a bunch of professionals, but you're not showing me that's who you are. So now we're going to do it *my* way."

What the team didn't know was that their manager had endured an almost sleepless night while he pondered exactly what to say. He wrote out his speech and rehearsed it, then recorded it, different versions, again and again, to hear how it sounded. Dark had been waiting for his moment, and with its arrival he wanted to make sure nothing was left unsaid.*

---

* The entire exchange left a positive impression on most of the room, Billy North and Vida Blue being prominent exceptions. "I'm taking a beating, and I don't mean physically," North said afterward. As a means of protesting his $250 fine, Blue procured 5,000 nickels from a nearby bank, toted them to the ballpark in a burlap sack, then scattered them across the manager's desk. When Dark arrived to the mess, he immediately knew the source. The manager approached Vida at his locker and asked, "Is that my fine money in there?" Blue braced for the coming storm, but when he acknowledged that he was its source, Dark said only, "Thank you very much." Then he grabbed the empty sack from Vida's locker, returned to his office, and raked in the change without bothering to count it. "Do you know how heavy a big bag of nickels is?" Blue asked, chuckling at the thought years later. "That was a big bag of shit."

"We needed it," said Bando about the meeting. "We were playing dead." Oakland swept the twin bill that day. When the manager removed his starting pitchers — Hunter in the first game, Dave Hamilton in the second — each man dutifully handed over the baseball. Bando homered in both games, and North went deep as the first batter in the nightcap.

Dark's players still didn't trust him — not fully anyway, especially the pitchers — but they trusted him more than they had a day earlier, and they would do so in increasing amounts over the weeks to come. The A's swept the Orioles at Memorial Stadium and closed July on a 13-3 run that left them 61-42, nineteen games up in the division.

There were still hiccups, of course. As the calendar turned to August the team arrived in Chicago, where, with Finley in attendance for the series opener, Holtzman loaded the bases with one out in the seventh. The lefty had given up 11 hits and three runs to that point, and Dark's instinct was to remove him. This was a new chapter, however, and the manager was trying to change. Holtzman didn't like early hooks, so Dark let him respond under pressure.

Even as the Owner's screams of "No way! No way!" filtered from the lower boxes into the dugout, Holtzman gave up a two-run single to Ron Santo, icing a 7–3 loss. After the game, Dark was scheduled, at Finley's request, to address a group of supporters at a nearby restaurant. The Owner was to introduce him, an eventuality made more frightening for Dark with every drink Finley put down before the program began.

The manager's fears proved founded. "You all have heard of John the Baptist," Finley told the crowd, which included a contingent from a local church. "John the Baptist was a winner. Well, tonight we've got Alvin the Baptist. Alvin the Baptist is a loser. Alvin, tell us how you lost a game tonight."

Dark was dumbfounded. The remark seemed like a joke, and considering that Finley, for all his virtues, was not a funny man, it may have been intended that way. To judge from the confusion in the room, however, nobody knew how to take it, so Finley doubled down. "I want Alvin the loser to tell us how he lost the ball game," he repeated. Again from the crowd: nothing.

"Well," sighed the Owner, "I guess this wasn't the best introduction. Suppose I get Alvin to tell you about being a good Christian and about the Bible. Then he can tell you how we're going to win the pennant and the World Series in 1974."

Every day Dark felt like he understood Dick Williams better and better.

Unlike years past, Oakland never hit a particularly rough patch down the stretch and endured no losing streak during which its division lead crumbled. Instead, the A's suffered an almost methodological malaise, failing to win or lose more than three in a row over the season's final two months. They went 29-28 to close the schedule, during which time their lead shrank from nine games to four. Again, Finley was inspired to act.

On August 17, after trainer Joe Romo twice failed to check on players who were slightly injured during a loss to Detroit, Finley met with the coaching staff for five solid hours, during which he ripped Romo for his inaction. The following day the trainer sprinted onto the field every time a player so much as had to catch his breath, his six visits including a dash from the clubhouse, where he was examining Campaneris, to first base, where Rudi stood completely uninjured after being hit by the softest of breaking balls. During the meeting Finley also chastised Dark for failing to deploy Herb Washington frequently enough.* Feeling like the team was sluggish in games following airplane travel, the Owner banned booze from flights. In supporting the decision, Dark spoke of sacrifice, telling the club, "All of you want to give 100 percent when you come to the ballpark, but some of you wind up giving 70 percent. From now on, I want you to give 100 percent of 100 percent." This led to a new catchphrase among the players, "100 percent of 100 percent," which they used in coming weeks to poke fun at the manager.

One thing that didn't change was the pitchers sniping at Dark. Overall, clubhouse respect for the manager had improved, but pitchers were steadfastly holding out. With Blue and Holtzman having already said their pieces, the most outspoken among them was Darold Knowles.

The reliever had been in Dark's doghouse throughout the season,

---

* After being thrown out in three of his first four steal attempts, Washington swiped nine of 11 and was finally beginning to resemble a bona-fide big leaguer. "It's like driving a car just after getting your license," he theorized. "You're going to be too careful until you have an accident. And once you have that first little bump, you relax and just go out and drive. Hey, that's me. I wasn't comfortable. I was just too tight, too tense. I was afraid of getting picked off, afraid of being thrown out stealing. But now I've been tagged out. Been picked off. I've had that accident. Now I'm comfortable."

pitching only 12⅓ innings across July and August combined, and only once in a three-week stretch, when the manager called on him to relieve Paul Lindblad against the Rangers on September 7. The lefty allowed one of Lindblad's baserunners to score, then shut down Texas without incident for nearly two full frames until the ninth, when two walks and a single led to another run. The game was by then an 8–2 blowout, but with only two outs to go, Dark called for right-hander Bill Parsons to make his first big league appearance of the season. Knowles paid Dark the courtesy of waiting around until Parsons arrived from the bullpen, mostly so he could harangue the manager as they returned to the dugout. "When in the fuck are you going to let me pitch?" he barked. "How the fuck can a pitcher pitch well when you let him pitch only once a month?"

In the dugout, in front of the entire team, the left-hander demanded a trade. Dark was all too happy to accommodate him, snapping, "Make your own deal and you're gone." When the confrontation threatened to become physical, Knowles stomped off to the clubhouse and, after the game ended, went down the hall to see his old hunting buddy, Rangers manager Billy Martin. Upon learning about Dark's offer, Martin placed a call to his front office with orders to initiate trade talks. For Charlie Finley, of course, it was a nonstarter. The Owner did not abide player demands, and would certainly not tolerate his manager usurping any semblance of Finley's control as GM. The next day, under direct orders from Finley, Dark apologized to the entire team for his behavior toward Knowles.

The ongoing nature of that incident and others like it inspired Ron Bergman to run an informal poll for the *Oakland Tribune* in which he found that none of the nine A's pitchers who appeared regularly was willing to give Dark a vote of confidence. "It's tough to pitch when Hitler is the manager," said one starter. Another intoned that "it's not the moves he does make, but the moves he doesn't make." The man couldn't win for trying.

On September 2, the A's hosted the Angels for the first of what would be nine straight games at the Coliseum, marking Ray Fosse's first home appearances since returning from his neck injury. Even more dramatically, they were also Dick Williams's first games in Oakland since he removed his A's cap. Finley was far more occupied by the latter detail. In the top of the ninth inning, with the A's ahead, 6–4, the Coliseum scoreboard flashed huge letters reading, "Good night, Dick" — a phrase made famous

by the NBC comedy *Rowan & Martin's Laugh-In*. (Just before the closing credits, Dan Rowan would instruct co-host Dick Martin to "say good
night, Dick." Martin's inevitable reply: "Good night, Dick.") On the Coliseum scoreboard, of course, the phrase carried another connotation. The
A's were winning, Williams had the misfortune of no longer being at their
helm, and the Owner was rubbing it in.

The Family Night crowd of 25,640 wasn't sure what to make of it, but
those in the A's dugout had a pretty good idea. "It's the worst thing I've
ever seen on a baseball field," said Dick Green after the game. "It was
bad enough by itself, but before the game was over?" From the dugout,
Jackson tried to get the attention of the press box to have the message
removed.

Here's what none of the players knew: Just before the Angels came
to bat, Finley had phoned the broadcast booth. "It sounded like he was
drunk," recalled Jon Miller, who fielded the call. "He said, 'Okay, okay,
okay. Now, ahhh, ahhh, at the end of the game, the ahhh, ahhh . . .'—he
kept going on like that—'at the end of the game, the ahhh, ahhh, at the
end of the game the ahhh, the ahhh, the organist is going to play "Good
Night, Sweetheart." And then on the big message board in left it's going
to say, "Good night, Dick." Okay, okay, okay? You got it? You got it? You
got it?'"

Miller did not get it. He asked the Owner if those were instructions.
They were not. "Now listen," said Finley. "Now listen. . . ." The disjointed-
ness of the conversation was sufficient to distract Monte Moore, who shut
off his microphone for a moment to ask what the hell was going on. "It's
Charlie," whispered Miller. Moore winced.

Eventually the young broadcaster repeated his question: did Finley
want him to inform the organist and scoreboard operator about the plan?
"No," said Finley, growing exasperated. "They *already* know this, they already *know it*." The Owner had called merely to ensure that his prank
was mentioned on the radio in a way that seemed at once surprised and
delighted. To make sure he didn't forget, Miller wrote, in blue pencil at the
top of his scorebook, the phrases "Good night, Dick" and "Good night,
Sweetheart."

The problem with the jibe, apart from the jibe itself, was that even as
it was posted the Angels were mounting a comeback, putting the tying
run into scoring position with two outs against Fingers. On the radio
Moore said, "They just put up, 'Good night, Dick' on the scoreboard. I

don't know what that's all about. That looks really bad, because a base hit ties the game."

When Fingers finally struck out Bobby Valentine to end it, the organist played "Good Night, Sweetheart." On the air, Moore ignored the song entirely.

Afterward, Jackson went to the Angels clubhouse to apologize for the slight and told Williams that if anything similar happened again he'd walk off the field. Fingers expressed similar sentiments on the postgame radio show, saying, "I almost walked into the dugout. I didn't want to throw a pitch until they took it off."

Finley did put it up again, the same message, the very next night, but waited until the game was over to do so, by which point Reggie was walking off the field anyway. Following an A's victory over Texas only three days later, the Coliseum scoreboard read, "Good night, Billy Boy," a message directed at Rangers manager Billy Martin.*

If there was an aftermath to Finley's folly, it was not beneficial to his team. After flashing the message at Williams, the last-place Angels beat Oakland in three of their four remaining games. After Martin saw it, Texas beat the A's five straight across two series.

Oakland went only 6-8 through the end of the schedule, but nonetheless clinched on September 27 when the Rangers lost to Kansas City, eliminating themselves. It was the most anticlimactic triumph in the club's recent history. Equipment manager Frank Ciensczyk procured 40 bottles of champagne, but after the game most of the players simply grabbed one and left. Only three members of the starting lineup, most of whom were removed after the fifth inning, even bothered to stick around until the end. The only person really celebrating seemed to be Finley, and even that was mostly a calculated bullying of the local media. The Owner stalked through the clubhouse, a bottle in each fist, pouring them selectively over the heads of those he wanted to make miserable. Eventually he ordered the room to silence.

"I sweated blood for twelve years with this baseball team," he bellowed. "Oh, let me tell you, I lost sleep. I lost my hair. My family suffered. All

---

* As little as the players appreciated the tactic, Finley was not its originator. When the A's visited Kansas City in late June, the Royals drew 39,474 fans for a 2–0 victory—or 8,658 more than the same teams had drawn a week earlier in Oakland for an entire four-game series. The scoreboard at Royals Stadium punctuated the contrast with the message "Eat your heart out, Charlie."

for this splendid moment. I'm damn proud of my team and, frankly, I'm damn proud of myself. I don't mind taking bows at all, as hard as I work."

Nobody could deny that the man worked hard. Nor could they deny that he didn't mind taking bows.

The A's opened the American League playoffs on October 5, against an opponent that had been a long shot a month earlier to make it that far. On August 29, the Baltimore Orioles were a sub-.500 team, languishing at 63-65 and in fourth place in the American League East, eight games behind division-leading Boston. Then they won ten in a row, seized the division lead, and closed with 28 wins in 34 games, including their last nine in a row. Somehow Jim Palmer ranked as the team's fourth-best starter in the only season between 1973 and '76 in which he failed to win a Cy Young Award.

Catfish Hunter also closed the season on a tear, going 11-3 with a 1.77 ERA in his final 15 starts, vaulting himself — with overall marks of 25-12 and 2.49 — to the 1974 American League Cy Young Award. He was the obvious choice to start Game 1 against Baltimore's Mike Cuellar (22-10, 3.11), who finished sixth in the Cy Young balloting.

On Saturday afternoon at the Coliseum, Cuellar looked like the better pitcher. The lefty threw eight strong innings, while Hunter gave up three homers and six runs while failing to survive the fifth. The Orioles' 6–3 victory was their tenth straight, and even with some 8,500 empty seats, it was the largest playoff crowd in Oakland history. The loss was a setback for the A's, but by this point they were used to rebounding from impediments far more onerous than this.

If Game 1 was about the failure of one of Oakland's biggest stars, Game 2 was about the success of a guy decidedly on the fringe. Since returning from his neck injury, Ray Fosse had hit just .185 with a single homer over 32 games. That he was in the lineup at all was because A's pitchers loved throwing to him. In the three months Fosse spent on the disabled list, Oakland's team ERA was 3.21; after he came back, it was an even 2.50. Throwing out eight of 14 would-be base thieves over the season's final three weeks helped mitigate his horrid batting line. Finley, however, consistently agitated for playing time for Claudell Washington — a move that necessitated moving Joe Rudi to first base and Gene Tenace behind the plate, forcing Fosse to the bench. Dark put the Owner off whenever possible, including the opening games of the playoffs.

Fosse started Game 2 strong, throwing out Paul Blair on a steal attempt, which dissuaded the Orioles from further such efforts. Then he called a five-hit shutout from Ken Holtzman, whose 2.19 ERA when Fosse caught was nearly two points lower than with everybody else.

The catcher also provided Oakland's big blow on offense when, with a 2–0 lead and two runners on base in the eighth inning, he stepped to the plate against reliever Grant Jackson, having already singled and doubled in the game. As Fosse settled into the batter's box he recalled a dream he'd had two nights earlier about hitting a three-run homer off a southpaw. Jackson threw left-handed.

Sure enough, the catcher connected for a prophesy-powered three-run homer to cap a 5–0 victory.* It was a return to form for the Marion, Illinois, native, who as a prep had turned down Bear Bryant's pitch to play football at the University of Alabama in favor of baseball at Southern Illinois. Fosse was eventually selected seventh overall by Cleveland in the first-ever player draft in 1965, six slots after the A's took Rick Monday. A power hitter with a rocket arm, he won Gold Gloves and made All-Star appearances in his first two full seasons, in 1970 and 1971. The most notable moment of his career, however, was also its least fortunate. During the 1970 All-Star Game in Cincinnati, with the score tied 4–4 in the bottom of the 12th inning, Pete Rose decided to win the game in front of his hometown fans. Taking off from second base on Jim Hickman's single, Rose didn't break stride around third. The throw home from Royals center fielder Amos Otis sailed wide, forcing Fosse several steps up the third-base line to field it. Rose led with his left shoulder as he barreled into Fosse, knocking the catcher backward and sending the ball ricocheting toward the third-base dugout. Rose scored, the National League won, and Fosse said his shoulder "felt as though it had been mangled." When X-rays came back negative, Fosse, despite being unable to raise his left arm, opened the second half behind the plate for Cleveland, batting cleanup. The catcher, who collected 16 homers and 45 RBIs before the injury, accounted for only two and 16, respectively, in the second half. The following April, eight months after the injury,

---

* Prior to Game 2, Finley gave the team a pep talk — something about the difference between determination and desire, as best as any of the players could tell — which was ignored at best and mocked at worst after he left the room. Players were incredulous when multiple media accounts credited the speech for Sunday's Game 2 victory.

further X-rays detected the fracture through which Fosse had been playing.*

Now, after having missed more than half of the '74 season following the Jackson-North brawl, here he was again, relishing the opportunity to finally absorb some of the accolades that had grown increasingly infrequent over recent years. After the game Fosse was shepherded to a media session in the exhibition hall between the Coliseum and the adjacent Coliseum Arena, home to the NBA's Golden State Warriors. As usual, the Owner did his darndest to turn it into The Charlie Finley Show, bursting into the room and screeching, "Yeeeeeeah, Fosse — that's my boy!" almost as soon as the questions for the catcher had begun. In his hand was a glass that had until very recently been filled with champagne. Once every head in the room had spun his way, Finley enthused, "It wasn't the bat, it was the Fosse that swung it!" There was no moment, it seemed, beyond opportunity for the Owner to draw attention to himself. Fosse was incredulous. "Then why didn't you want to play me from the beginning?" he yelled. It was an instinctive response. Finley didn't even bother to answer. He didn't have to. He'd already taken what he wanted.

"Fuck Curt Gowdy and all that shit." That's what Vida Blue had to say prior to Game 3.

Back in 1971, people thought that Vida couldn't be beaten. Then, in the playoffs, Baltimore beat him. He took the loss in his only start of the 1972 World Series. He didn't make it out of the first inning in his Game 1 start against Baltimore in the 1973 ALCS, then gave up four runs in Oakland's Game 4 defeat. Vida pitched poorly as Oakland lost Game 2 of the '73 World Series against the Mets, and absorbed the loss in Game 5. Over four years, 13 appearances, six starts, and 39 innings, Blue was 0-4 in the postseason, with a 5.31 ERA. This was why Gowdy, broadcasting for NBC-TV, told a national audience that Blue had never won a big game — after

---

* It was only one example of the kind of injuries that seemed to happen only to Fosse. In 1970, for example, a cherry bomb thrown from the upper deck of Yankee Stadium exploded under the catcher's instep, burning through his shoe and two pairs of socks. In 1971, Tigers pitcher Bill Denehy kicked out as Fosse charged the mound, his spikes slicing through Fosse's right hand, a spot on his neck, and a ligament in his left wrist, sidelining him for the better part of a week. So thorough was the impression that Fosse was brittle that after the catcher injured his neck in the Jackson-North fight, Finley urged him to "tell it like it happened because I don't want people to think that you're getting hurt all the time."

which Vida went out on a clear, cool day in Baltimore and spun a master-piece. Nine innings, two hits, no walks, seven strikeouts. Ninety-three of his 101 pitches were fastballs. No Oriole reached second base. Vida was so good that Jim Palmer was saddled with the loss despite pitching his own complete-game four-hitter, his only mistake being a fourth-inning homer by Sal Bando after an 11-pitch at-bat. Oakland's 1–0 win gave the A's a two-games-to-one lead in the best-of-five series.

Vida had approached the game with particular fastidiousness. He went over Baltimore's lineup repeatedly for days. He sought out Holtzman for advice following the lefty's dominant Game 2 performance and listened when Holtzman told him to consistently pitch batters away. (Of Balti-more's 27 outs, only five were hit to the left side.) Afterward, North sat next to Vida in the clubhouse, the outfielder's words floating into the ether for general consumption. "Never win a big game," he sizzled. "Yeah, well choke on that one, motherfucker."

Not everything had gone smoothly for Oakland. In the seventh inning, Dark called for Herb Washington to pinch-run for Tenace, who kicked the bag in anger at being pulled and upon reaching the bench spiked his helmet to the dugout floor. It bounced all the way to the manager, who, fed up with intransigence from his players, picked it up and threw it the length of the bench. It bounced out the far end of the dugout and ended up near Finley's box, drawing the Owner's irritated attention.

Within moments Washington was thrown out trying to steal second. At the sight of it, Tenace grabbed a fistful of bats, walked down the dugout tunnel, and splintered them one at a time on the concrete walls. After the game he called Washington's insertion a horseshit move and lamented — as not only the league's third-leading home run hitter but also, since the off-season departure of Mike Hegan, the team's best-fielding first base-man — that close leads late in games merited tightening the defense, not diminishing it. He suggested that Washington's skills would have been better utilized subbing for somebody like Jackson, whose every move on the base paths was made in deference to his tender hamstring. Tenace yelled that he wanted to be traded, if possible before the playoffs ended.

"Well, that's the A's for you," said Jackson later. "We're back in form, popping off and having fun. All we need right now is a fight." He'd get one soon enough.

• • •

The crowds in Baltimore were even less inspiring than those in Oakland, with Memorial Stadium a bit over half-capacity for Games 3 and 4. Those who made it to the latter witnessed some historic weirdness on the part of the home team.

It was an elimination game for the Orioles, and Mike Cuellar, starting on short rest, was so stiff during warm-ups that Orioles manager Earl Weaver had reliever Ross Grimsley heat up in the first inning. The good news for Baltimore was that Cuellar was literally unhittable. The bad news for Baltimore was that it didn't matter. Cuellar walked five men over the first four innings, then another three in the fifth to load the bases. That brought up Gene Tenace — hitless in the series but the league leader in bases on balls — with no margin for error.

Tenace walked, bringing home Bando with the game's first run. When Cuellar went to a 2-1 count on the next hitter, Claudell Washington — his last pitch being his 122nd of the day — there was Weaver, trudging wearily to the mound to remove his pitcher, who was throwing a no-hitter and losing.

Grimsley shut down the A's until the sixth, at which point Bando walked, then scored on Oakland's first and only hit, an opposite-field double by Jackson. (It was really more like a medium-deep fly ball, which, thanks to the 309-foot left-field line, ricocheted off the wall.) Now it was 2-0, which was more than enough for Catfish Hunter, who allowed only two hits over seven shutout frames. Fingers handled things from there, ceding an RBI single with two outs in the ninth before slamming the door. Against the odds, Oakland was one-hit and won, 2-1, to secure the pennant. If clinching the division had been the picture of decorum for the A's, the winning clubhouse this time was the opposite, with players hugging and tousling and laughing. It was the third straight season in which they'd earned a spot in the World Series, but the first time they turned the trick in fewer than five games.

The good vibes carried all the way to the manager, who found himself not only doused with bubbly but unexpectedly feted. "I just wanted to win for Alvin Dark," Hunter told reporters. "Alvin has received a lot of bad publicity, and he's done a hell of a job. Sure, I got on him, Sal got on him, and it's bad to get on the manager. Everyone was against him at first, myself included. But he proved himself right by winning. Believe me, it's tough to take over a championship team and win again."

This was the type of recognition for which Dark had hoped early on. It took him a full season to gain it. "Praise the Lord," he said in closing his postgame meeting with the press. "Praise the Lord."

With the team flight to Los Angeles not scheduled until the next day to account for a possible Game 5, Finley hosted the team at the Chesapeake Restaurant, a long-standing Baltimore institution that provided some of the area's finest dining. About 70 people attended, including players and members of Finley's family, enough to fill eight large tables. It was a spectacle; the restaurant's capacity was 300 people, and Finley had booked only part of it. The rest of the establishment's patrons wanted only to quietly enjoy their meals, but as the evening wore on, quiet became an increasingly scarce commodity. Charlie Finley was throwing a party.

The Owner was in his element, running things however he saw fit. Also: the ladies. It's not that Finley was womanizing more now that he had a divorce on the table, it's that his womanizing was more out in the open. In the playoffs it started and ended with five-foot-nine blond bombshell Lucianne Buchanan, the reigning Miss California. Their relationship was platonic, she said, but the eye-candy factor was undeniable. The Owner brought her along through every step of the postseason, on planes and in team hotels. He set her up with a guitar on the flight to Baltimore, and she serenaded the players.

In the middle of dinner Finley banged on his glass with a spoon and offered a toast. "You guys probably heard it because we were right near the dugout, but whenever we needed good luck, Miss California would do this cheer," he said. Players looked at one another with bemusement. "It always paid off," explained the Owner, looking Buchanan's way, "so, Lucianne, go ahead."

"Right here in the restaurant?" she stammered, embarrassed by the unexpected spotlight.

Finley wanted what Finley wanted. "Yes," he said. "C'mon, it'll be great."

With that, the reigning Miss California, the loveliest woman many of the people in attendance had ever laid eyes upon, let loose with an outsized hog call: *Sooooweee piggy piggy piggy piggy! Soooooweeeee!* She'd learned it from her father, who grew up on a farm in Texas, and chances were good that she was the first person to ever make that sort of sound in that sort of place, at least during dining hours. A number of patrons who had nothing to do with the A's — otherwise known as "innocent bystanders" — looked on, appalled. So much for crab cakes in peace. As Buchanan wailed, Catfish Hunter leaped from his chair and raced to her side. "That's really good," he said. "Now do it again and I'll help you." So Buchanan did it again: *Soooooweee piggy piggy piggy piggy!* this time with Hunter snorting along in hoglike accompaniment. The A's were champions of the American League, and they were having themselves a time.

13

Hello, Hollywood . . . Goodbye, Catfish
(prelude)

Lady, this is the Oakland A's. There are no friends on the bus.

— Reggie Jackson to an autograph seeker who, after several
A's players had brushed past her, said to him, "Gee, you're
nice, but some of your friends on the bus are not so nice."

The Los Angeles Dodgers were the antithesis of everything Charlie Finley built his organization to be. The Owner's operation was a one-man
show, with a bare-bones staff geared toward passing both decisions and
praise to the top of the food chain. Finley was a born iconoclast, a man
of orange baseballs and green bats and white shoes and designated runners and Harvey the freaking Rabbit. There was nobody in the ranks of
baseball ownership further than he from the staid, old-moneyed, tradi-
tion-gripping stability of Dodgers owner Walter O'Malley. They were a
model franchise, those Dodgers, from player development to community
outreach to their charming ballpark in Chavez Ravine. They boasted pris-
tine white home uniforms (augmented with so-American blue and red),
All-Stars at nearly every position, huge attendance, and the distinct aura
of *What a ballclub*. Apart from playing great baseball, the Dodgers had
so little in common with the A's that on paper it was difficult to gauge
whether they were even in the same business.

The Dodgers were in no way cowed by Oakland, but neither did they
accord them respect befitting a two-time defending champion. Like the
Reds in 1972, many Los Angeles players viewed their recent victory over
Pittsburgh in the NLCS as the season's true test, then dived headlong into
the same type of rhetoric that came back to bite Cincinnati. "I definitely

think we have a better ballclub," said left fielder Bill Buckner, adding that "the A's have only a couple of players who could make our club." The insult was both familiar and ludicrous. Oakland players understood they'd never get the kind of reception that champions in other cities took for granted, but expected that, among their colleagues at least, sheer dint of accomplishment would be worth a hot damn. No such luck. "I don't know how they come up with this shit," said Fingers, looking back. "I thought to myself, do they know who they're taking about?"

Oakland's confidence was equally pronounced, of course — they just didn't feel the need to publicize it. In 1972 the A's had been unsteady champions, feeling their way through the spotlight. In 1973 they were driven to distraction by Finley and Williams. Now, however, they understood precisely who they were and what they could do. "By 1974 we had the swagger," reflected Joe Rudi. "We knew we were good. Everybody had matured, and we knew we could play with anybody. The Dodgers didn't scare us at all."

Even the Dodgers' pep-rally attitude got under Oakland's skin. Los Angeles players pilfered the Mets' slogan from a year earlier, "You gotta believe," and were almost collegiate in their fervor. Such a tenor played well in Southern California, but the curmudgeons in the state's northern climes wanted no part of it. "Team spirit doesn't apply here . . ." bristled Ken Holtzman. "With $27,000 on the line, I hate everybody."

The Dodgers were the National League equivalent to the Yankees — fistfuls of pennants over the years and almost no second-division finishes. They boasted an impervious infield that would stay together a record total of nine years, through 1981. At first base was the 1970s version of Mr. Baseball: Steve Garvey, a square-jawed, All-American hunk with huge forearms whose .312 batting average, 21 homers, 111 RBIs, and winning smile would earn him the National League MVP Award. At second base, Davey Lopes's 59 steals topped anybody on the A's. Bill Russell's slickness at shortstop earned him an All-Star nod in '73. At third base Ron Cey made what would be the first of six consecutive All-Star appearances.

The Dodgers' front-end rotation of Andy Messersmith (20-9, 2.59 ERA, runner-up in the Cy Young voting) and Don Sutton (19-9, 3.23) could match up with anybody. And if the A's thought that Rollie Fingers could lock down a game's late innings, Mike Marshall had some things to show them. The diminutive screwballer pitched for five teams over his first eight seasons, but this, his first with the Dodgers, had been revelatory. The rubber-armed reliever appeared a record 106 times, reaching 208 innings without starting a game. His 21 saves led the league, while his 15 wins and 143 strikeouts each ranked third on the Dodgers staff. Marshall coasted to the first Cy Young ever awarded to a reliever.

Three of the top five NL MVP finalists (Garvey, Marshall, and Jim Wynn). Three of the top five Cy Young finishers (Marshall, Messersmith, and Sutton). Five All-Stars. Up-and-comers like the 24-year-old Buckner (.314 batting average, 31 steals). The Dodgers' starting catcher, Steve Yeager, was among the league's best defenders, and their backup catcher, Joe Ferguson, was so strong of arm that he was also used in right field. Either catcher, said multiple members of the Los Angeles roster, would prove too much for would-be base thieves like North and Campaneris.

All of it was reinforced by the star-worshiping atmosphere of Los Angeles, and fermented into something that pushed beyond the boundaries of confidence and well into egoism. The A's didn't care for it. "Shit," fumed Dick Green to his teammates. "What the fuck have they ever won? Where were they last year? Not even in the postseason. Where were they the year before? Not in the postseason. What have they ever won, all these big shots? We won two straight years, and *we're* supposed to be afraid of *them*? Are you kidding?"

Little did the A's know that by the time the dust settled on the Fall Classic, the Dodgers' attitude would be the least of their problems.

The afterglow of Oakland's victory over the Orioles was eradicated two days later by Friday's edition of the *Chicago Sun-Times,* which announced that, following the World Series, Catfish Hunter would declare himself a free agent.

Prior to the season, as Hunter's teammates lined up for arbitration, Catfish set to negotiating with Finley. He'd always wanted to make $100,000 per year, but the only way the Owner would give it to him was with a two-year pact. Hunter assented, with a caveat: half the money would be paid in regular two-week installments through the season, while the other half would go to a party of Hunter's choosing. Finley agreed and made the two-week payments as scheduled. When Hunter indicated that he wanted the other half paid into an insurance annuity in North Carolina, however, the Owner balked. That would put the tax onus on Finley instead of Hunter, sticking him for an extra $25,000, give or take. The pair went back and forth over the season's final months with so little resolution that

Hunter began to talk openly to teammates about the possibility of contract default. If that was the case, he would be relieved of any obligation to the A's and after the season could sign with whichever club he wanted. It was lunacy, of course, not at all the way baseball worked, but Catfish was insistent. Somehow no word of the dispute reached the press until the *Sun-Times* story on the cusp of Game 1.

Hunter wasn't trying to use the timing for negotiating leverage. In fact, he'd wanted the topic tabled until after the season. One of the people he told about his situation, however, former teammate Mike Hershberger, mentioned it to reporter Jerome Holtzman, who ran with it. With little to lose once the story broke, Catfish opened up. "What happens if you don't make a payment on your car or your house?" he asked a newsman. "The contract says you've got to be paid."

Some said the pitcher was posturing as a means of renegotiating a contract that began to look bad the moment his teammates started winning arbitration cases. If Ken Holtzman got $93,000 for his first 20-win season, what was Catfish worth after his fourth? Finley, meanwhile, was in nearly complete denial. He believed that he wielded power in the situation because owners wielded power over players in virtually every situation. Anyway, compared to the multimillion-dollar lawsuit Mike Andrews had filed a day earlier, the disputed 50 grand was small potatoes.* "There's nothing to it at all," said the Owner to the gathered press. "You can say I refuse comment."

Friday was workout day at Dodger Stadium prior to Saturday's Game 1. For the first all-California World Series, it seemed like every member of the Los Angeles media, not to mention the usual throng from around the country, had packed into the visitors' clubhouse. Ken Holtzman was pulling on his uniform when a herd of Chicago scribes approached his locker, smiles on every face. Jim Enright, Dave Nightengale, and Dick Dozer, who all knew the left-hander from his time with the Cubs, sought two things: to offer congratulations and to figure out what the heck was

---

* Shortly after beating the Orioles, Finley was asked if he'd heard from Mike Andrews. "What kind of fucking question is that?" he asked. When the A's arrived in Southern California a day later, he found out: Andrews, having spent the 1974 season out of baseball, had just filed a $2.5 million lawsuit in Alameda County Superior Court against Finley and Dr. Harry Walker, the man who examined him. They eventually settled out of court.

up with this bawdy, brawling team. "We read about you guys all the time, and I can't believe some of it," said Nightengale. "Is it just hype? What's really going on?"

While Nightengale spoke, Rollie Fingers and Blue Moon Odom walked one after the other through the clubhouse door. As Fingers approached his locker, adjacent to the stall at which Holtzman was entertaining the Chicago media, Odom called out from his own locker across the room: "Hey, Rollie, do you need any extra tickets?" This was not an uncommon question, especially during the World Series, when tickets were scarce and requests could be overwhelming. Still, the timing was odd. Fingers looked up quizzically, unsure about Odom's motivation.

Even as the question was being asked, clubhouse attendant Jim Muhe was on the far side of the room, approaching Bando's locker. This was his 14th year as visiting clubhouse manager, and he felt a bit foolish about the question he wanted to ask. He looked around furtively to see if anybody was listening, then unloaded something that had been on his mind since the A's eliminated Baltimore. "I'm nervous with you guys in here," he admitted to the Captain. Bando was confused. Oakland only just arrived in town; there hadn't yet been time for anybody to pull any tricks. He asked Muhe what was on his mind. "All the stuff I've heard about, the way you fight all the time," Muhe answered. "I've never had to deal with anything like that." Bando chuckled.

Down the row of lockers, Fingers stared across at Odom. "No," he said curtly, "I don't need any extra tickets, thanks. I've got enough."

"Oh," said Odom. "I thought you might need one for your wife's boyfriend."

At that moment Holtzman knew what was about to happen. "Oh God, here we go," he said aloud.

Across the room Bando, still speaking with Muhe, smiled at the clubbie. He thought it patently absurd that his team's reputation could have such a profound effect on somebody who hadn't so much as met most of the players. Sure, the Jackson-North scuffle earned some headlines, but that was back in June. And Odom-Blue was in '72, a lifetime ago. "That stuff is overblown," Bando said. "We don't fight any more than any other team. As a matter of fact, we love each other."

With the phrase "love each other," Fingers charged, murder on his mind. The mustachioed reliever grabbed hold of a nearby cart used to transport dirty laundry and pushed it as hard as he could toward Odom.

It bounced along the floor, wheels squeaking, and crashed into Odom's ankle just before Fingers swooped in with a one-handed shove that sent his opponent sprawling. For Odom, it was only an opening salvo. The guy hadn't missed any time after being *shot,* for crying out loud; a laundry cart and an awkward right hand weren't about to slow him down. That he was the smaller man by some four inches and 15 pounds didn't faze him. Odom leaped to his feet, lowered his shoulder, and charged headlong into Fingers's chest, knocking the reliever backward into a locker. As the pitcher fell his head glanced off a clothes hook and was cut open, blood flowing freely down his neck and onto the floor.* Unlike earlier fights, this one didn't require anybody to break it up. Odom got up limping and Fingers didn't get up at all, remaining seated and gripping his head. Within moments a score of teammates raced between the players, shouting at Odom, at Fingers, at each other. The clubhouse had gone from a scene of cheery anticipation to something approaching an English soccer riot.

Dozer, wide-eyed, turned to Holtzman. "Kenny, I apologize," the newsman said. "I will never doubt you when you say that you guys are fucking crazy." Enright shook his head. "I thought it was all bullshit," he said in disbelief, "but you guys take the cake."

Across the room, Muhe, mouth agape, turned uneasily toward Bando. "Get out of here," he said, backing away. Upon realizing that he couldn't toss the A's out of their own dressing room, the clubbie ejected himself, running out the door and down the hall to the home clubhouse, where he announced, "Those guys over there are killing each other! There's blood all over the place!"

Hunter applied pressure to Fingers's scalp until trainer Joe Romo could wrap a towel around the reliever's head. As Fingers was helped up, Odom, ankle smarting from the cart's impact, limped over, hand extended in truce. Fingers took it. "The fighting A's!" screamed Gene Tenace. "I love it! I love it!"

An hour later Fingers was back from Lutheran Hospital, five stitches in his head. There were 25 hours to go before the first pitch of the World Series, and he volunteered to toss batting practice to see how he held up. Odom also worked out, but by the time he returned to team headquar-

---

* One of the nearby lockers belonged to Ray Fosse, the guy who lost half his season trying to break up a fight earlier in the year. He knew this story already and didn't like how it ended. Rather than trying to break it up, the catcher raced in the opposite direction, toward the trainer's room.

ters at the Los Angeles Hilton his ankle had begun to swell. He spent the evening on crutches.

Suddenly the A's were a team of self-inflicted walking wounded. What the hell, outsiders wanted to know, just happened?

The answer had to do with Fingers's marital situation and Odom's lack of common sense when it came to leaving a subject alone. More than anything, it had to do with the team's culture of goading each other right up to the point of rage, a well-honed process that kept everybody so on edge that the very idea of loafing through a game or series was impossible to entertain.

Fingers and his wife, Jill, had been high school sweethearts in Upland, California, about 40 miles east of where he and Odom knocked each other senseless. The couple came up through the minor leagues together, but things were going sour, and had been for some time.* Their fights grew progressively louder and more frequent, to the point that the pitcher nearly moved in with Jackson during the season. Fingers felt the need to reassure Dark that the chaos of his marriage would not affect his performance on the field.

Usually, wives were within the boundaries of acceptable needle topics. Usually, of course, players and their wives held a mutual understanding that they would remain married at least through the weekend. Rollie and Jill Fingers were not so certain. Jill filed for divorce in July, but then the couple reconciled ... and split up again ... and got back together. Rumors swirled that Jill was seeing a contractor who was remodeling their house.†

In early September, Hunter cut a cartoon out of a newspaper, showing a couple in bed, the woman saying, "I told Alvin we were washed up, but I said it soft in case I want to make up with him," and taped it to Fingers's locker. Most of the A's thought it was funny, but the reliever did not. He demanded to know who was behind it, and when nobody confessed,

---

* Fingers's honeymoon came courtesy of the Owner. Nine days after his wedding — opening day of Fingers's third professional season, in 1967 at Double-A Birmingham — a comebacker caught the pitcher squarely in the face, shattering his cheek and jaw. He missed nearly two months of action, part of which he spent in Florida with his new bride. Charles O. Finley & Company picked up the tab.

† Another rumor had Bando, Tenace, and others visiting the contractor at his construction site with a warning to stay away from Fingers's wife ... at least until after the season. The concept of "Don't fuck with our money" was prominent in their alleged dialogue.

made a general announcement. "I'm sick and tired of jokes being made about me and my wife," he said. "My personal problems are private, and I intend to keep them at home. I'm doing my job at the ballpark, I'm not letting anyone down, and I deserve a little respect. Fun is fun, but when it goes too far it stops being funny, so forget about me and my wife, and get down to business or there's going to be some head-busting that this team doesn't need." It was a threat, and it was enough. The jibing stopped . . . until the World Series.

Odom had fought with nearly all his teammates over the years. Usually, he was personable and outgoing, but those occasions on which he could not keep up with teamwide needling tended to set him off. Odom loved a good conversational joust but perpetually fell short of fully understanding the rules. When somebody got the better of him — a quicker zinger, a more biting jibe — instead of admitting defeat, taking stock of where things went wrong, and moving on, he frequently stayed the course. If this meant absorbing further abuse — usually this meant absorbing further abuse — Odom's thin skin would get scuffed, and he'd lash out physically.

"Moon, God bless him, was a star at instigating stuff," said Holtzman. Added Bando: "John didn't have any softness about him. He'd say things that would come out in such a way you'd want to strangle him."

As they walked from the bus to the visitors' clubhouse at Dodger Stadium, Odom began to ride Fingers. Hard. The closer, as prominent a needler as Odom, was considered one of the team's best practitioners of the form. On this day Blue Moon had some ammunition with which to fire back. Just before they reached the clubhouse, he jokingly brought up the verboten topic of divorce. "Moon," Fingers responded, "you can't even spell 'divorce.'"

"Yeah," replied Odom, "but your wife can."

"We had gotten into it a lot of times, but nothing personal to that point," said Fingers, looking back. "We'd get on each other about giving up a home run or screwing around in the clubhouse. You usually don't want to make it personal, especially when a guy is going bad. You don't want to bring family into it. But he took it to a higher level. I wasn't in the mood."

Afterward, everybody downplayed the incident. Fingers, Odom, and Dark independently referred to it as a "friendly scuffle," a fact that was pointed out to the manager, who augmented his response by adding that "it was a friendly scuffle and five friendly stitches." After a moment to reflect, he softly added, "It's really been a strange year."

As blood was cleaned from the clubhouse carpet and players filtered onto the field for their workout, another distraction took shape at the far end of the A's dugout, where Jerry Kapstein had planted himself for a conversation with Hunter. Until that point Kapstein was known in the Bay Area primarily as the nascent agent who won three arbitration cases against Finley earlier in the year. Now, though, he was taking things to a new level.

As soon as Hunter departed, reporters swarmed Kapstein. He rewarded them with contract details, information about how Hunter's designated recipient had not been paid, and a tidbit about two certified letters informing Finley of the discrepancy going unanswered. Kapstein noted that the IRS had signed off on the plan — Hunter having no control over the funds and owing no taxes until he collected the money after his retirement from baseball — way back in spring training.

Finally, a newsman raised the inevitable question: *Is Catfish a free agent?* "The contract has been breached," Kapstein said. "From a legal point of view, he is. Yes, he is." Court action, he declared, was imminent.

With Kapstein involved, the league office took notice. Bowie Kuhn weighed in with a three-paragraph press release distributed to the media during Game 2, acknowledging that he received letters from Hunter's lawyers in North Carolina and the Major League Baseball Players Association indicating that the A's had not fulfilled Hunter's contract terms and requesting the pitcher's unconditional release. Kuhn did not come off as sympathetic to their cause. "Under the pertinent rule provision," read the statement, "the Commissioner can declare a player a free agent if his club is in arrears for salary payments, but only if there is no bona fide undecided dispute as to whether the money is owed." The key to the quandary was the definition of "bona fide," which appeared to be up to the sole discretion of Bowie Kuhn.

The Owner, meanwhile, continued to downplay the affair. "Don't be concerned about Hunter, because I'm not," he told newsmen. "I did offer him the money any way he wanted it. This is just a little misunderstanding." Downplayed or not, there was no way to deny that this World Series already boasted some of the most pound-for-pound drama of any Fall Classic ever, and a pitch had yet to be thrown.

• • •

Game 1 couldn't come quickly enough. Despite his fresh stitches, Fingers looked ready to go. Odom, hobbling around on crutches, did not. (He spent the entirety of the opener in the clubhouse, icing his ankle.) The real health story, however, concerned Reggie Jackson's perpetually balky hamstring, injured 21 days earlier, which had Dark and Finley drafting contingency plans. They had been able to hide Jackson at designated hitter against Baltimore, where he managed only a single and a double in four games. Against the Dodgers, however, there would be no DH, a detail that Finley used to promote the prospects of his wunderkind, Claudell Washington. In a pregame meeting with Dark and the coaching staff, the Owner wondered whether it was time for Washington to step up from understudy and for Jackson to ride the bench. He was met with the unanimous opinion that Reggie should play, whatever his condition. "The hell with you guys," Finley muttered. But he relented.

When the game started, there was Reggie on the lineup card, in right field and batting fourth. And there he was, striding to the plate to lead off the second inning, neither team having scored. And there he was, turning on an Andy Messersmith fastball, hammering it deep over the wall in left-center. It was October, and this was Reggie Jackson.

It was a glorious piece of hitting. Because Jackson's hamstring prevented him from pulling the ball effectively, he took it to the opposite field. The homer served as a marker for his own self-confidence, and also for the Dodgers, who saw Messersmith, their ace — the league's ace — go into a quick hole, beaten more by will-to-win than anything else. With one swing, Jackson reinforced that there was more to Oakland's success than met the eye.

Ken Holtzman, pitching his third straight Series opener, wasn't particularly efficient, giving up six hits and a walk over the first four innings, but a double play and a pickoff helped keep Los Angeles off the board. The left-hander aided his own cause with a one-out double down the third-base line in the fifth (his third Series two-bagger in as many seasons), eventually scoring from third on a suicide squeeze that gave Oakland a 2–0 lead.

Holtzman lasted until the fifth, when Davey Lopes reached base on a Campaneris error, then scored all the way from first when Jackson bobbled Bill Buckner's ensuing single. After Holtzman walked the next hitter, Jim Wynn, Dark advanced toward the mound. Yes, the run scored because of two errors. Yes, it was only the fifth inning. Yes, Holtzman had a habit of exploding at early removals, but this was the World Series and it was never too early for Rollie Fingers. The closer came in and escaped the inning with Oakland's 2–1 lead intact.

The A's stretched it to 3–1 in the eighth on a single, a sacrifice, and an error by Ron Cey, but the story of the inning was that they did not score more. With one out and Bando on third, Jackson hit a medium-deep fly ball to center fielder Jim Wynn, who had a great bat but an unremarkable arm. The Captain would likely have scored without trouble were it not for Joe Ferguson in right. Ordinarily, a center fielder has priority on any ball he can reach, and Wynn was camped under this one. Ferguson, however, possessed one of the best outfield arms in baseball and had discussed this very scenario with Wynn before the game. Ferguson flashed past his teammate, snatched ball from sky, and, planting his right leg, unleashed a 300-foot strike to catcher Steve Yeager. Bando didn't stand a chance.

In the ninth, Fingers recorded two quick outs, but one out from victory Wynn again made his presence felt, hammering a hanging breaking ball into the left-field bleachers. That cut the lead to 3–2 and gave the crowd — at 55,974, a Dodger Stadium record — renewed hope.

The next hitter, Steve Garvey, was Fingers's 19th of the day. The pitch Garvey smacked into right field for a single was the pitcher's 68th — only two fewer than Holtzman had thrown. It was a heavy workload, even for Fingers, and it was only the first game of a Series in which he was likely to see heavy usage. With the power-hitting Ferguson at the plate, Dark's question was not whether he should replace the reliever, but with whom. Catfish Hunter made the decision easy.

Hunter was not accustomed to relief work, having appeared out of the bullpen only once in five years, but this was his regular throw day between starts. The right-hander was supposed to have gotten in his work during batting practice, but Dark, playing a hunch, suggested that he wait until the game's middle innings. When Hunter got up in the fifth, Dark asked how he felt. Hunter's answer — *Great* — confirmed him on the manager's short list of available relievers. Hold off for a few innings more, Dark told him.

Now it was his time. When Catfish reached the mound, Dark offered some quick advice. "This guy can't hit your curveball with a boat paddle," he said expectantly. The manager was surprised when Hunter told him that Ferguson would see nothing but fastballs.

"What do you mean, fastballs?" Dark asked. "He can't hit a curveball. Why do you want to throw him fastballs?"

Because, said Hunter, his Carolina drawl elongating the sentiment, "I ain't got no curveball today."

Five fastballs later, Ferguson went down swinging for the game's final out.

Afterward, the teams' respective attitudes reflected why the A's were two-time champions and why Los Angeles, despite its pre-series braggadocio, appeared unprepared for this level of competition. In one clubhouse sat Rollie Fingers and Catfish Hunter, the closer having entered the game four innings earlier than usual and thrown a starter's workload of shutdown ball, the starter closing the game without his full complement of pitches. Neither man said much about it. Had either pitcher failed, history held that he wouldn't have made excuses.

In the other clubhouse, Ferguson — Hunter's strikeout victim to close the game — offered scant respect to the man who bested him, barking, "He didn't show me anything." Nearby, Wynn paid Fingers similarly little credence, saying, "He's like any other relief pitcher. He's hittable." The Dodgers had nearly doubled Oakland's hit total, 11 to six, and put runners into scoring position in the second, third, fourth, fifth, and eighth innings. It was a game they felt they should have won, and they couldn't figure out why they didn't.

They would be wondering the same thing five days later when the A's repeated as champions.

In case the existing drama was insufficient, stories cropped up in multiple newspapers just prior to Game 2 suggesting that the A's might move to Seattle. Reasons abounded. Oakland's 845,000 attendance ranked 11th out of 12 American League teams and was down nearly 100,000 from a season earlier. The suit brought by Seattle against Major League Baseball for allowing the Pilots to move to Milwaukee after only one season had recently been resolved, renewing the Emerald City as a desirable location. Also, lord knows that Charlie Finley had done this sort of thing before.

The Owner was forced to vehemently deny what nearly everybody believed to be true. "I want you to write what I tell you, okay?" he told one newsman. "That is a bunch of shit. If you can't say that in your paper, then say it's a crock of horse manure. Absolutely nothing to it." Okay,

Charlie, came the collective response. Whatever you say. And the stories kept right on coming.

"There will come a time when Herb Washington will be the most devastating running force in baseball," said Billy North on Sunday evening. "It's not far off." The statement might have been truthful, but its timing was strictly a public show of support, spurred by the events of Sunday afternoon, when Washington was humiliated on national television.

Before that could happen, though, the early story of Game 2 was Los Angeles pitcher Don Sutton. In bright sunshine at Dodger Stadium, the 29-year-old right-hander toyed with the A's through eight innings, allowing only four hits while striking out nine. Vida Blue didn't pitch badly for Oakland, but neither did he have the dominant stuff he exhibited against Baltimore. Joe Ferguson's two-run homer off a waist-high fastball in the sixth gave the Dodgers a 3–0 lead.

That was where things stood when Sutton hit Bando in the left shoulder to start the ninth. Jackson followed with a check-swing double down the left-field line, moving Bando to third and bringing the tying run to the plate with nobody out. Suddenly, after barely registering a pulse all afternoon, Oakland was coming alive and Sutton was coming apart. Dodgers manager Walter Alston turned to Mike Marshall, as he had so many times throughout the season. It was the right-hander's 110th appearance, and though nearly all of them were splendid, their abundance may have taken a toll. Joe Rudi lined Marshall's second pitch into center field for a single that scored both runners. Now the score was 3–2, with the tying run on first and nobody out.

Marshall bore down, using his Cy Young stuff to strike out Tenace. At that point Alvin Dark made two moves. He sent up Angel Mangual to pinch-hit for Odom (who had shaken off his ankle injury to strike out two in one shutout inning of relief), and he had Herb Washington run for Rudi at first. This, then, was Finley's triumph, the manifestation of his long-touted experiment, on the game's biggest stage. Washington trotted from the dugout, yellow shirtsleeves flapping beneath his green A's jersey, and began stretching in earnest. Garvey greeted him warmly, taking note that every corner of their little triangle — Garvey and Washington at two points, Marshall at the other — were Michigan State alums. Marshall, in fact, was not only in East Lansing at the same time as Washington but, as an adjunct professor, taught a kinesiology course that Herb attended.

This was an anticipated matchup. For all Marshall's ability as a pitcher, one of his best tricks, despite being right-handed, was a devastating pickoff that delivered the ball to first more effectively than most lefties. Washington, of course, while historically fleet, was still learning how to read even adequate pickoff moves. Having taught him a thing or two in the classroom, Marshall now had a chance to extend his lessons to the ball field.

Washington slowly built his lead to two steps, then three, then three and a half. He crouched, arms dangling, awaiting the pitch. Marshall spun from the rubber and cocked his arm toward first, but did not throw. Washington darted back, standing up.

Again the runner inched off the bag. Again Marshall came set, but this time he merely flinched toward first. It was enough to get Washington leaning back toward the base.

Marshall set up a third time. Now he stripped his move even barer, merely jerking his rear foot off the rubber. By that point Washington was no longer falling for it and nonchalantly strolled back to first.

Marshall had the runner exactly where he wanted him. The pitcher's next move was a full spin, this time for real and far quicker than anything he'd yet shown. Washington was leaning toward second, his right knee bent slightly as if to run. The play wasn't close. By the time Washington dived to his left, Garvey's glove was already waiting, ball securely in place. The runner never even touched the bag.

Garvey skipped toward the mound after registering the putout, leaving Hurricane Herb to lie alone, face down on the base path, pounding a fist into the dirt. "It's simply experience over immaturity," intoned Vin Scully on the TV broadcast. Said Tenace later: "He really should have just put his foot on the bag like in Little League. That's the only way he *wasn't* getting picked off."

Two pitches later Mangual whiffed at an eye-high fastball and the Series was tied at one game apiece.

Nobody berated Washington when he reached the bench. They didn't have to — it was obvious how bad he felt. A's players had denigrated his role throughout the season, but now they went out of their way to soften a blow that hurt him so much *they* could feel it. In the postgame clubhouse, Jackson talked about how much Washington's instincts had improved. Blue said that it could have happened to anybody. Dark gave him a supportive pat on the rear as he walked by, a wordless reassurance that, said Washington later, meant as much as anything. When the sprinter boarded the bus, Reggie sat down next to him, and the two spoke softly all the way to the airport.

As the Series moved to Oakland, Monday's workout day at the Coliseum was supposed to be a low-key affair, a chance to get loose in the sunshine and give the national media access to players. The A's, of course, had a poor history with workout days. The one in Los Angeles put Rollie Fingers in the hospital and Blue Moon Odom on crutches. A year earlier, the one in New York featured insurgent players wearing Mike Andrews's uniform number on their sleeves. The one in Cincinnati the year before was all about the reaction to Campy Campaneris's bat toss in Detroit. It wouldn't take long for this one to join the litany.

The drama's genesis occurred back in mid-September, when *Sport* magazine published a cover story for which Reggie Jackson posed while wearing military regalia from the movie *Patton*. He had been interviewed for the issue by the film's star, George C. Scott, and found the resulting copy to be entirely bland. He couldn't say the same, however, for the second feature about him in the same issue. That one was by Murray Olderman, a Bay Area–based 52-year-old syndicated writer and cartoonist who had been desperate to schedule an interview with Reggie for his quick-turnaround piece. After doing a five-hour photo shoot for the cover, however, Jackson was in no mood to talk. He agreed only to let the writer informally hang out for a while at his condo in the exclusive Hiller Highlands neighborhood of Berkeley.

When Jackson saw the ensuing feature, he was miffed. Olderman described Jackson as "utterly charming or maddeningly harsh, depending on the situation," and said that he "has more than a little ego, more than a limited belief in his own glorious destiny." He spent close to a third of the space recounting Jackson's fights with Epstein, Williams, and North.* For Reggie, though, the crux came in two parts. One was Olderman's description of a Bible set next to a handgun atop the television, juxtaposed

---

* Olderman also gently mocked Jackson in the story's first two paragraphs by describing how the player was willing to pose for the cover wearing military gear, but when a World War II–era jeep was rolled in as an additional prop, Reggie said, "Hey, man, I don't want to be *that* far removed from my peers." Reggie was used to taking grief from the media, but for a photo shoot that they themselves arranged? That was something else.

with copies of *Penthouse* and *Playboy* strewn around the apartment. In the player's mind, this insinuated that holiness was subjugated by the baser aspects of his life. The other part was the depiction of former A's ball girl Mary Barry, who was described as wearing a green bikini and spending hours in the apartment. (It did not explicitly say that the two were dating, but the notion was strongly implied.) Barry's teenage employment with the team lent negative connotations to the description, but she'd graduated from high school by the time the story came out and was no longer in Finley's employ. Both she and Jackson were single. "I don't expect everyone to write nice things about me," Reggie said after the piece was published, "but I don't want a sarcastic treatment that makes me look like something I'm not. I'm not a hypocrite, but his story suggests it."

Reggie's teammates, some of them, anyway, were aware of his anger. He spoke openly of revenge fantasies, the most prominent of which involved telling Olderman off amid his journalist colleagues, returning some of the embarrassment Jackson felt. The reality, of course, was that Reggie was keenly aware of his public image and what such a plan would do to it. His teammates were somewhat less concerned.

As the A's worked out Blue saw Olderman on the field, pointing out various members of the A's to his 16-year-old son, and got an idea. Grabbing the writer by the hand, he said, "Come with me, there's someone who wants to see you," and led him to Jackson. Reggie had decided weeks earlier that it was not in his best interests to pursue a confrontation, but with it thrust upon him he reversed course. It was the only way to save face in front of teammates who had heard him talk repeatedly about what kind of trouble Olderman would be in the next time they met.

So Reggie began to yell. He profanely told Olderman what he thought of the article, and what he thought of the man who wrote it. And the more he yelled the angrier he became. What started as show became genuine hostility.

The scenario was just how Reggie pictured it. The field was littered with newsmen from across the country, and the moment he began to shout they gathered like pigeons to bread crumbs. Jackson was dressed for battle — batting helmet, batting gloves, dark glasses, windbreaker over his uniform — making him all the more intimidating. He screamed that Olderman was "a horseshit writer who had written a horseshit story," told him that he didn't want to see him again, and threatened to "punch him in his fucking mouth." It was as if Reggie was trying to taunt the scribe into a physical altercation. Olderman did not bite.

"You better never get around me alone, that's all I can say," Jackson finally hollered, pointing his finger. "If you do, you'll be in trouble."

Olderman, wearing thick-framed glasses and a blazer, was an Army veteran and about the same size as Jackson. He was hardly cowed.

"Are you threatening me?" he asked coolly. Vida stood next to them, gazing sheepishly at the ground.

Jackson clenched his fists and told the writer he was not welcome in the Oakland clubhouse.

"Are you going to keep me out?" Olderman asked.

"Yeah," Reggie said.

That was when Joe Reichler, MLB's director of public relations, raced over to separate the men. "Walk away with me," he sternly ordered Jackson. When Reggie refused, Reichler laid down the law right there: "Threaten him again, or lay a hand on him, and you won't play the rest of the series." Jackson backed down.

Things were quiet until the next day, when, prior to Game 3, Reichler approached Reggie as he warmed up in front of the A's dugout. The Commissioner, he said, was "very disturbed" over Jackson's behavior. If it happened again, Reichler said, "there's going to be a problem, a very serious problem, and I think you know what I mean by that."

Reggie smiled. "As far as I'm concerned," he said, "everything is over."

It was too early for everything to be over, of course. The A's had already sent two players to the hospital, were still trying to make sense of their best pitcher's claims that he would soon be playing elsewhere, had to fend off rumors of moving, tried to deflect questions about a lawsuit filed against their owner by one of their own, and lived down one of the most embarrassing pickoffs in big league history. Now they were also dealing with their star player verbally assaulting a member of the gathered media.

In passing, it seemed, the Series was tied, 1–1. It was easy to miss, but there was still some baseball to be played.

Before he could take the mound for Game 3 in Oakland, Catfish Hunter had to field questions about his contract being a distraction, and what it meant in terms of his relationship with the Owner. He put it as clearly as possible. "I've got a job to do and I'll go out and do it," he said. "The court case comes later. The World Series is now. When I put on this uniform, I give 100 percent. I don't care if it's in a cow pasture or a stadium full of people."* Then he went out and showed why he was worth every penny Finley didn't want to pay him, thrilling a sellout Coliseum crowd by pitching shutdown ball into the eighth inning. Hunter was opposed by Los Angeles's Al Downing, a spot starter with 20 fewer wins on the season than Catfish who was pitching only because Dodgers ace Tommy John had recently undergone the elbow ligament surgery that would one day bear his name.†

The key moment in Oakland's scoring came in the third, when Jackson drove in Billy North with a high hopper in front of the plate that catcher Joe Ferguson dropped for an error. It was the A's first run, but even more exhilarating was the vigor with which an increasingly healthy Reggie motored down the line, showing more power in his stride than he had in weeks. Downing would record only three more outs before being yanked midway through the fourth, having given up four hits, four walks, and three runs. From there, both Hunter and the Dodgers bullpen put up a string of zeroes.

Catfish began to tire in the eighth, hanging a slider that lead-off hitter Davey Lopes blasted to deepest center field. North managed to track it down just in front of the wall, but it was concerning. The next batter, Bill Buckner, hit a slow fastball just a bit farther, this one reaching the center-field bleachers for the Dodgers' first run. Catfish was cooked.

With the score now 3–1, Dark called for Fingers, who was coming off his four-and-a-third-inning epic in Game 1. The first batter he faced, Jim Wynn, slapped a slider between Tenace and Green for a single, bringing the tying run to the plate in the person of the Dodgers' best hitter, Steve Garvey. Visions of a 2–1 series deficit began to dance through Oakland's dugout.

Garvey smoked a liner to virtually the same spot as Wynn's single, but this time Green was standing there to swipe it from the air above his

---

* Hunter probably didn't mean to intone Finley's 1964 stunt — as grand a *fuck you* to the politicians of Kansas City as he could muster — in which the Owner threatened to move his team to a cow pasture if his demands for a more favorable stadium lease were not met, and even went so far as to secure a location. That was the year before Hunter joined the A's. Now his cow pasture comment appeared to be more prophetic than Finley's. And more genuine.

† Downing was a 14-year veteran who spent an unremarkable half-season with the A's in 1970. His enduring notoriety had come six months earlier, from throwing the pitch that Hank Aaron hit for his record-breaking 715th home run.

shoe tops. In one fluid motion he fired to first to double off Wynn. Threat erased, inning over.

The A's would need every bit of their lead. Willie Crawford led off the top of the ninth with a homer that brought the score to 3–2. Perplexed, Fingers fiddled with his cap. The next batter, Joe Ferguson, topped an easy two-hopper to shortstop that kicked off the heel of Campaneris's glove. Fingers scuffed at the dirt in front of the mound. The error brought Ron Cey to the plate as the winning run, still with nobody out. Knowles and Odom heated up posthaste in the bullpen.

Fingers bore down to strike out Cey, but the next hitter, Bill Russell, slapped the first pitch he saw toward right field. It looked like a surefire single, but Green was perfectly positioned — as he had been all game and all series — and didn't have to move from his spot deep in the hole to tie a World Series record by starting his third double play of the night, this one a game-ender. Oakland's victory was the Series' third straight 3–2 score.

Afterward, the defeated Dodgers offered typically scant praise. "They got away with murder, to say the least," said Ferguson.

"We definitely have a better team," added Buckner, moaning, "We can't fight luck."

The only disrespect emanating from the A's clubhouse was directed at Oakland's own grounds crew. When Green was told of the double-play record, he took it as a soapbox opportunity. "When you take into account how bad the infield is in the Oakland Coliseum, making three double plays in any game, let alone a World Series, is something," he said. "We've complained about our infield for years, and sometimes I wonder why we keep bothering. No one is going to do anything about it."

In that he was correct. The A's home ballpark was far worse than Dodger Stadium, as were their amenities, their transportation, their community standing, and the players' relationships with their owner. What did the A's have? A 2-games-to-1 lead. They would take it.

Charlie Finley stood before his team, eyes burning bright enough to light the Coliseum during a blackout. He loved this kind of pep talk, truly believed that what he said mattered and that the players thought so too. He held a copy of that day's *San Francisco Examiner,* which offered some frank assessments from the Dodgers' Bill Buckner, who, wrote Glenn Schwarz, "discussed the A's as if they were the San Diego Padres." Among the things Buckner said: "If we played them 162 times, we could beat them 100."

Finley read the account aloud, with contempt. He called Buckner "horseshit." His voice rose. "I get sick and tired of National League teams laughing at us," he fumed. "They have all the mouths and we have all the trophies in the clubhouse."

Finley was correct, of course, but the players already knew everything he had to say. If there was any benefit to the moments he spent before them, it was that time spent listening to the Owner was not time spent beating each other senseless.

Before Finley left the clubhouse, he stopped by Dark's office and made some personnel changes, never mind that the lineup had already been posted and distributed to the media. The A's led the Series, but they'd managed only eight runs in three games. The Owner saw this as an opportunity. His new configuration featured Claudell Washington — Finley's pulled-from-obscurity superstar-in-the-making — in left field, and Joe Rudi at first base. With the Dodgers stealing more bases than all but one National League team, Ray Fosse was indispensable behind the plate — which meant that, with no DH, the American League's third-leading home run hitter, Oakland's resident World Series hero, Gene Tenace, would be relegated to the bench. To make matters worse, Tenace had already seen his name on the original lineup card. So had everybody else. He would spend the game seething.

It wasn't an elimination game for the Dodgers, but there was little denying that it was their last, best hope. With their top starter, Andy Messersmith, on the mound, anything short of a win would mean finding three subsequent victories from a batch of pitchers so unappealing that manager Walter Alston was considering Mike Marshall for a potential Game 6. It didn't work out as they'd hoped.

In the sixth inning, Oakland turned three walks, two singles, and an error by Garvey into four runs, transforming a 2–1 deficit into a 5–2 lead that they never relinquished. Ken Holtzman pitched two-run ball into the eighth and continued his solo crusade against the designated hitter, following his Game 1 double with a third-inning homer off Messersmith, which made him four-for-his-last-five World Series at-bats, including three doubles and a homer.

The play of the game was also the game's final play. In the ninth, with Fingers on the mound, Ron Cey on first, and the A's two outs from victory, Dick Green shaded pinch hitter Von Joshua up the middle. Seeing Fosse call for an outside pitch, the second baseman adjusted even more, sliding farther to his right as Joshua swung. That was how Green's momentum carried him toward a bullet over the bag that he had no business catching, hit so hard that he barely had time to dive into a full-bore sprawl toward center field. Snaring the ball on its fourth hop just before hitting the ground, Green pushed onto his knees and shoveled it to Campaneris at second for the out. Campy's powerful sidearm relay barely beat the speedy Joshua. Game over. "You can't smuggle a ball past second base," marveled Winkles after the game. "If it stays above ground and doesn't explode, Greenie will get it."

Green was the longest-tenured of the A's, so veteran that he had not even been signed by Charlie Finley, but by the Arnold Johnson administration the year before Finley bought the team. By 1974 he was an 11-year vet, having played under ten managers, counting Bauer and Dark twice each. One of his former teammates, Wes Stock, was now the A's pitching coach, and one of his former opponents, Jerry Adair, was coaching at first. Each was more contemporary than mentor.

Green grew up in Yankton, South Dakota, about 80 miles southwest of Sioux Falls. When he was 18, his father took over a North American Van Lines moving franchise in Rapid City, first as manager, then using part of his son's $12,000 signing bonus to purchase it outright. The junior Green worked there during his off-seasons, and eventually used the firm as leverage against Finley. It was a foolproof system: Green could make just as much money manning the family business, and was willing to sacrifice baseball to do so. It led to four annual retirements and four off-seasons with the Owner scrambling for extra cash to convince his second baseman about the merits of another summer in Northern California.

Early on Green fancied himself a hitter — his 11 homers in 1964 and 15 in '65 each ranked second among American League second basemen — but starting in 1970, his emphasis shifted. He hit bottom that season, which was pretty much the only thing he *could* hit, his .190 batting average so deeply affecting his confidence that he stopped fielding too. By necessity, Green taught himself to disassociate the two facets of his game, and from that point on was content to hit a punchless .240 while producing the American League's most spectacular defense. Green's true strength as a ballplayer — the quality that was discussed throughout the winter of 1974 following his magical World Series performance — was his power of anticipation. Contrary to what the Dodgers might have believed, it involved neither luck nor magic.

"I needed to be in the right place," he said, looking back. "If I knew where the pitchers were going to put the ball, I knew where the batter was going to hit it." Because he couldn't set up in advance lest he give away some strategy, he tended to stay constantly in motion. "Those plays he made against the Dodgers?" said Rudi. "He made those plays all the time."

The Dodgers — or at least Bill Buckner — appreciated none of this. "[Green] has to be lucky, because he hasn't seen us enough to know where to play our hitters every time," Buckner said among his litany of dismissive comments. "It's pretty obvious we're the better club."

The other prominent conversation topic in Oakland's postgame clubhouse concerned Tenace's benching. Dark told reporters that playing the left-handed Claudell Washington against right-handed pitchers had long been in the back of his mind. Nobody believed him. Tenace told reporters that Dark was acting on orders from Finley. This, people believed.

"I have no respect for Dark for not backing me up," Tenace told some 20 newsmen, a remarkable show of interest in a man whose participation had been limited to defensive-replacement duty in the ninth inning. "I like him, but I can't respect him as a man. Down deep he probably felt I should have played, but he didn't say anything. I don't see how a man can let himself be dominated that way." Tenace added that while he'd settled some from his trade demand during the ALCS, were Finley intent on keeping him on the bench, he *did* want a trade — and he wanted it soon.

It might have been hard to tell, but the A's were on the cusp of winning the World Series. They knew no other way.

Oakland had been bristling at the Dodgers' arrogance all series long, and all series long that arrogance failed to abate, even as Los Angeles's chances did, day by day. In Game 5 it spilled out onto the field, and it cost the Dodgers the clinching game of the World Series.

It was Vida Blue against Don Sutton in a rematch of Game 2 on a clammy, 81-degree night at the Coliseum. Billy North opened the scoring on Bando's first-inning sacrifice fly, and Ray Fosse — starting again in a lineup that saw Claudell Washington in left field and Gene Tenace on the bench — made it 2–0 with a second-inning homer. From his front-row seat, Charlie Finley — accompanied not by his wife, as had been the case in the previous two World Series, but by Miss California, Lucianne Buchanan — cheered with gusto.

As the innings ticked by the Dodgers grew increasingly desperate. Vida set them down in order in four of the first five frames. When Sutton's turn to bat came up leading off the sixth, LA skipper Walter Alston opted for offense — a move that paid off when pinch hitter Tom Paciorek hit Blue's first offering to the left-field wall for a double. It was an early indication that a tiring Vida, pitching his 303rd inning of the season, was beginning to leave the ball up in the zone. When the left-hander walked the next hitter, Lopes, Dark sprang from the dugout. The man on deck, Bill Buckner, represented the winning run, and Vida had a history of quick meltdowns. The master of the early hook, however, had a surprise up his sleeve, even in a 2–0 game: he left Blue in.

Buckner bunted the runners over for the inning's first out, and Jim Wynn lofted a sacrifice fly to left for the second, scoring Paciorek and narrowing the deficit to 2–1. With Paul Lindblad and Blue Moon Odom warming in the bullpen, Blue continued to struggle, giving up a single to Steve Garvey that drove in Lopes from second. Tie game.

Somehow, after a season spent yanking his starters at the earliest provocation, this was *still* not enough for Dark to make a move. Vida got Ferguson to fly out to end the inning and went back out at the start of the seventh. It was only after the southpaw issued a two-out walk to Steve Yeager, then ran the count to 2–0 on pitcher Mike Marshall, that Dark finally pulled the plug. In the 1972 ALCS, Vida had saved Odom; now it was Blue Moon's turn to return the favor. The right-hander finished the walk to Marshall but rebounded with four straight sliders to Davey Lopes, the last of which was hit to Green to end the threat.

As Los Angeles took the field in the bottom of the seventh, fans in the Coliseum bleachers unloaded a barrage — Frisbees and apples primarily — upon Buckner in left field. Perhaps they'd finally had time to digest his derogatory remarks, or maybe seven innings' worth of beer was catching up to them. When a whiskey bottle landed nearby, Buckner strode toward umpire Doug Harvey and threatened to vacate his position the next time an object came close.

Play was halted while the field was cleared and an announcement made imploring fans to keep their possessions to themselves. Marshall did a number of things during the delay. He stood on the mound, arms akimbo. He fiddled with his mustache. He joined the left-field conference composed of Walter Alston, two outfielders, the shortstop, and all four umpires, who were discussing what to do should the bombardment fail to abate.

What Marshall did not do was throw a practice pitch, even after plate umpire Andy Olsen asked if he'd like to warm up before play resumed. By the time the right-hander unloaded his first offering to Joe Rudi, it had been five minutes and nine seconds since he thought the inning was going to begin. It was a fastball, and Rudi pummeled it like he knew what was coming, the ball landing ten rows into the left-field bleachers to give the A's a 3–2 lead. For the hitter, it was a simple matter of deductive reasoning. Prior to the inning, Rudi figured that Marshall would start him off with a breaking ball, but during the delay he took note of the pitcher's lack of interest in keeping his arm loose. The Dodgers had been jamming Rudi with inside fastballs throughout the series, and he understood that a fastball is easier to throw cold than something with movement.

"I don't know what the hell Marshall was doing out there in the outfield, but he wasn't doing anything on the mound," said the outfielder, looking back. "That was his Mr. Macho thing—he didn't need to warm up, he was ready to pitch right now. Well, the guy hadn't thrown a pitch in five minutes, and his pitches were fastball and screwball. I couldn't imagine him throwing a screwball without warming up a little bit, so I sat on the fastball."

A salvo of toilet paper from the upper deck followed Rudi's homer, and while the field was cleared once again, Marshall *again* refused to take a warm-up pitch as Yeager watched from behind the plate, arms folded, with nothing to do. Upon resuming play, Marshall went to a first-pitch breaking ball to Claudell Washington, which, true to Rudi's prognosis, sailed outside and high. It took the reliever three pitches to get loose, after which he was again dominant, retiring Washington on a foul pop-up, then striking out Fosse and Green to end the inning.

The Dodgers's conceit resurfaced with their first batter of the eighth. It was, suitably, Buckner. With the score still 3–2, Rollie Fingers came on as part of a double switch, Tenace taking over at first base and Rudi moving to left field. But something wasn't right. Fingers, feeling a twinge near his right triceps before the game, had told Dark that he'd be good for an inning, maybe two, but at first didn't look even that good. Buckner snapped a single into center field that after two hops unexpectedly passed beneath the glove of a charging Billy North. The error could have been disastrous, with the ball bouncing all the way to the wall as North gave chase. Buckner, having finished tenth in the league in steals, could run. Third base was in his sights, easy, with a real shot at a game-tying inside-the-park homer. "I had an opportunity to be Bill Buckner before Bill Buckner was Bill Buckner," laughed North looking back, referencing Buckner's infamous miscue on Mookie Wilson's grounder a dozen years later.* That North wasn't pre-Bucknerian was entirely thanks to the man playing alongside him. Those who say that Reggie Jackson turned it on only when it suited him might have a bevy of examples to back them up, but nobody ever hustled harder after a ball they had no business reaching than Reggie on that play. Before it had even reached North, Jackson was in full-sprint pursuit.

It was a dream scenario for Los Angeles: the tying run in scoring position with the heart of the order — Wynn, Garvey, and Ferguson — coming up in a one-run game. Then Buckner set his mind on third. It wasn't preposterous; against another team it might even have been a good idea. Jackson shouldn't have arrived so quickly to back up the play, but there he was. Even after corralling the ball, Reggie might have instinctively tried to throw it directly to third, but he knew his fundamentals. His relay to Green, standing 15 feet into the center-field grass, was strong, accurate, and without hesitation. Green's turn toward third began almost before the ball reached him, and he unleashed a perfect strike to Bando, who, with his glove raised 18 inches above the bag, blocked the baseline like a catcher in front of the plate. All the Captain had to do was drop his mitt onto the desperately diving Buckner and umpire Bill Kunkel punched his arm into the air. "Big money," said North later. "Whenever everybody's looking, Reggie comes through."

Now, instead of having a man on second and nobody out, Los Angeles had the bases empty and one down. Fingers quickly spun the odds back toward the Dodgers by walking Wynn, but then got Garvey to fly to Jackson for the second out. That brought up Ferguson, the fifth-place hitter, who did what he could to back up his ongoing claim that the Dodgers were the superior team, drilling a hanging slider into the second deck in left field, somewhere between 12 miles and 9 million miles according to two postgame assessments, both from Fingers. It was a monster shot . . . that went barely foul.

---

* In Game 6 of the 1986 World Series, with two outs in the bottom of the tenth inning, the bases loaded, and the game tied, Wilson topped an easy grounder to Buckner — playing first base for the Boston Red Sox — for what should have been an easy play to end the inning. Instead, it infamously rolled under Buckner's glove, clinching the game for the Mets, who won Game 7 two days later.

Lesson learned. It was the last breaking pitch Fingers threw. The right-hander promptly got Ferguson to flare a fastball into center that a hard-charging North caught on the run for the final out of the inning, Oakland's 3–2 lead intact.

In the ninth the closer worked without incident. A fly ball to right field by Cey. A pop-up to Green by pinch hitter Willie Crawford. Finally, Von Joshua topped a ball back to Fingers, who was so excited that he ran it most of the way to Tenace himself before tossing it over for the game's final out. Within moments a scrum of yellow shirts took over the infield. The A's were the first team to win three straight titles since the New York Yankees took five in a row between 1949 and 1954.

Four of the five games ended in 3–2 scores. The A's scored only 16 runs and batted a collective .211, but their pitching held the Dodgers to 11 runs. Oakland went through the entire postseason — four games against the Orioles and five against the Dodgers — using only five pitchers.

As fireworks exploded over the Coliseum, the A's retreated to their clubhouse to celebrate.* Darold Knowles, who set a record by appearing in every game of the 1973 World Series but was overlooked entirely against the Dodgers, stood atop his locker, the better to survey the landscape and soak it with champagne. Finley, viscerally appalled by the idea of appearing on TV alongside Bowie Kuhn, designated Bando, Hunter, and Campaneris to receive the championship trophy on the team's behalf, then left to track down Jackson. Before the game he had instructed Reggie that if the A's won, he was to ascend the TV platform, approach the Commissioner, and spray a "whole fucking bottle of champagne over that son of a bitch." Jackson was instinctively disinclined to do favors for the man, but this one held some appeal. As the nation watched, Reggie performed as instructed, then punctuated the effort by kissing Kuhn on the cheek. "We won it three times in a row, and only the Yankees ever did better," he exulted moments later. "I want to win four in a row. I want to win five in a row. I want to win it six times in a row, the only team ever, a new dynasty, the best baseball team in history!"

---

* Within minutes the field was destroyed — bases, plate, and pitching rubber stolen, turf shredded. Even the telephone from Finley's box was pilfered. It showed up later that night in a paper bag at the Ringside Saloon on 13th Street. The men who had it, in town from Texas, recounted for the bartender their tale of prying it loose, downed a couple of drinks, then raced to the airport to catch a flight home.

Because the A's had barely hit the ball during the Series, the MVP went to Fingers for his work over the four games in which he appeared: a 1.93 ERA with a win and two saves, even though few of his appearances were easy. His best inning — one of only two three-up, three-down frames he threw — was the last one of the Series. The pitcher's father, George Fingers, broke through the crowd to embrace his son. "You've taken five years off my life," he deadpanned as they hugged. The elder Fingers faced the surrounding media. "Never raise a son to be a reliever," he shouted with a grin. (Many in the A's clubhouse thought that Dick Green should have been MVP for his defense alone, figuring that had he shown *any-thing* offensively he would have been a shoo-in. Fingers himself held this opinion. Instead, Green went 0-for-13, a detail that MVP voters could not reconcile.)

As the party died down and the A's clubhouse began to clear, Catfish Hunter sat on the stool in front of his locker, his uniform soaked through with champagne. He appeared distracted. When talking to reporters, the pitcher spoke at length about pride — in his team, in his performance — but said nothing about being happy. The idea was raised that if he followed through as promised, he had just completed his last game as a member of the A's.

"I don't want to talk about that," he said. And the interview was done.

14

Catfish Gone

> If Finley got the best of Catfish in business, it is not right.
> Finley is a businessman, Catfish isn't. If Finley was fair, he
> would offer to renegotiate Cat's contract. But Finley is not
> fair in terms of money.
>
> —Reggie Jackson, September 1974

> Nobody's going to do me out of $50,000.
>
> —Catfish Hunter, December 1974

The story really started in January 1970, when Charlie Finley loaned Jim Hunter $150,000 to buy a 485-acre farm adjacent to his existing property in North Carolina. Hunter was to repay the money at a minimum of $20,000 per year, plus 6 percent interest, for as long as it took to get square. At Hunter's salary — $21,500 in 1969, $33,200 in '70 — it was a stretch, but worth it. The land was almost on top of his own, and its closer proximity to the Perquimans River made its soil especially robust for the corn, soybean, and peanut crops the pitcher grew up tending. Like most of Finley's side deals with his players, the pact was consummated with a handshake, no contract necessary.

Just a few months later, however, the Owner purchased the Memphis Pros of the American Basketball Association, supplementing the hockey team he had already acquired, the NHL's California Golden Seals. This placed more strain on the financial reserves of Charles O. Finley & Company than anticipated. Recouping his loan to Hunter was among the Owner's quickest paths to solvency.

Except that Catfish had already spent the money on the farm. That wasn't good enough for Finley, who took to telephoning frequently from Chicago and haranguing the pitcher about finances. "He'd call me in the clubhouse," recounted Hunter. "He'd call me off the field. He called me at the hotels on the road. He called me at home. He called my father, who was furious." The curious part was that the calls would come only on days that Hunter was scheduled to pitch, frequently minutes before game time, after he had already taken the field. (Traveling secretary Tom Corwin found himself beating a familiar path to the bullpen to inform Hunter of yet another phone call in the clubhouse.) Perhaps Finley thought that if he caught Catfish at his moments of peak concentration, the pitcher would pay more credence to his debt. Like numerous instances of willingly hobbling himself to prove a point, however, the Owner either failed to consider that such harassment might be deleterious to the pitcher's performance, or he didn't care.

Growing increasingly spooked, Hunter tried to arrange alternative financing through multiple banks in North Carolina, but without showing up in person it couldn't be done. He asked Finley for a leave of absence between starts to pull something together, but he was dealing with the man who once chided Dick Williams for playing golf on an off day, and his request was denied. Hunter grew nervous, began losing sleep. Finley's bombardment peaked in August, his calls piling one atop the other. Hunter went 0-4 in his seven starts that month, while the A's went 1-6. When the 24-year-old finished the 1970 season with an 18-14 record — tantalizingly close to his first 20-win campaign — he knew just where to look for the two missing victories. "I asked [Finley] once why he only called me on the days I was due to pitch, but he said he didn't know when I was going to pitch," Hunter recalled. "That was a bunch of bull, because Charlie knows everything that's going on in this club. He tells the managers who to pitch and when. I tried not to think the worst of him, but it was impossible."

The land was important to Hunter, who as a local farmer possessed an innate understanding of its value. Desperate to find a suitable arrangement, he even offered up insanity: a ten-year contract at $15,000 per season in lieu of the $150,000 that he owed. It would have priced the pitcher's services at below half his current value, never mind inflation. Finley, unwilling to consider anybody's terms but his own, refused. As soon as the season ended Hunter raced home to arrange for a second loan to cover the first, but gave up when a boundary-line dispute delayed the proceedings. That winter he sold 80 percent of the farm to a family friend for his initial $150,000 investment and sent the money to the Owner.

Bitter feelings from that exchange stayed with the pitcher for a long time, and informed his future actions. From that point on, every deal Hunter made with Finley was extensively documented, with signatures from each party in all the appropriate places. That last detail, it turned out, would prove to be instrumental in the years to come.

On February 11, 1974, not long before he was expected to report for spring training, Hunter avoided arbitration by agreeing with Finley on a two-year deal at $100,000 per — only the second multiyear contract the Owner ever awarded. Hunter was among baseball's best pitchers, with three straight 20-win seasons, three All-Star appearances in four years, and back-to-back top-five finishes in the Cy Young voting. Although his contemporaries were earning much more — Tom Seaver made $173,000 in 1974, and Steve Carlton $165,000 — Catfish had no way of knowing that. He'd always wanted to earn six figures, and when Finley made the offer it seemed just fine.

There was only one caveat, Hunter said. His attorney back home in North Carolina, a man with the prototypically Southern gentleman name of J. Carlton Cherry, had advised him to defer some of it. Put it into a life insurance annuity, he said, which could be cashed in for additional income once Hunter's baseball career ended. The benefit to this arrangement was that instead of being in a high tax bracket in 1974, Hunter would be taxed later on, when he was effectively unemployed and on the hook for a smaller amount.

That is exactly how Cherry wrote the addendum: $50,000 per year, to be paid at regular intervals through the season, and $50,000 disbursed to an entity of Hunter's choosing. Finley agreed. Several of his players had similar deferred-payment arrangements; Reggie Jackson's 1973 contract called for more than half of his $73,000 salary to be paid out over a two-year period after he retired. The benefit to Finley was that he got to hold on to the money in the interim, earning interest on it all the while.

The difference with Hunter's stipulation was that the Owner wouldn't have the money at all — the annuity would. Even less palatable for Finley was the discovery that about $25,000 in taxes was due immediately, and he would be the one paying them. Before long the Owner denied having agreed to anything, claiming he never saw the wording appended by Cherry.

There were two flaws to this argument. One was that Finley, while poring over the contract, added revisions in his own handwriting — instructions to his payroll department to earmark payments to whomever Hunter designated. The other was that the Owner did not actually sign the document. On its surface, this seemed like a boon for him. If he hadn't agreed to the arrangement, after all, even if evidence right up to the point of signature suggested that was the case — it could hardly be valid. But the document in question was the only contract Hunter had. If it was not valid, that meant Catfish had been pitching contract-free, which would make him a free agent.

When the 1974 season opened, Finley made the standard payments every two weeks as agreed. Although Cherry provided specific directions for the annuity deposit — to be paid to the Jefferson Insurance Company of North Carolina, starting midseason — the Owner did not put a penny toward it. Hunter was effectively pitching for half the money for which he signed.

Cherry spent the summer's middle months peppering Finley with letters seeking fulfilment. At first the Owner didn't respond. Later he offered a bevy of excuses, saying that he didn't want to set a precedent for the rest of the team, and that his accountant was out of town, and that he didn't think his soon-to-be-ex-wife — the club's secretary, at least in title — would approve. When he finally tired of the charade, he simply claimed that the paperwork was lost.

By early August the Owner was sufficiently concerned to urge Hunter to accept a straight payment of $50,000. He did this over the telephone, just as in 1970, calling only on the days when Catfish was scheduled to pitch. As in 1970, the bombardment had an effect: after Finley started calling, Hunter turned in two of his worst outings of the season. The pitcher, irate, began to discuss his situation with members of the pitching staff. Word quickly filtered up the ranks.

In September, Hunter turned to Jerry Kapstein for help, and reported the pertinent details. "I did everything I could to live up to the contract, but he still has not paid the money," the pitcher told him. "I don't know much about this, Jerry. Do you think I'm a free agent?"

"Jim, let me ask you this," said Kapstein. "Did your lawyer, Mr. Cherry, give Finley official notice of the contract breach?"

"Yes, he did."

"Did the ten-day period [as stipulated in the contract] pass after Finley received the letter?"

Not only had the period passed, Hunter said, but Finley never even bothered to respond.

"Based on those facts, it would appear to me you will be a free agent," Kapstein said.

Telling the pitcher to lie low until the end of the season, the agent said that he'd visit Cherry in North Carolina over the winter to work out details. "Be sure no one else knows," he warned.

For that, it was already too late. Hunter had discussed his situation with a number of people — several A's pitchers; Jackson, in his capacity as player rep; and Billy North, as the best-read player on the team. It was Catfish's conversation with Mike Hershberger, however, that came back to bite him, in the form of his ex-teammate's leak to the *Chicago Sun-Times* a few days later.

When Miller and MLB Players Association counsel Dick Moss read the contract, they agreed with Hunter's interpretation and sent written notice to Finley about the violation. They also noted, as per the terms therein, that the Owner had ten days in which to comply. This was standard language found in every uniform player contract, placed there 40 years earlier by the owners themselves to provide a reasonable buffer against default claims. Once that buffer expired, however . . . well, they were breaking new ground. According to the union, Hunter could proclaim himself a free agent as of September 26, but he did not want to distract from Oakland's playoff push. On October 4 the MLBPA sent a telegram to Finley's Chicago office, notifying the Owner of his default and informing him that "because of the impending playoffs and World Series, the effective date of termination [of Hunter's contract] shall be the day following the last game played by the Oakland Athletics in 1974."

The ALCS began at the Coliseum the following day. Finley was there, as was American League president Lee MacPhail. Seizing the opportunity, the Owner brought MacPhail into the clubhouse, where he found Hunter and offered him a check for the outstanding $50,000 on his contract. "Let's get this out of the way," he told the pitcher. "I'll give you the money, and we can go try to win the World Series." Catfish, heeding Cherry's advice, turned him down. "Mr. Finley," he said, "you pay it the way the contract reads, and everything will be just fine." Finley launched into histrionics, crying to MacPhail, "What can I do? I offer him the money and he won't take it. What can I do?" The Owner's distress may have been played up for the executive in the room, but it was also informed by recent advice he received from the Player Relations Committee, which told him that he was obliged only to pay the pitcher directly.

The display swayed MacPhail, who later said, "The Oakland club offered everything to which [Hunter] is entitled. I can't see how anyone can say he's a free agent." The trouble with that logic was that Hunter, like any employee in any profession, was entitled to the terms of his contract, and accepting a check for which he'd have to pay taxes was not within those terms. When Hunter claimed to become a free agent after the season, he had little idea whether it would actually come to pass. There was no questioning, however, that Catfish meant every word he said.

On October 10, two days before the World Series was to start, Jerome Holtzman's story about Hunter's contract ran in the *Chicago Sun-Times*. All the details were there — the amount, the annuity, the timeline, the unanswered letters to Finley. Also, the bombshell: the best pitcher on the best team in the league was attempting to jump ship. By October 11 it was national news. There was no hiding it now.

The Los Angeles–based Kapstein heard about it just in time to hightail over to Dodger Stadium for Friday's workout. The Fingers-Odom fight drew much of the day's attention, but the agent's presence was impossible to miss. With the news already out, Catfish instructed Kapstein to disclose details. In the Dodger Stadium press box, the agent laid it all out for the assembled media, adding that Hunter was not talking because his focus was on the World Series. The press ate it up.

Catfish broke the news of his possible departure to Tenace, Bando, and Rudi that night over dinner with their wives. "What the heck are you drinking?" asked Tenace, who spent the ensuing days humming "If I Were a Rich Man" around the clubhouse.

Union leader Marvin Miller, meanwhile, sent a letter to Bowie Kuhn seeking official recognition of Hunter's free agency. As expected, Kuhn — citing tax complications and Finley's attempt to pay the pitcher on October 4 — declared such a penalty to be too severe. He even suggested mediating the dispute himself, which Miller countered with a clause in the Basic Agreement mandating an impartial arbitrator for contract disputes between players and owners.

Only an hour after the World Series ended, even as Oakland play-ers celebrated in their clubhouse, the union filed two grievances — one against Finley for breach of contract, another against Kuhn and Major League Baseball for failure to declare Hunter a free agent. Finley remained bewildered, at least publicly. "I cannot believe that Catfish would do this to me," he said. "I'm sure that he will be with us next season." Privately, the Owner was less reticent. When Hunter approached him with a solution to both their problems — a long-term contract at $200,000 per season, with a $200,000 bonus — Finley rejected him outright and did not counter.

An arbitration hearing took place on November 26 in New York. Hunt-er's team claimed that Finley knew everything about the annuity arrange-ment from the beginning and willingly defaulted. Finley argued that he believed the deal to involve deferred money, paid after the pitcher's career ended — not a sum due right away. Tasked to make sense of it was a three-person panel. The votes of the first two members — Miller, on behalf of the players, and John Gaherin, the owners' chief negotiator — canceled each other out. That left things up to Peter Seitz, a 69-year-old litigator with nearly two decades of arbitration experience across numerous in-dustries whose most relevant decision to date allowed Warriors star Rick Barry to sign with the rival American Basketball Association after playing out his one-year option in 1967.

Seitz took 20 days to announce his decision, and when he did it was groundbreaking. He sided with Hunter completely. Finley was on the hook for the outstanding $50,000, plus interest, for Hunter's services in 1974, and because he had not fulfilled the player's contract, it was there-tofore terminated. Just like that, Major League Baseball had its first true free agent.

The Owner immediately sought a court order overturning Seitz's ruling. Bowie Kuhn said it was "like giving a life sentence to a pickpocket," and imposed a moratorium on other teams negotiating with Hunter.

They both knew it was folly. An arbitration ruling had to possess seri-ous discrepancies to be overturned — "capricious, arbitrary or dishonest conduct" was how Kuhn described it, even as he noted that none of the above factored into Seitz's decision. The courts agreed, refusing Finley's plea at two levels of the judiciary.

On a personal level, Finley could not understand Hunter's ingratitude. Hadn't the Owner been the one to personally scout him in the backwoods of Hertford? Hadn't he stuck with him through his hunting accident, nursed him to health through visits to the Mayo Clinic, showered him with a $75,000 signing bonus? What about the five grand he gave him for pitching a perfect game, or the cost of a new Cadillac for winning 21 in 1971? The Owner went out of his way to invest money for Catfish, generating an after-tax profit of $15,000 in 1972 alone. And what about the farm loan? When Hunter needed money most, Finley came through. Such was the Owner's myopia that he refused to acknowledge that his actions in recalling the loan undid any goodwill that may have previously been fostered. Finley was aggrieved, and he was furious. More than that, he found himself in the wildly uncomfortable position of victim. The Owner was used to controlling every situation, and when he couldn't . . . well, through his lawsuits and ongoing bloviation he continued to act as if he was still in charge.

On December 18, Kuhn, seeing no other option, lifted his moratorium. The race was on. Catfish had won 106 games over the previous five years, plus another six in the postseason. He had just been voted the American League's best pitcher and, while a ten-year vet, was still only 28 years old. If ever the sky was the limit for a ballplayer in terms of contract leverage, this was it. Early speculation said that it might take as much as $1 million to lock him up.

Ahoskie, North Carolina, population 5,500, was the "big city" close to Hunter's home in Hertford, about an hour's drive to the northwest. It was also the location of the law offices of J. Carlton Cherry, Hunter's 68-year-old longtime attorney, who had maintained a practice in town for some 45 years. For three weeks in December 1974, Cherry's firm became the most prominent entity on baseball's landscape, the result of the lawyer's decision to avoid sending his client on a tour of interested parties and instead bring the parties to him. Thus began a parade of excess the likes of which Ahoskie — or, really, any small town — had never before seen. Hunter and his team entertained between three and five clubs a day, 48 executives in all by the time things wrapped up. "Shit, I love this place," said Catfish's old pitching coach in Oakland, Bill Posedel, in town representing his new employer, the San Diego Padres. "I bought the whole town of Ahoskie drinks last night, and it only cost me two dollars."

Suitors could fly their private planes to the diminutive Tri-County Airport just outside the city, but most opted for the much larger facility in Norfolk, some 60 miles up State Highway 13. Without so much as an Edgewater Hyatt nearby, they booked rooms at the Tomahawk Motel and made the best of things. Main Street featured three stoplights, two restaurants, a bus station, and the law offices outside of which baseball's royalty began to congregate.

It didn't take long for the $1 million predictions to be blown from the water. The first team to make an offer, the Cleveland Indians, opened with $2.4 million over ten years. By day's end the Red Sox had upped it to $3 million over five. After that, teams got creative.

The Rangers discussed a generous straight salary, plus a farm annuity, plus $30,000 a year for 15 years. Pittsburgh offered $3.75 million for five years, plus, among other perks, limited partnership in five new Wal-Mart stores. The Royals weighed in with $137,500 per year for six years, money for the farm, college tuition for Hunter's kids, and a figure that nearly got the pitcher to sign on the spot — $50,000 a year for life. When Hunter asked, however, what would happen to the contract after he died, Kansas City GM Joe Burke told him that his demise would be the termination point. "How about my wife?" asked Catfish. Joked Burke, "Well, we won't have to worry about that, will we? You'll be dead." It was not a good joke, and it continued to sour Hunter even after the Royals added $30,000 per year for the rest of Helen Hunter's life as well.[*]

As it all unfolded Hunter received a personal letter — not at his lawyer's office but at his own PO box in Hertford — reading, in part, "I naturally feel that the arbitrator, in making his decision, exceeded his authority and jurisdiction . . . however, I hereby offer, without qualification, to purchase and own the annuity on your life as you requested on or about August 1, 1974."

It was from Finley. Amid the fervor for the pitcher's services, he was supplicating himself — or coming as close to it as he knew how. (Even then the Owner was unable to refrain from mentioning that his position had been correct.) A contract to play for the A's in 1975, he said, would be arriving shortly.

• • •

---

[*] The only teams to refrain from bidding were the Orioles, whose GM, Frank Cashen, was unwilling to buck club policy forbidding multiyear player contracts, and the Giants, whose owner, Horace Stoneham, was trying desperately to unload a 90-loss team that had sold fewer than 520,000 tickets in 1974, and was in no position to shell out anything approaching big bucks.

Upon seeing how poorly his five-year, $1.5 million proposal stacked up, Yankees president Gabe Paul conceded defeat and made the two-and-a-half-hour road trip to Raleigh for his return flight to New York. One thing Paul had working in his favor, however, was Yankees director of minor league scouting Clyde Kluttz. Also, Kluttz's wife, Wayne.

Kluttz, who visited Hunter along with Paul, was the former A's scout who had been vital in steering the pitcher toward the A's in the first place. As a fellow North Carolinian, woodsman, and hunter, he'd endeared himself to the Hunter family. He earned extra points shortly after Hunter first signed when Finley tried to backtrack and get the teenager to agree to a second contract — dated 1965 instead of 1964 — that would have allowed him to be sent to the minors without penalty owing to the expiration of the bonus baby rule. "Don't sign nothing else," Kluttz advised. Hunter listened, and never spent a day in the minors. A decade later it was Kluttz, still tight with the pitcher, who suggested Hunter's $200,000-per-year compromise offer to Finley.

When Kluttz called his wife from the airport to tell her that he and Paul were homeward bound, she surprised him with instructions to stay put. "You have breakfast with that boy tomorrow morning," she insisted. "You know Jim and he knows you. You talk to him once more." Unable to find a flaw in her reasoning, Kluttz did exactly that.

He was greeted at the farm with open arms and found Hunter chock-full of questions. *Can I live in New York City?* Kluttz was no fan of the urban environment, but there were places on the outskirts with space to breathe. *Steinbrenner?* Couldn't be worse than Finley, Kluttz reasoned, plus he's just as serious about winning. Kluttz talked about the rabid fan base and increased opportunities in the country's largest media market. Ultimately, though, it didn't matter — New York's offer wasn't close enough to merit serious consideration.

Hunter wanted to make a decision by the next day, December 31. He was tired of the hour-long drive into Ahoskie, not to mention that the baseball season ended two months earlier and he hadn't so much as dusted off his hunting rifle. Catfish was leaning toward San Diego, although Cherry was still championing the Royals. Boston, the Angels, Pittsburgh, and the Mets had outside chances.

On the morning of the last day of the year Hunter drove to Ahoskie prepared to finalize a deal. Before seeing Cherry, however, he stopped at the Tomahawk Motel to meet Kluttz for a cup of coffee. That was where the old scout shot the final arrow in his quiver. "Jimmy," he asked, "what would it take for you to come and play for the Yankees?" Kluttz had no power to make an offer, but he had a direct line to somebody who did. Hunter told him — a five-year deal with 15 years of deferred money at $100,000 per season, plus college funds for his kids and a variety of perks to be determined. It was a longshot, but it was something. The two men went to Cherry's office, where one of the attorney's partners, Joe Flythe, called Paul with details of the contractual benchmarks that could seal the deal.

It put the executive in a tight spot. Ordinarily, Paul could go directly to owner George Steinbrenner for approval, but the Boss had been suspended by Bowie Kuhn for making illegal campaign contributions to Richard Nixon and was temporarily banned from contact. They were talking about nearly $3.5 million over five years, and Paul needed help. He placed a call to Yankees minority partner Ed Greenwald, a prominent tax attorney in Cleveland, and together they concluded that they could make it work. Paul was vibrant when he called Flythe back. "That's more money than we wanted to pay," he exuded, "but we'll do it."

There was only one catch. That kind of financial outlay required the Yankees to squeeze every penny they could from the contract, and for tax purposes it made sense to put the deal on their 1974 books. That left them about 12 hours to finalize things. With that, the sprint was on. While Paul and Flythe made travel preparations for New York, Greenwald was already on his way to the airport in Cleveland to charter a plane to North Carolina. In the midst of the mayhem, the phone rang. It was Padres GM Buzzy Bavasi, who had just received approval from owner Ray Kroc to increase his already enormous offer, worth $4.5 million, including cash, stock, and a McDonald's franchise. "If you come to San Diego," he barked into the telephone, "you can write your own check."

Bavasi was informed that at that very moment Hunter was heading out the back door, to the airport and New York City. The executive raged about being used as a pawn to drive up other offers, but there was little he could do. Hunter, Kluttz, and a coterie of lawyers from Cherry's office met Greenwald's plane at the Suffolk Airport in Virginia, some 45 minutes away. For the duration of the flight, Greenwald, yellow legal pad in hand, drafted an addendum to the standard player's contract, conferring with Hunter's team every step of the way. By the time they reached New York it was ten pages long and barely legible, owing to a bumpy trip. The document would come to be known around Yankees HQ as "the Catfish Hunter Manifesto."

Upon landing in New York at 6:00 P.M., the group sped to Paul's office, where they pored over the details, point by point. Shortly after 7:00 P.M., Paul had a staffer schedule a news conference for 8:15. There was no indication what it was about, but newspeople summoned from New Year's Eve parties across New York could imagine only one possibility. As the room began to fill, the men of the hour were still finalizing details. It seemed for a moment that the midnight deadline might come and go . . . and then it was done. A souvenir Yankees cap was propped atop Hunter's head, and out he went, smiling, to face the crowd.

That room was the time and place — the very moment — that George Steinbrenner became utterly relevant to baseball's landscape, and Charles O. Finley became an afterthought.

Part 3

DESCENT

1975–1980

15

Retool

I'm happy as hell for Jim. He came off like a robber. It should
happen to all of us.

—Sal Bando

As soon as Catfish Hunter became a member of the New York Yankees, the
A's franchise focus underwent a dramatic shift. The team's initial stages in
Kansas City under Charlie Finley were based around player acquisition,
a movement that morphed over time into player development and, upon
arrival in Oakland, plugging roster holes around the existing core. Now
that the team's most essential player had flown the coop, however, the
Owner began to cast about desperately for ways to replace him. Forget
easy — nobody knew whether it was even possible. "There never has been
a challenge like this in the history of baseball, losing a twenty-five-game
winner and trying to repeat as world champions," worried Alvin Dark.
Finley, the kind of guy who invented work when there wasn't any to do,
faced this actual crisis with a frenetic flurry of activity.

He began by extending a training camp invitation to 36-year-old
Juan Marichal, who was so over the hill that Finley's best compliment
about him was "He says he can still pitch." The Owner brought back ag-
ing pitcher Lew Krausse, who had just been released by the Braves, his
fifth team, 14 years after Finley first lavished a massive $125,000 contract
on him as a prep phenom in 1961. Finley purchased another ex-Athletic,
Horacio Pina, from the Angels, and Jim Todd from the Cubs. He called in
White Sox castoff Roger Nelson and tried to acquire 35-year-old Claude
Osteen, released by St. Louis. No longer having access to quality, the
Owner went whole hog after quantity . . . and fooled nobody. "The loss

of Catfish Hunter is the dumbest thing that's ever happened to a baseball team," lamented Reggie Jackson. "They say that Finley is a business genius. You call that smart?"

Airlifting aging pitchers into camp was only half the plan. The other part involved goosing the offense, starting with the Owner's third major trade with the Cubs in four years. In 1972 it had been Ken Holtzman for Rick Monday. In 1973 he acquired Billy North for Bob Locker. This time Finley got himself a bona-fide Hall of Famer. Almost before the champagne on the clubhouse carpet was dry, Finley sent Locker, Darold Knowles, and Manny Trillo to the North Side in exchange for Billy Williams and his 392 career home runs. The guy was 36 years old and in clear decline, but Finley, hoping Williams would take to DH-ing, extended a two-year deal for the same $150,000 per year that he had been making in Chicago.

Williams proved his ability to fit in within minutes of arriving at the spring training clubhouse in Mesa, when Joe Rudi asked him if he had a first baseman's glove.

"I've got every type of glove," joked Williams. "An outfielder's glove, a first baseman's glove, a golf glove, a soccer glove. . . ." *How about boxing gloves?* somebody asked. The question was loaded, and Williams was ready.

"I was going to come in here wearing boxing gloves," he said. "I've read so much about you guys I figured let's get it over the first day and have it out one at a time." He was a natural fit.

The move forced Claudell Washington into left field, which forced Joe Rudi back to first base, which forced Gene Tenace to catcher. The defensive liabilities of this alignment were proven, but Williams's bat was unquestionably more potent than Ray Fosse's. Without Catfish, Finley figured it was the best hope the A's had.

"You know, I'll be surprised if we don't win again," said the Owner, taking full credit for a move — the loss of Hunter — that everybody else viewed as a mistake. "Losing Catfish will make these men play all the harder. This is a great baseball team, and I'm proud to be the man who assembled it."

In case there was still doubt about Finley's feelings toward his holdover players — the ones who, despite winning three titles, had rebelled against him in every imaginable way, up to and including their public support of Hunter — his handling of their contracts settled it. The largesse the Owner heaped upon Billy Williams was in direct contrast to the offers he made to his long-standing veterans. Joe Rudi had just finished second in American League MVP voting, and Rollie Fingers made his second straight All-Star team and was the World Series MVP. Each was offered a token raise. Everybody else — including Sal Bando, who finished third in the MVP vote, and Reggie Jackson, who finished fourth — either got no bump at all or received cuts up to the maximum-allowable 20 percent. Finley wasn't going to pay his players what they were worth under the best circumstances; now that arbitration forced him to undercut them out in the open, he figured that he might as well do so with gusto. "I'm mad as hell," responded Bando when he saw his offer. "So are more than half the guys on the club. . . . You win the third straight World Series and you don't get a raise? Can you believe that?"

Finley's intransigence led to mass participation in the second year of arbitration hearings. Thirteen Oakland players signed up, all according to the Owner's plan. Finley then set to furious negotiating sessions, coming to last-minute compromises — using his own lowball offers as starting points — with seven of them. In the wake of Hunter's deal with New York, Bando tried to withdraw from his hearing six days before it was scheduled, looking to play out his contract and test baseball's reserve clause as a potential free agent. According to the process, however, once a name was submitted it could be withdrawn only by mutual consent. Finley turned the Captain down flat, publicly bashing him as a "pop-off" and "one of the worst-fielding third basemen in baseball."[*]

Ultimately, Finley won, and won big. He beat Bando, Fosse, Holtzman,

---

[*] Finley took particular issue with a speech that Bando made a month earlier in Gresham, Oregon, in which he said, "[Finley] just doesn't have a first-class operation. It's not run smoothly. It's not run in the best interests of the community and baseball. It's run in the best interest of one man. . . . He just doesn't understand how to treat players. To him, everything is cut and dry, a challenge or a fight, when it really doesn't have to be." The words hit the press wire, and when they reached Chicago Finley was not timid with his response. He resented Bando's assertion "that the Oakland A's have the worst front office staff in baseball," he said, even though Bando never used such language. The Owner went on to question whether, once everything was over, he would even allow Bando to retain his captaincy. "Bando has been a very unappreciative individual," he said. "He doesn't seem to like anything we do. Who appointed him team captain? Yours truly, Charles O. Finley, that's who, and I paid him for being captain. He's always received his checks on time, so what's the reason for his complaints? If he wishes to become the village idiot, let him be my guest."

and Jackson. Among the Owner's primary arguments in each case was that players had already augmented their salaries with a $22,219 winner's share from the World Series. The arbitrator bought it.

The only guy who did not seem concerned about his salary situation was Dick Green, who, predictably, retired for the fifth straight season. This year was different, however — without Hunter around, Green figured that the A's were no longer of championship caliber, and Finley wanted offense, something Green could not provide. With minor league second baseman Phil Garner waiting in the wings, the Owner was content to cut the cord.

That meant training camp opened without Hunter or Green, and with a spate of new pitchers battling for space on the roster. Amid it all, one thing remained consistent: when the championship rings were passed out sans ceremony for the second year in a row, players discovered that they again contained green glass in place of diamonds. By that point, however, the Owner's cheapness was old hat and outrage was minimal.

In the middle of March, Marichal signed with the Dodgers, who, unlike Oakland, offered a guaranteed contract. ("We don't believe in taking chances," explained the Owner, whose primary strategy in replacing Hunter was the taking of chances.) Osteen signed with the White Sox. Krausse couldn't even crack the rotation at Triple-A Tucson. Salvation, it turned out, came from a source that nobody expected, not even Finley.

Mike Norris, who turned 20 in the middle of spring training, was coming off a middling, injury-riddled season at Double-A Birmingham. Then he showed up in Mesa, shut out the Angels in his first exhibition appearance, and never let up. By the end of training camp he was Alvin Dark's number-three starter. "I look at him like Jeremiah," said the manager. "He's like a prophet sent down to save us." "Jeremiah" quickly became Norris's tag around the clubhouse. Better still was the fact that he was a local kid, out of San Francisco's Balboa High School. So taken was Finley that he gave the youngster Hunter's old number, 27.

Jeremiah's first start came against the White Sox in the third game of the season. The anticipation was stunning. With more than 100 friends and relatives in attendance, Norris faced 32 batters, five over the minimum, and gave up only three hits in a 9–0 complete-game victory. Dark went so far as to provide a Bible to the press box so that reporters might look up appropriately reverent passages for their stories.

In Norris's next start, he allowed one hit over seven innings and again did not cede an earned run. People wondered whether he might be able to fill Catfish's shoes for about $3.5 million less. People wondered whether he might actually be *better*.

In his third start, Norris broke.

It was April 20 at the Coliseum, a Sunday afternoon against the Twins. The right-hander walked Rod Carew to open the game, felt a twinge in his elbow, and departed immediately. All Dark could say in the aftermath was, "I told Jeremiah that God is in charge and everything will work out." The manager did not address the fact that it was Norris's first Sabbath start as a big leaguer.

Ten days later the right-hander underwent surgery to remove calcium deposits from his pitching elbow and was effectively lost for the season. The hunt for a number-three starter resumed apace, with new urgency added to the hunt for a number-four starter, which had never slowed in the first place.

The Owner's first step in mitigating the impact of Norris's injury was, oddly, to acquire another pinch runner. Finley had already released Jesus Alou to make space for Don Hopkins and his 222 stolen bases over four minor league seasons, but at the end of April the Owner acquired a third rabbit, utility man Matt Alexander, from the Cubs. Unlike Herb Washington, the two new guys could play the field, and with roster space at a minimum owing to the panoply of pitchers acquired in response to Hunter's departure, the impending doom of Hurricane Herb was ever clearer. Finley broke the news of Washington's unconditional release to him in person on May 4, in Chicago, the two departing White Sox Stadium together, the Owner's arm across the shoulder of his great failed experiment.[*]

Finley's first real admission that his Hunter replacement plan was not working came when he traded Ted Kubiak to San Diego for veteran right-hander Sonny Siebert, sacrificing bench depth for some proficient

---

[*] As popular a personality as Washington was in the A's clubhouse, his teammates didn't exactly struggle with his departure. "I'd feel sorry for him if he were a player," said Bando in the majority opinion.

innings. Siebert was 38 and had been only marginally effective for the Padres, but he was a pitcher, and Oakland needed pitchers. Four days later the Owner took an even bigger step, sending Blue Moon Odom to Cleveland for right-handers Dick Bosman and Jim Perry, effectively crafting a five-man rotation. Odom had regressed so badly that he could not crack an A's staff with as many as three vacancies, and his refusal to work things out at Triple-A left Finley little choice.[*]

Perry was 39, and Bosman 31. They shared the dual traits of being mediocre and expensive, and neither factored into Cleveland's long-term plans. Three weeks later Finley moved again, sending Dave Hamilton and prospect Chet Lemon to the White Sox for veteran righty Stan Bahnsen, 30, a competent innings-eater and a natural fit for the new abundance of come-what-may pitching. With six starters at their disposal, Finley and Dark worked out a rotation in which Blue and Holtzman pitched on a regular schedule, with the other four slotted behind them in whichever way made the most sense at the time.

It was ingenious. The older pitchers thrived with the extra rest, Blue embraced his new role as staff ace, and Jim Todd bolstered the bullpen, more than compensating for the departure of Knowles and Locker. Oakland stormed out of the gate, cruising into the All-Star break at 55-32, eight and a half games up in the American League West. Seven A's — Blue, Campy, Fingers, Reggie, Rudi, Tenace, and, in his first full season, Claudell Washington — were selected for the Midsummer Classic in Milwaukee.

Of more lasting importance than the All-Star Game itself, however, was the concurrent owners' meeting held across town at the Pfister Hotel. The agenda included two major topics — a presentation by the Major League Franchise Committee concerning options for relocating either the Giants or A's away from the Bay Area, and an extension for Kuhn, whose seven-year contract was set to expire the following season. Both held enduring interest for Finley.

To retain his post the Commissioner needed 75 percent of the vote,

---

[*] Odom did not endear himself to his new employers when, after three appearances — two awful relief outings and one complete-game shutout over Kansas City — he demanded an $8,000 raise as compensation for the postseason bonus he would miss now that he was no longer with the A's. On one hand, it was the same mentality Finley used to justify the low salaries he handed out. On the other, an owner could get away with that kind of nonsense, but a player could not. Within three weeks Cleveland brass flipped Blue Moon to the Braves for spare parts.

or approval from nine of the 12 teams per league. With only two own-ers standing against him — Finley and Baltimore's Jerry Hoffberger — the procedure was pro forma, a simple matter of tallying votes to make it official. As Cardinals owner Gussie Busch took the floor to support the Commissioner's reelection, however, Finley spoke up — "a sound from Dante's Inferno," as Kuhn later described it. The Owner proclaimed with certainty that *four* American League owners were now against Kuhn — that he and Hoffberger had been joined by the Yankees and Rangers — a sufficient number to topple the Commissioner. The cadre was quickly labeled the "Dump Bowie Club."

George Steinbrenner was serving a two-year suspension at Kuhn's behest, so the Yankees' participation made sense. The Rangers', how-ever, did not. Brad Corbett had purchased the team only a year earlier, and turned out to be more of a wild card than most anticipated. He was heeding advice from the man who sold him the club, Bob Short, whose increasingly personal clashes with Kuhn while moving the Senators from Washington to Texas left him bitter.* A pastiche of chaos settled over the meeting. When Finley called for an immediate vote, Kuhn supporters, led by Finley's longtime antagonist, Dodgers owner Walter O'Malley, did the only thing they could to staunch the tide: they ad-journed the meeting via a parliamentary procedure and carried things over to the following day. Wrote Kuhn in his autobiography, *Hardball:* "There was professional baseball being pushed around on a critical issue by four owners whose motives had nothing to do with baseball's general welfare. Over eighty percent of the voters were stopped in their tracks by a petulant minority of four. That Charlie Finley was the public spokes-man for this minority was the ultimate degradation."

Kuhn may have held little sway with the revolutionaries, but O'Malley was a different matter. Corbett had already left town, but the Dodgers owner tracked him down at a Florida hotel and via long-distance phone lines convinced him to flip. That was all it took; without four votes, Finley

---

* Corbett went so far as to enlist Rangers manager Billy Martin, in Milwaukee as one of the All-Star coaches, to lobby other owners on behalf of Kuhn's ouster. Martin did him one better, getting old pal Mickey Mantle — in town because Kuhn had named him an honorary captain of the Amer-ican League squad — to canvass for votes. It did little for Martin's standing in Arlington; Corbett fired him precisely one week later.

was powerless. (As soon as Steinbrenner learned that his vote no longer mattered, he seceded as well.)

When the owners reconvened the following morning, they made it official: National League approval was unanimous, and the AL voted 10–2 in favor of another term for Kuhn.* It was easy to surmise that Finley had suffered a crushing defeat, but by filibustering Kuhn's reelection vote, he forced the tabling of the resolution calling for the A's or Giants to find someplace else to play. Had the establishment thought that Finley would be entranced by the cost of relocation being divided evenly among all franchises — either the Giants would leave town or the league would foot the bill for the A's to do so — they had no clue about how the Owner worked. The plan left a modicum of control over his team to somebody else, a term by which Finley could never abide. "If you see [Kuhn]," the Owner told a reporter, "tell him what I said: Nobody is going to tell Charlie Finley what to do."

From Finley's very first efforts at buying a team, he was never afforded the respect from fellow owners that he felt he deserved. His grassroots movement to ice the Commissioner had brought the establishment to its knees, proving to every one of his baseball peers — particularly O'Malley, the patriarch of them all — that being paid no heed was not the same as wielding no power. He knew going in that the odds of unseating Kuhn were long, but even so, he was able to prove his ability to interject bedlam on a whim. And that was worth something, wasn't it?

Oakland kept right on rolling after the break, increasing its division lead to as many as 11 games. The All-Stars were shining, the front end of the rotation was terrific, and the back end was holding things together. Everything was humming. Enter Finley.

The A's opened their second half in Cleveland with two wins in three

---

* Despite his victory, Kuhn was outraged at the way things played out. In addressing the owners in the aftermath, he said, "Thank you, gentlemen, especially those who voted for me. It's too bad it took so long but it's not surprising, considering the quality of the opposition." From across the room, Finley shouted, "What a joke!" At the press conference afterward, when Kuhn concluded his remarks, Finley announced that he, too, had something to say. By this time, the Commissioner's patience had been stripped bare. Leaning into the microphone, he said sternly, "Charlie, you may leave my room." The Owner was livid. "Thank you, Commissioner," he spat. "That just shows more class."

games. Rather than board a postgame charter to Baltimore, however, they flew commercial. This meant that, following a night game after which they did not leave the ballpark until close to midnight, players had to wake near dawn in order to reach Maryland for that day's doubleheader. Baltimore swept the exhausted A's and took three of four in the series. The next stop was Detroit for another doubleheader, again without an off day. Again no plane was chartered, and again players' schedules were thrown out of whack by an early morning flight — not to Detroit, but to Washington, where they caught a connection. "If Charlie could have put us on a bus," said Rollie Fingers, "he would have."

The ensuing road trip offered more of the same. The A's left Texas at dawn for a same-day game in Kansas City. (Steve Busby shut them out on six hits.) They went 3-5 on the trip, then waited around Arlington for a 1:30 A.M. commercial flight to Oakland that didn't get them home until 5:00 A.M., and were back at the ballpark hours later to face Boston. Wiped out, the A's scored 15 runs over a nine-game span, were one-hit by Kansas City's Paul Splittorff, and won only nine of their next 21, by which point their lead had shrunk to five.

Things crumbled everywhere. Joe Rudi tore a ligament in his left hand and missed five weeks. Finley released Jim Perry after 11 middling starts and didn't replace him, leaving the roster a player short. "All Charlie is interested in doing is saving money and making money," Rudi said. "You can see he's not interested in winning."

The Owner's cutbacks spread throughout the system. The A's drafted 27 players in 1975, but farm director John Claiborne complained that funds were allocated to sign only nine of them. Those players were especially needed because Finley had systematically purged the system of prospects in exchange for low-ceiling veterans. The long-term results were not pretty. Chet Lemon (three All-Star appearances over a 16-year career) for Stan Bahnsen (15-16 record in parts of three seasons with Oakland). Dan Ford (11-year big league career) for Pat Bourque (never played again for Oakland). Manny Trillo (17-year career, four All-Star appearances, three Gold Gloves, two Silver Sluggers) as part of the package for Billy Williams (.231 average and 34 homers across two seasons in Oakland). Finley further scrimped by joining the Central Scouting Bureau, a collective service with group rates, and cut loose many of his most trusted scouts. He found even more savings when his farm director, John Claiborne, resigned at the end of July under the rationale that he "just couldn't take it anymore."[*] His replacement was Norm Koselke, the brother-in-law of Charles O. Finley Jr., who was already on the payroll. "It was a disaster," said Rudi, looking back. "Just a disaster."

Oakland's front office was reduced to six people: the Owner; the Owner's cousin, Carl Finley (handling PR and promotions); Koselke; controller Chuck Cottonaro; traveling secretary Jim Bank; and ticket manager Lorraine Paulus. Finley took a liking to a clubhouse kid named Stanley Burrell and made him an honorary executive — complete with a ball cap that read "VP" — based partly on his charm and partly on his willingness to fetch drinks and provide play-by-play over the phone to the Owner in Chicago.[†] Four secretaries and two phone operators rounded out the operation.[‡] This was Major League Baseball's three-time defending champion. The playoffs were imminent.

Just because Finley spent the season proclaiming that the A's could win without Catfish Hunter didn't mean he wanted them to. His attorney filed a 50-page brief in Alameda County Superior Court claiming that meeting the terms of Hunter's contract would have necessitated income tax fraud. He also said that the contract failed to specifically mention an insurance annuity, and that the arbitrator exceeded his authority in ruling for Hunter. He called the revocation of Hunter's rights "punitive damages" and said that it was like "giving the death penalty for a parking violation."

Finley lost. Again. He filed an appeal to overturn the decision, and another appeal to prevent Hunter from playing for any team but the A's, and another appeal about the arbitrator's overreach.

---

[*] "Unlike most office help hired by Finley in his baseball operations, Claiborne had some unusual handicaps," explained Ron Bergman in *The Sporting News.* "He wasn't related by either blood or marriage to the owner. He had some baseball experience before joining the A's. And he was competent." Claiborne said that in his three years on the job he was fired four times and quit five times. "I told Finley a few years later that I won, 5–4," he said.

[†] When Brewers second baseman Pedro Garcia noted that the kid bore a resemblance to Hank Aaron, the nickname "Hammer" was born. (Burrell's other nickname around the team was "Pipeline," because many players believed him to be a source of inside information for the Owner.) After Burrell left the A's and entered the music business, he kept the moniker and reached new levels of success as MC Hammer.

[‡] By season's end the Owner added two more positions, shifting cousin Carl to postseason ticket sales and bringing in former Seals PR guy Shep Goldberg, then hiring Syd Thrift to run the minor league operation.

Catfish, meanwhile, was doing everything he could to make Finley miserable. He won a league-leading 23 games for the Yankees, finished second with a 2.58 ERA, and trailed only Jim Palmer in the Cy Young voting. Even more painful for Oakland was that Hunter won all four of his starts against the A's, each of them a complete game, while giving up a total of three runs. In case that didn't hurt enough, he *lost* all three of his starts against Oakland's closest competitors, the Kansas City Royals. After the season, Finley went so far as to send Hunter a contract for 1976, just to avoid the presumption that he'd given up. "We still feel like Hunter has been kidnapped," he said. By that point he was the only one harboring such thoughts.

The A's clinched the division on September 24, and their celebration was 45 minutes of mayhem. Jackson spun Billy North helicopter-style while teammates doused them with champagne. Newcomers made up fully half the roster, with longtime vets like Billy Williams and Tommy Harper — 31 years in the big leagues between them with nary a playoff berth — especially jubilant. The A's had passed their first post-Catfish test, and that was worth celebrating. Left unspoken was that, without Hunter, the likelihood of a fourth straight title was considerably diminished. Spray 'em if you got 'em.

Still unanswered was the question about the team's third starter. It was the same shortcoming the A's had faced the last time they lost a playoff series, in 1971. Dick Bosman, the presumptive favorite, spent September in a protracted fade. Siebert pitched so poorly that he was shunted to the bullpen. Bahnsen had shuttled in and out of the rotation all along. There was talk that reliever Jim Todd would take the spot, despite having not started a game all year.[*]

On the final day of the regular season, a Coliseum crowd of 22,131 got to see Vida Blue make a tune-up start against the Angels in advance of the playoffs. Dark said beforehand that Vida would pitch no more than five innings, so the pitcher wasn't surprised when he was removed prior to the sixth. Many of those in the crowd, however, could not believe that Dark was pulling a pitcher who hadn't given up a hit. The relievers who fol-

---

[*] Dark held outside hope for Mike Norris, but Jeremiah came back for an exploratory appearance four games before the end of the season, gave up two hits and two walks in two-thirds of an inning, and was shut down again.

lowed — Glenn Abbott, Paul Lindblad, and Rollie Fingers — didn't allow a baserunner between them, making it only the second time in baseball history that multiple pitchers combined to win a no-hitter.* The 5–0 victory was Blue's 22nd of the season. Jackson hit two homers to tie Milwaukee's George Scott for the league lead, with 36.

Oakland's 98-64 record was the league's best, better than any championship season with Hunter. They finished second in the AL in runs scored (758), home runs (151), and stolen bases (183). Tenace's 29 homers were tops among big league catchers, while Rudi hit 21 despite missing six weeks with a thumb injury, and Billy Williams chipped in 24. For all the worries about their pitching, the A's ERA was second in the league, while their bullpen was baseball's best, with Fingers, Lindblad, and Todd combining for 27 wins and 43 saves.

The Owner's summation was classic Finley. "When I look where [Dick] Williams is with the [last-place] Angels and where Hunter is with the [third-place] Yankees, and where the A's are without them, I feel like I'm having the last laugh," he gloated. "Williams didn't win for the A's. Hunter didn't win for the A's. If anyone won for them, *I* won for them. They are a team, they win as a team, and the team is bigger than its individuals. No man is indispensable here. Except maybe me."

In the East, the Red Sox won 95 games and finished four and a half games ahead of Baltimore. They averaged nearly five runs per game thanks to an exceptionally young and outrageously talented outfield featuring 22-year-old Rookie of the Year runner-up Jim Rice (who would miss the series after breaking his hand in September) and 23-year-old Fred Lynn, who won the Rookie of the Year Award *and* the American League MVP.

Even more worrisome for the A's was the specter of Fenway Park, the location for the first two ALCS games. With its left-field wall only 310 feet from home plate, Fenway struck special fear into the hearts of left-handed pitchers — including Oakland's only two reliable starters. A's pitchers had put up a 6.18 ERA at Fenway during the regular season, with Blue (two homers and six runs over four and two-thirds innings) and Holtzman (two homers and seven runs over six and a third) being particularly awful.

---

* In 1917, Babe Ruth walked the game's first batter and was ejected for arguing balls and strikes, then was relieved for 27 consecutive outs by Ernie Shore. In 1967, Baltimore's Steve Barber and Stu Miller no-hit Detroit but lost, 2–1.

The A's had myriad problems in Game 1, but Holtzman was not among them. In the very first inning, Carl Yastrzemski stroked a two-out single and advanced to second when Washington misplayed the ball. Carlton Fisk then hit a chopper through Bando for Oakland's second error, Yaz scoring when Washington, backing up the play, airmailed Campaneris with his throw. Fisk took second on the play, then scored when second baseman Phil Garner booted Lynn's ensuing grounder. One hit, three physical errors, one mental error, 2–0 Boston. It was more than the Red Sox needed as Luis Tiant spun a three-hitter in a 7–1 victory.

The loss hardly gave the A's reason to panic. It was their third straight playoff-opening loss, and they'd managed to come back before. Oakland's lack of a third starter, however, lent particular gravity to Game 2, which would be the game in which Fenway made all the difference. The left-field wall — the infamous Green Monster, rising more than 37 feet above the warning track — simply swallowed baseballs. Bando cracked four hits off it in Game 2 — two doubles and two singles that would have been home runs anywhere else, each of which was played perfectly by Yastrzemski. Although Yaz won six Gold Gloves in 12 years as a Red Sox left fielder, the 36-year-old had long since transitioned to first base. Rice's injury forced him back to his original position, however, where he turned in a sublime, series-long defensive masterpiece. He also hit a two-run homer in the fourth inning of Game 2, part of a three-run frame that ended Vida's night. Boston won, 6–3.

The A's had faced elimination before, against the Tigers and Reds in '72, and the Orioles and Mets in '73, but those series were played on the A's terms, with the best they had. This series, though, seemed to be defined by the team's weaknesses. *If we can win in Boston, we might have a chance.... Fenway is fearsome, and we hope our pitchers can survive.... If we had Catfish, everything would be better.* Such phrases did not belie a championship mind-set. The A's were reading the script as it played out before them, and they were frightened.

In Game 3, back in Oakland, Dark bypassed Dick Bosman in favor of Holtzman on two days' rest. Then Claudell Washington committed a fourth-inning error that led to a Red Sox run. A double and two singles in the fifth scored another, chasing Holtzman. Todd and Lindblad ended the frame by allowing two more. Boston led, 4–0, and Oakland was running out of chances.

Even then, the A's might have come back had it not been for Yastrzemski. In the fourth inning the aging star raced into the corner to corral what looked like a certain double by Jackson, then spun and threw out the startled runner at second base. In the eighth, with the Red Sox leading 5–2 and two men on base, Reggie drilled what looked like a sure triple into left-center. Yastrzemski's all-out effort — diving, he reached backward toward the wall to snare the ball after it was by him — prevented extra bases, holding Jackson to a single and one RBI. Instead of Reggie serving as the tying run at third base, he was still on first with the A's down by two. Dick Drago got Joe Rudi to ground into what was essentially a game-, series-, and season-ending double play. The A's went down with barely a whimper in the ninth. It was the first time in four years that their season concluded with anything but champagne.

In the Coliseum's near-silent home clubhouse, players went about the business of packing up for the winter. There would be no victory parties at which to assault each other, no championship rings to complain about next spring. Gene Tenace wandered to a bathroom sink and shaved off his mustache. It no longer represented what it used to.

All anybody from outside the team wanted to talk about was Hunter, and what he would have meant to the series. Somebody asked Bando if losing the A's ace was the biggest blunder in the history of the sport. "If it isn't," the Captain said, "I haven't heard of any bigger."

Finley wasn't even there to see it. He was in New York, testifying in a multimillion-dollar securities violations suit he filed over stock purchased back in 1970. When sportswriters tracked him down for comment, one of them raised the idea that Finley the owner should fire Finley the GM for losing Hunter to the Yankees. At that, the Owner simply walked back into the courtroom, leaving the question hanging in the air behind him.

26

Housecleaning

We were always mad at Charlie. Couldn't beat up Charlie.
Had to beat up each other.

— Reggie Jackson

Prior to the 1975 season, Dodgers pitcher Andy Messersmith rejected his team's salary offer, then played the entire campaign without a signed contract. Marvin Miller and the Players Association filed a grievance on his behalf, with the goal of overturning baseball's reserve clause. At its core was section 10(a) of the Uniform Player's Contract, which read that if player and club had not agreed to terms by March 1, "the Club shall have the right . . . to renew this contract for the period of one year." The owners saw this as indefinite, with the clause reapplied each time the option was exercised, one year at a time, in perpetuity.

It wasn't until the Players Association rose to prominence in the 1970s that the interpretation of the phrase came under meaningful question. The way Miller read it, an owner's right to unilaterally renew a player was enforceable for one year only, after which the player would be sans contract, making him a free agent at season's end. It was the same principle that freed Catfish Hunter from the A's, though that case was built around contract default, not lack of agreement.

Miller and the MLBPA enlisted pitcher Dave McNally — who, despite having effectively retired following the 1975 campaign, was still on the Montreal Expos' reserve list — to join Messersmith as a symbolic hedge against the Dodgers subverting the process with an exorbitant offer to their pitcher. The grievance hearing was conducted across November and December by Peter Seitz, the same man who decided Hunter's dispute with Finley.

Seitz again came down on the side of the players, and when the Eighth Circuit Court of Appeals upheld the decision, it was settled: automatic contract renewals were a thing of the past. Players who were not signed would, after the season, become free agents.

Ideas for compromise measures flew from all corners of the baseball landscape, but Finley was the only one lobbying for baseball to make every player a free agent at the end of every season. The idea was shot down as lunacy by the rest of ownership's ranks, but it was the only proposal that scared the union half to death. Finley "seemed to be the only one smart enough to recognize that opening the floodgates by making all players free agents would work to the owners' advantage by holding salaries down," Miller said later. Put another way, a handful of free agents each year would be a scarce commodity, but a league full of them would not. As was usually the case, Finley's idea was encumbered among his peers by the fact that it came from Finley.

Back in Oakland the Owner appeared set on making as many home-grown free agents as possible. For the second year in a row nearly every contract he mailed out called for minimal raises or no raises at all. When nine A's — Vida Blue, Sal Bando, Campy Campaneris, Rollie Fingers, Ken Holtzman, Reggie Jackson, Billy North, Joe Rudi, and Gene Tenace — returned their pacts unsigned, Finley responded by cutting each of them the maximum amount. It was a bitter act, but it was also the only leverage he had; to get the difference reinstated, the players would have to put pen to paper.

Jerry Kapstein represented five of Oakland's nine (Campy, Fingers, Holtzman, Rudi, and Tenace) and was rejected out of hand when he informed Finley that his clients all sought multiyear deals. The agent sent proposals anyway, each calling for more than $100,000 per season.

No matter how much money any of them made, the A's would be playing the 1976 season under a new manager. Alvin Dark had followed his chaotic 1974 campaign with a masterful 1975, working his Blue/Holtzman/cast-of-thousands rotation with precision. The Owner, however, grew so uncomfortable with Dark's religiosity that even the manager's strongest selling point — overt subservience — was no longer sufficient to save him. Dark was effectively finished when Finley saw a headline on the front page of the *Hayward Daily Review* reading "Alvin Dark Says That Unless He Changes His Ways, Finley's Going to Hell."

The story in question was short on context. Omitted entirely was that the quote came from a longer monologue delivered on September 30, a few days before the playoffs, at the Redwood Chapel Community Church in Castro Valley, just south of Oakland. "Charlie Finley feels that he is a fantastic, big person in the game of baseball, and he is," Dark told the congregation. "I give him credit for building up a great ballclub. But to God, Charlie Finley is this little, bitty thing that is lost. And if he doesn't accept Jesus Christ as his personal savior, he is going to hell. And I've told him that so many times. He has to turn his life over to the Lord. Before it's over with, with all the Christians praying for him, I definitely think he's going to be saved."

In response, the Owner not only fired Dark but hurled the most personal insult possible, saying that his own mother did not agree with the manager's assessment, and "she knows more about those things than Alvin Dark."

On December 19, Finley hired Dark's replacement, Chuck Tanner, saying that he "possesses the qualities I have been looking for." Primary among them was the fact that Tanner had been fired by the White Sox a day earlier with three years remaining on his five-year contract. That left Chicago owner Bill Veeck to pick up all but $25,000 of the manager's contract. Said Tanner, "I feel outstandingly exotic."*

The manager was upbeat and energetic. More pertinent to his new post, he was also capable of handling Finley. The media put Tanner immediately to the test at his introductory press conference, re-creating the situation in which Alvin Dark said that Ray Fosse would play shortstop should the Owner demand it. With Finley having sold Fosse to Cleveland only nine days earlier,† Tanner was instead asked what he would do if the Owner insisted that Gene Tenace play shortstop. "When we're losing, Charlie will be running the team," he answered. "When we're winning, I want all the credit. I know Charlie isn't stupid enough to ask Gene Tenace to play shortstop." When asked about his new team's propensity for beating each other up in the name of competitive spirit, Tanner said, "There are a lot of good kids who go to bed at eight every night, are no trouble

---

* In five years with the White Sox, Tanner received nearly universal praise for maximizing talent. He also had a unique perspective on the A's, having helmed the opposition on four of the five occasions that Oakland clinched a division championship.

† Technically, Finley owed the Rangers $25,000, the Rangers owed the Indians $25,000, and the Indians needed another catcher.

at all, are great to be around, and hit .130. Give me the outspoken, good player."

The A's most outspoken player was also the one guy Finley was actually making an effort to woo. The Owner went bigger and better than he ever thought possible for Reggie Jackson, putting three years on the table for a total of $525,000 — and was genuinely shocked when it turned out to be not nearly enough.* Reggie's camp requested an additional $75,000 per season of deferred money, at which point Finley categorized Jackson as unsignable.

Then he traded him.

On April 2, a week before opening day, Finley sent Jackson and Ken Holtzman (who had requested $480,000 over three years) to Baltimore in exchange for outfielder Don Baylor, right-hander Mike Torrez, and minor league pitcher Paul Mitchell. The banishment served multiple purposes. For one thing, the Owner no longer needed to worry about clearing out his bank account to make Reggie happy. Also, he notified the remaining holdouts that he could unmake his team just as easily as he made it. Nobody was untouchable, and those unwilling to abide by Finley's terms were taking their chances.

Jackson learned about the trade at the ballpark in Mesa. His teammates were in Tucson for an exhibition game, but Reggie had remained in camp for extra batting practice. Somebody shouted from the clubhouse about a phone call. Chicago was on the line.

"Reggie, this is Charlie," Finley said. "We've traded you to Baltimore. Good luck." No *thank you*. No nothing. It couldn't have come as a surprise, what with it being the third straight season of rumors pegging Reggie to the Orioles. Hell, Jackson himself had recently approached Dodgers GM Al Campanis on a beach in Hawaii with a request to bring him to Los Angeles. Ultimately, though, Reggie felt that he'd stick around. All those years' worth of crap he'd been through with Finley had managed to work themselves out in the end. Why couldn't this too?

It just couldn't. Reggie knew that leaving would be sad, but it would also be a cause for celebration — not only with his new ballclub for what was to come, but with his old one for what had been. But there he was,

---

* A year earlier Reggie described his contract demands in terms of bullion: "Gold is $192 an ounce. I weigh 217 pounds. That means under the gold standard I'm worth $654,624 — over three years." The comment was facetious, but Finley did not forget it.

nobody in the room save for a few clubhouse kids to accept his tearful goodbyes. Finley didn't so much as acknowledge Reggie's contributions during that phone call. What Jackson wanted in the end was what he wanted in the beginning, which was something he never really got: to be treated like a man. He packed his green A's duffel and headed to the parking lot, alone.

When word of the deal reached the A's, they were dumbstruck. The clubhouse atmosphere, which provided the team so much of its edge, would not be the same. "A guy grows on you when you've been around each other for so long," lamented Bando. Players talked about the talent inequity in the deal, and the breaking up of a champion, and about how they no longer felt support from above when it came to fielding the best team possible. "It started unwinding," said Gene Tenace, looking back, "and it didn't stop."

The only one who seemed delighted was Finley. "The deal was made because it will lead us to another world championship," he puffed in the immediate aftermath. "I would have made the deal even if all three of the players were signed. I think that under the circumstances it will turn out to be one of the best trades we ever made." Baylor, 26, was a speedy outfielder with moderate power and terrific potential. Torrez, 29, slotted into Holtzman's spot in the rotation. The wild card was Mitchell, a 26-year-old who went 10-1 at Rochester of the International League in 1975 and was 3-0 — including a five-hitter over the A's — in limited big league duty. He was among Baltimore's prized prospects, and Finley hoped that he could mitigate the loss of Hunter.

It took only a week for the Owner to admit that he was indeed motivated by Jackson's salary demands, but even that much was calculated spin. The Owner gave the dollar amounts sought by each of his would-be free agents to the *San Francisco Examiner* — Rudi wanted a three-year deal for $400,000, Tenace three years at $320,000, Fingers $310,000 over two, and Campaneris $600,000 for five — thinking that the information would inspire fans to side with him. He never acknowledged that his behavior over the years — all of it, collectively, on a persistent basis — made him beyond siding with when it came to public perception.

The players were mortified that their requests, which the Owner had assured them would remain confidential, were now on the record. "When I found out about it, Charlie didn't have enough money to sign me," Tenace said later.

What Finley couldn't see was that each of the requests was below a quickly rising market rate. When it became clear what the new financial tableau might bring — Messersmith soon landed with the Braves for three years and $1 million — the unsigned A's players realized what a bargain they'd offered. On April 2, the same day Jackson and Holtzman were traded, Kapstein withdrew every one of his proposals. They'd sat unanswered on Finley's desk for 34 days.

If the Owner thought he'd have it easier with his new players, he was mistaken. Like the recently departed, Baylor was also unsigned, not to mention represented by Kapstein. The outfielder arrived in Oakland with a request for two years at $230,000, which Finley summarily rejected. Mitchell, slated as the number-four starter, shocked Oakland brass when he told them upon arrival that he had pitched only four innings all spring because of muscle spasms in his leg. As starts to a season go, this one was inauspicious before it even began.

Throughout spring training Chuck Tanner had been planting bugs in Reggie's ear about what a big season could be worth financially in the new marketplace, so it was with money in mind that Reggie decided to take advantage of his change in employers and hold out for more. Baltimore GM Hank Peters traveled across the country to negotiate with the slugger in person, but by that point Jackson was talking about more than a million dollars over multiple seasons. The Orioles seemed like a great fit; they were contenders in the AL East, Reggie's mother lived in Baltimore, and he'd be reunited with pal Dave Duncan. Jackson's sister was even married to the brother-in-law of Orioles catcher Elrod Hendricks. It wasn't enough. Reggie sat as the remaining days of the spring schedule ticked away. Then the season opened without him.

Baltimore struggled out of the gate offensively, winning only six of its first 16. Peters finally got Jackson on board with a one-year pact worth close to $200,000, which still allowed him to play out his contract and seek free-agent riches at season's end. Reggie suited up three weeks into the season, then needed more than a month to regain his timing. When he finally caught up with the rest of the league (.309, 18 homers over the season's final three months), the Orioles were in fourth place, ten games behind New York.

Without Reggie in the lineup, the A's weren't doing much better. Baylor, hampered by a wrist injury, hit .150 with two homers through 30 games.

Bando batted .189. Third and fourth starters never emerged behind Blue and Torrez. Mitchell tossed up a 5.90 ERA through May as Oakland lost four of his six starts. Even Fingers and Todd struggled in relief. Playing in a nearly empty ballpark, the defense made lazy errors and appeared to forget the bulk of the fundamentals that had been so maniacally drilled by Dick Williams. "They don't look right without Reggie Jackson," observed Kansas City's John Mayberry. "They just look like they're waiting to get beat."

The A's were short on power and pitching, but they did have speed for days and a manager who knew a good thing when he saw it. Under Tanner's direction, the A's reached 100 steals faster than any AL team ever, at one point swiping 17 consecutive bags. It mostly just made for more exciting losses. Oakland set a modern record in May by stealing nine bases in a single game without being caught, but still lost to Minnesota. In one five-game stretch, the A's stole 20 bases against the White Sox and Twins, including beating their own record with 12 in one contest, while getting caught only once . . . and didn't win any of them.

It came at a cost. Two of the team's best hitters, Tenace and Rudi, were hurt on steal attempts. Tenace missed five weeks with strained knee ligaments, after which he could not squat to play catcher for an additional seven weeks, leaving the team with punchless backup Larry Haney—who, despite leading Oakland catchers in games played, collected *two* extra-base hits all season. Rudi missed ten days, then spent a month struggling to regain his form. As a team, the A's hit .231 through early June, by which point they were 27-31 and ten and a half games out of first.

On June 15, Charlie Finley threw in the towel.

Upon concluding that he had little hope of signing his key free agents, the Owner opened his phone lines and made everybody available to teams around the league. When he tried to swap combinations of his own big-name players for the likes of Fred Lynn, Thurman Munson, and equally unavailable talent, nobody bit. So he took a different tack. The A's weren't winning anyway, so Finley figured that he might as well enrich himself.

His first target was Boston. The offer: Red Sox GM Dick O'Connell's choice of Vida Blue, Joe Rudi, Rollie Fingers, Gene Tenace, and Don Baylor, for the low, low price of $1 million per head. For another $500,000, Finley'd throw in Bando too. For O'Connell, the timing was terrific. Team patriarch Tom Yawkey was 73 years old and in rapidly failing health, and in his 43 years of owning the team had never won a World Series.

The GM called Red Sox manager Darrell Johnson, in Minnesota for a series against the Twins, to get his input. He figured Blue to be a lock for acquisition, considering Boston's dearth of left-handed starters, but Johnson said that he preferred Rudi — who made little sense given that Boston already had the league's best young outfield — and Fingers. O'Connell promised to think about it, but when he tried to reconnect with Johnson, the Red Sox had already finished their game and were en route to Oakland for their next series.

O'Connell had heard rumors that Yankees GM Gabe Paul was also interested in purchasing some of Finley's players, and had even traveled to Chicago for a face-to-face meeting with the Owner. Unable to harbor the thought of being outmaneuvered by his team's fiercest rival, he called Finley back and went with his manager's instincts rather than his own.

"Are Rudi and Fingers still available at $1 million apiece?" he asked.

"Yes, they are," Finley said.

"Well, we just bought both of them."

O'Connell was momentarily elated, but in a precursor to Yankees–Red Sox salary wars to come, New York negated Boston's $2 million effort by securing Blue a day later for $1.5 million. The arms race was officially on.

There were, however, details. While the Red Sox were purchasing players who would be free to bolt after the season, Paul's willingness to go a half-million more for Vida came with a caveat: he wanted the pitcher under contract. Finley got right on it, dialing Blue's agent, Chris Daniels, to discuss an extension. Daniels proposed a three-year pact at $200,000 per — an amount that should have been fine with Finley, considering that it was New York's money he was offering. But that was not the Owner's way. Finley called the proposal astronomical, then spent the next three hours bending a little bit at a time. Pleading poverty and claiming that Vida had him over a barrel, the Owner finally offered a three-year deal worth a total of $485,000.

Daniels quickly got Blue on the phone. "Hey, V, listen — that crazy son of a bitch finally came to his senses," he said. "If you could get down to the Coliseum to sign the papers today, we can get it done." Blue made a beeline for the team offices, where Finley's secretary, Carolyn Coffin, patched him through to Chicago. Speaking directly to the Owner, Vida asked for assurances that the rumors surrounding his departure were only that.

Finley lied. He wanted Blue to be a member of the A's for the rest of his career, he gushed, adding, "Vida, you know I would never trade you."

That night Finley traded Blue to the Yankees for a pile of money. Less than three years earlier he had rejected $150,000 from the Yankees in exchange for Dick Williams, saying, "You can't play cash." Now his tune had changed. Noted *Sports Illustrated* two weeks later, the three departing players represented "the biggest sale of human flesh in the history of sports."

New York announced the Blue deal the following day. Vida heard about it while driving home from lunch, and learned that the Yankees paid Finley three times more for his services than they'd be paying him. When the left-hander showed up at the Coliseum, he was not happy. Not happy at all.

Finley delivered the news to the Coliseum clubhouse himself, phoning from Chicago to speak to Chuck Tanner. Ever vigilant about perception, the Owner invited *Chicago Tribune* reporter Don Pierson to record his end of the call. Thus was he on the record when he tried to explain: "I can't afford to pay these astronomical salaries they're all demanding when we're drawing so poorly in Oakland." And when he tried to rationalize: "We will rebuild it, Chuck. I'm sorry we had to do this today." And when he tried to pin the blame squarely outside his own office: "The big thing, Chuck, as I'm telling the press here, was the agent, Jerry Kapstein, who represents five of my players. He kept me in the dark continuously, right up to the last minute. Never made one trip to come in and talk to me." This, of course, was classic Finley spin. Technically, he was correct; Kapstein had not gone to Chicago to negotiate. He did, however, make overture after overture in an attempt to *begin* negotiating, none of which got him anywhere.

The presence of the press may have influenced the Owner's mother-hen attitude. "Is Vida there?" he asked Tanner. "I can't find him. The damn Yankees released the story on me and it makes me look bad because I didn't tell him. The damn Yankees even tried to deny it was for a million-and-a-half. . . . Let me talk to them, Chuck. All of them. One at a time." *Sophie's Choice* wouldn't be published for another three years, but Finley was doing all he could to make like he had been shoehorned into just such a position. Blue came on the line.

"Vida, this is Charlie Finley," the Owner said. "I know how you feel. The goddamn Yanks jumped the time on me. They promised they wouldn't make the announcement, and then we all heard it on the news . . . What do you mean what announcement? . . . I traded you to the Yankees . . . just you . . . for money." Vida saw through Finley's attempt to position himself as an aggrieved victim, and pressed the Owner with faux ignorance about what the hell was going on. He wanted to see the bastard sweat.

Finley continued: "Vida, this will mean an awful lot to you. I've appreciated all you've done to help me and all the contributions you've made. . . . We couldn't have won three straight world titles without you. The whole thing was brought about by one agent, Jerry Kapstein. Now your man [Chris Daniels], Vida, I've never dealt with a man so respectful. I love you, buddy, and believe me when I tell you that." Blue was scheduled to pitch that night in the opener against Boston. Instead, he made plans to head to Chicago, where the Yankees were about to begin a series with the White Sox.

Joe Rudi learned about his sale from a radio report he heard while driving home from an off-day visit to Sacramento with his family. That Boston was in town made things easy; when Rudi arrived at the Coliseum the following day he saw his gear being carted down the hallway to the visitors' clubhouse. He was the first of the three sold players to arrive, and after tearful commiseration with his former teammates he made the short walk to meet his new ones. He was already gone when Finley called.

Rudi's Red Sox uniform felt foreign. Because the A's wore white spikes, clubbies got busy with black shoe polish. Fingers walked in a short time later and was given the locker next to Carl Yastrzemski. When the visitors took the field to warm up, it was impossible for the ex-A's to think about the proceedings in anything but surreal terms.

The idea of playing for Boston held a certain appeal. Rudi thought about hitting in Fenway Park, where the 390-foot center-field fence was a recipe for chip-shot home runs when it came to an up-the-middle hitter like himself. Fingers didn't need even that much. "I was happier than a pig in shit to get away from Charlie," he said.

When the news broke, Bowie Kuhn was in Chicago — at Comiskey Park, in fact, watching the White Sox play the Orioles. After Chicago general manager Roland Hemond handed him a minutes-old print-out off the newswire announcing the sales, the Commissioner called O'Connell, who told him that if Finley was selling, he sure as hell was buying. Kuhn requested that the Red Sox exec keep the players out of the lineup until things could be sorted out, and issued orders to delay Blue from reporting to the Yankees. Finally, he called Finley's office across town.

It was after 9:00 P.M. by that point, but the Owner answered the phone. Kuhn labeled the player sales a "disaster" and told Finley that an investigation would occur before — and if — he allowed them to go through. Finley responded with his typical bombast, forgoing any sense of politics in favor of raw, effervescent emotion. "Commissioner," he said, "it's none of your damn business. You can't stop me from selling players. Guys have been selling players forever, and no commissioner has ever stopped them."*

Kuhn arranged to meet the Owner that night at the coffee shop in the Pick-Congress Hotel, a block from Finley's office. It was just after 10:00 P.M. when he arrived with his top aide, attorney Sandy Hadden, in tow. With Finley was his son Paul. The Owner started the meeting by ordering a round of Black Russians — vodka and Kahlua — despite (or perhaps because of) being the only one at the table who could stomach the things. He pulled out New York's bill of sale for Blue and again told Kuhn that it was none of his business. He said that he had built his franchise out of nothing, and now, facing mass exodus, he was eager to do so again. Baseball was working under a different financial system in 1976 than it had been in 1961, Finley pointed out, and he needed money to reload. He insisted that the A's would win more World Series, but that they couldn't do so from a bankrupt state — and selling 600,000 full-price tickets per season was not exactly keeping him flush. "Commissioner, I can't sign these guys," the Owner pleaded. "They don't want to play for ol' Charlie. They want to chase those big bucks in New York. If I

---

* When Finley claimed that owners "have been selling players forever," he had precedent to back him up. As early as 1887, the Chicago White Stockings of the National League sold King Kelly to the Boston Beaneaters for $10,000. In 1919, when American League president Ban Johnson disapproved of Boston's efforts to sell pitcher Carl Mays to the Yankees, New York obtained an injunction upholding the transaction; Mays pitched the next four years for New York. Bolstered by their court victory, the Yankees then purchased Babe Ruth from Boston for $125,000. In 1934 the Senators sold shortstop Joe Cronin — MacPhail's predecessor as AL president — to the Red Sox for $250,000.

sell them now, I can at least get something back. If I can't, they walk out on me at the end of the season and I've got nothing, nothing, nothing at all."

Finley's true goal, of course, was to pocket the cash and, in the face of an untenable financial landscape, dump the depleted A's. "He knew the price of the team would be the same with or without those players . . ." said Paul Finley, looking back, "so why not unload them, pick up the $3.5 million, and sell the team for the same amount of money?"

It was powerful motivation. The Owner spoke for nearly two hours, by which point the diner had all but shut down. Kuhn kept thinking about a term he had recently coined: *competitive balance*. He feared enduring repercussions if rich teams could simply purchase whichever players they wanted in the heart of a pennant race. The draft was instituted in 1965 to mitigate this very sort of inequity. "I'm still very troubled by this situation," Kuhn told the Owner. "I'd like to think about it overnight and get back in touch with you."

When Kuhn returned to New York the next day, he was still thinking. He set up a conference call with his executive council to solicit opinions. The league presidents, MacPhail and Feeney, along with Tigers owner John Fetzer (who had bid on Blue before the Yankees secured him), thought he should let the sales go through. Three others — Dodgers owner Walter O'Malley, Brewers owner Edmund Fitzgerald, and Expos president John McHale — urged Kuhn in the opposite direction. A consensus worried about Finley taking the league to court if things didn't go his way. Considerable friction still existed between owners and players about the impending free-agency class, and it was suggested that tampering by the Commissioner could be seen as an effort to impair the process.

The following day Kuhn called the principals to his Fifth Avenue office to discuss the matter. The 18 people in attendance included MacPhail, Finley, George Steinbrenner and Gabe Paul of the Yankees, Dick O'Connell, Marvin Miller, and ten attorneys. The meeting was drama-free. Kuhn alleged no misdeeds and allowed the parties to speak for themselves. Finley revisited his rationale for the sales being approved. The entire process took 95 minutes. Upon departing, Steinbrenner flashed a hopeful thumbs-up for reporters. Miller announced, "I don't understand what the furor is about. No rules have been violated. What has happened here has happened hundreds of times — namely, the selling of players for cash."*

The following day, June 18, Kuhn ruled. In a prepared statement delivered at a packed press conference in his office, he said, "If, as contended by the participants, the Commissioner lacks the power to prevent a development so harmful to baseball as this, then our system for self-regulation for the good of the game and the public is a virtual mirage. I think the Commissioner's power is clear and binding, and its exercise vital to the best interests of the game." With that, he negated the sales.

Kuhn didn't quite call Finley a liar about his claims to sink the money back into the franchise, but he might as well have. "Whether other players will be available to restore the club by using the money involved is altogether speculative, although Mr. Finley vigorously argues his ability to do so," he wrote in his decision. "Public confidence in the integrity of club operations and in baseball would be gravely undermined should such assignments not be restrained."

Finley reacted as anticipated. Seven days later he filed a $10 million federal lawsuit in Chicago and proclaimed that until the matter was settled, none of the players involved would suit up for the A's. He called the action a "personal vendetta," said Kuhn sounded "like the village idiot," and labeled him "a twenty-four-carat kook."

Oddly, Marvin Miller — naturally opposed to virtually everything the Owner did — was squarely in his camp on this one. Calling Kuhn's ruling "sheer insanity," the union head said that the Commissioner was trying to circumvent the rights of the owners. "Whenever there's a trade made, he can decide that one team did not get enough value and he can veto the deal," he said. "He has single-handedly plunged baseball into the biggest mess it has ever seen." Finley, altogether ignoring his own initial objection to Miller's presence at the meeting, responded: "When both Marvin

---

* Pertinent examples existed even within Finley's own franchise. In 1914 Connie Mack dismantled his famous million-dollar infield following a World Series loss to the Boston Braves, selling his players to the highest bidders and dooming the Athletics to seven straight last-place finishes. After rising to prominence again in 1931 — the A's came within an extra-base hit of winning their third straight World Series — Mack held another fire sale, shipping off his best players for the 1976 equivalent of $2,553,085.70. (That number was provided 45 years later by Finley, who added that it was the *after*-tax figure.) In the latter instance the A's didn't recover. Over the next three decades they finished in last place 13 times, and next to last another six. In the 30th year, Finley bought the team.

Miller and the owner of a ballclub are thinking the same way, the other person *has* to be wrong."

Meanwhile, the players at the heart of the controversy were in limbo. Blue canceled his flight to Chicago, then held tight awaiting further news. When the Red Sox left for Anaheim, Rudi and Fingers remained in Oakland. They were no longer members of the Boston club, but they weren't exactly A's either, having been banned by Finley from both field and clubhouse despite Kuhn's ruling that they were immediately eligible to return. Soon a compromise was arranged: the players would work out with the A's, then decamp to the press box once games began. The Owner explained that appearing in games might compromise his legal claims that they were not under his employ. If they got injured, who would compensate Boston, and how? This was it, then. The game's most pressing questions had officially become the dominion of courtrooms. Until things were settled, Oakland would compete with only 22 players.*

Day after day, Rudi, Fingers, and Blue showed up at the Coliseum, warmed up with their teammates, then departed for the showers. Day after day the A's were angry about it, all of them, frustrated by the helplessness of their position. The league was angry that three star players had been nullified for reasons contrary to the Commissioner's orders. The calendar ticked toward July.

On June 25, a Friday, with the players in question having sat for the better part of two weeks, the rest of the A's took action. Their method was a by-then familiar tactic: player strike. Led by Bando, players closed the clubhouse doors to vote on the matter. The tally in favor of a walkout if their banished teammates were not reinstated within three days was unanimous — 21–0, with two abstentions. Bando informed Marvin Miller that the A's would not play on Sunday without resolution. Miller

---

* Additional fallout landed in New York, where the Yankees — thinking they had Blue in hand — pulled the trigger on a win-now trade aimed at securing the American League East. They acquired Ken Holtzman from Baltimore — ostensibly reuniting Oakland's Big Three — along with unsigned Doyle Alexander and backup catcher Elrod Hendricks, and mortgaged the farm to do so. Lost in the deal were three players who would become Orioles cornerstones through the mid-1980s: Tippy Martinez, Scott McGregor, and Rick Dempsey. Without Blue, however, the Yankees were still one dominant pitcher short of contention, not to mention three prospects short for the foreseeable future. Responded a pissed-off Billy Martin: "[Kuhn] has opened a big can of worms. Is this in the best interest of baseball, having lawsuits all over the country?"

disapproved, but held no power in the matter. He urged Bando to keep things cool, then sat back to see what would happen.

After that day's game, a victory over Minnesota, Bando informed Tanner about the development. The manager wanted the players back as badly as did their teammates, and got the Owner on the phone. "Mr. Finley," Bando told him, "I want you to know that we had a team meeting and we all agree that if we don't have Joe in the lineup Sunday, we're going out on strike." (Rudi was the only one mentioned because Blue's start would have to be slotted appropriately, and Fingers was never in the starting lineup.) Finley cursed. Then Finley screamed blood and torture. The volume grew so piercing that Bando had to hold the phone away from his ear. Suddenly, however, the Owner realized that his time could be spent more productively. He hung up on Bando and called the Coliseum's radio booth, smack in the middle of the postgame show, demanding to be put on the air. When Monte Moore patched him through, Finley proceeded to rip his team for selfishness and lack of foresight, informing the Bay Area about the players' plans. The outburst was designed to garner sympathy, but it did something else — it got people to pay attention.

Sunday was deadline day, and media — national media, in enormous numbers — flocked to the Coliseum for Oakland's finale against the Twins . . . or whatever was going to happen instead of it. "This was going to be the first in-season, one-team strike since the early 1900s," said clubhouse man Steve Vucinich, looking back. "Nobody wanted to miss that." Before the game players closed the clubhouse doors and took another vote to confirm that everybody was still on board. Given time to think it over, some changed their minds, but the measure still passed overwhelmingly, 14–7. The players got dressed, took batting practice, and loosened up according to the standard timetable. Then they returned to the clubhouse and began removing their uniforms. It was 12:50 P.M. The game was scheduled for 1:05. The only player on the field was starting pitcher Dick Bosman, warming up with a coach in case the issue was resolved.

Tanner immediately repaired to his office and got Finley on the telephone. "They're taking off their uniforms, Charlie," he said with no small amount of urgency. The players knew where their manager was and what he was doing. Jim Todd, the player representative since Reggie was traded, was talking to Marvin Miller on a hallway telephone, providing a blow-by-blow account of the action.

When Tanner emerged from his office, all eyes turned his way. The packed room grew still. First pitch was minutes away.

The manager held up the lineup card. "Here it is," he said. "North, center field . . . Campaneris, shortstop . . . Baylor, designated hitter . . . Bando, third base . . . Tenace, first base . . . Rudi, left field . . ."

The recitation of the names spurred a clubhouse eruption, the ensuing shouts of joy clearly audible to the 40 or so reporters waiting outside the doors. Players raced to their lockers, pulled on their uniforms, and bounded down the stairs, through the tunnel, and onto the field. "It was mass hysteria," said Bando. "It was like the World Series."

The game started about a half-hour after it was scheduled, but the 4,798 fans at the Coliseum didn't seem to mind — they were nearly as delighted as the A's to see Rudi back in the lineup. "We put Finley up against the wall and won," exulted Billy North later. "Didn't nobody jump up in Charlie's face. Didn't nobody tell Charlie what he couldn't do. But *we* did."

The A's won, 5–3, and Rudi's 0-for-4 from left field didn't even matter. Fingers pitched three and a third innings of shutout relief (he was well rested) to pick up his ninth save. The A's had gone 7-5 in the players' absence, reducing their deficit in the West from ten and a half games to seven and a half games, but, said Billy Williams, "we could have won all [of them] if they'd been able to play." With their comrades returned, the momentum was undeniable.

Finley went quickly into face-preservation mode. "Since all members of the American League have agreed not to protest any of the games in which these players will appear, I have decided to acquiesce to Commissioner Kuhn's directive . . ." he said in a statement. "At the same time, however, I strongly dispute and protest his decision that his actions are in the best interest of baseball. If having Fingers, Rudi and Blue play against the two teams that now own them is in the best interest of baseball, so be it."

Finley failed to acknowledge that Kuhn's directive was days old by that point and had nothing to do with the timing of his decision. Nor did he mention that he had been warned by the MLBPA that the players could be made free agents immediately if he did not abide by Kuhn's instructions within ten days. Also omitted was his serious attempt to field his Triple-A Tucson Toros roster at the major league level, an idea that was shot down by both Lee MacPhail (who warned Finley that he would not approve any player suspensions, a prerequisite for replacing them with minor leaguers) and the Pacific Coast League, which threatened its own legal action.

Finley's lawsuit was tried in January and lasted 15 days. It was there that Kuhn came clean about his distrust of Finley's motivation for the sales, owing to the Owner's uncertain finances with his insurance business and the fact that he was facing not only an IRS investigation into back taxes but support payments to his soon-to-be-ex-wife. On more than one occasion during the hearings Finley showed up in the company of leggy blondes, who heard his legal team object to as many motions — up to 49 in a single day — as possible.

In his six-page decision handed down on March 17, Judge Frank Mc-Garr clarified that "the question before the court is not whether Bowie Kuhn was wise to do what he did, but rather whether he had the authority." Then he made it official: Kuhn had the authority. McGarr rejected Finley's claims that the Commissioner's action was personally motivated, and effectively shut the door on the Owner's final hope for baseball solvency. As Finley said afterward, it was "eighteen years of blood, sweat and sacrifice down the drain."

Upon returning, Rudi talked about how, as much as he would have loved to play at Fenway Park, Oakland was where his family wanted to be. Blue wasn't saying much of anything to anybody, inside the clubhouse or out. "Maybe if the Yankees and A's get in the playoffs I could pitch for both sides," he muttered in his most in-depth public analysis of the situation. "I'd be tired, but that might end all this crap."

Fingers picked up a win and two saves in his first three games following the layoff, but it took some time for the others to return to form. Rudi hit .148 in his first weeks back. Vida gave up six runs over five innings against the Royals in his first start. The two games Oakland made up in the standings during their absence were quickly handed back. The A's didn't play terrible baseball — Bando was red-hot, hitting seven homers in seven games, and Phil Garner was named an All-Star in just his second season — but they weren't playing well enough to keep up with Kansas City. In early August they fell 12 games back, inspiring Finley to label the situation "a disaster."* Said the dispirited Owner: "I don't even know if I want to go out and see them play." The fans were similarly uncertain; 22 of the 50 home dates through July failed to draw even 5,000 patrons.

Then Mike Torrez and Stan Bahnsen shut down the Angels on consecutive days. Blue threw a complete-game five-hitter over Milwaukee. Mike Norris, back from the minors, raised hopes with six and two-thirds innings of two-hit ball against Boston. Before anybody knew what was happening, the A's won nine in a row and were only seven games behind the Royals. With time running out on the season, Finley reversed his fire-sale ways and purchased a duo of 38-year-old sluggers, Willie McCovey and Ron Fairly, and canceled an agreed-upon sale of Bando to the Yankees.

The Owner even flew to Rhode Island to meet with Kapstein in a last-ditch effort to lock up his would-be free agents, presenting three-year deals across the board — $420,000 for Rudi, $410,000 for Fingers, $375,000 for Campaneris, $360,000 for Tenace, and $300,000 for Baylor. Each figure was higher than he had been willing to go at the beginning of the season, but it was by that point far too little, far too late. The players had spent the previous months bitter about the 20 percent cuts Finley imposed in March, not to mention his release of their initial contract proposals and his aborted player sales and his ongoing public disparagement. They wanted out, and any hometown discounts they might have considered six months earlier were no longer in play. All five proposals were rejected, none countered.

With that, Finley turned again. He went back to court to obtain judicial approval for the sales of Rudi, Fingers, and Blue, effective for the final two weeks of the season. He renewed efforts to sell Bando — tied for the league lead in home runs — to Texas for $500,000, a deal that the Rangers rejected when Bando said that it would take $600,000 over four years to lock him up.

Oakland ended the season on an 18-14 run, knocking games off their deficit at a rapid-fire pace, but never quite caught up, finishing two and a half games behind Kansas City. It was the first time in six years that the

---

* Among the losses was a no-hitter thrown by old friend Blue Moon Odom, who had just been recalled from the minors by the White Sox. He lasted only five innings on account of surrendering nine walks, and reliever Francisco Barrios pitched the last four hitless frames. It was the final victory of Odom's career.

A's ended a season anyplace but first. Their final road trip was to Chicago; Finley did not even show up.*

At least one thing didn't change: for the sixth straight year the regular season's final game was toasted with champagne. This time, however, the celebration was about escape. The team's seven unsigned players — six from the beginning of the season, plus McCovey — had fulfilled their obligations to Charles O. Finley and were free to seek outside employment at going rates. Thirty-six bottles of champagne appeared in the clubhouse.

"This is to celebrate the liberation of the Oakland Seven," gushed North, who, having signed a two-year contract at the beginning of the year, was not among their ranks. Also not among their ranks was Vida Blue, who since June had been choking on the three-year pact he was tricked into signing prior to his aborted sale to New York.† Two days earlier Blue had broken nearly three months of public silence, erupting in a clubhouse monologue intended for reporters. "I hope the next breath Charles O. Finley takes is his last," he shouted in the published version, scrubbed of obscenities. "I hope he falls flat on his face or dies of polio. I have no respect for that man. He didn't do one thing this year to help this ballclub. Instead, he sat back there in Chicago and ate with all those bankers. I hope he makes 10 zillion dollars, but he isn't going to get one copper nickel from me when he goes to hell."

Across the clubhouse Fingers put it more genteelly, saying only that "I feel sorry for anyone who has to play for this club next year." When somebody asked Bando if it was difficult to leave, he joked, "Was it difficult leaving the *Titanic*?"

The room also contained a healthy dose of pathos. It was the finale for a team that nobody wanted to end — a team that had until very recently

---

* For Oakland, second place still merited some pride. Blue's 18-13 record didn't reflect it, but he was more dominant than at any time since 1971, with a 2.35 ERA that ranked second in the league. Torrez won 16 games with a 2.50 ERA. Bando's 27 homers tied with Jackson for second in the league, while Tenace's 22 ranked seventh. Most notable was their running. Oakland set an American League record with 341 stolen bases, becoming the first team in major league history to have three players with 50 or more — North with a league-leading 75, Campaneris with 54, and Baylor with 52. Three more had 30-plus, and two additional nabbed at least 20. The pinch runners, Larry Lintz and Matt Alexander, combined for 51 bags while collecting one hit in 31 at-bats.

† The following May, Blue filed a $1.5 million suit against Finley, claiming fraud and bad faith in the three-year contract he had signed the previous June, stemming both from the lies that the Owner told him and the fact that nobody from the A's signed the contract. The amount sought was, not coincidentally, how much the Yankees were willing to pay for his services.

possessed the talent to contend for many more championships. Within three months even Charlie O was dead — the mule, not the Owner — succumbing to liver disease in a turn that seemed darkly representative of the club as a whole. The end had started with the departure of Catfish Hunter and was accelerated by the trades of Jackson and Holtzman, but this was the end of the end, and everybody knew it.

The Royals were beaten in the playoffs by the Yankees, who were beaten by the Reds in the World Series. In December outside offers for the Oakland Seven began in earnest, and players fell away from the team, one by one. Baylor to the Angels, five years for $1.4 million. Rudi joining him in Anaheim, five years, $2.09 million. Tenace and Fingers to the Padres —five years, $1.815 million for the catcher; six years, $1.5 million for the closer. Bando to Milwaukee, five years and $1.4 million. Campaneris to the Rangers, five years, $950,000. Reggie, traded by Finley over a demand for $700,000, signed a five-year pact with the Yankees worth $3 million. Finley's players could have been locked up back in March for a combined $2.98 million; instead, they looked elsewhere and pulled in $12.25 million between them. Once they were scattered across the landscape, Finley cried persistently that he had tried to sign them, that he offered more even than they had asked. He said that other owners could afford to pay exorbitant salaries because they wrote them off against income from outside industries. He said that baseball suffered from a lack of leadership and forethought. He acknowledged deserving precisely none of the blame.

It was done.

Long Slope Down

During spring training, even the Seattle Mariners laughed at them. Come back when you grow up, they heckled. Writers were picking them last in the American League West and calling them the Oakland Apathetics and the Oakland Triple-A's.

— *Los Angeles Times,* May 18, 1978

The A's were essentially a rubble pile by the middle of winter. Their free agents were gone. Billy Williams was released and subsequently retired. They needed starters at first base, third base, shortstop, left field, catcher, designated hitter, and up and down the pitching staff.

Things got worse when Finley traded Chuck Tanner — whose salary, Lee MacPhail ruled, no longer had to be paid by Bill Veeck — to the Pirates for catcher Manny Sanguillen and $100,000. Finley's new farm director, Syd Thrift, and traveling secretary, Jim Bank, both quit. The Owner even fired broadcaster Monte Moore after 15 seasons. Finley had long been known for effectively running a one-man operation, and the label was looking more literal by the day.

The next three years were a blur of more-of-the-same. Finley continued to attack Bowie Kuhn, who in the wake of the aborted fire sale ordered all clubs to apprise him in advance of major deals. The Owner responded by selling Paul Lindblad to the Texas Rangers for $400,000 without notice, then suggested that Kuhn buy a newspaper if he wanted information. Because it occurred during the off-season, and because at age 36 Lindblad would not by himself swing the balance of power in the American League West, Kuhn eventually allowed the sale.

Finley traded Phil Garner to the Pirates for a handful of prospects. He traded Claudell Washington, Mike Torrez, and Stan Bahnsen in separate deals, getting little back outside of what he himself described as "a substantial amount of cash." He sold second-line players up and down the roster, pocketing nearly $2 million. Oakland finished last in the league in batting, slugging, runs scored, and on-base percentage. The pitching staff featured a disinterested Vida Blue and a company of rookies and castoffs. Two seasons after winning their fifth straight division title the A's lost 98 games and finished in last place, behind even the expansion Mariners. Jack McKeon, Finley's 14th manager in 17 years, was replaced midseason by Bobby Winkles. Attendance plunged, despite the expansion of half-price Mondays into half-price Monday-through-Thursdays. Things grew so bad that when the team learned that the Oakland tailor who stitched letters and numbers onto the backs of the uniforms was actually a jewel thief with little interest in either baseball or sewing, it seemed almost normal.

In September 1977, after another bypass operation and with finances ravaged by his impending divorce, Finley finally decided to sell the A's. His buyer of choice, willing to meet the $12.5 million reserve price, was a six-foot-four, 300-pound billionaire oilman named Marvin Davis, who intended to move the team to Denver.

For that to happen, of course, the Owner needed help divesting himself from the 20-year lease in Oakland, which still had another decade to run. Only too happy to pitch in, Bowie Kuhn convinced the Coliseum commissioners that, in light of their negligible revenues and the legal headaches that Finley was certain to bring if they impeded him, they'd be well served to compromise. He talked Bob Lurie — who had purchased the Giants from the Stoneham family in 1976, then suffered through two seasons in which his team finished last in the National League in attendance — into a scenario in which the Giants would play half their games in Oakland, at the enticing cost of sweeping the area free of competition. Then the Owner mucked up the works.

With so many wary parties involved, the only way to reach complete consensus was a guarantee that Finley — the sport's most litigious owner — would waive his right to sue. Already on the books, however, was Finley's appeal of his suit over the voided player sales, plus one in the pipeline concerning a recently squashed effort to sell Blue to Cincinnati. The courts were Finley's final assurance that his voice would be heard, and he refused to give them up, but without such a guarantee Marvin Davis was unwilling to proceed. Referring to Finley as "that nut," he withdrew his offer.

Back in the saddle for the foreseeable future, Finley unloaded Blue — legitimately this time — to the San Francisco Giants for six marginal players (the best of whom, Gary Thomasson and Gary Alexander, were themselves traded for lesser players by midseason) and $300,000. In May 1978 he traded Billy North — the final tie to the championship teams — to the Dodgers for less talented (and less expensive) outfielder Glenn Burke. He released mediocre veterans to make room for even more mediocre rookies. His payroll was devoid of full-time scouts and minor league hitting and pitching instructors. The A's front office was so thin that secretaries and clubhouse men were listed on the executive register simply to give it some heft. The Owner reached a new low when, convinced the team was moving, he opted against securing a radio contract, instead appointing the 10-watt college radio station out of UC Berkeley as the team's flagship station. Broadcasts didn't even reach the Coliseum.*

Amid these shortcomings, Winkles somehow led a team of youngsters into an early division lead. But on May 21 — with the A's 24-15 and in first place — the manager, no longer able to tolerate Finley's interference, quit. He was replaced by the man he himself had replaced a year earlier, Jack McKeon. Oakland went into free fall, losing 93 games. Even the *Oakland Tribune* pulled its reporters from the road; for the first time since moving west, the A's played games completely devoid of local media presence. After the season Finley replaced McKeon with Jim Marshall, a man selected based in no small part on his willingness to take the job.

In 1979 things somehow got even worse. Oakland lost 108 games, and Coliseum attendance submarined to 306,763, or 3,787 per game. On April 17 against the Mariners, 653 people paid to get into the ballpark. The city of Oakland sued Finley for breach of contract based on a complete lack of interest in attracting fans.

Those were the first events that led to the A's being ripped from the Owner's grasp. The next came courtesy of the former Miss Shirley Mc-

---

* Until Finley gave in 16 games into the season and signed with professionally run KNEW, the team's lead broadcaster was Cal undergraduate Larry Baer, who later went to Harvard Business School and eventually became the president and CEO of the San Francisco Giants.

Cartney, who, thanks to the appeals process dragged out by her husband, had been in the apparently endless process of divorcing Finley since shortly after the 1973 World Series. He testified that he owned nothing but a stake in a joint $25,000 checking account with Shirley, plus a bunch of stock he'd used as collateral against millions of dollars in loans. Besides, he said, Shirley already owned 30 percent of Charles O. Finley & Company. Also, profits were way below forecasts. Also, he wasn't even able to pay his 1973 income taxes without borrowing money.

Ordered to provide documentation, Finley shuffled his feet to the point of being charged with contempt of court. He presented reams of unrequested material and let the opposition lawyers figure out what was pertinent. He claimed to have trouble finding the documents he *was* asked for. He said that Shirley already had access to it all anyway. He filed for a change of venue. After two years he claimed that the discovery process was too burdensome. The judge penalized him for the delays by ordering him to pay $15,000 for his wife's legal fees. After more delays he was ordered to pay another $50,000. In all, Finley's tactics bought him six years. He needed them.

The Owner's obfuscation was hardly justified, but neither was it based on fiction. Finley was battling the IRS over more than half a million dollars it claimed he owed on back taxes from a five-year span in the mid-1960s. More pertinently, Charles O. Finley & Company had been in steep decline for a number of years, in 1974 losing its biggest client, the American Medical Association.

Kuhn reintroduced Marvin Davis to the equation and even helped renegotiate another deal with the Coliseum commission to let the A's out of their lease. He nearly pulled it off, until Raiders owner Al Davis announced his intention to move his football team to Los Angeles. The city of Oakland, deciding that it could not afford to lose both franchises, canceled the arrangement.

By that point the Owner was desperate. The A's were the least desirable franchise in the major leagues, and the opportunity to realize his $12 million asking price was growing slimmer by the day. He made a splash in 1980 by hiring Billy Martin as his 18th manager in 20 years, a move that resulted in an inspired 29-game swing, with Oakland's 83-79 record good for second place in the American League West. Featuring an AL record 100 stolen bases from Rickey Henderson, 35 homers from young slugger Tony Armas, a glorious return to form by Mike Norris (22-9, 2.53 ERA), and stout pitching from newcomers Rick Langford, Matt Keough, and Steve McCatty, Oakland drew nearly 850,000 fans — an increase of more than half a million.

It was Finley's final hurrah. The A's had served as an extension of himself, a symbol of the man as magnate, as overlord, as creator, but it all ended in August 1980, when the Owner agreed to sell the team to the Haas family for $12.7 million. Walter H. Haas Jr., the great-grandnephew of Levi Strauss, ran the San Francisco–based clothing company that bore his ancestor's name. His son Wally and son-in-law Roy Eisenhardt came aboard in official capacities. The family viewed the purchase in terms of civic goodwill as much as anything, figuring that keeping the A's in Oakland would bolster regional pride and give their product some marketable associations with sports.*

Assets being stripped from every side, the Owner was able to use the sale money to settle into a comfortable retirement, but the loss of the team he spent most of his adult life either trying to acquire or forging in his own image was devastating. "I know how a man feels without a country," he lamented shortly after the sale went through. "A man without a country. The thought just occurred to me yesterday. I feel like him, me without a ballclub."

Shirley Finley ended up with the farm in La Porte, so Charlie moved into one nearby that he'd initially bought for his parents, who had since passed. It was half the size, but still boasted a ten-room house, which he remodeled to resemble a storied Southern manor. He commissioned a series of six stained-glass windows for the barn, one featuring a nearly life-size depiction of his old nemesis, Reggie Jackson. The hayloft was outfitted with an upstairs ballroom, complete with grand piano, and above that a faux press box. "I always wanted my own," said the man who had been vexed by his inability to eject reporters from actual ones.

Finley continued to dabble in sports, notably patenting an "inverted pebble" football with golf-ball-like dimples that he said would improve both accuracy and distance. He even convinced the University of Michi-

---

* When Eisenhardt showed up at the Coliseum toward the end of the year to familiarize himself with the front office, he was stunned by the organizational wasteland before him. "Here I was," he said, "in the office of what was supposedly a major-league franchise in the middle of a season, and all I could find was a switchboard operator, a controller who collected the gate receipts, and Charlie's cousin, Carl Finley, answering phone calls and practically running the whole show himself." The team's three championship trophies were on a secretary's desk, propping up file folders.

gan to use it from 1990 to 1992, during which time Desmond Howard won the Heisman Trophy.

Finley's health deteriorated through the 1980s, a result of high cholesterol and ongoing heart problems. He underwent emergency vascular surgery in 1981. His diet, heavy on butter and oils, and his longtime smoking habit took a devastating toll. The man who built his entire persona on being indomitable — on rebounding from anything an unloving world might hurl his way — was finally out of rebounds. Charles Oscar Finley passed away somewhat suddenly on February 19, 1996, three days before he turned 78.

His funeral was held on his birthday, in overcast weather in Merrillville, Indiana, about 45 miles west of La Porte. Although Finley had employed hundreds of players over his 20 years of team ownership, only two showed up for his funeral—the same two he managed to alienate most: Reggie Jackson and Catfish Hunter.* Former Braves owner Bill Bartholomay, Finley's peer in the Chicago insurance industry, was the lone baseball executive on hand. New A's owner Steve Schott sent clubhouse manager Steve Vucinich, one of three people still in the club's employ from the Owner's time, to represent the organization. After years of pushing people around and away, both within his organization and throughout baseball, it made sense that Finley would not draw the masses to his side one last time.

Still, there was no mistaking the sadness, beyond even the end of a life. At his core, Finley equated power with importance and importance with love, even in the empiric absence of actual affection. As it turned out, fear and enmity did not equal respect, a fact borne out by the lack of representation at his funeral from a sport he helped shape more than any other during his time within it.

For Charlie Finley, it was lonely at the top. In the end he discovered that it was even lonelier at the bottom.

---

* The players, traveling from Yankees camp in Fort Lauderdale, were an hour late because of flight delays. The start of the funeral was held up until they arrived.

Epilogue

> We were the team everybody wanted to come see: the freaks with the mustaches, with the long hair, that took batting practice in black shoes but came out to play in white shoes.
>
> —Vida Blue

On opening day 1972, Ken Holtzman made the most of his first American League start, toying with the Twins through eight innings in his Coliseum debut before passing off a 3–2 lead to his roommate, Rollie Fingers. The closer opened the ninth with two quick outs, leaving center fielder Bobby Darwin as the Twins' final hope. Fingers had never faced Darwin, a career minor leaguer, and called Sal Bando over for a quick scouting report. The Captain knew only one detail: for the first eight years of his professional career, Darwin had been a right-handed pitcher.

Fingers couldn't have been more delighted. If the guy was a pitcher, that meant he couldn't hit, and if he couldn't hit, all the closer had to do was pummel him with fastballs. What Bando did not tell him, because Bando did not know it, was that Darwin had transitioned to hitting because he was good at it. Darwin unloaded on Fingers's 3-1 offering, blasting the ball farther than anybody thought possible, through the last exit of the upper deck in left field, 377 feet from the plate and four stories above field level. The ball had barely slowed when it vanished from view down a rear-facing staircase. Fingers later called it the longest home run he ever gave up in Oakland.

Although the A's went on to win in 11, the closer's miscue deprived Holtzman of a deserved first victory. In the postgame clubhouse Fingers approached the deprived starter. "I only hope you don't win 19 this year," he said, "because I just cost you one right there."

Holtzman finished the season with 19 victories.

In 2012 the team reunited in Oakland for the 40th anniversary of the '72 championship. The men were older, balder, grayer, and heavier, but otherwise it was as if no time had passed. As soon as they saw each other Holtzman — who in the interim had stayed close with Fingers, serving as best man at one of his weddings — approached his old pal. Before a pleasantry could be exchanged, however, he had something to get off his chest. "You know, roomie," he said, loud enough for the room to hear, "on the landing pattern coming into the Oakland airport I saw that ball Darwin hit off you. It's still flying."

It was the kind of sentiment — mutual accountability, even decades after accountability ceased to matter — that propelled those A's. Fingers and Holtzman were unique — close friends, ragging each other about everything, at length and in public — but they were also representative. Their Oakland team was talented, but it did not possess the most talent. What got the A's over in ways both middling and profound was an ingrained understanding about maximizing potential. It wasn't that they did things differently than other teams, it was that they did them with more intensity, with better focus and more precision. They did not yield. The players' incessant needling of each other ensured that regression among their ranks was never anything more than a temporary affair, beaten away verbally and occasionally physically. If continually walking the line of social propriety meant that they might cross it on occasion, so be it; an occasional fistfight was worth the results the process wrought. "It was one big group therapy session," said Phil Garner, looking back. "They'd literally have you crying, and when you started crying it was even worse."*

That was one way to look at it. Dave Duncan had another: "The thing that helped the team more than anything else was the fact that Reggie Jackson was on that team, and Reggie Jackson felt that he was the leader of the team. Sal Bando was on that team. Sal Bando felt that he was the leader of the team. Mike Epstein was on that team. Mike Epstein felt that he was the leader of the team. Joe Rudi was a quiet leader, but really influential in his attitude and advice to the players. Everybody felt that they

---

* "You have to pass the crazy test," laughed Blue Moon Odom, looking back. "You fill out that application: are you crazy? If the answer is no, we don't want you."

were the leader of the team, so nobody tolerated any kind of lackadaisical attitude or lackadaisical play or not doing what needed to be done to succeed. You didn't have one or two guys who were team leaders, you had nine or ten."

It was Hunter delivering a devastating put-down with such genuine affection that its target couldn't help but laugh . . . before heeding the message and fixing his behavior. It was Bando making sure that a pitcher was where he needed to be, mentally and mechanically, prior to every pitch. It was Rudi working harder than anybody to turn himself into the league's best left fielder, and then accepting an unwanted transfer to first base because he was a good soldier with the team's interests in mind. But the man who best typified those A's — whose success was predicated on a brand of baseball that barely registered with the viewing public — was the second baseman whose 12 years in green and gold were longer than any of his championship teammates save for Campaneris.

Dick Green learned early on that standing around on a baseball diamond, even between plays, is not a productive use of time. He communicated incessantly with the defenders around him. He relayed the catcher's signals to right field so that Jackson might get a better jump on a batted ball. He searched for the perfect pre-pitch position — close to where he wanted to play a batter, but not so close that he would give away anything about the upcoming pitch. Then he earned his money getting a jump on the ball before the pitch ever reached the plate.

It was this type of preparation, Green's and everybody else's, that showed up in the relay to nail Bill Buckner during the 1974 World Series. Reggie would not have been able to back up North's error had he not been hustling from the outset. Based on extensive drilling, his throw to Green, the cutoff man, was instinctive and seamless, aimed and released before Reggie even saw where Green had set up, because he already knew where Green would be. The relay strike to third was precisely where Bando wanted it because the infielders knew every detail about each other's games — because they had taken the time to learn every detail about each other's games. It was in every way a cooperative effort. "We were so much more than individuals," reflected Green. Years of postseason experience impressed upon the A's the importance of every pitch, that they all matter in crunch time, and that relaxing one's attention for even a moment is detrimental to winning baseball games. And winning baseball games was what those A's did best.

It was Holtzman getting on Fingers about untimely home runs. It was Bando getting on himself for untimely strikeouts. It was Reggie getting on teammates with accusations of flagging hustle, which, justified or not, helped others avoid falling into similar traps. Even if players disagreed with the specifics therein, they unequivocally spoke each other's language.* One can talk about Bando's leadership and Rudi's will and Vida's mercurial ability and Hunter's indomitability, but these men were world-beaters as members of an ensemble cast. Despite their star power, the A's were a team of supporting players who understood precisely how to support each other.

Above them all was the specter of Finley.

The Owner's legacy is one of pure duality, a study in extremes. On one hand, the man was a visionary, a perpetual mover for whom rest was never an option, let alone enjoyment of the ride. His ideas came at a tommy-gun pace, rat-a-tatting across baseball's landscape without care for their chances of adoption. There is something to be said for undeterred perseverance when accolades arrive in inverse proportion to achievement. Charlie Finley had perseverance in spades. For all the animosity he engendered, for the lack of respect he received from his own players and around the league, for the enmity that flew toward his office in amounts commensurate with his enduring ability to win baseball games, the man made a profound mark on America's pastime.

At Finley's final press conference upon selling the A's, American League president Lee MacPhail finally bestowed some of the credit that had to that point been so rare. "Baseball has lost its number one innovator," he said. "The designated hitter, divisional play, night World Series games, colorful uniforms and opening the World Series on Saturday were all ideas that Charlie pushed before others did."

---

* This dynamic with the A's explains why Reggie Jackson had so many problems upon going to the Yankees. His teammates in Oakland didn't necessarily approve of his brashness, but they understood that, for all his faults, and despite the overload of annoyance he could deliver in a surprisingly compact package, the man was essentially benign. Jackson's ego was beyond compare, but his goal was never ruination. Similar consideration did not greet him in the Bronx. "We understood Reggie, but when he went to New York, the Yankees didn't," said Gene Tenace. "And they didn't want to until he started hitting home runs in the World Series. After that they may still not have liked him, but at least they respected him."

Such single-mindedness came with a downside, of course—the demons that fed his virtues. Finley's success was predicated on his essential Finleyness—the ability to seize whatever he sought, primarily through sheer force of will. Softening his personality might have been deleterious to his effectiveness, and without his ability to gather information, to make assessments and bold decisions, and above all to sweat and to sacrifice, the A's would invariably have been diminished.

However, Finley's narcissism and relentless self-promotion were abiding. The Owner systematically propped himself up at the expense of others, in the process alienating nearly everybody who worked for or alongside him. He was in thrall by the power he held, wielding it fully lest it somehow go to waste. Cheapness was certainly a factor in the man's decision to barely staff his team's front office, but there was also his uncompromising need to have a say—to have *the* say—in whatever went on. Other voices could be heard, of course, but only with the understanding that they merely provided suggestion. The Owner made the decisions and the Owner took the credit.

For all of Finley's accomplishments, the man's corrosive methodology was pernicious. He made a habit of firing, fining, and downright tormenting those upon whose talents his team's fortunes rode, far less concerned with long-term well-being—theirs or his own—than the simple ability to make a point and stand by it. "All he wanted ever in his life," reflected Billy North, "was to always be right."

Meanwhile, Finley's systematic alienation of the team's fan base came at the cost not only of local acclaim but of historical standing. If a ballclub's own fans can't bother with it, after all, why should a national audience? The Owner's presence in Oakland was negligible, his interest in community affairs nonexistent. He spent his first five years in Northern California believing that a winning product would trump his own civic apathy, and did not realize until far too late just how wrong he was. The Owner rarely got good press because he rarely deserved it, and his perpetual skirmishes with the media inspired few journalistic explorations of the man's positive side. Once Finley's despotic turns gathered momentum, he cut a national figure somewhere between tyrant and punch line.

When Coliseum crowds continued to disappoint, Finley's efforts to goose attendance dried up entirely. The man who in Kansas City painted the stadium and moved the bullpens and lit the dugouts and constructed a petting zoo in the name of improving the fan experience stopped giving a shit. He provided a winner for the people of Oakland, and when they did not hold up their end of the bargain, he chose to not hold up his.

The arc mirrored the one Finley took with his players. He doled out expensive clock radios that first spring training in 1961, and marked the move to Oakland in '68 by presenting gold watches as Christmas gifts. He passed around $25 bonuses to the entire clubhouse to mark a double-header sweep. When the A's won their 100th game in 1971, the Owner handed every player a $100 bill. (The following night, after Oakland won its 101st and final game of the season, he returned to the clubhouse and, in an appreciated token of joviality, handed everybody a $1 bill.) He awarded new suits to players who performed heroic feats, and doled out Cadillacs like candy — to Vida Blue, to Alvin Dark (the first time around, in Kansas City), to Catfish Hunter (who opted instead for cash).

Finley could also be unexpectedly thoughtful. When Hunter made his big league debut in 1965, the Owner called Abbott and Lillie Hunter in North Carolina, propped up the receiver next to the radio, and told them to listen for as long as they'd like, long-distance phone rates be damned. When longtime minor leaguer Marcel Lachemann failed to qualify for a $5,000 bonus in 1969 because he did not remain in the majors for ninety consecutive days, Finley paid him anyway. When Dick Williams's daughter Kathi graduated from high school in Florida in 1973, the Owner gave the manager three days off to attend. When two All-Star rings were stolen out of Jackson's hotel room in 1973, Finley replaced them himself. In 1967, when the wife of Double-A pitcher Joe Grzenda had a medical issue, Finley chartered a plane to fly her from Birmingham to the Mayo Clinic in Minnesota. "He'd fight you over a $100 raise, but he flew a jet down for Joe's wife," marveled Joe Rudi years later. "It just never lined up."

The catch was that these gestures were enacted, every one of them, with an eye toward the care and maintenance of Finley's own ego. Doing nice things, bestowing nice gifts, providing nice favors — those actions placed the Owner squarely in charge. Roster moves and payroll decisions were obvious manifestations of power, but Finley's array of generosity afforded him so much more. There was always a point to it, some karmic debt to be collected later. For this, his players forever viewed his largesse with a wary eye and kept him at a remove far greater than such kindnesses would otherwise suggest.

Through it all the Owner insisted on serving as a foil for his team, giving his players something against which to rail. It was his nature — the man cared far more about getting his way than how anybody felt about him — but there may also have been a calculation to it, a means of providing a unified front for his roster. To whatever degree he intended, it worked. That the A's did not splinter despite the parade of verbal and physical assaults originating among their own ranks was largely due to the fact that, no matter how much hatred coalesced between them, it was always trumped by their collective disdain for the man at the top. When all else failed, they had at least that much in common.

Ultimately, Finley is impossible to define without consideration of the undefinable — the question of how great his A's might have been if not for his perpetual, shortsighted meddling. He built a team capable of winning four, five, six, or even seven championships, had he not run off his core players in one of the greatest examples of squandered potential in baseball's long history. The hard evidence, borne still on the fingers of the 77 men who played for those title teams, 16 of whom appeared on all three, suggests a far better outcome than what actually occurred. Said Reggie: "We were talented and mean and hungry, and we might just have turned out to be the greatest team of all time." The sentiment is valid. When the A's beat the Dodgers for their third straight World Series victory in 1974, Jackson, Tenace, Rudi, and North were all between 26 and 28 years old, just entering their primes. Bando was 30. Hunter, Blue, Holtzman, and Fingers were 28 or younger. Players like Claudell Washington, Phil Garner, Chet Lemon, Manny Trillo, and Mike Norris were waiting in the pipeline to bolster the roster and eventually turn it over.

For all the hypothetical pondering, however, one fact is beyond dispute: no executive during the Owner's tenure could approach his championship pedigree. The A's didn't win just three straight championships, but six consecutive postseason series, topping by one the previous mark of five, set by the Yankees of 1949–1954. That New York's victories all came in the World Series — divisions and divisional playoffs did not yet exist — makes the distinction significant. "The Yankees might not have won five straight if they'd had to play a series first," noted broadcaster Jon Miller. "That alone puts the A's right there with those Yankees as one of the greatest teams ever."

On the day of the home opener in 1974 — two years after Rollie Fingers cost Ken Holtzman what would have been his first victory with the A's

— the two pitchers passed time during pregame batting practice the way most pitchers do — shagging balls in the outfield. They were idling in right field, making chatter and lobbing loose baseballs toward the collection bucket, when they were surprised by the sight of the Owner emerging from the clubhouse tunnel. Finley rarely appeared on the field, but there he was, some 350 feet away, for a pregame interview in front of the home dugout along the third-base line. This, realized the pitchers, was an opportunity. They still burned hot over the Mike Andrews incident the previous October, and from the shoddy World Series rings that had been presented only days earlier. Fingers turned to his teammate. "Grab a couple baseballs," he said. "We're going to fire them at his ass." Holtzman concurred, and the countdown began. "On three," said Fingers. "One . . . two . . . *three!*" With that, the men — one righty, one lefty — let loose with a four-ball fusillade, two shots each in rapid succession, flying on arcs over the infield and toward the dugout. Did any of them connect? The players weren't sure — they began doing sit-ups while the balls were in flight, to provide cover in case Finley tried to identify his assailants.

It takes a certain type of owner to inspire physical assault from his players, which is itself a testament to the power of Charlie Finley. On every front, the Owner delivered to his players the success for which they'd dreamed, then ripped it away from them simply because he could. Finley's ego squashed his legacy by depriving his team of unknown championships, and squashed it further by affecting how the championships he did win were perceived. Take a walk down Main Street in Cooperstown, New York, and poke your head into any one of the dozens of shops surrounding the National Baseball Hall of Fame. There you will find copious commercial homages to the Yankees and Dodgers and Red Sox and Cubs, but you will be hard-pressed to find evidence that the A's even existed during the 1970s, let alone defined the era.

Somehow that didn't bother the Owner as much as it should have. Or did it? After a spring training game in Tucson in 1972, Finley hitched a ride back to Phoenix with beat writers Ron Bergman and Jim Street. Upon spying two 20-something hitchhikers, the Owner issued orders to pick them up, and the kids slid into the backseat alongside him. Finley's motivation quickly became clear. "Have you ever heard of Charlie Finley?" he asked the new passengers. *No,* they said, *we have not.*

So the Owner pulled out a copy of *Sports Illustrated,* featuring Vida's holdout. "Have you ever heard of Vida Blue?" he asked. Again, the passengers demurred. Undeterred, Finley began flipping pages, stopping to point out every quote he had provided for the story. *Sorry,* came the response. *We still have no idea who you are.*

It was the one thing that could stop Finley dead in his tracks. The man was expert when it came to leveraging power, knew precisely how to brandish his personality in ways that perpetuated whatever myths he was peddling at the moment. Now, however, stripped of baseball and the bully pulpit he so exactingly built atop it, he was little more to his seatmates than a means to an end, somebody to tolerate in exchange for a ride. The description fit in ways big and little.

The rest of the drive, nearly two hours' worth, passed in silence, until Finley got home, back to the people who would listen.

Cast of Characters

Sal Bando

> Sal Bando was the godfather. Capo di capo. Boss of all
> bosses on the Oakland A's. We all had our roles, we all con-
> tributed, but Sal was the leader and everyone knew it.
>
> — Reggie Jackson

Bando was drafted by the A's in the sixth round of the first-ever amateur
draft in 1965, made his debut in Kansas City the following September, and
was the starter at third base when the team moved to Oakland in 1968.
Three top-five MVP finishes. Four All-Star Games. Unremitting respect
from his teammates. After eleven years with the A's, the Captain sought
free-agent riches in Milwaukee, where he played the final five seasons
of his career, settling down there with his wife — then and now — Sandy,
and eventually serving as the Brewers GM for eight years.

Vida Blue

I would go down to the bullpen in 1971 and watch Vida warm
up. Then I'd walk down to the dugout and say, "Game's over,
boys. Shutout."   —Rollie Fingers

Blue's incandescent 1971—a 24-8 record, 1.82 ERA, and 301 strikeouts,
leading to the Cy Young and MVP awards—helped overshadow the rest
of his career, which, despite numerous hiccups, held considerable success. Despite Vida's slow start after holding out in 1972, he still finished
with a 2.80 ERA. He averaged 19 wins between 1973 and 1976, then tailed
off to a 14-19 record in '77 as the A's crumbled around him, leading the
American League in hits and earned runs allowed. Finley traded him to
San Francisco in 1978, and several months later Vida started the All-Star
Game for the National League. The Giants sent him to Kansas City prior
to the 1982 season, and he fell into heavy cocaine use that resulted in 81
days in prison and his suspension for the entire 1984 campaign. Blue enjoyed moderate success in a comeback with the Giants as a 36-year-old
in 1986, but abruptly retired prior to the '87 season—for which he was
to have rejoined the A's—after reportedly failing another drug test. He
lives in the Bay Area, working as a pre- and postgame analyst for the San
Francisco Giants telecasts.

Campy Campaneris

> You can talk about Reggie Jackson, Catfish Hunter, and Sal
> Bando, all those great players, but it was Campy who made
> everything go. —Charles Finley

Signed out of Cuba in 1961, Campaneris debuted with the A's three years later, and was a full-time starter by 1965. The guy could run, leading the American League in steals in six of his first nine seasons. He leveraged that speed, as well as a rocket arm and a fantastic ability to track down balls hit to his left, into six All-Star appearances. In 1977, Campy left Oakland for the Texas Rangers, who traded him to the Angels in 1979. He closed his career in 1983 by talking his way onto the New York Yankees roster at age 41, then batting .322 across 60 games.

Dave Duncan

> Dave is our quarterback, you might say. You can't write
> enough good about him.   — Dick Williams

Duncan signed with the A's in 1963 and debuted in Kansas City the following season. He took over as the team's full-time catcher in 1968, the year they moved to Oakland, but it wasn't until meeting hitting coach Charley Lau in 1970 that he blossomed at the plate, raising his batting average from .126 in 1969 to .259 a season later. The year after that, in 1971, he hit 15 homers and was an All-Star. Duncan followed his A's career with two seasons each in Cleveland and Baltimore, but his lasting contribution to the game came as a pitching coach under manager Tony La Russa. He spent 30 seasons with the White Sox, the A's, and the Cardinals, with his former teammate, in the process becoming the most storied pitching instructor in baseball history. His sons, Chris and Shelly, had major league careers of their own.

Mike Epʃtein

This is a mighty hunk of rough-hewn physique, the kind of
guy you want on your side in a street brawl.

—*Oakland Tribune*, May 10, 1971

Epstein played football at Cal under Marv Levy (and assistants Bill Walsh
and Mike White), and professional baseball under Gil Hodges, Ted Williams, Dick Williams, and Whitey Herzog. That's a lot of brainpower. The
guy was one of baseball's biggest power threats for a five-year span, averaging 24 homers per season from 1969 to 1972, including 44 in the season-
plus after Oakland acquired him from the Senators. Epstein faded quickly
after Charlie Finley traded him to Texas, batting just .188 in 27 games.
After only six weeks he was shipped to Anaheim, where he spent the final
two years of his career. Epstein eventually opened his own baseball school
outside Denver, Colorado, the Epstein Hitting Academy, where, with his
son Jake, he certifies instructors across the country in his model plate
approach.

Rollie Fingers

We call him "buzzard" because he's off in his own world. Nothing bothers him. Him and that handlebar mustache of his—he's cool.   —Reggie Jackson

The transition from being a distracted and ineffective starter over his first three seasons to a world-beating reliever over his final 13 was comprehensive. Fingers, with the help of Dick Williams, rewrote the idea of what a closer could be, averaging 10 wins and 21 saves for the A's between 1972 and 1976, earning four All-Star appearances during that span while striking out nearly a hitter per inning. Fingers departed for San Diego via free agency after the 1976 season, and led the National League in saves in each of the next two years. Rejoining Sal Bando with the Milwaukee Brewers in 1981, he had the best year of his career at age 35, again leading the league in saves while putting up a 1.04 ERA and winning the American League's Cy Young and MVP awards. He was inducted into the National Baseball Hall of Fame in 1992.

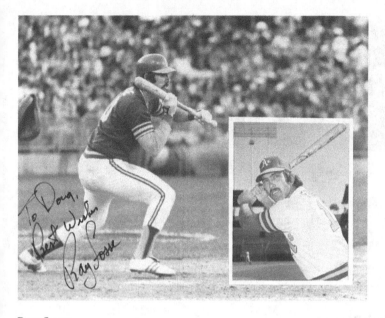

Ray Fosse

You've got to be kidding. How can they trade our quarterback?

—Cleveland's Gaylord Perry, upon learning that Ray Fosse had been traded to Oakland

Fosse hit his peak as a player during the three full seasons he spent in Cleveland prior to joining the A's, during which time he won his only Gold Glove awards and made his only All-Star teams. His three years in Oakland, however, provided him the only playoff appearances of his twelve-year career, not to mention two World Series rings. Always a defensive stalwart, his offensive production tumbled after the neck injury he suffered in the Bill North–Reggie Jackson fight in 1974, and he fell into disuse in '75 before being sold back to the Indians. He has worked on the A's radio broadcasts since 1986 and on their TV broadcasts since 1988.

Dick Green

> It looks as if a little man no one can see whispers in his ear,
> "Psst—a little more to your left. Now, back up. Yeah—there.
> It'll be along in a minute."
>
> —Longtime manager Bill Rigney on Dick Green

Signed out of Yankton, South Dakota, in 1960, Green took pride in two primary areas: his ability to make plays in the field, and his aptitude for disassociating his fielding from whatever he did — or, far more frequently, didn't do — at the plate. Green somehow averaged nearly 10 homers per season over a 12-year career, but his lasting impression on offense was set by the five he hit, total, over the three years of the A's championship run. He earned his paycheck on defense, however, his ability to anticipate where batted balls would end up being unsurpassed among his peers. As he long promised, Green took over his family's moving company in Rapid City upon leaving baseball, and eventually sold it to finance his retirement. He continues to hunt and fish in and around Rapid City.

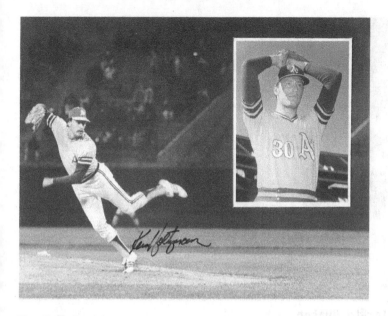

Ken Holtzman

Holtzman would give all this bluster about "I hate this goddamn game." Every day I'd stand beside him just to hear him
go through his routine about how the game sucked and how
he wanted to get out — but then he'd put on his uniform and,
I'm telling you, he'd just out-compete the other guy.

— Phil Garner

After coming over from the Cubs in exchange for Rick Monday, Holtzman won 59 games across Oakland's three championship seasons, and 174 over a 15-year career. He earned two All-Star berths with the A's and started the opener of all three of their World Series during the 1970s. Finley traded Holtzman to Baltimore to start the 1976 season, and the Orioles traded him again that June, to the Yankees, where he spent parts of three seasons before finishing his career back in Chicago, with the Cubs. After averaging nearly 20 wins per year in Oakland, Holtzman won a total of 23 games over his final five seasons, never again approaching the success he had with the A's.

Catfish Hunter

> You think you can hit him, but you can't. Not when it counts.
> Not often. He's human, but he's less human than the next guy.
> —Reggie Jackson

Five straight 20-win seasons, four with Oakland and one with the Yankees. One Cy Young Award, and three other top-five finishes. Eight All-Star games. Hunter pitched for contact and let his fielders make plays behind him to a greater degree than maybe any other successful pitcher in history. (It's why he never struck out 200 men in a season, and ten times ranked among the American League leaders in homers allowed.) He left the A's for free-agent riches in 1975, closing his career with five mostly injury-riddled seasons with the Yankees. About ten years after Hunter was elected into the National Baseball Hall of Fame in 1987, he was diagnosed with amyotrophic lateral sclerosis — ALS, or Lou Gehrig's disease. The condition eventually cost him the use of his arms, which left him unable to brace himself when, in 1999, he fell on the concrete steps in front of his house in Hertford, North Carolina. He hit his head and died shortly thereafter at age 53, leaving his wife and former teenage sweetheart Helen, and three adult children.

Reggie Jackson

> Reggie Jackson was the strongest, most dynamic personality I ever saw play the game. Of course, Reggie would be the first to tell you that. —Catfish Hunter

Fourteen-time All-Star. American League MVP in 1973. Five-time top-five MVP finalist. Number six on the all-time home run list when he retired. Struck out more than anybody in history. Jackson was the second player selected in the 1966 amateur draft and made his big league debut less than a year later. Within two seasons he was a superstar. Reggie spent the 1976 season with Baltimore, and then an incendiary five years with the Yankees that included two championships and one legendary World Series game in which he hit first-pitch homers in three straight at-bats. Five years with the Angels followed, including leading the league in homers at age 36, before he wrapped up his career with a final campaign in Oakland, in 1987. Jackson was inducted into the National Baseball Hall of Fame in 1993.

Billy North

> I was ten years old, a little black kid hitting rocks in my back-
> yard in Seattle, and I said to my brother, "I want to play in
> the World Series." I was obsessed with baseball. And I got to
> play in the World Series. You tell me, is this not a wonderful
> life?
> — Billy North

Known among the A's as "Paperboy" for the stack of periodicals he brought with him on airplanes, North was among the best-read and sharpest-witted members of the team. He joined the A's after the 1972 season in a trade for reliever Bob Locker, and over his first four seasons in Oakland twice led the league in steals. He hung around into the 1978 campaign, a victim of the two-year contract he signed just before the team broke apart, then spent a lackluster season with the Dodgers and closed his career with three years in San Francisco, where he led the team in stolen bases three times and was reunited with Vida Blue. North went on to become a financial advisor in Kirkland, Washington.

John "Blue Moon" Odom

> Johnny had incredible stuff. I hated putting on the pickoff
> play with him, because he'd throw that goddamn sinker to
> second base and it would just tear me up.
>
> — Ted Kubiak

John "Blue Moon" Odom was snapped up by Charlie Finley out of high
school in 1964, in the final year before the amateur draft. He made his
big league debut that same season, but it wasn't until the A's moved to
Oakland in 1968 that he earned national attention. Over the 1968 and
1969 campaigns, Odom went 31-16 with a 2.68 ERA, and was an All-Star
both years. Elbow problems curtailed his success over coming seasons,
and even though he rebounded in 1972 with a 15-6 record, he managed to
strike out more men than he walked only once more over the final seven
seasons of his career before wrapping things up with the White Sox in
1976.

Joe Rudi

He's just the best goddamn winning ballplayer around.

—Dick Williams

Rudi's lasting impression was one of quiet excellence, a man content to leave the headlines to others because his focus was squarely on his job, which he did as well as anybody in the sport. Rudi signed with the A's in 1964 out of Modesto, California — and left money on the table to do so, turning down $20,000 from the Yankees in favor of $15,000 from the A's, motivated by Kansas City's thin roster and what he saw as a more direct route to the big leagues. Twice a runner-up in AL MVP voting, Rudi was so accomplished as a left fielder that he won a Gold Glove at the position in 1975 despite playing twice as many games at first base (91) as he did in left field (44). He spent four years with the Angels after joining them as a free agent in 1977, then closed his career with two seasons in Boston, finally making the aborted trip Charlie Finley tried to send him on in 1976. Rudi lives in Baker City, Oregon, with his wife — then and now — Sharon.

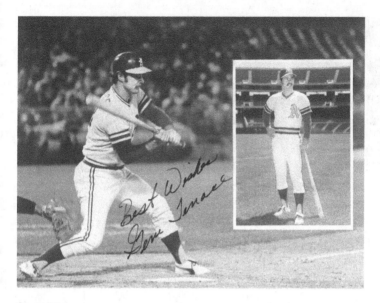

Gene Tenace

I've become kind of famous for my signature catch-phrase,
"WHAMMY!" Like, "Gene Tenace at the plate, and . . . WHAMMY!"

—Champ Kind (David Koechner) in
Anchorman: The Legend of Ron Burgundy

Tenace joined the A's as a shortstop in the 20th round of the 1965 draft, then transitioned to outfield and finally to catcher. Although he did not seize a starting role until the 1972 stretch run, he finished among the American League leaders in home runs in all four of his seasons in Oakland thereafter. (Ranking second in the American League with 398 walks over that span allowed him to also finish among the league's OBP leaders three times despite batting only .244 overall.) After eight years in Oakland, Tenace bolted for San Diego, where he led the National League in bases on balls in 1977, before finishing his career as a backup in St. Louis and Pittsburgh. Four top-ten finishes in home runs. Seven top-five finishes in walks. A Baseball-Reference.com rating above that of Hall of Fame catcher Ernie Lombardi. Also, an unsurpassed ability to tell a great story, even if the topic is four decades old and the details have grown fuzzy. Tenace lives in Redmond, Oregon, with his wife — then and now — Linda.

Herb Washington

> This guy actually outran the baseball sometimes.
>
> —Gene Tenace

Washington's final stat line with the A's included 105 games, 33 runs scored, 31 stolen bases, 17 times caught stealing — and zero at-bats. After being released by Finley, Washington never again played major league baseball. Between his salary, his signing bonus, and his World Series share, however, he had enough capital to open a fast-food franchise in his hometown of Detroit, a venture that he eventually grew to 25 outlets in Ohio and Pennsylvania. This made him among the most financially accomplished of his ballplaying peers, and solidly atop the list when it came to non-baseball-related income.

Dick Williams

> We would not have won anything without Dick Williams. He taught us how to win. We didn't know how before he came. We were just some guys who could play, but he taught us how to play together.
>
> — Reggie Jackson

Williams made up for a mediocre 13-year playing career — in which he was traded five times, sold once, waived once, and released once — with an outsanding managerial tenure. In his three seasons helming the A's, Oakland averaged 96 wins per year, winning three division titles and two World Series. Williams went on to manage the Angels, Expos, Padres, and Mariners over the next 16 years, taking Montreal to the playoffs in the strike-shortened 1981 campaign, and the Padres to the World Series in 1984. He was inducted into the National Baseball Hall of Fame as a manager in 2008, and passed away in 2011, at age 82.

Alvin Dark

> Alvin's recall amazed me. He was always comparing what he'd seen on the field that day to a situation that had come up six weeks earlier. A pitcher who had thrown a slider when he should have thrown a fastball. What the count was. How many runners were on base. How did he remember, I wondered? I assumed all managers had that gift. But I've never met another who could recall the little things that happen in a game as clearly as Alvin Dark did.   —Jon Miller

Dark was one of Charlie Finley's two-time managers, helming the A's in Kansas City in 1966 and part of 1967, and again in 1974 and 1975. In so doing he showed his versatility, shepherding a band of inexperienced youngsters to the team's best record in 14 years the first time around, and leading the veteran A's to their third straight championship in the second. After being fired by Finley for a second time, Dark received one more managerial opportunity, with the San Diego Padres in 1977 (reuniting with Rollie Fingers and Gene Tenace), but was dismissed after 113 games. After becoming the oldest living manager of a postseason team, Dark passed away in 2014 at age 92.

Acknowledgments

To say that this book would not have been possible without gracious participation from the players involved would not quite be accurate. The book could have been written — it just wouldn't have been nearly as good. It wasn't only that players took time with me, it was that the time they took was spectacular.

Dick Green drove me to Mount Rushmore in a negative-15-degree North Dakota chill, and we sat behind picture windows under one of the greatest backdrops I've ever experienced for an interview.

Joe Rudi toured me with no small amount of pride around Baker City, Oregon, and demonstrated the wondrous array of ham-radio equipment in his home office.

Sal Bando saved me a car rental in Phoenix by picking me up at the airport.

Gene Tenace spent four hours with me in a booth at Shari's Restaurant in Redmond, Oregon, without once getting up to use the restroom or even so much as spitting into a cup in acknowledgment of the chaw he packed into his lip midway through. At his house he showed off the most impressive display of memorabilia I encountered during the course of this project . . . save possibly for that of broadcaster Monte Moore, or maybe Rollie Fingers.

Billy North let me shadow him for an entire day in and around Seattle, including ferrying his 94-year-old mother to a medical appointment. If his genes even remotely resemble hers, Billy's going to be needling his teammates for a long time to come.

The list goes on and on. Blue Moon Odom gave me an up-close look at the '72 World Series trophy sitting on a TV tray in his living room. Dave Duncan made time for me in southern Missouri just a day before he was to move to Arizona. Mike Epstein showed me his hitting school outside Denver, and Ken Holtzman found his way to my hotel near St. Louis. Irv

Noren pulled out his scrapbooks and Bobby Winkles bought me coffee. Ted Kubiak and I crossed paths at a restaurant on the road, him returning to Southern California from the north, me returning to Northern California from the south. I lunched with Vida Blue in the Berkeley hills, and spent time at the Oakland Coliseum with Ray Fosse, who carved out periods in which to chat prior to his broadcasting duties.

Suffice it to say that while Oakland's roster included only two Jews, it was a team filled with mensches.

Additional thanks go to two journalists of the time, Glenn Schwarz and Jim Street, for making extraordinary efforts to fill me in on their perspectives. To my lasting regret, Ron Bergman was in failing health while I reported this book, and passed away in May 2015. His exceptional skills in covering the team for the *Oakland Tribune* and *The Sporting News* turned what could have been dreary research into a delightful task. He was connected, insightful, and so witty it makes one's teeth ache, to borrow one of his own phrases.

In-person interviews took place mostly between November 2013 and February 2014, while phone interviews continued to trickle in until 2016. To all those who spent time with me, thank you: Mike Andrews, Marty Appel, Sal Bando, Jim Bank, Mary Barry, Vida Blue, Lucianne Buchanan, John Claiborne, Tom Corwin, Tommy Davis, Dave Duncan, Mike Epstein, Rollie Fingers, Paul Finley, Ray Fosse, Phil Garner, Robert Gerst, Dick Green, Johnny Holliday, Ken Holtzman, Darold Knowles, Ted Kubiak, John Lindblom, Jeff Logan, Jon Miller, Monte Moore, Irv Noren, Billy North, Blue Moon Odom, Joe Rudi, Glenn Schwarz, Charlie Silvera, Sam Spear, Ed Sprague, Roy Steele, Wes Stock, Jim Street, Paul Tarnopol, Gene Tenace, Steve Vucinich, Herb Washington, Rick Williams, and Bobby Winkles.

Special mention goes to the current staff of the Oakland A's, whose assistance made my job a whole lot easier. Clubhouse manager Steve Vucinich has been there since the beginning, and offered unique perspective on everything that's gone down in Oakland since day one. Particular adoration goes to Debbie Gallas, mover of mountains, whose fabulousness knows no bounds.

Invaluable photographic help was secured from John Horne at the National Baseball Hall of Fame, and a couple of Bay Area sharpshooters from back in the day, Jonathan Perry and Ron Riesterer. Special thanks and kudos go to Doug McWilliams, whose portraits — first assembled in 1975 in an effort to persuade Charlie Finley to include them in the team yearbook — grace the Cast of Characters section of this book. Finley turned him down, and the images spent most of the next 40 years sitting in a file in Doug's office. Massive thanks, Doug, for sharing your images with me and the world.

Also, thanks to my editor Susan Canavan and the team at HMH, and my agent, Jud Laghi, who championed this book from the start and without whom it never would have been published.

Finally, they say that behind every book about 1970s baseball dynasties is an encouraging spouse. And if they don't say that, they should. Without willingness from my wife to temper our children while I secured myself behind a too-thin office door, and to watch them while I left town to write undisturbed for extended periods (those kids are pretty great when it comes to everything but Dad's productivity; hi Mozi, hi Reuben), things would have turned out differently and not nearly as well. Thank you, Laura, a million times, for your enduring love and support.

Notes

INTRODUCTION

page

xii   *"I still owe you $45,000"*: Reggie Jackson, with Mike Lupica, *Reggie: The Auto-biography* (New York: Random House, 1984).

xiii   *"You doing all right in Baltimore?"*: Ibid.
       "You're all going to do all right": Ibid.

xiv   *"You should be proud of yourself"*: Ibid.

1. WELCOME TO OAKLAND

3   *"Thank you for everything"*: *Hayward Daily Review,* September 30, 1968.
     "I can't even get in": Ibid.

4   *"tell me to move to Oakland"*: *New York Times Magazine,* July 15, 1973.

5   *"Oh my God"*: Tom Corwin interview.

6   *"Of all the possible answers"*: *Sports Illustrated,* March 30, 1970.

7   *"Finley's one-man band"*: *Sports Illustrated,* October 9, 1972.
     "Does that mean you're going": Rick Williams interview.

8   *"If this is what it takes to win"*: Dick Williams and Bill Plaschke, *No More Mr. Nice Guy: A Life of Hardball* (San Diego: Harcourt, 1990).
     "I'm the only chief around here": Ron Bergman, *Mustache Gang* (New York: Dell, 1973).

9   *"The best baseball brains available"*: Ibid.
     "'You ain't hitting until'": Gene Tenace interview.
     "He made us all managers on the field": Maury Allen, *Mr. October: The Reggie Jackson Story* (New York: Times Books, 1981).
     "Where were you supposed to be?": Rollie Fingers interview.

10   *"Dick had this emotional distaste"*: Allen, *Mr. October.*
     the bench-jockey skills: *New York Post,* December 13, 1973.

11   *"I have no small fines"*: *Sports Illustrated,* May 3, 1971.

"*Hey, you reckon that megaphone*": Catfish Hunter, with Armen Keteyian, *Catfish: My Life in Baseball* (New York: McGraw-Hill, 1988).

"*You could be talking to Mr. Finley*": Jim Bank interview.

"*If you've got a fucking problem*": Williams and Plaschke, *No More Mr. Nice Guy.*

12   "*We never even saw the ball*": *Life,* June 18, 1971.

"*There are some guys you go*": *New York Times Magazine,* July 25, 1971.

"*That's funny*": *Time,* August 23, 1971.

13   "*We didn't want him to pitch*": *Oakland Tribune,* June 16, 1971.

"*I'm going to tell Greenie*": Reggie Jackson, with Mike Lupica, *Reggie: The Autobiography* (New York: Random House, 1984).

"*George, you my man*": *Sports Illustrated,* July 12, 1971.

14   "*This young fellow is going to be*": *Time,* August 23, 1971.

"*There are times when I can*": *The Sporting News,* July 12, 1971.

"*Baseball is a business*": *New York Times Magazine,* July 25, 1971.

"*Vida was my father's name*": Ibid.

15   "*It sounded suspiciously as if*": Ibid.

"*You want me to disrespect my*": Vida Blue interview.

16   "'*The man's too much*'": *Oakland Tribune,* July 8, 1974.

"*I've never been more tired*": *New York Times,* August 16, 1971.

"*I wake up and then I'm at*": *New York Times Magazine,* July 25, 1971.

"*I want to sign 'em all*": Vida Blue and Bill Libby, *Vida: His Own Story* (Upper Saddle River, NJ: Prentice-Hall, 1972).

"*I sometimes feel like*": Associated Press, August 16, 1971.

"*hostile*": *The Sporting News,* August 21, 1971.

"*There was no monkey*": Ibid.

17   "*There you go again*": Ibid.

18   "*complete fatigue*": *Oakland Tribune,* August 9, 1971.

"*We didn't blow this thing*": *The Sporting News,* October 23, 1971.

"*Now we understood*": Sal Bando interview.

2. THE OWNER

19   "*[Charlie Finley] has made himself a thorough student*": *Los Angeles Times,* July 7, 1987.

22   "*I'm not in this for a fast buck*": Bill Libby, *Charlie O. and the Angry A's: The Low and Inside Story of Charlie O. Finley and Baseball's Most Colorful Team* (New York: Doubleday, 1975).

23   "*I like to see what's going on*": *Sports Illustrated,* June 5, 1961.

"*Thirty thousand dollars' worth*": Ibid.

24   "*The greatest mule search in history*": *Sports Illustrated,* July 19, 1965.

"*Brother, I mean to tell you*": Herbert Michelson, *Charlie O: Charles Oscar Finley vs. the Baseball Establishment* (Indianapolis: Bobbs-Merrill, 1975).

3. VIDA'S BLUES

29 *"Vida Blue is beautiful"*: Vida Blue and Bill Libby, *Vida: His Own Story* (Upper Saddle River, NJ: Prentice-Hall, 1972).

30 *"How come you didn't get more money"*: "Would you pitch for the same" (videotape transcript), *The Sporting News*, January 22, 1972.
   "Do you know what floor we're on?": Ron Bergman, *Mustache Gang* (New York: Dell, 1973).

31 *"I know you pitched 300 innings"*: Vida Blue interview.
   "This creates an inequity": Bill Libby, *Charlie O. and the Angry A's: The Low and Inside Story of Charlie O. Finley and Baseball's Most Colorful Team* (New York: Doubleday, 1975).
   "It doesn't help [Blue] one cent": *Oakland Tribune*, February 10, 1972.

32 *"There were a lot of things he said"*: Robert Gerst interview.

33 *"A club doesn't release"*: *The Sporting News*, August 11, 1973.
   "just fade away": *Black Sports*, August 1974.
   "This is a wonderful opportunity": *The Sporting News*, April 1, 1972.

34 *"I'm a mixed-up kid"*: *Oakland Tribune*, April 3, 1972.

35 *"I'd like to see Vida take the"*: *Oakland Tribune*, February 17, 1972.
   "I'm for a guy getting all he can": Associated Press, March 11, 1972.
   "a damn cent": *Time*, April 17, 1972.

37 *"don't think we're ballplayers"*: Libby, *Charlie O. and the Angry A's*.
   "I guess I'm a lousy businessman": *The Sporting News*, April 1, 1972.

38 *"Finley had a way"*: Bowie Kuhn, *Hardball: The Education of a Baseball Commissioner* (New York: Crown, 1987).
   "You know where he went": Robert Gerst interview.

39 *"Had Mr. Finley been willing"*: *Oakland Tribune*, April 29, 1972.
   "in the best interests of baseball": Herbert Michelson, *Charlie O: Charles Oscar Finley vs. the Baseball Establishment* (Indianapolis: Bobbs-Merrill, 1975).
   "I will obey his order": Libby, *Charlie O. and the Angry A's*.
   "Charlie, either you show in Boston": Kuhn, *Hardball*.

40 *"menace to baseball"*: *Sports Illustrated*, July 21, 1969.
   "I signed it and I'm happy": Bergman, *Mustache Gang*.
   "no comment": Associated Press, May 3, 1972.
   "I'll be lucky if I win ten": *Oakland Tribune*, May 2, 1972.
   "I just kept thinking": Vida Blue interview.
   "if the plane would have left": *Oakland Tribune*, May 4, 1972.
   "He treated me like a damn": Ibid.

41 *"Tonight isn't tell it like it is"*: Ibid.

4. SWEET SMELL OF SUCCESS

42   *"We finally built those big names"*: Blue Moon Odom interview.

43   *"Moodiness is an outgrowth"*: *Sports Illustrated*, July 31, 1972.
    "Don't buy more than you can handle": *Sport*, October 1974.
    "Those are family tickets": Mike Epstein interview.
    "This was not a typical": Ken Holtzman interview.
    "Reggie's eyes are spinning": Gene Tenace interview.

44   *"Who the hell grabbed Epstein"*: Catfish Hunter, with Armen Keteyian, *Catfish: My Life in Baseball* (New York: McGraw-Hill, 1988).

45   *"Who the fuck do you think you are"*: Mike Epstein interview.
    "any time from eight in the morning": Tom Corwin interview.

46   *"tell him I'm not here"*: Darold Knowles interview.
    "How do the shoes fit?": Jay Johnstone, with Rick Talley, *Temporary Insanity: The Uncensored Adventures of Baseball's Craziest Player* (New York: Bantam, 1986).
    "Once an Athletic, always": The Sporting News, August 5, 1972.

47   *"Vida was still real good"*: Sal Bando interview.
    "Evidently he's not interested": *Oakland Tribune*, July 15, 1972.
    "Shit, I would've hit": Vida Blue interview.
    "Charlie would see the bill": Steve Vucinich interview.

48   *"Hey man, I just throw"*: Bill Libby, *Catfish: The Three Million Dollar Pitcher* (New York: Coward, McCann & Geoghegan, 1976).
    "Yes, I'm bitter": *Sports Illustrated*, July 31, 1972.
    "I sat next to Vida": Reggie Jackson, *Reggie: A Season with a Superstar* (Chicago: Playboy Press, 1975).
    "His soul is broken": *Oakland Tribune*, March 20, 1973.

49   *"Is Ken a big eater?"*: *Oakland Tribune*, November 30, 1971.
    "A kosher Lou Gehrig": *Pittsburgh Press*, May 24, 1967.
    "We just wanted to be": Mike Epstein interview.
    "This is who I am": Ibid.

50   *"Believe it or not"*: Ken Holtzman interview.
    "Reggie had no business putting it on": Mike Epstein interview.
    "Mr. Jackson knew some Hebrew": Ken Holtzman interview.

51   *"It was sorrowful"*: Ibid.
    "It was an emotional period": Mike Epstein interview.
    "it sure did affect my confidence": Dick Green interview.

52   *"The last place you wanted to be"*: Rollie Fingers interview.

53   *"I was on my way to Sakizukiland"*: Ibid.
    "He just threw the ball": Dick Green interview.

"a rubber arm and a rubber head": *The Sporting News*, August 19, 1972.

"Shit, I didn't even know anything": Rollie Fingers interview.

"All relief pitchers have a reputation": Ken Holtzman interview.

"He was pitching to Brooks Robinson": Jackson, *Reggie: A Season with a Superstar*.

54 "It's my identity now": Bill Libby, *Charlie O. and the Angry A's: The Low and Inside Story of Charlie O. Finley and Baseball's Most Colorful Team* (New York: Doubleday, 1975).

"There was no way I was shaving": Rollie Fingers interview.

55 "listening to the A's play-by-play": *The Sporting News*, September 16, 1972.

"look like prostitutes": *Sarasota Herald-Tribune*, September 23, 1972.

56 "We would go into a city": Jon Miller interview.

"He'd call Twombly in the office": Glenn Schwarz interview.

57 "Before his first World Series": Libby, *Charlie O. and the Angry A's*.

"I've tried to tell him": Ibid.

"You lying little fucker": Herbert Michelson, *Charlie O: Charles Oscar Finley vs. the Baseball Establishment* (Indianapolis: Bobbs-Merrill, 1975).

"The reason Finley got a lot": Dick Green interview.

58 "probably beneath my dignity": *Sports Illustrated*, October 9, 1972.

"Oooh, goddang, they had a team": Blue Moon Odom interview.

"I cracked his ribs": Ibid.

59 "I'm going to use him": *Oakland Tribune*, September 1, 1972.

"Angel, no, no, NO!": Irv Noren interview.

"I was right in the middle": *Oakland Tribune*, August 23, 1972.

"Available" column: *Oakland Tribune*, August 24, 1972.

5. TEETERING IN TIGER TOWN

60 "Every time Billy Martin battles": *Oakland Tribune*, October 3, 1972.

61 "If I get to pinch-hit": *Oakland Tribune*, October 8, 1972.

"I felt fast as Campaneris": Ibid.

62 "It was so different": Ken Holtzman interview.

63 "I don't want you to know": Darold Knowles interview.

"There is something withdrawn": *The Sporting News*, April 25, 1970.

64 "prevent further riot": *Oakland Tribune*, October 9, 1972.

"[Campaneris] has got to be suspended": Ibid.

"It was deliberate as hell": Ibid.

"What do you think": Charlie Silvera interview.

"The plan was to actually": Matthew Silverman, *Swinging '73: Baseball's Wildest Season* (Guilford, CT: Lyons Press, 2013).

65 "He told us to call him dad": Herbert Michelson, *Charlie O: Charles Oscar Finley vs. the Baseball Establishment* (Indianapolis: Bobbs-Merrill, 1975).

"In a few days": The Sporting News, October 28, 1972.

67 "If there's a fight on the field": Oakland Tribune, October 9, 1972.
    "The only way I find out": Oakland Tribune, October 11, 1972.

69 "I feel sick": Oakland Tribune, October 13, 1972.
    "It was like a pep talk": Dave Duncan interview.
    "Reggie came around and told us": Baseball Digest, January 1973.

70 "We just wanted to keep him": Joe Rudi interview.
    "I didn't go to school": Blue Moon Odom interview.

71 "What are you doing?": Ron Bergman, Mustache Gang (New York: Dell, 1973).
    "Maybe the shooting is what": Ibid.

72 "What the hell do you want?": Dick Williams and Bill Plaschke, No More Mr.
    Nice Guy: A Life of Hardball (San Diego: Harcourt, 1990).
    "I say with all sincerity": Associated Press, October 12, 1972.
    "read a note": Oakland Tribune, October 13, 1972.
    "I was to take over the A's": Oakland Tribune, October 10, 1972.

73 "I'm sorry": Associated Press, October 12, 1972.
    "Cronin was sleeping, God bless him": The Sporting News, October 28, 1972.
    "You could be damn sure": Oakland Tribune, October 13, 1972.

75 "I was hot and my stomach was": New York Times, October 13, 1972.
    "I'd never felt pressure like that": Darold Knowles interview.
    "I don't care what Vida's record was": Ken Holtzman interview.

76 "I was gagging": UPI, October 13, 1972.
    "Oh man, I know why": Ibid.
    "I bet Blue Moon": Williams and Plaschke, No More Mr. Nice Guy.

77 "one of the most draining": Catfish Hunter, with Armen Keteyian, Catfish: My
    Life in Baseball (New York: McGraw-Hill, 1988).
    "Hey man, I was only": Bill Libby, Charlie O. and the Angry A's: The Low and
    Inside Story of Charlie O. Finley and Baseball's Most Colorful Team (New York:
    Doubleday, 1975).
    "We won the motherfucking playoffs": Steve Vucinich interview.
    "We have to get to the World Series": Williams and Plaschke, No More Mr.
    Nice Guy.
    "I'm sorry": UPI, October 13, 1972.

78 "Don't you ever say that": Ibid.
    "I'm still pissed": Blue Moon Odom interview.
    "John is a very sensitive guy": Vida Blue interview.

6. WORLD SERIES, 1972

79 "I really would have liked": Tom Clark: Champagne and Baloney: The Rise
    and Fall of Finley's A's (New York: Harper & Row, 1976).

"This should have been our greatest day": Reggie Jackson, with Mike Lupica, *Reggie: The Autobiography* (New York: Random House, 1984).

81   "Reggie was being his basic hot dog self": Rollie Fingers interview.

"I would grow hair": Bill Libby, *Charlie O. and the Angry A's: The Low and Inside Story of Charlie O. Finley and Baseball's Most Colorful Team* (New York: Doubleday, 1975).

"Mr. Bando, I would like": Sal Bando interview.

"Jesus, Irv, when are you": Irv Noren interview.

82   "Not for the Cincinnati Reds": Joe Posnanski, *The Machine: A Hot Team, a Legendary Season, and a Heart-Stopping World Series: The Story of the 1975 Cincinnati Reds* (New York: William Morrow, 2009).

"How can a baseball team": *Oakland Tribune*, November 8, 1972.

"Hey, . . . get my bat!": Irv Noren interview.

"We just didn't think": Dick Green interview.

"We were going to get": Rollie Fingers interview.

83   "I had double-play balls hit": Dick Green interview.

"one of the most amazing": *Oakland Tribune*, October 24, 1972.

"Our scouting report was so good": Ted Kubiak interview.

85   "Nervous?": Ken Holtzman interview.

86   "That's odd": Gene Tenace interview.

"I didn't even feel the ball": Ibid.

"How strange": Ibid.

87   "It never dawned on me": Ibid.

88   "We were looking around like": Ken Holtzman interview.

"He will get a substantial": *The Sporting News*, October 28, 1972.

"All right": Baseball Hall of Fame Research Library clip file, October 18, 1974.

90   "Go back on that one": Joe Rudi interview.

"Oh no": Sal Bando interview.

91   "the best catch I've ever seen": *Oakland Tribune*, October 16, 1972.

"[Hunter] is a good pitcher": *San Francisco Chronicle*, October 16, 1972.

92   "They're one game ahead": *Chicago Daily News*, October 16, 1972.

"I'm not going to panic": *Baseball Digest*, January 1973.

"I could have done the same thing": *Oakland Tribune*, October 16, 1972.

"I feel you don't appreciate": Ibid.

"I've been busting my ass": Dick Williams and Bill Plaschke, *No More Mr. Nice Guy: A Life of Hardball* (San Diego: Harcourt, 1990).

"I'll do whatever I want": *Oakland Tribune*, October 16, 1972.

93   "Mr. Levitt, you can": Ibid.

"Here we are, two wins": Williams and Plaschke, *No More Mr. Nice Guy*.

"If he feels bad about coming out": *Oakland Tribune*, October 17, 1972.

"Dick Williams and his players": *Oakland Tribune*, October 16, 1972.

94   "I won't mention any": *Oakland Tribune*, October 18, 1972.

95   "In the crepuscular light": *Oakland Tribune*, October 19, 1972.
"I'm not sore": *Oakland Tribune*, October 19, 1972.

96   "Gene, I want you to stand": Williams and Plaschke, *No More Mr. Nice Guy*.
"Wait until Rollie picks": Rollie Fingers interview.
"Do you understand?": Gene Tenace interview.
"What is this, Little League?": Rollie Fingers interview.
"I had never seen that play": Gene Tenace interview.

97   "Be alive! They're going to": *New York Daily News*, October 20, 1972.
"the best slider I ever": *Oakland Tribune*, October 19, 1972.
"Bench might not have hit it": Sal Bando interview.
"Man, you guys made me": Gene Tenace interview.
"He called it the best one": *Oakland Tribune*, October 19, 1972.

98   "Go up swinging": *San Francisco Chronicle*, October 20, 1972.
"All you could hear was noise": Ibid.

99   "It's unbelievable": *Oakland Tribune*, October 20, 1972.

100 "Son of a bitch": Williams and Plaschke, *No More Mr. Nice Guy*.

101 "For a man who throws as hard": *Oakland Tribune*, October 21, 1972.

102 "one base hit, anyhow": *Cincinnati Inquirer*, October 22, 1972.
"I'm not going to lie": *Instream Sports*, October 22, 2012.
"It was from him": Gene Tenace interview.

103 "What in the hell are you doing?": Gene Tenace interview.

104 "Gosh doggit, that ball looked": Ibid.
"It's a known fact": *Oakland Tribune*, October 23, 1972.
"He didn't even know where the hitter": Gene Tenace interview.

105 "Right down the middle": Gene Tenace interview.
"Three fastballs, game's over": Irv Noren interview.
"I thought he would be looking": Ibid.
"I know what you're going to do": Ron Bergman, *Mustache Gang* (New York: Dell, 1973).

106 "If it's not against the boards": *Oakland Tribune*, October 23, 1972.
"the greatest kiss of them all": Ibid.
"As good as their hitters were": Sal Bando interview.
"The A's have a great bench": *Oakland Tribune*, October 23, 1972.
"It's just the first one": Bergman, *Mustache Gang*.
"money, sweat and sacrifice": *The Sporting News*, November 4, 1972.

107 "It's one thing to be pitched to": Mike Epstein interview.
"The equation was simple": Joe Rudi interview.
"How the hell can you win": *The Sporting News*, November 4, 1972.
"They couldn't drink it all": Bergman, *Mustache Gang*.
"We're number one!": *Oakland Tribune*, October 23, 1972.
"God, your wife can kiss": Mike Epstein interview.

108 "I don't even know": *Oakland Tribune*, October 23, 1972.

"Who do we have here?": Bill Libby, *Charlie O. and the Angry A's: The Low and Inside Story of Charlie O. Finley and Baseball's Most Colorful Team* (New York: Doubleday, 1975).

"there's only one man who manages": The Sporting News, October 17, 1970.

"One day I found out": Bergman, *Mustache Gang.*

109   *"You've never taken"*: Libby, *Charlie O. and the Angry A's.*

"I would like to open the bomb bay": New York Times Magazine, July 15, 1973.

"Finley was trying to be friendly": Dave Duncan interview.

"I had been of no help": Mike Epstein interview.

110   *"I just can't stand scenes"*: Bergman, *Mustache Gang.*

"It was a madhouse": Sal Bando interview.

"You better get [the players] all": Jimmie Piersall, with Dick Whittingham, *The Truth Hurts* (New York: Contemporary Books, 1985).

"Let's keep this trophy": The Sporting News, November 11, 1972.

"We worked as one": Ibid.

"Season's over and I had enough": Vida Blue interview.

111   *"baseball's executive of the year"*: Oakland Tribune, November 16, 1972.

7. SPRINGTIME FOR CHAMPIONS

112   *"Charlie Finley thinks he invented"*: The Sporting News, February 3, 1973.

"I just couldn't see sitting through": Mike Epstein interview.

113   *"Sometimes there just isn't any justice"*: Ibid.

114   *"With all credit to the A's"*: Baseball Digest, January 1973.

"there was a time when most": Bill Libby, *Charlie O. and the Angry A's: The Low and Inside Story of Charlie O. Finley and Baseball's Most Colorful Team* (New York: Doubleday, 1975).

115   *"Dr. Walker advised me"*: Oakland Tribune, January 21, 1973.

"He called me a fucking idiot": Libby, *Charlie O. and the Angry A's.*

116   *"More offense"*: Oakland Tribune, March 13, 1973.

"I don't know how to say this": Oakland Tribune, March 30, 1973.

"They should take the orange baseball": Oakland Tribune, April 3, 1973.

117   *"Vida called me on my birthday"*: The Sporting News, March 17, 1973.

"In spite of [Blue] reporting": Oakland Tribune, March 12, 1973.

118   *"you will never hear from us"*: Dave Duncan interview.

"I didn't think a lot of it": Ibid.

"I was bullied into signing": Oakland Tribune, March 5, 1973.

"What will you do if": Dave Duncan interview.

"You've been traded to Cleveland": Ibid.

"I am a human being": The Sporting News, April 3, 1973.

120   *"Nothing ever has been given"*: The Sporting News, January 6, 1973.
      "I'm going to make that [ring]": The Sporting News, March 24, 1973.

8. DEFENDING YOUR FLAG

121   *"People expect more of us"*: The Sporting News, June 2, 1973.
      "Are you guys 3-0": Oakland Tribune, April 11, 1973.
122   *"If it keeps up"*: Oakland Tribune, April 23, 1973.
      "I just feel like I want": Oakland Tribune, May 29, 1973.
      "We're being out-designated": Oakland Tribune, May 1, 1973.
123   *"When your name's on the lineup"*: Oakland Tribune, June 7, 1973.
124   *"Reggie, if you played defense"*: Irv Noren interview.
      "I can't play here and be happy": Oakland Tribune, July 5, 1973.
      "I couldn't believe I got off the hook": Sal Bando interview.
      "Superstar, my ass": Reggie Jackson, with Mike Lupica, *Reggie: The Autobiography* (New York: Random House, 1984).
125   *"We just don't get along"*: Oakland Tribune, July 6, 1973.
      "I just work here": Ibid.
      "Tension-filled flight": Dick Williams and Bill Plaschke, *No More Mr. Nice Guy: A Life of Hardball* (San Diego: Harcourt, 1990).
128   *"That big asshole"*: The Sporting News, June 6, 1970.
      "It inflated my ego": Ron Bergman, *Mustache Gang* (New York: Dell, 1973).
      "You can't print it": Ibid.
129   *"What you think of this?"*: Ibid.
      "Last Saturday, I made gestures": Bill Libby, *Charlie O. and the Angry A's: The Low and Inside Story of Charlie O. Finley and Baseball's Most Colorful Team* (New York: Doubleday, 1975).
      "I'd never been so alone": Sports Illustrated, June 17, 1974.
130   *"I don't want any more big years"*: Libby, *Charlie O. and the Angry A's*.
      "You've talked for a half-hour": Bergman, *Mustache Gang*.
      "It was just another indication": Sal Bando interview.
133   *"I don't think I could live"*: Oakland Tribune, May 19, 1973.
134   *"We were all looking at each other"*: Joe Rudi interview.
      "We're trying to win a championship": Ray Fosse interview.
135   *"Reggie, I can't play you"*: Oakland Tribune, October 22, 1973.
      "[Vida] has really dominated": Oakland Tribune, August 21, 1973.
136   *"no staff, no marketing"*: Sal Bando interview.
      "The ballpark was horrible": Rollie Fingers interview.
      "When we have a winner": Libby, *Charlie O. and the Angry A's*.
137   *"With the mustaches, the characters"*: Joe Rudi interview.
      "That's it, that's a promotion?": Jon Miller interview.
      "Thanks a Million": Williams and Plaschke, *No More Mr. Nice Guy*.

9. BEATING THE BIRDS

138 "If everything the press says": The Sporting News, October 27, 1973.

139 "Man throws like that": The Sporting News, October 20, 1973.
"hit one [Bumbry] won't": New York Daily News, October 8, 1973.

140 "he was doing the job anyway": The Sporting News, June 14, 1969.
"Take him away and that team": Tuscaloosa News, September 13, 1978.
"If there was one guy": Wes Stock interview.
"we all knew that Sal": Reggie Jackson, with Mike Lupica, Reggie: The Autobiography (New York: Random House, 1984).

141 "I've got a big Columbus Day crowd": Oakland Tribune, October 8, 1973.
"You sanctimonious little shit": Bill Libby, Charlie O. and the Angry A's: The Low and Inside Story of Charlie O. Finley and Baseball's Most Colorful Team (New York: Doubleday, 1975).
"I don't give a fuck": Oakland Tribune, October 9, 1973.
"I started thinking that": Dick Williams and Bill Plaschke, No More Mr. Nice Guy: A Life of Hardball (San Diego: Harcourt, 1990).

142 "We'd be the only three guys": Ken Holtzman interview.
"It was all gray-haired old ladies": Rollie Fingers interview.
"She doesn't care what I do": Los Angeles Times, May 21, 1969.
"I am now the best lefthanded": Oakland Tribune, November 30, 1971.
"I hear rumbles that Finley": Oakland Tribune, June 30, 1972.

143 "I've never seen a pitcher": Glenn Dickey, Champions: The Story of the First Two Oakland A's Dynasties and the Building of the Third (Chicago: Triumph Books, 2002).
"If we don't get this one": Oakland Tribune, October 10, 1973.
"If you pull me out": Ibid.
"Revenging myself?": Oakland Tribune, October 9, 1973.

144 "We had them by the nostrils": Libby, Charlie O. and the Angry A's.
"You shouldn't be talking": The Sporting News, October 27, 1973.
"we'll probably score": Ibid.

145 "Winning isn't everything": Oakland Tribune, October 15, 1974.

146 "almost earned him a spot": Catfish Hunter, with Armen Keteyian, Catfish: My Life in Baseball (New York: McGraw-Hill, 1988).
"Do you have a nickname?": Ibid.

147 "I don't understand why": Ibid.

148 "Don't walk him": Williams and Plaschke, No More Mr. Nice Guy.
"I felt so great": The Sporting News, October 27, 1973.
"Fabulous, fabulous, fabulous": Ibid.
"a special case": Oakland Tribune, October 12, 1973.

149 "He is our obstacle": Libby, Charlie O. and the Angry A's.

10. SCAPEGOAT NATION

150 *"We had to get Charlie off"*: Dick Williams and Bill Plaschke, *No More Mr. Nice Guy: A Life of Hardball* (San Diego: Harcourt, 1990).

153 *"There were these great big desks"*: Joe Rudi interview.
"You've heard the expression": *New York Daily News*, October 14, 1973.

156 *"my fault"*: Williams and Plaschke, *No More Mr. Nice Guy*.

157 *"I have no excuse for what happened"*: Bill Libby, *Charlie O. and the Angry A's: The Low and Inside Story of Charlie O. Finley and Baseball's Most Colorful Team* (New York: Doubleday, 1975).
"Do you feel any pain?": G. Michael Green and Roger Launius, *Charlie Finley: The Outrageous Story of Baseball's Super Showman* (London: Walker Books, 2010).
"The commissioner is going to ask": John Claiborne interview.

158 *"Oh yes he did"*: Williams and Plaschke, *No More Mr. Nice Guy*.
"Not in this way": *Oakland Tribune*, October 18, 1973.

159 *"We'll get through it without you"*: Ibid.

160 *"Do what you feel is best"*: Herbert Michelson, *Charlie O: Charles Oscar Finley vs. the Baseball Establishment* (Indianapolis: Bobbs-Merrill, 1975).
"We want Mike!": UPI, October 16, 1973.
"That's a great idea": Libby, *Charlie O. and the Angry A's*.
"It finished him": Williams and Plaschke, *No More Mr. Nice Guy*.

161 *"Believe me, that was the wrong bunch"*: Ken Holtzman interview.
"Everybody was pissed": Rollie Fingers interview.
"I can't believe what I just saw!": John Lindblom interview.

162 *"This is chickenshit"*: Ken Holtzman interview.
"I never saw so much press": Ibid.
"Are you nuts?": Ibid.
"This thing is a real embarrassment": *Oakland Tribune*, October 16, 1973.
"if you make an error": *Kansas City Star*, October 16, 1973.

163 *"The press ate it up"*: Rollie Fingers interview.
"to give the players": *Oakland Tribune*, October 16, 1973.
"You must have a letter": *The Sporting News*, November 3, 1973.
"this press conference": Libby, *Charlie O. and the Angry A's*.

164 *"the handling of this matter"*: Bowie Kuhn, *Hardball: The Education of a Baseball Commissioner* (New York: Crown, 1987).
"destroy": *New York Post*, October 17, 1973.
"sometimes all of us have to be": Michelson, *Charlie O.*

165 *"to give even a quick and superficial"*: Williams and Plaschke, *No More Mr. Nice Guy*.
"This is the hardest thing I've ever done": Ibid.

"I'm going to deny this": *The Sporting News*, November 3, 1973.

"It was pure quiet": Sal Bando interview.

"Dick said he didn't really give": Gene Tenace interview.

167 "If it gets this cold": *New York Daily News*, October 17, 1973.

168 "I had a little bit": *Oakland Tribune*, October 17, 1973.

"Blind people come to the park": *New York Daily News*, October 17, 1973.

"Dissention does it again": Libby, *Charlie O. and the Angry A's*.

"Maybe we could use a good fight": *Oakland Tribune*, October 17, 1973.

"There's another fight among the A's": Ibid.

169 "friendly persuasion": *Kansas City Times*, October 18, 1973.

"Mr. Finley never threatened": Libby, *Charlie O. and the Angry A's*.

"Hey man, where's my five?": Michelson, *Charlie O.*

"Seeing him was like an energy": Sal Bando interview.

"like a hero, like a king": Darold Knowles interview.

170 "Signing that piece of paper": Michelson, *Charlie O.*

"None of this baseball stuff": Ibid.

"He'll probably get fired": Ibid.

171 "Take that, you son of a bitch": Williams and Plaschke, *No More Mr. Nice Guy.*

"I played with great players": Gene Tenace interview.

"I started falling in love": Darold Knowles interview.

172 "Goodbye Charlie / Goodbye Charlie": *New York Daily News*, October 19, 1973.

"I wondered why the third-base coach": *Oakland Tribune*, October 20, 1973.

"Yogi played right into our hands": Williams and Plaschke, *No More Mr. Nice Guy.*

173 "He was Tom Seaver": *Baseball Digest*, January 1974.

174 "The kook said he had": *The Sporting News*, November 3, 1973.

"You can't expect to have": *Baseball Digest*, January 1974.

175 "I didn't want to come in": *Oakland Tribune*, October 22, 1973.

176 "Thanks for all you did": *St. Louis Post-Dispatch*, October 23, 1973.

"I'm looking for a great big diamond": *New York Daily News*, October 12, 1973.

"Please don't give that man": *Oakland Tribune*, October 22, 1973.

"This doesn't look like a": Libby, *Charlie O. and the Angry A's*.

177 "This is a great day for me": Williams and Plaschke, *No More Mr. Nice Guy.*

"I'm sorry, I'm sorry, I'm sorry": *Oakland Tribune*, October 22, 1973.

"I am, too, Reggie": Libby, *Charlie O. and the Angry A's*.

"I won't stand in his way": *Oakland Tribune*, October 18, 1973.

"There's a certain amount of glamour": Ibid.

"I would love to manage the Yankees": *Oakland Tribune*, October 22, 1973.

"I have great regard": Michelson, *Charlie O.*

"Mike and I are very, very close": Ibid.

178 "If anybody gets Williams": *Oakland Tribune*, October 24, 1973.

"It was the first time": Ibid.

"I never said I would not": Libby, *Charlie O. and the Angry A's*.
"Would I want a manager": Ibid.

179 "Bando grabbed Campaneris": Sal Bando interview.

11. WHEREFORE WILLIAMS?

180 "And Vida Blue and Blue Moon Odom": Dick Williams and Bill Plaschke, *No More Mr. Nice Guy: A Life of Hardball* (San Diego: Harcourt, 1990).

181 "You can't play cash": Bill Libby, *Charlie O. and the Angry A's: The Low and Inside Story of Charlie O. Finley and Baseball's Most Colorful Team* (New York: Doubleday, 1975).
"We've waited long enough": *Oakland Tribune*, December 13, 1973.
"record of achievement": *Oakland Tribune*, December 19, 1973.

182 "A man can't divorce his wife": Herbert Michelson, *Charlie O: Charles Oscar Finley vs. the Baseball Establishment* (Indianapolis: Bobbs-Merrill, 1975).
"I can get up tomorrow": *Oakland Tribune*, January 25, 1974.
"constitutes breaches, both actual": *Oakland Tribune*, February 12, 1974.

183 "further conduct not in the best interest": Libby, *Charlie O. and the Angry A's*.
"The Commissioner is saying Finley is lying": *Oakland Tribune*, December 1, 1973.
"I live with it every day": *The Sporting News*, March 20, 1976.

184 "None of your fucking business": Michelson, *Charlie O*.

185 "Him and her": Ibid.

12. ANOTHER RUN

187 "We will be the nation's biggest assholes": John Helyar, *Lords of the Realm: The Real History of Baseball* (New York: Villard, 1994).
"We learned that, wait a minute": Ken Holtzman interview.

188 "can go bleep himself": *San Francisco Chronicle*, February 13, 1974.
"Even if they're completely innocent": Ibid.

189 "I bet you mention this game": Ken Holtzman interview.
"Now, Mr. Arbitrator, let me tell you": Ibid.
"Fingers here": Marvin Miller, *A Whole Different Ball Game: The Sport and Business of Baseball* (New York: Birch Lane Press, 1991).
"Charlie just tried to downgrade you": Rollie Fingers interview.

190 "I had tears in my eyes": Gene Tenace interview.
"Finley actually told the arbitrator": Ted Kubiak interview.

191 "Mr. Reggie Jackson and his representative": Miller, *A Whole Different Ball Game*.
"they had to give it to somebody": *Sports Illustrated*, June 17, 1974.

"Babe Ruth was a superstar": Miller, *A Whole Different Ball Game.*

192 *"I just knew had I gone to arbitration"*: G. Michael Green and Roger Launius, *Charlie Finley: The Outrageous Story of Baseball's Super Showman* (London: Walker Books, 2010).

"He likes to be the lord": Herbert Michelson, *Charlie O: Charles Oscar Finley vs. the Baseball Establishment* (Indianapolis: Bobbs-Merrill, 1975).

"was arbitration": *Dallas Morning News*, January 22, 1989.

193 *"Alvin Dark? Again?"*: Jon Miller interview.

"Really, I haven't even looked": *Oakland Tribune*, February 20, 1974.

194 *"You can't make most Negro and Spanish players"*: *Newsday*, July 23, 1964.

"colored boys": *Oakland Tribune*, February 24, 1974.

"mission field": Alvin Dark and John Underwood, *When in Doubt, Fire the Manager: My Life and Times in Baseball* (New York: Dutton Adult, 1980).

"For a team to be successful": Bill Libby, *Charlie O. and the Angry A's: The Low and Inside Story of Charlie O. Finley and Baseball's Most Colorful Team* (New York: Doubleday, 1975).

195 *"I will call Mr. Finley"*: Ibid.

"take a day-to-day": Dark, *When in Doubt, Fire the Manager.*

"Be strong and of good courage": Ibid.

"When you have a championship club": *Oakland Tribune*, February 21, 1974.

"Finley manages this team anyway": Reggie Jackson, *Reggie: A Season with a Superstar* (Chicago: Playboy Press, 1975).

196 *"Fuck Charlie Finley"*: Herbert Michelson, *Charlie O.*

"look silly": *Oakland Tribune*, March 2, 1974.

"The new rings are horseshit": Ibid.

"cheap so-and-so": Libby, *Charlie O. and the Angry A's.*

"the worst in World Series history": Michelson, *Charlie O.*

197 *"I went on national television"*: *Oakland Tribune*, March 2, 1974.

"Finley changed": Dick Green interview.

"He hated the ballplayers": Rollie Fingers interview.

"Pigs get fat, hogs go to market": Libby, *Charlie O. and the Angry A's.*

198 *"Herbie, you better be glad"*: Herb Washington interview.

"That's a joke": *Oakland Tribune*, March 18, 1974.

199 *"Charlie Finley, owner of the world champion"*: Herb Washington interview.

"He couldn't throw a baseball": Rollie Fingers interview.

"He has as much business playing baseball": Libby, *Charlie O. and the Angry A's.*

"He got his running in": Gene Tenace interview.

"I'd never shaved a day in my life": Herb Washington interview.

"Anyone who can start as fast": *Oakland Tribune*, March 18, 1974.

"I'd come back to the dugout": Herb Washington interview.

200 *"Herbie didn't know about baseball"*: Gene Tenace interview.

"I think a happy ballplayer": Dark, *When in Doubt, Fire the Manager.*
201 "I want to play 162 games": *Oakland Tribune,* April 5, 1974.
"John McGraw must be turning over": Jackson, *Reggie: A Season with a Superstar.*
"the only twenty-game winners": *Oakland Tribune,* April 9, 1974.
202 "I knew Alvin Dark was a religious man": *Oakland Tribune,* April 9, 1974.
203 "I don't think Rollie is tired": *Oakland Tribune,* April 22, 1974.
"I don't agree with the way": *The Sporting News,* May 11, 1974.
"Hey, genius, Knowles is ready": Jackson, *Reggie: A Season with a Superstar.*
"Walk him": *San Francisco Chronicle,* July 15, 2004.
"Hey, Bando, why'd you do it?": Sal Bando interview.
204 "If we were too hard on our teammates": Jackson, *Reggie: A Season with a Superstar.*
"So what if he brings in the wrong pitcher": Ibid.
"Accept his moves": Ibid.
"overbearing down": *Oakland Tribune,* May 5, 1974.
"I'm not doing a good job": *Oakland Tribune,* May 3, 1974.
205 "He's horseshit": *Oakland Tribune,* May 21, 1974.
"Oh, no, you don't!": Ray Fosse interview.
206 "Well, hell, Alvin, I'm coming back": Jackson, *Reggie: A Season with a Superstar.*
"I'm not sure he knows he's a bigot": Ibid.
"I don't know what the fuck": Ibid.
207 "You're the one that wanted him": Ibid.
"He ain't ever going to learn": Ibid.
"Just sit down and relax": Dark, *When in Doubt, Fire the Manager.*
208 "Great peace have they": Jackson, *Reggie: A Season with a Superstar.*
"How do you stand it?": Dark, *When in Doubt, Fire the Manager.*
"You see this?": *Oakland Tribune,* June 3, 1974.
"When he begs like that": Ibid.
209 "Here we had just had": Jackson, *Reggie: A Season with a Superstar.*
"Who the fuck are you?": *New York Post,* June 8, 1974.
"I'm the man who's telling you": Jackson, *Reggie: A Season with a Superstar.*
210 "I'm not afraid to tell": Ibid.
"I wouldn't know what color I was": Ibid.
"taking over the president's office": Billy North interview.
"Never speak to me again": Jackson, *Reggie: A Season with a Superstar.*
"What motherfucker is managing": *New York Post,* June 8, 1974.
"Reggie is a great player": *Sports Illustrated,* June 17, 1974.
211 "Superstar my ass": Herb Washington interview.
"You're a fucking jerk": Jackson, *Reggie: A Season with a Superstar.*
"It was surreal": Herb Washington interview.

"*I had a slam bid*": Dick Green interview.

"*They're just going to fight later*": Rollie Fingers interview.

212 "*You know damn well*": Jackson, *Reggie: A Season with a Superstar.*

"*Hey man, I don't know*": Ibid.

"*What are you doing?*": Gene Tenace interview.

"*Well, that's it*": *Oakland Tribune*, June 6, 1974.

213 "*Being on this club*": *Oakland Tribune*, June 7, 1974.

"*It's very bad*": *Oakland Tribune*, June 6, 1974.

"*It's my fault*": *New York Post*, June 8, 1974.

"*punch him in his damn mouth*": Jackson, *Reggie: A Season with a Superstar.*

214 "*You're world champions*": *Oakland Tribune*, June 8, 1974.

"*as if they were ten-year-olds*": Dark, *When in Doubt, Fire the Manager.*

"*For the first time in years*": Jackson, *Reggie: A Season with a Superstar.*

215 "*Hey, Skip, you'd better tell that boy*": Herb Washington interview.

"*The shit between me and you*": Billy North interview.

"*I don't have to love or hate anybody*": *New York Daily News*, June 8, 1974.

216 "*I can't control the bat*": *Oakland Tribune*, June 17, 1974.

"*He couldn't manage a fucking meat market*": *Oakland Tribune*, June 20, 1974.

217 "*Did you mean that?*": Dark, *When in Doubt, Fire the Manager.*

"*Shit, I didn't mean it*": Catfish Hunter, with Armen Keteyian, *Catfish: My Life in Baseball* (New York: McGraw-Hill, 1988).

"*we were fine*": Sal Bando interview.

"*He's had twenty-five different*": *Oakland Tribune*, June 24, 1974.

"*If you think running a meat market*": Sal Bando interview.

218 "*I'm not a .200 hitter*": *Oakland Tribune*, June 17, 1974.

"*Attention: To All Players*": Ibid.

219 "*He's the best player for his age*": *The Sporting News*, September 28, 1974.

"*Nothing surprises me anymore*": *Oakland Tribune*, July 11, 1974.

220 "*What can you expect*": UPI, July 10, 1974.

"*I've never been more disappointed*": Dark, *When in Doubt, Fire the Manager.*

"*Vida, you and I are even*": Ibid.

221 "*Outfielders aren't paid to flip the ball*": Jackson, *Reggie: A Season with a Superstar.*

"*you all said in the papers*": Jon Miller interview.

"*I'm taking a beating*": *Oakland Tribune*, July 15, 1974.

"*Do you know how heavy*": Vida Blue interview.

222 "*We needed it*": *Oakland Tribune*, July 15, 1974.

"*No way! No way!*": Dark, *When in Doubt, Fire the Manager.*

"*You've all heard of John the Baptist*": Ibid.

"*I guess this wasn't the best*": Ibid.

223 "*It's like driving a car*": *The Sporting News*, May 25, 1974.

"*All of you want to give*": Jackson, *Reggie: A Season with a Superstar.*

224 *"When in the fuck are you going to let"*: Ibid.

"Make your own deal": Darold Knowles interview.

"It's tough to pitch": Oakland Tribune, September 11, 1974.

225 *"It's the worst thing I've ever seen"*: Oakland Tribune, September 3, 1974.

"It sounded like he was drunk": Jon Miller interview.

226 *"I almost walked into the dugout"*: Oakland Tribune, September 3, 1974.

"Eat your heart out": Oakland Tribune, June 30, 1974.

"I sweated blood for twelve years": The Sporting News, October 19, 1974.

228 *"felt as though it had been mangled"*: Oakland Tribune, July 13, 1975.

229 *"tell it like it happened"*: Ray Fosse interview.

"Yeeeeeeah, Fosse — that's my boy!": The Sporting News, October 26, 1974; Ray Fosse interview.

"Then why didn't you want": Ray Fosse interview.

"Fuck Curt Gowdy": Oakland Tribune, October 9, 1974.

230 *"Never win a big game"*: Ibid.

"Well, that's the A's": Jackson, Reggie: A Season with a Superstar.

231 *"Alvin has received a lot of bad publicity"*: Oakland Tribune, October 10, 1974.

232 *"Praise the Lord"*: Ibid.

"You guys probably heard it": Jon Miller interview.

13. HELLO, HOLLYWOOD . . . GOODBYE, CATFISH (PRELUDE)

234 *"Lady, this is the Oakland A's"*: Oakland Tribune, October 12, 1974.

235 *"I definitely think we have a better ballclub"*: Time, October 28, 1974.

"I don't know how they come up": Rollie Fingers interview.

"By 1974 we had the swagger": Joe Rudi interview.

"Team spirit doesn't apply": Time, October 28, 1974.

236 *"What the fuck"*: Jon Miller interview.

237 *"What happens if you don't make"*: Oakland Tribune, October 11, 1974.

"What kind of fucking question": Reggie Jackson, Reggie: A Season with a Superstar (Chicago: Playboy Press, 1975).

"There's nothing to it at all": Ibid.

238 *"We read about you guys"*: Ken Holtzman interview.

"I'm nervous with you guys": Sal Bando interview.

"Oh God, here we go": Ken Holtzman interview.

"That stuff is overblown": Sal Bando interview.

239 *"Kenny, I apologize"*: Ken Holtzman interview.

"Get out of here": Joe Rudi interview.

"The fighting A's!": Oakland Tribune, October 12, 1974.

240 *"I told Alvin we were washed up"*: Jackson, Reggie: A Season with a Superstar.

241 *"I'm sick and tired of jokes"*: Ibid.

"Moon, God bless him": Ken Holtzman interview.

"John didn't have any softness": Sal Bando interview.

"We had gotten into it a lot": Rollie Fingers interview.

242 "It was a friendly scuffle": Oakland Tribune, October 12, 1974.

"From a legal point of view": Ibid.

"Under the pertinent rule provision": Oakland Tribune, October 14, 1974.

"Don't be concerned about Hunter": Ibid.

243 "The hell with you guys": Wes Stock interview.

244 "This guy can't hit your curveball": Catfish Hunter, with Armen Keteyian, Catfish: My Life in Baseball (New York: McGraw-Hill, 1988).

245 "He didn't show me anything": Bill Libby, Catfish: The Three Million Dollar Pitcher (New York: Coward, McCann & Geoghegan, 1976).

"He's like any other relief pitcher": The Sporting News, October 26, 1974.

"I want you to write": Oakland Tribune, October 14, 1974.

246 "There will come a time": Oakland Tribune, October 15, 1974.

247 "He really should have just": Gene Tenace interview.

248 "Hey, man, I don't want to be": Sport, October 1974.

249 "I don't expect everyone": Jackson, Reggie: A Season with a Superstar.

"Come with me": Oakland Tribune, October 15, 1974.

"a horseshit writer": Ibid.

250 "Walk away with me": New York Daily News, October 16, 1974.

"very disturbed": UPI, October 16, 1974.

"As far as I'm concerned": Ibid.

"I've got a job to do": Libby, Catfish.

252 "They got away with murder": Oakland Tribune, October 16, 1974.

"We definitely have a better team": San Francisco Chronicle, October 16, 1974.

"When you take into account": Ibid.

"discussed the A's as if they were": San Francisco Examiner, October 17, 1974.

253 "I get sick and tired": Oakland Tribune, October 17, 1974.

254 "You can't smuggle a ball": Ibid.

255 "I needed to be in the right place": Dick Green interview.

"Those plays he made": Joe Rudi interview.

"[Green] has to be lucky": Oakland Tribune, October 17, 1974.

"I have no respect for Dark": San Francisco Chronicle, October 17, 1974.

257 "I don't know what the hell": Joe Rudi interview.

258 "I had an opportunity to be Bill Buckner": Billy North interview.

"Big money": Ibid.

259 "whole fucking bottle of champagne": Jackson, Reggie: A Season with a Superstar.

"We won it three times in a row": Maury Allen, Mr. October: The Reggie Jackson Story (New York: Times Books, 1981).

260 "Never raise a son to be a reliever": San Francisco Chronicle, October 18, 1974.

"I don't want to talk about that": Libby, Catfish.

14. CATFISH GONE

261 "If Finley got the best of Catfish": Reggie Jackson, *Reggie: A Season with a Superstar* (Chicago: Playboy Press, 1975).
"Nobody's going to do me": *Oakland Tribune*, December 18, 1974.

262 "He'd call me in the clubhouse": Bill Libby, *Catfish: The Three Million Dollar Pitcher* (New York: Coward, McCann & Geoghegan, 1976).
"I asked [Finley] once": Ibid.

264 "I did everything I could": *San Francisco Examiner*, December 17, 1974.

265 "Let's get this out of the way": Darold Knowles interview.

266 "What can I do?": Catfish Hunter, with Armen Keteyian, *Catfish: My Life in Baseball* (New York: McGraw-Hill, 1988).
"The Oakland club offered everything": *Oakland Tribune*, October 14, 1974.
"What the heck are you drinking?": Gene Tenace interview.

267 "I cannot believe that Catfish": *The Sporting News*, October 26, 1974.
"like giving a life sentence": Bowie Kuhn, *Hardball: The Education of a Baseball Commissioner* (New York: Crown, 1987).
"capricious, arbitrary or dishonest": Ibid.

268 "Shit, I love this place": Hunter, *Catfish*.

269 "How about my wife?": Ibid.
"I naturally feel that the arbitrator": Ibid.

270 "Don't sign nothing else": Ibid.
"You have breakfast with that boy": *Cleveland Plain Dealer*, January 5, 1975.

271 "what would it take": Hunter, *Catfish*.
"That's more money than we wanted": Ibid.
"If you come to San Diego": Ibid.

272 "the Catfish Hunter Manifesto": *Cleveland Plain Dealer*, January 5, 1975.

15. RETOOL

275 "I'm happy as hell for Jim": *New York Daily News*, January 31, 1975.
"There never has been a challenge": *Oakland Tribune*, February 9, 1975.
"He says he can still pitch": *Oakland Tribune*, February 15, 1975.
"The loss of Catfish Hunter": *The Sporting News*, February 22, 1975.

276 "I've got every type of glove": *Oakland Tribune*, March 3, 1975.
"You know, I'll be surprised": *The Sporting News*, April 26, 1975.

277 "I'm mad as hell": *New York Daily News*, January 31, 1975.
"pop-off": *Oakland Tribune*, February 15, 1975.
"[Finley] just doesn't have a first-class": UPI, January 25, 1975.

"That the Oakland A's have the worst": *Oakland Tribune*, February 15, 1975.
"Bando has been a very unappreciative individual": Associated Press, February 16, 1975.

278 "We don't believe in taking chances": *Oakland Tribune*, March 15, 1975.
"I look at him like Jeremiah": *Oakland Tribune*, April 2, 1975.

279 "I told Jeremiah that": *Oakland Tribune*, April 21, 1975.
"I'd feel sorry for him": *Oakland Tribune*, May 5, 1975.

281 "a sound from Dante's Inferno": Bowie Kuhn, *Hardball: The Education of a Baseball Commissioner* (New York: Crown, 1987).
"There was professional baseball": Ibid.

282 "Thank you, gentlemen": Kuhn, *Hardball*.
"If you see [Kuhn]": *Oakland Tribune*, July 13, 1975.

283 "If Charlie could have put us on a bus": Rollie Fingers interview.
"All Charlie is interested in": *The Sporting News*, September 18, 1976.

284 "just couldn't take it anymore": John Claiborne interview.
"Unlike most office help": *The Sporting News*, August 23, 1975.
"I told Finley a few years later": John Claiborne interview.
"It was a disaster": Joe Rudi interview.
"punitive damages": *Oakland Tribune*, January 4, 1975.

285 "We still feel like Hunter": *The Sporting News*, March 27, 1976.

286 "Williams didn't win for the A's": Bill Libby, *Catfish: The Three Million Dollar Pitcher* (New York: Coward, McCann & Geoghegan, 1976).

288 "I haven't heard": *Oakland Tribune*, October 8, 1975.

16. HOUSECLEANING

289 "We were always mad at Charlie": Reggie Jackson, with Mike Lupica, *Reggie: The Autobiography* (New York: Random House, 1984).

290 "seemed to be the only one smart enough": Marvin Miller, *A Whole Different Ball Game: The Sport and Business of Baseball* (New York: Birch Lane Press, 1991).
"Alvin Dark Says That": *The Sporting News*, November 1, 1975.

291 "Charlie Finley feels that": *The Sporting News*, November 29, 1975.
"she knows more about those things": Joe Posnanski, *The Machine: A Hot Team, a Legendary Season, and a Heart-Stopping World Series; The Story of the 1975 Cincinnati Reds* (New York: William Morrow, 2009).
"possesses the qualities I have been looking for": *The Sporting News*, January 3, 1976.
"I feel outstandingly exotic": Ibid.
"When we're losing, Charlie will": *The Sporting News*, February 14, 1976.
"There are a lot of good kids": Ibid.

292 *"Gold is $192 an ounce"*: Oakland Tribune, November 25, 1974.

"Reggie, this is Charlie": Maury Allen, *Mr. October: The Reggie Jackson Story* (New York: Times Books, 1981).

293 *"A guy grows on you"*: The Sporting News, April 17, 1976.

"It started unwinding": Gene Tenace interview.

"The deal was made because": The Sporting News, April 17, 1976.

"When I found out about it": Gene Tenace interview.

295 *"They don't look right"*: The Sporting News, June 12, 1976.

296 *"Are Rudi and Fingers still available"*: John Helyar, *Lords of the Realm: The Real History of Baseball* (New York: Villard, 1994).

"Hey, V, listen — that crazy son of a bitch": Vida Blue interview.

297 *"Vida, you know I would never"*: New York Times, June 25, 1976.

"the biggest sale of human flesh": Sports Illustrated, June 28, 1976.

"Is Vida there?": Chicago Tribune, June 16, 1976.

298 *"I was happier than a pig in shit"*: Rollie Fingers interview.

299 *"disaster"*: Bowie Kuhn, *Hardball: The Education of a Baseball Commissioner* (New York: Crown, 1987).

"it's none of your damn business": Ibid.

"Commissioner, I can't sign these guys": Ibid.

300 *"He knew the price of the team"*: Paul Finley interview.

"I'm still very troubled": Helyar, *Lords of the Realm*.

"I don't understand what the furor": Sports Illustrated, June 28, 1976.

301 *"If, as contended by the participants"*: The Sporting News, July 3, 1976.

"Whether other players will be": Ibid.

"personal vendetta": Ibid.

"sheer insanity": Ibid.

"Whenever there's a trade made": Ibid.

"When both Marvin Miller": New York Times, June 20, 1976.

302 *"[Kuhn] has opened a big can"*: New York Daily News, June 19, 1976.

303 *"I want you to know"*: Sal Bando interview.

"This was going to be the first": Steve Vucinich interview.

"They're taking off their uniforms": Sal Bando interview.

304 *"Here it is"*: The Sporting News, July 10, 1976.

"It was mass hysteria": Ibid.

"We put Finley up against the wall": Billy North interview.

"we could have won all": The Sporting News, October 30, 1976.

"Since all members of the American League": Associated Press, June 28, 1976.

305 *"the question before the court"*: Chicago Tribune, July 19, 1992.

"eighteen years of blood": Kuhn, *Hardball*.

"Maybe if the Yankees and A's": The Sporting News, July 17, 1976.

306 *"a disaster"*: The Sporting News, August 28, 1976.

307 *"This is to celebrate the liberation"*: The Sporting News, October 23, 1976.

"I hope the next breath": Ibid.
"I feel sorry for anyone": Ibid.
"Was it difficult leaving the Titanic?": *The Sporting News*, December 4, 1976.

17. LONG SLOPE DOWN

309   "During spring training": *Los Angeles Times*, May 18, 1978.
310   "a substantial amount of cash": Associated Press, March 26, 1977.
311   "that nut": *The Sporting News*, April 15, 1978.
313   "Here I was . . . in the office": *Inc.*, June 1, 1982.
        "I know how a man feels": *New York Daily News*, September 3, 1980.
        "I always wanted my own": *Los Angeles Times*, July 7, 1987.

EPILOGUE

315   "We were the team": Vida Blue interview.
316   "I only hope you don't win 19": Rollie Fingers interview.
        "You know, roomie": Ken Holtzman interview.
        "It was one big group": Phil Garner interview.
        "You have to pass the crazy test": Blue Moon Odom interview.
        "The thing that helped the team": Dave Duncan interview.
317   "We were so much more": Dick Green interview.
318   "We understood Reggie": Gene Tenace interview.
        "Baseball has lost its number one innovator": *Sporting News Official 1981 Baseball Guide*.
319   "All he wanted ever in his life": Billy North interview.
320   "He'd fight you over a $100 raise": Joe Rudi interview.
321   "We were talented and mean and hungry": Reggie Jackson, with Mike Lupica, *Reggie: The Autobiography* (New York: Random House, 1984).
        "The Yankees might not have won": Jon Miller interview.
322   "Grab a couple baseballs": Ken Holtzman interview.
        "Have you ever heard of Vida Blue": Jim Street interview.

CAST OF CHARACTERS

327   "Sal Bando was the godfather": Reggie Jackson, with Mike Lupica, *Reggie: The Autobiography* (New York: Random House, 1984).
328   "I would go down to the bullpen": Rollie Fingers interview.
329   "You can talk about Reggie Jackson": *The Sporting News*, October 4, 1980.
330   "Dave is our quarterback, you might say": *The Sporting News*, June 12, 1971.
331   "This is a mighty hunk": *Oakland Tribune*, May 10, 1971.

332   "We call him 'buzzard'": Reggie Jackson, *Reggie: A Season with a Superstar* (Chicago: Playboy Press, 1975).

333   "You've got to be kidding": *Sporting News*, April 14, 1973.

334   "It looks as if a little man": *Oakland Tribune*, October 17, 1974.

335   "Holtzman would give all this bluster": Phil Garner interview.

336   "You think you can hit him": Bill Libby, *Catfish: The Three Million Dollar Pitcher* (New York: Coward, McCann & Geoghegan, 1976).

337   "Reggie Jackson was the strongest": Catfish Hunter, with Armen Keteyian, *Catfish: My Life in Baseball* (New York: McGraw-Hill, 1988).

338   "I was ten years old": Billy North interview.

339   "Johnny had incredible stuff": Ted Kubiak interview.

340   "He's just the best goddamn winning": *Boston Globe*, February 1, 1981.

342   "This guy actually outran": Gene Tenace interview.

343   "We would not have won anything": Maury Allen, *Mr. October: The Reggie Jackson Story* (New York: Times Books, 1981).

344   "Alvin's recall amazed me": Jon Miller, with Mark Hyman, *Confessions of a Baseball Purist* (New York: Simon & Schuster, 1998).

Index